The Craft of Innovative Theology

The Craft of Innovative Theology

Argument and Process

Edited by John Allan Knight and Ian S. Markham

WILEY Blackwell

This edition first published 2022
© 2022 John Wiley & Sons Ltd.

All rights reserved. No part of this publication may be reproduced, stored in a retrieval system, or transmitted, in any form or by any means, electronic, mechanical, photocopying, recording or otherwise, except as permitted by law. Advice on how to obtain permission to reuse material from this title is available at http://www.wiley.com/go/permissions.

The right of John Allan Knight and Ian S. Markham to be identified as the authors of the editorial material in this work has been asserted in accordance with law.

Registered Office
John Wiley & Sons, Inc., 111 River Street, Hoboken, NJ 07030, USA

Editorial Office
9600 Garsington Road, Oxford, OX4 2DQ, UK

For details of our global editorial offices, customer services, and more information about Wiley products visit us at www.wiley.com.

Wiley also publishes its books in a variety of electronic formats and by print-on-demand. Some content that appears in standard print versions of this book may not be available in other formats.

Limit of Liability/Disclaimer of Warranty
The contents of this work are intended to further general scientific research, understanding, and discussion only and are not intended and should not be relied upon as recommending or promoting scientific method, diagnosis, or treatment by physicians for any particular patient. In view of ongoing research, equipment modifications, changes in governmental regulations, and the constant flow of information relating to the use of medicines, equipment, and devices, the reader is urged to review and evaluate the information provided in the package insert or instructions for each medicine, equipment, or device for, among other things, any changes in the instructions or indication of usage and for added warnings and precautions. While the publisher and authors have used their best efforts in preparing this work, they make no representations or warranties with respect to the accuracy or completeness of the contents of this work and specifically disclaim all warranties, including without limitation any implied warranties of merchantability or fitness for a particular purpose. No warranty may be created or extended by sales representatives, written sales materials or promotional statements for this work. The fact that an organization, website, or product is referred to in this work as a citation and/or potential source of further information does not mean that the publisher and authors endorse the information or services the organization, website, or product may provide or recommendations it may make. This work is sold with the understanding that the publisher is not engaged in rendering professional services. The advice and strategies contained herein may not be suitable for your situation. You should consult with a specialist where appropriate. Further, readers should be aware that websites listed in this work may have changed or disappeared between when this work was written and when it is read. Neither the publisher nor authors shall be liable for any loss of profit or any other commercial damages, including but not limited to special, incidental, consequential, or other damages.

Library of Congress Cataloging-in-Publication Data
Names: Markham, Ian S., author. | Knight, John A., author.
Title: The craft of innovative theology : argument and process / Ian S. Markham and John A. Knight.
Description: Hoboken, NJ : John Wiley & Sons Ltd., 2021. | Includes bibliographical references and index.
Identifiers: LCCN 2021025870 (print) | LCCN 2021025871 (ebook) | ISBN 9781119601555 (paperback) | ISBN 9781119601579 (pdf) | ISBN 9781119601562 (epub)
Subjects: LCSH: Theology, Doctrinal. | Theology--Methodology. | Christianity and other religions. | Religious pluralism--Christianity.
Classification: LCC BT78 .M384 2021 (print) | LCC BT78 (ebook) | DDC 230--dc23
LC record available at https://lccn.loc.gov/2021025870
LC ebook record available at https://lccn.loc.gov/2021025871

Cover Image: © agsandrew/Shutterstock
Cover design by Wiley

Set in 10/12 pt Warnock Pro by Integra Software Services Pvt. Ltd, Pondicherry, India

10 9 8 7 6 5 4 3 2 1

For Melody and Lesley – our companions on the journey of life

Contents

The Acknowledgments		ix
Contributors		xi
Introduction		xiii

Part I God and the Incarnation — 1

1 Knowing God through Religious Pluralism — 3
Tinu Ruparell
Research Level 2 — 3

2 Is It Possible for the Eternal Word to Be Made Manifest in a Person with Down's Syndrome? — 19
Ian S. Markham
Research Level 1 — 19

Part II God and Church — 31

3 Racial Stigma and Southern Baptist Public Discourse in the Twentieth Century — 33
Pamela D. Jones
Research Level 1 — 33

4 The Plugged-in Church: Is it Appropriate to Baptize Artificial Intelligence — 50
Ian S. Markham
Research Level 1 — 50

Part III God and the World — 63

5 Humanity: Where on Earth Have We Come From and Where Are We Going To? — 65
Celia Deane-Drummond
Research Level 3 — 65

6 What Challenges Does the Theory of Biological Evolution Pose to Christian Theology? — 81
Christopher Southgate
Research Level 3 — 81

Part IV God and Ethics — 97

7 Sin and the Faces of Responsibility — 99
Leigh Vicens
Research Level 4 — 99

8 A Good Story: Human–Animal Friendship and Meat Eating — 114
Trevor Bechtel
Research Level 2 — 114

9 Just Business: It's Not What You Think — 127
Kathryn D. Blanchard
Research Level 2 — 127

Part V The End of the World — 149

10 Relentless Love and the Afterlife — 151
Thomas J. Oord
Research Level 1 — 151

11 Hell: Retributivism, Escapism, and Universal Reconciliation — 164
Andrei A. Buckareff
Research Level 3 — 164

12 Christ Will Come Again — 183
Keith Ward
Research Level 2 — 183

Part VI Method in Theology — 195

13 Theological Language and Method in Liberal Theology: Schubert Ogden's Response to the Falsification Controversy — 197
John Allan Knight
Research Level 4 — 197

14 Does Culture Determine Belief? The Relationship between the Social Sciences and Theology — 212
Martyn Percy
Research Level 3 — 212

15 Theological Reference and Theological Creativity in Judaism — 226
Cass Fisher
Research Level 4 — 226

16 Marshall's Slingshot: Truth Theory, Realism, and Liberal Theological Method — 245
John Allan Knight
Research Level 4 — 245

Glossary — 261
Index — 266

The Acknowledgments

From the Editors

We are grateful to Catriona King, the commissioning editor from Wiley Blackwell, who saw the potential in this idea. It has been delightful to work with Catriona. The subsequent readers' reports transformed the project and added depth and texture. Thanks to Conant Fund of the Episcopal Church, we had sufficient funds to cover the costs of – what became – a virtual conference and our talented and capable research assistant.

Jean Cotting was our research assistant for this project. She is organized, efficient, and extremely capable. Along with working with all the contributors (and becoming the master of the gentle reminder), she organized the discussion sessions, shared the results of the sessions with contributors, and put together the entire glossary. All of this was done during the great pandemic of 2020; and all of this was done with humor and graciousness. Thank you Jean. Then in the concluding stages of the project, Sam Burke stepped forward and assisted the editors by finalizing the manuscript and helping with the copyediting and the proof stage. Thank you Sam. We are grateful to Taryn Habberley, who did a marvelous job with the index.

Finally, we are grateful to all those who added this assignment to their busy lives. We are proud and delighted by the quality of the essays. This was not a regular writing assignment; each contributor needed to shape their essay for the book. They all did it so well. Thank you.

From John Knight

First, of course, I'd like to thank Ian Markham, my co-editor. It has been a delight to work with Ian, who brought all kinds of gifts to the project that I simply don't have. I could not have asked for a better co-editor.

I am also grateful to Marty Shaffer, Dean of Liberal Arts, and Thom Wermuth, Vice President of Academic Affairs, at Marist for supporting my research over the years. I'm also grateful to Andrei Buckareff, my colleague at Marist, whose friendship I value greatly and whose knowledge and expertise has kept me from many philosophical mistakes over the years.

Finally, of course, I'm grateful to my family: Ella, Johnny, and Melody. Their patience with me is completely undeserved. I'm especially thankful for the wise advice and counsel, companionship, friendship, incisive but kind critique, and unfailing love from my wife, Melody. My life has been fortunate and blessed in many ways, but their presence is the best part of it.

From Ian Markham

The idea of a "research methods textbook" that takes people to a place where they can write complex research articles was birthed in endless conversations at The Grape and Bean pub with John Knight. It has been a privilege to work with John. He saw possibilities in the project that I did not see. I am grateful for John's expertise and sense of fun that he brought to this project as co-editor.

I am blessed with a board of trustees that understands that the writing of books is part of my duties as dean and president of Virginia Theological Seminary. In particular my board chair, Dr. David Charlton, is not just one of the wisest voices of counsel that I have ever known but also has been completely supportive of my writing and teaching. I am deeply grateful for his leadership of the board.

My senior staff – Melody Knowles, Jacqui Ballou, Katie Glover, and Linda Dienno – provide me with much needed space to write. Cassandra Gravina is a remarkable executive assistant. I appreciate them all so much.

Please allow me to acknowledge my debt our US family. To Elaine and Ian, we love you. I am grateful every day for the joy that Luke, my son, brings to the lives of his parents. Lesley and I find life all the richer because of his presence. The editors have decided to dedicate this book to our wives. For Lesley, one is never sure what exactly is around the corner of life, but I am so pleased that I am making the journey with you.

Contributors

Trevor Bechtel, Student Engagement Director, University of Michigan
Kathryn D. Blanchard, Charles A. Dana Professor of Religious Studies and Chair of Religious Studies, Alma College
Andrei A. Buckareff, Professor of Philosophy, Marist College
Celia Deane-Drummond, Director – Laudato Si Research Institute and Senior Research Fellow in Theology, Campion Hall, University of Oxford
Cass Fisher, Associate Professor, University of South Florida
Pamela D. Jones, Assistant Professor (retired), Central Michigan University
John Allan Knight, Associate Professor of Religious Studies, Marist College
Ian Markham, Dean and President of Virginia Theological Seminary and Professor of Theology and Ethics, Virginia Theological Seminary
Thomas J. Oord, Doctoral Program Director, Northwest Nazarene University
Martyn Percy, Dean, Christ Church, University of Oxford
Tinu Ruparell, Associate Professor of Indian and Comparative Philosophy, University of Calgary
Christopher Southgate, Professor of Christian Theodicy, University of Exeter
Leigh Vicens, Associate Professor of Philosophy, Augustana University
Keith Ward, Regius Professor of Divinity Emeritus, University of Oxford

Introduction

Most professors are better at imparting content than they are at imparting research skills. Professors are good at explaining the complexities of Aquinas or the details of Kant's categorical imperative. But they are less good at helping a student learn how to *think* about a new way to interpret this thinker or *defend* an unfashionable position. Beyond the basics, such as thinking critically and avoiding plagiarism, many professors usually don't teach a student how to move the discipline on to a new set of questions or a new approach or a potential solution to an old problem. For the Masters' student trying to write a thesis or a student starting on a Ph.D. dissertation, we have an old-fashioned system of "trial and error" – you try, the professor tells you that it is wrong, and you try again. There is a need for a book that explains *how* to write in such a way that you advance a discipline; there is a need for a book that explains *why* this article is great and that it should be a model of great research writing.

This book sets out to solve this problem. We do so in two ways. First, toward the end of this introduction we set out what we take to be the basics of writing publishable research essays. Second, we offer sixteen model "research" articles. Surrounding each article is an apparatus that explains precisely why this is a model research article. We make explicit what is often implicit. We explain about the importance of the signpost, the accurate representation of positions you do not hold, the way in which objections are anticipated, why this footnote is important, and how a good piece of writing ultimately drags the reader to feel that this argument might be right even if his or her instinct is to find the argument mistaken.

Therefore, the first purpose of this book is to teach the art of writing good, creative, research-orientated theology. Our target readers are all those trying to write a Masters' thesis or beginning work on their doctorate. But the book is also intended to provide the basis of an "innovative theology" course. This is a course that takes a group of students through a set of issues, loosely clustered around the key themes in systematic theology, that are models of good theological writing with theses that are provocative. A professor can select certain chapters or simply work through each chapter and in so doing teach both content and the art of research writing.

We did try to make sure that the book touches a range of different approaches to the writing of innovative theology. So Pamela Jones, primarily, employs a historical approach to the theme of race in the Southern Baptist Conference. Keith Ward attends closely to the biblical text in his discussion of eschatology. Andrei Buckareff brings the rigors of analytical philosophy to the issue of hell. In addition, we were interested in writing that crosses disciplines. As a result, the engagement of science is prominent with articles on anthropology (Celia Deane-Drummond), biological evolution (Christopher Southgate), and artificial intelligence or AI (Ian Markham). We wanted

---

The Craft of Innovative Theology: Argument and Process, First Edition. Edited by John Allan Knight and Ian S. Markham.
© 2022 John Wiley & Sons Ltd. Published 2022 by John Wiley & Sons Ltd.

articles that connected with the dilemmas of living. Trevor Bechtel explores the issues around the eating of animals, while Kathryn Blanchard takes COVID-19 as a case study in business ethics. We wanted some essays that exhibited an interfaith sensitivity. Therefore, Tinu Ruparell writes about religious pluralism and Cass Fisher reflects on the whole concept of Jewish theology. We wanted some texts that are very accessible – Thomas Oord eases the reader into a controversial thesis in a very gentle and readable way – and we wanted other articles to illustrate what participation in a highly technical discussion, where the scholar is completely on top of the literature and the current conversation – Leigh Vicens and John Knight met this goal perfectly. We wanted different writing styles, from those who love stories and illustrations – Martyn Percy and Trevor Bechtel – to those who appeal primarily to precise logical distinctions – Andrei Buckareff. For the teacher and the reader working through this book, the result is that you are introduced to a vast spectrum of approaches. But they all share the virtue of being great examples of provocative, innovative research writing.

Approaching the Book

There are two ways that this book can be used. First, a professor can start at the beginning and treat the book as a textbook for "creative theology." Second, a professor can move around the book focusing on those chapters that are easier for a beginner to access first and moving on to those chapters that are more advanced. This works for a "research methods" course. Now there are many "research methods" books on the market, but none do the work of providing research method techniques for the student who is going to start writing at the level of a Ph.D. or a research Master's Degree. This text teaches research writing at the highest academic level. If used for a research methods course, then the result is that the student at the end of the course will have a real sense of the different types of research levels and different types of research writing.

Research Levels

We deliberately wanted a book that embraced a full spectrum of research writing, from the very accessible to the very difficult. To give the reader a sense of the level, each chapter has a ranking. Level 1 means that the article is accessible and teaches basic research skills. Level 2 means that the article has certain concepts that will require explanation, but a good student can grasp the issues. Level 3 means that the article assumes some knowledge of the field and, without such literacy, the argument will be difficult to grasp. One assumption we are making here is that reading articles that are technically beyond the reader actually helps the reader to grow. With the help of the glossary (all words in bold in the text are explained in the glossary at the end of the book) and with the sheer discipline of reading to the end, the reader will learn how to read at such a technical level. Level 4 means that there is a level of technical understanding and background knowledge that is essential for understanding the article. In the end, research articles are an act of participation in a pre-existing conversation. To have credibility, one must know the existing participants in the conversation. The essays included in this book exhibit this kind of credibility and exemplify the ultimate goal of great innovative academic writing.

We have four articles at each ranking. At the first research level, Ian Markham offers an essay in Christology that argues that Jesus (the first-century Jewish male) could have been Eternal Word made flesh in a different human form; he takes as his case study a person with Down's Syndrome and argues that the Eternal Wisdom could have been made manifest in such a life. Also at this level, there is Pamela Jones offering a historical survey of the Southern Baptist Convention (SBC) and its journey to overcome the stigma of racism; she suggests that shifting attitudes in the SBC are partly linked to declining membership. Ian Markham has a second article at this level, in which he explores AI. He argues that it is possible that the church might have to face the emergence of "self-conscious" AI entities that then should be granted human rights. And finally Thomas Oord's chapter "Rentless Love and the Afterlife" argues that God would not compel a person to be either in heaven or hell. God's character is unchangeable and that character does not compel.

At the second level, the book starts with Tinu Ruparell exploring the implications for theology of religious pluralism. He makes the case that all theology must take interreligious conversations seriously. Trevor Bechtel takes a serious look at the eating of animals; he argues that factory farming is deeply wrong and that no animal should be eaten that has not had a good life. Kathryn Blanchard looks at the debate in the US over COVID-19 – health or business. She argues for a vision of business that takes seriously the full range of stakeholders. The last chapter at this level is written by Keith Ward; his essay argues that Christians should treat the language about the return of Christ in the same way as the creation narrative. To harmonize with the scientific narrative, we need to recognize that the language is not descriptive of the return of the resurrected Christ to Earth, but instead an affirmation that ultimately God's providential plans for creation will be realized.

At the third level, we have two chapters on science and religion. Celia Deane-Drummond reflects on what it means to be distinctively human. She advocates for getting away from "Image of God" language and instead drawing on Christology. Christopher Southgate argues that although evolution is true, it does create real problems for theology. His suggested solution is a compound theodicy. Andrei Buckareff looks at hell, suggesting that persons in hell will not necessarily be "unhappy" and that there is always an option to escape. Finally, in this third level, Martyn Percy invites the reader to see how all faith is conditioned in different ways by the culture in which it grows.

At the fourth level, we have Leigh Vicens who provides a nuanced account of the concept of responsibility. Given that no human can avoid sinning, in what sense should we be held responsible? Demonstrating mastery of the literature, she sees blame as a moral protest concept; it is not so much the person that is blamed but the actions that we do. The other level four essays are all in Part VI. John Knight teases out some linguistic assumptions underpinning liberal theology. Cass Fisher looks at the way in which Jewish studies should be developing the arguments for "theological reference" (namely you can properly refer to God) rather than continuing to deny the legitimacy of theological reflection. And finally, John Knight in the last essay in the book, takes a particular argument – the slingshot argument of Marshall – and shows that it does not invalidate correspondence theories of truth.

One goal here is to create the "self-conscious" reader who can see and appreciate good academic writing. At the end of this book, you will understand the achievement of these different essays. In so doing, when you read other articles and books you will be able to place and recognize the achievement of those texts. But before moving on to the chapters we've just mentioned, let's turn to the basic elements of publishable academic writing.

For the Student: Basics of Writing for Publication

In this section we'll do three things. We'll first talk about the importance of asking a good question (which in your writing you'll attempt to answer). Next, we'll introduce the basic parts of any good essay. Finally, we'll say a few words about the process of producing a publishable essay.[1]

Every Good Piece of Writing is an Answer to a Question

When reading any source, whether it's an ancient text or a scholarly book or article, it's important to figure out just what question the author is asking. That is the first step in any good interpretation. But focusing on the question is important not only for reading well but also for writing well. When you're setting out to write an essay, make sure you have a good question. But what makes a question a good one? To our minds, a good question has several characteristics. First, it should be authentic – that is, it should be original to your essay. That doesn't mean that no one has ever asked it before. Rather, it should be a question that either has not been answered or has not been answered to your satisfaction. In your hands it is a question that can yield an original contribution to scholarship in theology. And making an original contribution will be the most important consideration in determining whether your essay is publishable.

Second, a good question is one that is answerable. There are two parts to this characteristic. First, there must be evidence or arguments capable of supporting a reasonable answer. Take, for example, the following question: "What did prehistoric people think were the most persuasive forms of argument?" Since the people in question are prehistoric, there won't be any evidence to support an answer. Second, it must be capable of an answer within the space constraints of the journal – normally around twenty pages or so. "How have the relations between church and state changed in Europe between the middle ages and the present?" It's questionable whether a book would have sufficient room for an adequate answer to that question; certainly an article is too short.

---

[1] As you begin to write your dissertation, keep in mind that you will eventually want to publish it as a book. The following works are very helpful in this task: William Germano, *From Dissertation to Book* (Chicago: University of Chicago Press, 2005); idem, *Getting It Published: A Guide for Scholars and Anyone Else Serious about Serious Books* (Chicago: University of Chicago Press, 2001); Beth Luey, ed., *Revising Your Dissertation: Advice from Leading Editors* (Berkeley and Los Angeles: University of California Press, 2004); and Susan Rabiner and Alfred Fortunato, *Thinking Like Your Editor: How to Write Great Serious Nonfiction—and Get It Published* (New York: W.W. Norton & Co., 2002). While revising our dissertations for publication, however, we found it extremely useful to submit some portions (usually not a whole chapter) to journals for publication. We found the feedback from the anonymous reviewers to be extremely helpful. Thus, we have focused most of our comments on writing article-length essays. In our comments here, we are indebted to Victoria Reyes, "How to write an effective journal article and get it published (essay)," *Inside Higher Ed*, https://www.insidehighered.com/advice/2017/05/09/how-write-effective-journal-article-and-get-it-published-essay; "How to get published in an academic journal: top tips from editors," *The Guardian*, Jan. 3, 2015, https://www.theguardian.com/education/2015/jan/03/how-to-get-published-in-an-academic-journal-top-tips-from-editors; and Faye Halpern, Thomas A. Lewis, Anne Monius, Robert Orsi, and Christopher White, *A Guide to Writing in Religious Studies*, https://hwpi.harvard.edu/files/hwp/files/religious_studies.pdf.

Third, a good question is one that is consequential. If the answer to the question – your thesis – is shown to be true, there will be consequences for the field. Perhaps it will open up new ways of thinking about some particular question; perhaps some conventional view will have to be changed. These consequences tie into the question of motivation. What is motivating you to write this essay? Very often it will be to provide a counterargument to some view you think mistaken. It might be to lay the groundwork for a new direction in addressing some theological issue. Essentially, a good question can provide a follow-up answer to "So what? So what if you're right?" If you've formulated a good question, you'll be able to answer the "So what?" question by articulating the consequences of your answer. And these consequences should be spelled out in your conclusion.

Every Good Piece of Writing Has a Beginning, a Middle, and an End

A Beginning: The Introduction

We find it helpful to write the introduction first, to make explicit how we want to proceed. But most often it will need to be rewritten after the essay is substantially completed, as arguments regularly change a bit during writing. But in the final draft of your introduction, make sure the argument is clear. How do you know if it's clear? Suppose you're on the subway and strike up a conversation with the person seated next to you. If that person asks you to explain the argument in your paper before she gets off at the next stop, could you explain it without resorting to technical vocabulary? That clear, concise explanation should be included in your abstract and your introduction.

The introduction should serve four functions. First, it should contextualize your essay. A good introduction will describe previous work on the subject and show that there is a problem or a lacuna in the literature that needs to be addressed. Second, the introduction should show exactly how your essay addresses the problem. This is where you will state the precise question you will be answering and the thesis for which the essay will argue. Third, it's very helpful if the introduction provides a brief roadmap of your argument that states in a concise and orderly way the explanation you gave to the hypothetical person on the subway. Editors are busy people; don't make their job harder than it needs to be. When an author makes their job easier by making clear, right in the introduction, what the essay will argue, the whole process goes more smoothly and quickly. Fourth, make sure to mention the broader implications of your essay for contributing to some ongoing conversation. You can spell this out in more detail in the conclusion, but it should be mentioned in the introduction.

B Middle: The Argument

The middle section is where you make your argument. In general, we find it helpful if each step in your argument has its own section. The sections may or may not have a title (i.e. the sections may just be numbered); the journal you pick may have guidelines for this.

Not all arguments rely on textual evidence (a purely logical or *a priori* argument won't), but even those that don't will likely involve some text that you are disputing. If your argument involves textual evidence, you'll need to do more than simply quote the texts. You will need to interpret them. This will require several steps. First, either simply quote the text or re-state in a summary fashion what the author is saying. Next, if there are ambiguities, state the various meanings that the text might have, then specify which meaning is most supportive of your argument. Then show how, in the context of the entire text, this meaning is the best one. You can do this by noting a contradiction or an adverse logical ramification to the alternate meanings. Finally, explain exactly how the text in question supports your argument.

On the other hand, if you are criticizing a text, state the various meanings that the text might have, then specify which meaning is most resistant to your critique. Then you have two alternatives. First, you can show that this is the only meaning that can withstand your critique. Second, you can show that even this most resistant meaning cannot withstand your critique.

You will also need to consider and refute counterarguments. If there are counterarguments in the literature, you need to find them and argue against them. And if there are other possible counterarguments that have not yet been raised, you'll need to articulate them and refute them as well.

C End: The Conclusion

Your conclusion should include three elements. First, summarize concisely the findings of your essay, including the thesis. Second, without trivializing your essay, specify the limitations of your argument. Claiming to have done more than you actually have will reduce your credibility. Third, explain your original contribution. How has your essay done something that other publications have not? Finally, propose possibilities for future work, describing how such possibilities have been made possible by the work your essay has accomplished.

Process

Now that we've mentioned some of the basic elements of a publishable essay, let's talk about the process of writing it.

Read, Read, Read!

The first thing to do, of course is research and read. Read a lot. Make notes on the reading. Make sure your research is current and complete. As you're reading, think about the way you will explain to the reader how your essay relates to work that has already been published. It's not necessary to mention every previous publication on your topic, but situating your essay in the context of previous work in the field is necessary to demonstrating your specific contribution. In addition, as you're reading and doing research, think about how to formulate the question your essay will answer. As you're considering various formulations, remember the elements of a good question as we discussed earlier. It is not uncommon to begin with an overly broad question and, as you read more, narrow the question down until finally it is narrow enough to be answerable within the space of an article-length essay.

Decide on a Journal

First, submit your essay to only ONE journal at a time. Often, authors write the essay first and then decide on a journal. The process will probably be faster and easier, however, if you decide on the journal first. The problem of writing the article first and then deciding on the journal latter is that the guidelines of each journal varies significantly. Hours can be wasted as you change the citation system and delete pages of text that exceed their word limit.

Know the audience and the most common topics of the journal. The best way to do this, in addition to reading the description on their web site, is to read several articles from the journal to get a sense of the kinds of discussions they publish. If your preferred journal is published in the UK and has primarily British readers, you should not assume, for example, that they all know the American system (and similarly for British writers publishing in the US). You can ask your advisor to recommend a couple of journals. Look at the journal's web site for submission guidelines (citation style, word limit, etc.), and follow them carefully as you're writing. This will not only save you time but will also avoid irritating the editors right out of the box.

In addition, note that journals have a specific identity. *Religious Studies*, for example, focuses on philosophy of religion; submitting an essay to that journal discussing the relationship between Canaanite and Israelite religion would be pointless. *Theology Today*, while it publishes scholarly articles, also publishes essays pitched to a broader readership than practicing scholars. So it's helpful to decide on the audience to which you wish to speak and pick your journal accordingly. This may seem obvious, but we hear from editors that it is surprising how many essays are submitted to journals whose focus has almost nothing to do with the essay.

Finally, think about how quickly you want your work to be published. Some journals are more prestigious than others and have a higher rate of rejection. In addition, some journals are known for their lengthy wait before publication. We have had articles accepted as is, but it took two years after acceptance until the articles appeared in print. Some journals with lengthy wait times will publish your essay online while it is waiting; listing the "doi" number on your cv will show prospective employers that your work is publishable.

Formulate a Good Question

Remember the elements of a good question we discussed earlier. Your essay will be an answer to the question you have formulated. Confine your paper to answering that question. The strongest papers answer one question convincingly, provide plenty of evidence and arguments to support the answer, and position the argument within the overall conversation in the field. This will often mean that you cannot publish a whole dissertation chapter in a journal article. Instead, you may need to take one argument or sub-argument from the chapter and resituate it into a contemporary conversation in the literature.

Outline

The structure of your paper is as important as the content. Structure your outline so that it's as easy as possible for a reader to follow your argument from beginning to end. Every good essay follows a strong narrative arc, and this should be displayed in your outline. This narrative arc can be a logical or historical progression, and it will constitute the structure of your argument. We like to have an outline in mind before we start writing. Others like to start writing and get inspiration and ideas before they start writing. However you begin, a good essay will follow a well-structured outline.

Write

Make sure to explain clearly how your work is an original contribution. Even if your essay is an interpretation of an aspect of another scholar's work, or a reinterpretation of a theological concept, you must still have something original to say in order for the piece to be publishable. This contextualization is crucial and is a common reason for rejection of articles after peer review. Don't be bashful when you write. Make sure your paper demonstrates a strong authorial voice that is neither unduly modest nor overconfident. Above all, seek clarity. Writing that is clear and easy to read is also easier to understand and more persuasive. Keep in mind that clarity does not equate to superficiality, and clear writing does not necessarily involve overgeneralizations. Generally speaking, language that is more specific is clearer and less conducive to misunderstanding.

Always keep your audience in mind as you're writing. Write your essay in such a way that it answers questions that they are asking and is appropriate for their level of expertise. Scholars and other experts in the field can be expected to be familiar with technical language, while lay readers may need technical concepts explained.

The structure of your paragraphs should follow the roadmap in your introduction. Each paragraph should have a topic sentence that states the overall point of the paragraph. And at the beginning and end of each section (remember that each section is a step in the overall argument) you should include a "signpost" that references the roadmap in the introduction and indicates where the overall paper is going. If the argument is especially complex, your signposts can include summary reminders of the points in the argument that you have already established can be helpful. Topic sentences and signposts keep your reader oriented to the overall direction of the paper and how far along in the argument they are.

Revise

Once you have finished a draft and completed your first revision, ask a colleague to read it. This may become less necessary after you have become more experienced in publishing articles. Still, even experienced writers sometimes find it helpful to have a colleague read their essays. As the author, you know and have been living with your argument for some time. It's therefore difficult for most authors to know how clear the essay's argument is to someone reading it for the first time. It's common in graduate school, however, to form dissertation groups of three or four students who read and discuss each other's work before submitting it. This is especially helpful if you're writing in a language other than your first language. Even if you don't have a colleague read it, it's a good idea to let it sit for a couple of days and then do a significant revision.

Proofread

It's very important, after your essay is finished, to proofread it carefully for typographical and grammatical errors, misspellings, etc. (including errors introduced by autocorrect!). Don't rely on spellcheck! You may want to have a friend proofread your piece – after having gone over it repeatedly, it can be very difficult to see small errors. Some schools still offer proofreading services, though these are becoming rarer.

Submit!

When you're submitting your work, many journals ask for a cover letter. Don't repeat the abstract in the cover letter or go through your argument in any detail. Instead, focus on the bigger picture, explaining what you think is most significant about your essay and why it is a good fit for the journal. This is a chance to emphasize your original contribution, but keep it brief.

Revise and Resubmit!

After submitting an essay to a journal, unless the editor rejects it for being outside the scope of the journal, you will likely receive comments from reviewers (two, or possibly three) with their suggested changes. At this point, it is amazing how many writers who receive revise and resubmit letters never actually resubmit the essay. After receiving the reviewers' comments, it's probably a good idea to read them and then wait a couple of days before responding. More than once we have received reviews with comments we initially thought quite wrong, only to find ourselves agreeing with them after a few days. When resubmitting your essay after receiving reviews, you should submit a cover letter detailing the changes suggested by the reviewers and describing any changes you have made to the essay in response. Respond directly and professionally to every reviewer comment. You don't necessarily have to comply with every suggestion; but if you disagree with a comment and disregard the suggestion, you should provide your justification for doing so.

Celebrate!

You may experience some hesitation before submitting the essay. This is understandable, for once it's submitted you lose some degree of control over it. It's a difficult thing to submit a manuscript for publication. Even if it's rejected from your first-choice journal, submitting it is still an accomplishment and your work during the submission process will make it more likely that your second-choice journal will accept it. So reward yourself in some way!

In Conclusion

Learning to write at the highest level of the academy is hard. But we are committed to the view that stating complex and technical arguments with stylistic clarity can be learned through examples. We chose models of writing that reinforce certain basic principles – a good piece of academic writing has a signpost, it is fair to the opponents, it illustrates a grasp of the literature, and it always goes back to the primary sources.

We are hopeful that this book will assist those who aspire to write research articles. We hope the ultimate result is a growth in the academy, in the church, and in the world of thoughtful exponents of creative theology.

John Allan Knight and Ian S. Markham

Part I

God and the Incarnation

1

Knowing God through Religious Pluralism

Tinu Ruparell

RESEARCH LEVEL 2

Editors' Introduction

Good academic writing is clear and elegant. This opening essay meets both of those conditions. It is a provocative thesis: All serious theology must be shaped by religious pluralism. He believes that this has always been the case; and now it must continue to be "consciously" so in the future. He suggests five characteristics of such theology, which he sets out as the heart of the essay. He then concludes by responding to some of the objections that the reader might have to his argument.

Theology is always hybrid (see Box 1.1).

Box 1.1
Tinu Ruparell puts his thesis front and center. All theology draws on a range of traditions and sources. He then unpacks this assertion by insisting that all serious theological systems must take religious pluralism seriously. This is a shocking assertion. It means that all those who primarily work as theologians within a tradition are, in the view of Ruparell, not doing serious theology. The opening of this essay is controversial and provocative. The reader is invited to engage with the argument.

I propose this statement as axiomatic for any theology which takes religious **pluralism** seriously, and of course *all* theology must take religious pluralism seriously. Indeed I contend that no theological system can be taken seriously if it does not countenance the facts of religious plurality at its very foundation. To fail to do so is to be blind to the conditions of human thinking about the religious. The religious traditions we encounter, study, may participate in, critique, and/or promote have all originated, developed, and continue to exist within a context of religious plurality. This, I submit, is an empirical fact needing little further argument.[1] Moreover, all

---

[1] Due to space I cannot here justify this claim fully, though even a cursory reading of most of the world religions' founding texts shows regular references to a religiously plural context. Ancient theologians are also well aware of their pluralistic context. For instance Clement attributes to Xenophanes the view that the Thracians "gods are red haired and blue eyed, the Ethiopians' black as apes" in the process of his argument that the "heathens made Gods like themselves, whence springs all superstition" *Stromata* VII, chapter 4.

theology, like all theorization, is inherently comparative.² In order to understand and create theology the scholar partakes in comparative and generalizing activity, which requires **emic** and **etic reference**. Religious pluralism is thus an intra-religious concern as much as it is an interreligious one. No tradition, and therefore no theology, can thus be considered without conscious reference to the Other since all traditions were originated and continue to develop with explicit or implicit reference to other traditions which form their contexts. The importance of religious pluralism for our understanding of the theology, as well as for the production of novel, creative theology, cannot be understated. In what follows I will argue that the practice of theology must be recast to be explicitly pluralistic in a way that has not hitherto been the case. Theology must be more obviously interreligious and hybrid because theology is *already* interreligious and hybrid, but currently does not recognize itself as such (see Box 1.2).³

Box 1.2

Footnote 3 is a lovely note. The author is anticipating an obvious objection: If all theology is – as a matter of current reality – hybrid, then why is this program so radical and provocative? He uses the footnote to answer this objection. He is writing alert to potential criticisms to his arguments.

In redescribing theology through religious pluralism, I argue, it becomes more powerful, more relevant, and more useful. More powerful in its increased capacity to accurately describe the human condition; more relevant as it breaks out of its chains as a chauvinist practice of merely priestly interest; and more useful as it regains a role in broader economic, social, political, and cultural spheres.

Before I proceed to describe some elements of a pluralistically remade theology, an issue of terminology needs to be clarified (see Box 1.3).

Box 1.3

Ruparell is a careful scholar. He knows that there is considerable discussion over the language. So he clarifies precisely what he means by the terms "religious pluralism" and "a theology of religious pluralism." He does not want the reader thinking of a different meaning of these terms that then leads to a misunderstanding of his argument.

Religious pluralism refers simply to the existence of many different religious traditions in any given context (let us avoid for now the question of the definition of religion or religious tradition.) A *theology of religious pluralism*, however, has most often signified a particular view or theory concerning the status of multiple, different religious traditions – their beliefs, truth claims, and practices, etc. – in terms of one tradition held to be normative. So, for instance,

---

² I take this as a central thesis of J.Z. Smith's famous characterization of religion in his *Imagining Religion: From Babylon to Jonestown* (Chicago: University of Chicago Press, 1982), xi.

³ I realize the irony of proposing a somewhat radical program to transform theology into something I point out it already exhibits. My argument is not that theology must become pluralistic in a way it never was, but rather that it should fully and thoroughly recover the vigor and creative potential of the pluralism out of which it was born.

theological projects with which many will be familiar, using well-worn distinctions such as religious **inclusivism, exclusivism,** and pluralism, describe views from within a given (mostly Christian) tradition considering the truth claims and the **soteriological** status of other (mostly non-Christian) traditions. In what follows I do not intend to propose a theological redescription in this vein – though certain kinds of theologies of religious pluralism may follow from what I argue. What I wish to do, in keeping with the general aim of this collection, is to propose how one should do creative, novel, interesting, and useful theology in the light of religious pluralism, viz. allowing the facts of religious plurality more forcefully and creatively to impinge directly on theology. Eschewing a "view from nowhere," I wish to highlight what any attempt at doing theology should look like if it is shaped and guided by the facts of religious plurality from the outset. I shall use the terms *pluralistic theology* to refer to this project. While I will focus on Christian, or broadly Semitic, traditions, there is no reason why the claims and arguments should be limited to Christian theology. Indeed, creative theologizing concerning any religious tradition should be thoroughly pluralistic in the senses I shall elaborate. A throughgoing pluralistic theology thus construes its religious tradition to be merely one among others, even if it shows special concern for its "home" tradition. The nuances of the tension inherent in this definition should become clearer as we proceed.

What does it mean, then, to speak about God – that is, do theology, and specifically creative theology – in the face of our religious Others? I suggest that it will or should display, minimally, the following characteristics (see Box 1.4):

Box 1.4

He helpfully lists the characteristics of a theology that takes religious pluralism seriously. The following five characteristics are his own listing. Although he is drawing on approaches found throughout the literature, his own listing of these five characteristics is his contribution to the debate.

---

1. Theology must be radically humble (principle of **fallibilism**).
2. Theology must be radically flexible (principle of indeterminacy).
3. Theology must be radically open (principle of contingency).
4. Theology must be radically poetic (principle of attraction).
5. Theology must be radically risky (principle of irony).

These are in no way meant to be an exhaustive set of characteristics, nor should we imagine that they will be present in equal measure, however, I argue that these are at least necessary features of knowing and speaking about God in the context of religious plurality. We will see, moreover, that these principles are interwoven, one often implying or melding into the others. Let us take them in turn before drawing some concluding insights and responding to some potential concerns.

Radical Fallibilism: The Principle of Humility

Pluralistic theology must be conducted according to the fundamental idea that on matters both large and small, *we may be significantly wrong in the end.* One must therefore engage in creative theology with a spirit of humility. There are both internal and external reasons for this **epistemic fallibilism** (see Box 1.5).

> **Box 1.5**
>
> One feature of this essay is to draw a contrast with other approaches to theology. So this pluralistic theology will operate with a spirit of humility. It is not a conceited theology – one that is sure that it is right and everyone else is wrong. This is an important part of Ruparell's argument.

Firstly, within Christian scriptures and theological tradition, there are many proscriptions against the idea that human beings can adequately grasp the true nature of the divine. The Hebrew Bible and New Testament clearly state that God is beyond all reckoning,[4] and that to believe and act as if one knows God's being, nature, and acts is liable to leave one mistaken in the end, as evidenced by the parable of the sheep and goats (Matthew 25: 31–46)In this parable, those who presumably followed religious law but failed to act according to its deeper meaning were judged to be wicked. Surely one lesson to take from this parable is that one shouldn't be quite so certain that one's religious beliefs and practices are correct, or that one has fulfilled all of God's requirements. And in the Hebrew Bible perhaps no greater scriptural evidence for fallibilism can be had than the epiphany of Job. While notoriously difficult to square with traditional teaching about God's nature as well as the **theodical** questions which give rise to the narrative, God's blustery appearance in the whirlwind very clearly puts human knowledge in its place: limited, mistaken, overweening. However else one might interpret the book, Job clearly emphasizes human ignorance and fallibility.

Theologically, the doctrine of **transcendence**, when fully realized, makes it impossible to know God, truly, in any positive sense; that is, we cannot literally attribute any predicates to God, only negations – as in the *via negativa* of Aquinas or Augustine's depiction of God as *wholly other* (see Box 1.6).[5]

> **Box 1.6**
>
> It is worth pausing and looking closely at footnote 5. In the text, the author is explaining that God's transcendence means that we cannot know precisely what God is like. The author is aware that this is the realm of **apophatic** theology. To discuss this at any length in the text would be a major distraction. Instead, the author uses the note to invite the reader to read an essay on apophatic theology. In this way, he reassures the reader that he is aware of this strand in the literature; and he helpfully directs the reader to a text that can provide a helpful discussion of this approach to theology, namely, Andrew Louth, "Holiness and the Vision of God in the Eastern Fathers," in *Holiness: Past and Present*, ed. Stephen C. Barton(London: T&T Clark, 2003), 217–239.

The transcendence of God puts hard limits on what human beings can know about the divine, highlighting the humility with which we must hold theological statements. Of course the doctrine of transcendence, and indeed the scriptures on which they are based, are also balanced by statements that positively ascribe actions and characteristics to God. Aquinas's theory of analogy makes certain forms of positive religious language possible and sensible, but of course

---

[4] See for instance Isaiah 55:8–9; Acts 17:24; 1 Kings 8:27; Job 38–42.

[5] Thomas Aquinas, *Summa Theologiae* I.2.a.2; Augustine of Hippo *Confessions* 7.10.16. For a discussion of the roots of apophatic theology, see Andrew Louth, "Holiness and the Vision of God in the Eastern Fathers", in *Holiness: Past and Present*, ed. Stephen C. Barton (London: T&T Clark, 2003), 217–239.

analogical language cannot be said to refer to God directly. We must rely on figurative language to speak, as it were, above our heads,[6] while maintaining strict adherence to Divine Otherness lest our words refer to something other than God.[7] To be clear, transcendence logically forbids the possibility of literal, positive predication, so the characteristics of God described in scripture and tradition must be suspended in analogical tension. In the light of this tense suspension, the most consistent perspective is that when humans hold a particular view about the divine it must be held lightly, as with an open palm. This is a performance of our humility: we cannot presume to truly *know* God, yet we are able to *understand* our relationship to the divine only when we continually recognize the tentative, fallibilistic nature of our ideas.

Most religious traditions accept that language cannot literally refer to God, only analogically or figuratively. Just as the idea of transcendence necessitates a theology which requires epistemic fallibilism as an axiom, analogical predication opens up possibilities of understanding that facilitate and even encourage a religiously plural, creative theology. The flexibility and **polysemy** inherent in analogical/metaphorical[8] language allows for a wide variety of images, metaphors, and symbols to be used in religious language, not all of which necessarily derive from a single tradition. This opens up the possibility of using figures of speech (along with their semantic horizons) deriving from "foreign" language games, resulting in hybrid or creole predication. This is indeed the case for Christian tradition itself, as the first few centuries of its theological development show a synthesis of Jewish and Greco-Roman concepts, language, images, narratives, and symbols: the marriage of Jerusalem and Athens. So if, following George Lindbeck,[9] we understand the relationship of theology to religious belief, practice, and tradition on the model of the relationship of grammar to its natural language, then a thoroughly pluralistic theology can be forged through explicit and implicit synthesis of ideas, images, and concepts derived from a variety of religious forms of life. What begins with a humble recognition of fallible and limited human abilities to know the divine leads to a freedom to borrow from a variety of languages and conceptual schemes in order to express what *can* usefully be said. A humble, creative, pluralistic theology must therefore leave space for such hybridity.

Radical Flexibility: The Principle of Indeterminism

I expect some may be rather queasy about the skeptical trajectory of the principle of fallibilism just described. If we must resist the drive toward certain knowledge and conviction, maintaining, rather, that when all is said and done we might be significantly wrong about central beliefs and practices of a tradition, then in what sense could we hold religious beliefs and practices to be true? Surely, contends the critic, even a theology thoroughly inflected by the facts of religious plurality must have some criteria of justifiable belief? Pushed too far, does not the principle of fallibilism lead to Pyrrhonian skepticism?

---

[6] See Janet Martine Soskice's *Metaphor and Religious Language* (Oxford: Clarendon, 1987).

[7] Augustine, *Sermons* 117.3.5.

[8] I suggest that analogy is a species of metaphorical predication however cannot develop this view fully here. It is worth distinguishing, at this point, polysemy with hybridity: the prior belonging to a term's reception and the latter its semantic content.

[9] George Lindbeck, *The Nature of Doctrine: Theology in a Post-Liberal Age* (Louisville: Westminster John Knox press, 1984), 33–34.

The question of truth in theological discourse is, of course, still much debated, and a thorough discussion of it is beyond the scope of this chapter. However, I suggest that a pluralistic theology of religion must avoid the **scylla** of a strict **correspondence theory of truth**, and the charybdis of mere coherence theories, opting, rather, for a pragmatic theory.[10] The principle of indeterminism at work here describes a position which maintains that the truth of religious propositions is constructed, negotiated, dynamic, and provisional. Religious truth refers to what particular, historic, and changing religious communities, broadly construed, accept as valuable, constitutive, and trustworthy. "True" is what such communities label the propositions which, generally, work for them; that is, help to deliver the kinds of goods and forms of life commonly valued by those communities. For pluralistic theology, religious truth cannot be fixed forever in objective certitude, for, as Kierkegaard reminds us, objective facts per se do not impinge on our lives. Facts about the universe must be appropriated subjectively in order to have meaning for us.

Box 1.7

In this description of the second characteristic notice how he goes back to the original sources when outlining the views of Kierkegaard. He does not draw on secondary sources, or descriptions of Kierkegaard's views, but quotes the actual relevant section of Kiekegaard's journal.

In his journal of 1835 Kierkegaard writes (see Box 1.7):

> What would be the use of discovering so-called objective truth, of working through all the systems of philosophy and of being able, if required, to review them all and show up the inconsistencies within each system [...] what good would it do me if truth stood before me, cold and naked, not caring whether I recognised her or not, and producing in me a shudder of fear rather than a trusting devotion?[11]

Subjectivity is thus the tell-tale of religious truth, as Kierkegaard makes clear through his definition of truth as an "objective uncertainty held fast in an appropriation process of the most passionate inwardness."[12] However, to function as a general theory of truth, this subjectivity must be tested through negotiation and contestation within the relevant religious communities.[13] These negotiated settlements shape subjective truth toward the ends valued by particular communities

---

[10] I follow Rorty's development of a pragmatic theory of truth as found in his *Philosophy and the Mirror of Nature*, 35th anniversary ed. (Princeton, NJ: Princeton University Press, 2009) and elsewhere in his writing. While the pragmatic theory of truth he presents there has undergone much critique and development, I suggest the nub of his argument presented in this book remains compelling, particularly for the project of pluralistic theology. **Correspondence theories of truth** cannot simply apply to religious propositions since it would require an impossible Archimedean vantage point and coherence theories fail to break from the perhaps more serious threat of non-realism.

[11] Søren Kierkegaard, *The Journals of Kierkegaard*, trans. A. Dru (London: Collins, 1958), 44.

[12] Søren Kierkegaard, "Truth is Subjectivity," in *Concluding Unscientific Postscript*, ed. A. Hannay (Cambridge: Cambridge University Press, 2009), 171.

[13] In William James's construal of pragmatic theories of truth, this test, negotiation and contestation *is* the verification treasured by proponents of correspondence theories of truth. See lecture IV in his *Pragmatism* where he states: "True ideas are those that we can assimilate, validate, corroborate, and verify. False ideas are those that we cannot".

at particular times and places. Truth is thus at the same time the product of contingent, historical processes while being held fast to subjectivity with the greatest trust. It plays an essential and foundational role in the creation and maintenance of a religious community while at the same time continually arising from and responding to the needs, desires, best practices, and values of that dynamic, interactive community. Religious truth understood pragmatically is a continual work in progress, much as even the most established scientific theories are always provisional. Insofar as religious beliefs and practices continue to be effective in bringing about the forms of life cherished by communities, exemplified in their narratives, performed in their rituals, made relatively more permanent in their institutions, held fast to in subjectivity, they are thereby labeled "true."

This picture of truth as it pertains to religious statements demonstrates the flexibility and indeterminacy at the heart of a pluralistic theology. The test for such a theology will focus on how the "grammar" of the beliefs and practices of a community facilitate its shared ends and values. Where a question arises as to the truth or legitimacy of a particular belief, doctrine or practice, the final arbiter must be the community itself, and as communities are by nature dynamic, so too will its reflected picture of religious truth. A pluralistic theology cannot be ossified since the negotiation of what counts as "true belief," i.e. "warranted practice," will necessarily emerge from contestation, negotiation and provisional acceptance. Within this framework, again, lies an openness to new possibilities and hybrid expression.

Radical Openness and Poesis: The Principles of Contingency and Attraction

I will consider the next two characteristics together as they form two sides of the same coin. Pluralistic theology must be both expansive and comprehensive in terms of its creative power and potential, as well as integrative and discriminative in terms of its manifestation or **instantiation** into particular, beautiful, and useful forms. Openness and contingency here refer to the scope and freedom of this creative power: there is an effervescence, an overflowing nature to pluralistic theology which reflects the plethora of creative possibilities made possible following the loosening of theological strictures wrought by the principle of indeterminism. At the same time this **centrifugal** openness and expansiveness is (not so much restricted as) given form and structure, through a parallel, contrary pressure toward "felicitous particularity." Importantly, this **centripetal**, poetic[14] pressure is guided, as we shall see, by aesthetic criteria. These two forces work together through a tense dialectic: a fecund mutual interanimation encompassing a simultaneous centrifugal expansion shaped by a centripetal particularization. Energized by this dialectic, pluralistic theology is opened up to the voice of the religious Other in ways that recognize the creative and indeterminate potential of mutual engagement, while at the same time **kenotically** offering its own tradition as a substrate for differentiation. The effect is that theology, characterized by radical openness, tempered by radical poesis, invites the creation of novel insight, greater solidarity, and a more comprehensive consolation.

It is worth elaborating these mutually opposed yet creative forces further, not only to clarify their activity but also to intimate the ironic nature of pluralistic theology we shall describe later. Two processes are at the heart of the centrifugal/centripetal tension I have described: the

---

[14] I use the term "poetic" to refer to *poesis/poiesis*, the Greek term for "making." The poetic here signifies the movement from potentiality to actuality, a movement effected by a poet, or maker.

centrifugal, creative revelation of metaphorical predication, and the centripetal, coalescing manifestation into forms regulated by aesthetic attraction. This dialectic both/and movement between creatively opposed forces recapitulates the dynamics of metaphor. Indeed this dynamic is the fountainhead at the center of creative theologizing. It will be useful to rehearse Paul Ricoeur's highly influential "interactionist" account of metaphor in order to describe this dynamic.

Following Ricoeur, we can define metaphor as a figure of speech whereby one thing is referred to in terms which evince another.[15] On this view, metaphor is a semantic generator whereby the terms of the metaphor – importantly understood as statements rather than individual words – work to redescribe each other in a **hermeneutic** spiral. Furthermore, as these metaphorical "poles" are each connected by a web of reference to both their horizons of language and to their corresponding aspects of lived experience, what metaphor brings together are not individual elements of language – semantic sound bites so to speak – but connected aspects of life. Pluralistic theology thus brings into creative tension interrelated webs of belief and practice in the same way as when holding together two corners of a seamless fabric what is connected to the corners is also brought together. This is important for a number of reasons. Firstly, for a metaphor to be fertile, its terms' associated commonplaces must be readily summoned. Only then can metaphor engage the imagination so that the statement evinces a "semantic twist" (in Monroe Beardsley's words) such that novel interpretations are created. Secondly, this aspect of metaphor also guards against the decontextualization which naïve comparisons often effect. Pluralistic theology doesn't simply substitute an emic term or idea for its **etic** counterpart, but rather seeks to knit together the webs of reference contextualizing those terms. By leveraging the action and structure of metaphor in the ways which I shall shortly describe, pluralistic theology seeks to bring into conversation fuller and more detailed areas of lived religious experience to create a more robust hybrid theology.

As just mentioned, metaphor works by redescribing each pole or element of the metaphor in terms of the other.[16] The dialectic of metaphor must begin with and maintain difference,[17] for only with this alterity is the necessary logical or semantic incoherence, which is the spur to the metaphorical imagination, present. In meeting a metaphorical statement there is a disjunction which the interpreter sees as logically incoherent. This is illustrated by "Man is wolf" to take Freud's famous example. The pressure of this disjunction imaginatively calls forth a term's associated commonplaces – what Gadamer calls a horizon of meaning and Voloshinov[18] the apperceptive context – and from this horizon new descriptions are associated with the other term in the metaphor; humans are seen to be more lupine, in our example. The process is bidirectional or multidirectional so that each term in the metaphor is redescribed in terms of the others; wolves are thus seen to be more human. In this way the semantic field of a metaphor is effectively stretched to include these new connections. Ricoeur calls metaphors "semantic generators" as these new connotations, this new metaphorical interpretation, exists between the parent terms of the metaphor, owing allegiance, as it were, to its sources while differing from each. Metaphor

---

[15] This is Janet Soskice's definition, which while wholly in line with Ricoeur's, is more succinctly expressed. See Soskice, *Metaphor and Religions Language* (Oxford: Clarendon, 1984) and Ricoeur *The Rule of Metaphor* (Toronto: University of Toronto Press, 1977).

[16] While metaphor is not limited to this dyadic structure, it is useful here to explain it in these terms.

[17] This is an important point for those who fear that in a full-blooded pluralistic theology, Christian distinctiveness may be obfuscated. The dialectic at the heart of pluralistic theology *must* maintain the coherence and alterity of its sources.

[18] There is some debate in the literature as to whether Voloshinov is a pen name for Mikhail Bhaktin.

is a semantic hybrid which loses not its foundation in its sources but neither can it be contained by them. It is the result of an imaginative, mutual redescription of its constituent terms and succeeds through its **dialectical** both/and in maintaining the alterity of its terms while creating new shared references between them. It creates new meaning from bringing together, in the mind, established terms and contexts in new and unforeseen ways.

This model of metaphorical dialectics explains how novel, hybrid significations are formed *de novo*. Theology, as alluded to at the beginning of this chapter, is inherently hybrid – a nexus of multiple narratives and sources continually reacting to changes in the environment, as well as its inherited tradition of interpretation. A thoroughly pluralistic theology, like metaphor, is also a tense nexus of intrinsic and extrinsic sources redescribing each other according to the inner dialectic of metaphorical predication, but also guided by the frame in which theologizing takes place. Importantly, the dialectics of metaphor succeed in revealing the frame since metaphor begins in semantic rupture. This disruption allows us to see the otherwise hidden frame, making a hybrid, pluralistic theology potentially a corrective for negative pressures underlying the frame. What I am suggesting is that the dynamics of consciously hybrid, pluralistic theology can be leveraged for revelatory and liberative ends. Not only can this happen; I argue that it should happen. Pluralistic theology here makes possible a prophetic voice, illuminating injustice and revealing the scars and cracks long hidden under the carapace of doctrine and accepted religious tradition.

Pluralistic theology never loses sight of the fact that it is a human response to the needs of the day, relying on human creativity, energy, and improvisation. Given the wide and varied needs of communities across the world, a genuinely pluralistic theology must make use of every source of insight available in order to "humbly follow truth wherever we find it."[19] In order to take advantage of the sheer wealth of creative thinking about God, pluralistic theology must remain open to all sources at hand, eschewing comfortable closure. The metaphorical dynamic at the heart of pluralistic theology allows it thus to be characterized as a form of *bricolage*, that is, a construction out of many, ready-to-hand, diverse sources – continuously being built, torn apart, and rebuilt toward a more useful form.

As I stated at the outset, I contend that all theology is inherently hybrid. Pluralistic theology reveals this feature more clearly in order to better use this creative source. As bricolage, pluralistic theology draws attention to the contingent, diverse nature of its components and contexts, while at the same time celebrating the metaphorical, expansive, and revelatory power of its compilation. Married to this centrifugal force, however, is the centripetal, particularizing, and poetic force which gives shape to pluralistic theology's eventual results. The workings of this force can be seen through the issues of criteria and poesis, that is, if metaphorical predication gives rise to a plethora of possible forms of bricolage, how is one to choose which possibility is excellent and worth pursuing? Are all such instances of hybrid bricolage equally valid, valuable or effective? By what criteria is the centripetal force guided? Moreover, what is the role and responsibility of the theologian in creating a thoroughly pluralistic theology?

To illustrate these questions, imagine an example of pluralistic theology along the lines I have drawn so far. Liberated from both the worries that theology must be done according to the given, proper, and correct forms and traditions, as well as the illusion of objective certainty and conservative fetishes for precedent, a theologian sets out to consciously bring together significant aspects of, for instance, particular Christian and Hindu religious beliefs and practices. The object might be to develop a novel theological model for understanding the nature of prayer, for

---

[19] Francis X. Clooney S.J., *Theology after Vedanta: An Experiment in Comparative Theology* (Albany NY: SUNY Press, 1993), 5.

instance.[20] After painstakingly studying the constituent traditions' notions of prayer, their histories, varieties, and critiques, as well as partaking in both forms of prayer with great sincerity, the theologian brings into metaphorical "conversation" aspects of these concepts and practices from both traditions in a pluralistic theology. The question to be asked is: Given the necessarily limited scope of religious knowledge and practice available to the theologian-bricoleur, the particularities of their religious, social, theological, and cultural background, as well as the explicit and **inchoate** agenda(s) driving their project, how can anyone know whether the hybrid pluralistic theology they create has any cogency, legitimacy, or usefulness for themself or the communities they are bringing together? Just as an instance of bricolage can be relatively valuable, surely pluralistic theologies can be relatively good or bad, useful or irrelevant, beautiful or crass, delightful or tawdry. If pluralistic theology, in its expansive phase, celebrates the plethora of possible hybrids, by what measure, in its contrary precipitative phase, can one identify and determine the felicity of its results?

I suggest the criterion to be used should be aesthetic, in the sense not merely of inherent beauty, but also the comprehension, elegance, and simplicity through which it both delivers the goods desired by the relevant community and expands the senses in which these goods suffice.[21] A pluralistic theology should be guided by the aesthetic qualities inherent in the hybrid: those fearful symmetries which reveal harmonious form, figure, unity in variety, fitness, utility, adaptability, goodness, and truth. Here I rely on the ancient Greek equivalence of the good, true, and beautiful when, in *Philebus*, we find Socrates stating "the good has retired into the region of the beautiful,"[22] and again, in *Gorgias* we see him explicitly arguing that what counts as beautiful is to be judged so not only by the pleasure it gives, but, importantly, its utility also.[23] However, harmonious expression of qualities is not in itself a sufficient marker. The beauty of a pluralistic, hybrid theology will lie also in its ability to bring to light some new, perhaps hitherto hidden, aspect of religious experience, knowledge, understanding, and/or feeling. The revelatory nature of pluralistic theology will be an aesthetic measure of its value. This revelation is not merely to shine light on inchoate wisdom brought to the surface through the action of metaphorical recombination but to show how the interstitial space constructed between the "home" and "other" tradition constitutes a possible locus of habitation. What pluralistic theology seeks to create is not just more knowledge or wisdom but a new, attractive, form of religious life. Its ultimate value will be found in the kinds of experience of being it makes possible. Just as the constant action of currents and waves builds sand bars in between opposite shores, the interstitial space between religious traditions is filled by a mobile region of intersection, sustained by the ongoing recombinant conversation between its parent religions. This shared locus of meaning is intended to be a potentially new way of being religious for adherents of its source traditions, as well as a new option for living for those outside of these religions. Importantly, this recombinant religious tradition will naturally reflect the implicit and explicit commitments, biases, and presuppositions of its poet, the pluralistic theologian. His/her responsibility in its creation will be to both

---

[20] It is not required that a pluralistic theology bring together analogous notions of prayer, ritual, etc. Such comparative exercises too often form the basis of illegitimate cultural appropriation. The dialectics of metaphor can be used to avoid such substitutionary appropriation. I focus on analogous notions of prayer here for illustrative purposes only.

[21] I should note that Rorty would add within the concept of sufficiency, the call to solidarity with those who suffer.

[22] Plato, *Philebus*, accessed April 20, 2020, https://www.gutenberg.org/ebooks/1744, 278.

[23] Plato, *Gorgias*, accessed April 20, 2020, http://classics.mit.edu/Plato/gorgias.html.

create as beautiful, elegant, and useful a hybrid as they can, while allowing it to reshape themselves in its creation.[24] The production of pluralistic theology – as is true for all theology, I would argue – thus becomes an expression of **autopoesis** as well. With this in mind the pluralistic poet-theologian must expand their minds in order to create something truly lovely. In so doing they autopoeticize in order to create, and create to autopoeticize. This formula aptly describes the experience of the dialectic at the heart of pluralistic theology.

Radical Risk: The Principle of Irony

We finally arrive at the quality of radical risk, characterized by irony. Irony is, I suggest, characteristic of all theology. It is present in the very attempt to speak about something over our heads, in the sense that we cannot hope to refer to a transcendent realm with immanent ideas and terms, yet this is exactly what we do. I have already alluded to the problems of religious language, fallibilism, and truth, and won't rehearse these points here. But irony cuts deeper into the body of theology by revealing the absurdity with which we must all struggle. Perhaps no other philosopher has wrestled more profoundly with the idea of absurdity than Søren Kierkegaard, who bound irony and absurdity together at the heart of religious life.

Kierkegaard considered the basic facts of a religious life to be absurd. Christians are supposed to believe in an eternal, simple, infinite, transcendent God who simultaneously became **incarnate** as a temporal, composite, finite, human being. There are two possible responses to this paradox: to have faith or to take offense. What we cannot do, according to Kierkegaard, is to believe by virtue of reason. If one chooses reason, the absurdity of the choice causes offense and dismissal. If one chooses faith, one must suspend reason in order to believe in something which is higher than reason. Belief then can only be had *by virtue of the absurd*.[25]

What this means is that one must decide to believe, as an act of will, in something one knows to be unreasonable, illogical, preposterous, inappropriate, and incongruous: that is, the absurd. To do this one is required to regularly and constantly renew one's commitment to God, repeating the decision to believe and form one's life according to the teachings of Jesus. The act of belief is a continual, repeated, decision to follow Christ. Repetition is the substance of faith, for Kierkegaard, and the only way to become one's true self. But in the face of absurdity these decisions cease to be decisions at all, for deciding in itself requires the existence of decidables, that is, options which express sensible propositions. The absurdity of the options amounts to either believing in something which is paradoxical, or taking offense at an irrelevant paradox. The former is clearly nonsensical, the latter utterly foolish. In either case these are not "live options," as William James puts it.[26] Absurdity evacuates the decision of its weight; it ceases to be a decision at all. The only way out of this conundrum is to embrace, as a knight of faith, irony.

A dictionary definition of irony describes it as *the expression of meaning, in language which normally signifies the opposite*. This is not simply to experience a bit of bad luck like "rain on your

---

[24] The biblical virtue of kenosis drives the authentic pluralistic theologian.

[25] William McDonald, "Søren Kierkegaard," *The Stanford Encyclopedia of Philosophy*, ed. Edward N. Zalta (Winter 2017), accessed February 4, 2020, https://plato.stanford.edu/archives/win2017/entries/kierkegaard, accessed 4 Feb 2020.

[26] William James, *The Will to Believe*, a lecture first published in *The New World* Vol. 5 (1896): 327–347.

wedding day" or a "free ride when you're already there,"[27] but rather a *conscious act of saying while at the same time unsaying*, a position which undermines itself in the process of its expression. It is to deliberately steer a path between two contrary positions: affirmation and negation – but irony is much closer to negation since in saying anything at all we implicitly affirm the existence and significance of what we are talking about. To speak ironically, then, is to layer the *unsaying* part on to what we are saying, to add simultaneous negation to our positive affirmation.

Kierkegaard spent quite a lot of time considering irony and the absurd. In *Repetition* he shows that Job gets everything back by virtue of the absurd, and in *Fear and Trembling* he argues that Abraham's reprieve from having to sacrifice Isaac is also due to the absurd. Faced with a religion such as this, what attitude could we take other than irony? Indeed Kierkegaard goes further and argues that all human life must be understood through the ironic. He claimed that:

> Just as scientists maintain that there is no true science without doubt, so it may be maintained with the same right that no genuinely human life is possible without irony[28]

More importantly Kierkegaard sees irony as a way of liberating us and in this freedom giving us a permission to play in the infinite possibilities of being human:

> Irony is a qualification of subjectivity. In irony, the subject is negatively free, since the actuality that is supposed to give the subject content is not there. He is free from the constraint in which the given actuality holds the subject, but he is negatively free and as such is suspended, because there is nothing that holds him. But this very freedom, this suspension, gives the ironist a certain enthusiasm, because he becomes intoxicated, so to speak, in the infinity of possibilities.[29]

This infinity of possibilities is just what intoxicates the pluralistic theologian. By drawing into sharp relief the porous boundaries of our traditions, their hybrid constitutions, their freedom from constraint, the dynamic dialectic of expansion and precipitation at their heart, and the beauty of its bricolage, pluralistic theology responds to the facts of religious plurality in a more authentic and fruitful way than traditional theological forms. The irony at the heart of both theologizing and indeed religious life is revealed to a greater extent when Christian theology borrows heavily from non-Christian traditions and is open to being transformed by these traditions. Moreover, pluralistic theology can set free prophetic voices calling attention to the papered-over fissures of injustice revealed by pluralistic theology itself. What results is a panoply of possible hyphenated, hybrid traditions: Hindu-Christian, Buddhist-Christian, Christian-Jewish, Buddhist-Jewish, Muslim-Hindu, and so on. Of course all of these possible combinations will be unique to their particular sources and poets, and shaped by their contexts, aims, communities, and times. Not all of them will be beautiful and good. Not all of them will "catch on" as inhabitable for those who have been alienated by religion. It is impossible to decide **a priori** which hybrids will survive and which will perish. But, crucially, those which *do flourish*, attracting others through their inherent beauty and the elegance by which they reveal new, inhabitable forms of religious life, will form the basis of new traditions of religion more adequate to the needs of their communities. Some will last, some will not, but all will have at least been more

---

[27] Alannis Morisette has a lot to answer for.

[28] Kierkegaard *The Concept of Irony with Continual Reference to Socrates (1841)*, 326.

[29] Kierkegaard *The Concept of Irony with Continual Reference to Socrates (1841)*, 262ff.

aware of and responsive to the facts of religious plurality, and thus be truer to our current awareness and experience. Theology conducted *through* religious pluralism will then rise to the needs of the day, making religious traditions more relevant and bringing life to people in new ways. Surely this is the goal of creative theology (see Box 1.8).

Box 1.8

The author is alert to the controversial nature of his argument. So he introduces a delightful device. He has an "objections and responses" section. He is well aware that plenty of theologians would not be sympathetic to his approach. So he wants to articulate the objection and offer a response. In so doing, he is making it harder to simply dismiss his argument. He is alert to why someone may find the argument problematic and wants to explain how the problems can be overcome.

Objections and Responses

In this section I wish briefly to consider some of the issues, objections, questions, and concerns usually brought against the vision of pluralistic theology I have championed. I understand that for many, what I have suggested will strike them somewhere on the continuum between uncomfortable and preposterous. What, they ask, would motivate the "average" creedal, churchgoing, tradition-respecting Christian to follow such a strange and potentially "dangerous" program? Should we not worry about appropriating an other's religious form of life? Does countenancing the possible value of an other's religious tradition negate or weaken one's own? These and other possible objections might be laid at the door of the erstwhile pluralistic theologian and a proper response to them would necessitate a volume of its own. What I propose to do instead is to particularize and personalize my responses to a few significant issues as an invitation to the conversation I hope this chapter will evince.

In traditional presentations of philosophical theology one normally seeks to avoid speaking from a particular and personal location. This detached, abstract, pseudo-objective "voice from nowhere" is sadly all too common in discourses from theology to science.[30] However, one of the noted salient features of pluralistic theology is the rootedness of the pluralistic theologian/bricoleur in her or his context, history, and particularities. Moreover, the theologian/bricoleur must meet their responsibility to speak authentically from their location while producing as beautiful a recombination as they can. In this spirit, then, while avoiding self-indulgent autobiography in favor of autopoesis, I propose to respond to some key issues from the perspective of my own history and social location: that is, a first-generation immigrant, born in East Africa to Indian parents, having grown up in a (somewhat) multicultural context in Canada. Like many others, my perspective is that of a multiply hybrid person (or "intersectional" hybrid, in today's parlance). Culturally, religiously, socially, politically … I find myself in between many overlapping and interwoven identities, and it is from this hybrid, interstitial position that I argue for a more pluralistic theology. I hasten to add that, by indicating my hybridity, in no way do I want to

---

[30] The absence of the subject as origin and context of all knowledge claims is a glaring and regrettable omission in our current scientific, philosophical and theological discourses; a point well made in Frank, Gleiser, and Thompson's discussion of "the blind spot." See: https://aeon.co/essays/the-blind-spot-of-science-is-the-neglect-of-lived-experience, last accessed May 2020.

suggest that somehow my responses to any issues concerning pluralistic theology are dependent on my own unique experience. In many ways I share my social location and my immigrant story with countless others, and pluralistic theology does not rely on any particular history nor require a certain kind of perspective. Rather, in locating myself, I seek to disclose (at least partially) my own biases, presuppositions, and commitments, as well as to specify these responses in the belief that, ironically, the universal resides in the particular. As literature shows us, the story of one is often the story of many.

> **Box 1.9**
>
> The author makes this exercise manageable by dividing the objections into three major concerns. Notice the elegant way they are organized, each one is a "question."

Three major concerns are typically raised in response to pluralistic theology (see Box 1.9): the question of *truth*, the question of *purity*, and the question of *possibility*. For lack of space, as well as to avoid repeating much of what I have (however inadequately) already covered regarding a pragmatic conception of truth, I shall concern myself with only the last two questions here.[31]

The issue of purity is at the base of concerns regarding mixing, miscegenation, syncretism, crossbreeding, hybridity, and recombination. Pluralistic theology, in bringing together "foreign" religious beliefs, concepts, and practices with their traditional Christian counterparts, is thus suspected of an illegitimate mixing and/or adulteration of Christian tradition. So deep is the worry over purity that in defining religious syncretism as "incorporation by a religious tradition of beliefs and practices incompatible with its basic insights"[32] Hendrik Vroom makes extrinsic religious sources incompatible a priori with (in this case) Christian "insight."

The motivation to conserve what is held dear at one level can often turn into fear, ethnocentrism, chauvinism, and bigotry at the other, and the frequency and ease with which reasonable concern to hold on to what is good slides inexorably into distrust, hatred, and violence cannot be underestimated. This is not to say that all conservative motivation concerning the production of a pluralistic theology is inherently chauvinistic; however, we must be ever vigilant regarding this possibility. Our sensitivities concerning purity itself touch deep into our psyches and social structures. Mary Douglas's seminal work on purity, pollution, and danger shows us that whenever our sense of purity is threatened by pollution, in this case the interpolation of foreign theological ideas, "our pollution behavior is the reaction which condemns any object or idea likely to confuse or contradict cherished classifications."[33] Religious syncretism is most often the

---

[31] Some readers may feel I am ducking the really significant philosophical issue. A thorough discussion and defense of a pragmatic approach to religious truth is, of course, far beyond the scope of this paper. However I suggest that the worry about getting at the Truth of religion is, to my mind, a holdover of an anachronistic **epistemology** as well as theologically unsustainable. The latter due to the commitment to divine transcendence at the heart of Semitic religion (which I discussed above) and the former the result of having ceded the rules of engagement while in the process of defending against the (now dubious) claims of nineteenth-century and twentieth-century **positivism** and scientism.

[32] Hendrik Vroom, "Syncretism and Dialogue: A Philosophical Analysis," in *Dialogue and Syncretism: An Interdisciplinary Approach*, ed. J.D. Gort, H. Vroom, R. Fernhout, and A. Wessels (Grand Rapids, MI: Eerdmans, 1989), 26.

[33] Mary Douglas, *Purity and Danger: An Analysis of Concepts of Pollution and Taboo* (New York: Routledge, 1966), 45.

category used to characterize the concern about purity within religious traditions; however, syncretism itself is a very contested term as applied to religious contexts. I would agree with Rosalind Shaw and Charles Stuart that such worries are generally manifestations not of religious or theological concerns but primarily of political anxieties. Stuart and Shaw point out that the term has no determinate meaning but one that has been construed in various ways through history.[34] To label something as "syncretic" therefore does not actually accomplish anything since, historically, all religious traditions are mixtures of various diverse elements. The vast weight of historical studies of religion put this beyond doubt. How syncretism is used in a particular context, then, depends on what is at stake, and these are primarily political questions. I suggest that the various religious or theological reasons for labeling something syncretic do not in the end bear scrutiny. What is left after these options are taken away are, simply, political pressures. So the concern regarding the very *idea* of recombining religious ideas, behaviors, practices, structures, and so on together, that is, the feeling of dis-ease at the possibility of pluralistic theology, must be considered on political grounds, that is, the question of who and what is to be included within the bounds of a particular religious tradition, and who/what is to be left out. This boundary-keeping function is undoubtedly part of what religions do; however, my understanding of the trajectory of Christian belief and practices is toward radical inclusion.[35] As someone who grew up outside of Christian tradition, the anomic, radical inclusivity of the teachings of Jesus struck me as one of its most distinguishing characteristics. It seems contrary to the spirit of Christian thought and witness to welcome the sinner into the fold, so to speak, but first require their sterilization of the worldviews which gave rise to and constitute them. My point here is that the program of pluralistic theology I am advocating will necessarily reveal the inchoate political pressures and ethnic boundaries in which we already exist. Bringing these to light is not a defeater for pluralistic theology but rather a virtue, since it is too easy for traditional theology to incorporate their underlying axioms and thus be subsumed by their political, social, and economic settlements (see Box 1.10).[36]

Box 1.10
The author knows that there are other questions the reader might have. Given he has written extensively on this approach to theology, he uses footnote 36 to acknowledge that there are outstanding questions and invite the reader to look at an essay where he focuses on this objection.

Before moving to the question of the possibility, it should escape no one that at the very center of Christian theology lies the great hybrid, God-man. The **Incarnation** represents the grossest

---

[34] Rosalind Shaw and Charles Stuart in the introduction to their edited collection, *Syncretism/Anti-Syncretism: The Politics of Religious Synthesis* (London: Routledge, 1994), 3–6.

[35] Of course many Biblical sources could be used here, not least the extended banquet story of Luke 14 and 15.

[36] Some may aver that I have not considered certain kinds of thorny problems which may arise from pluralistic theology, namely that its practice may require us to endorse and recombine views, practices, and structures from which we are rightfully repelled. This is a difficult question and well beyond the scope of this essay. I have considered it in the context of the "reluctant dialogian," that is, a person who not only rejects interreligious dialogue but considers us an enemy and means us harm. See "The Dialogue Party: Dialogue, Hybridity and the Reluctant Other," in *Theology and the Religions: A Dialogue*, ed. Vigo Mortensen (Grand Rapids: Wm B. Erdmann's), 235–248.

impurity imaginable in the Semitic context: a being who is fully God and fully human. Christ is the paradigmatic hybrid, through whom human beings are understood to be redeemed, transformed, and sanctified. Any concerns about purity must be put aside if we are to fully understand and appreciate this doctrine.

The question of the possibility of pluralistic theology revolves, I take it, not so much on the nature of its project but rather the likelihood of its acceptance and success in the contemporary Christian world. While I do not wish to avoid the question, to some extent it is a purely empirical matter and thus beyond my ability to settle here. Pluralistic theology may or may not be welcomed, developed, and come to fruition, depending on the particulars of the communities who respond to its challenge. As I have stated, much will depend on the beauty its hybrid theological visions manifest – its attractiveness, promise, and consolation – as well as countless other contingencies of history, identities, time, and space. Whether it is likely to be taken up by theologians or the communities they serve is thus hard to say. However, I suggest that for those of us who find ourselves very obviously to be hybrid – who accept the hyphenated life, whose histories, vocations, relationships, families, sense of self, and hopes for the future are thoroughly soaked in the water and wine of interstitial, liminal, hybridity –pluralistic theology does not represent an endlessly deferred alterity and alienation, but rather articulates the thrilling pluripotentiality of multiple belonging, of an excess of freedom, of ludic liberation, and authentic becoming. Surely, a program for creative theology should covet such an outcome.

2

Is It Possible for the Eternal Word to Be Made Manifest in a Person with Down's Syndrome?

Ian S. Markham

RESEARCH LEVEL 1

Editors' Introduction

This is a deliberately provocative article. The idea is simple: Could Jesus – the Incarnate Word – be someone else? Instead of being a first-century, Jewish male, could Jesus have been a first-century person with Down's Syndrome? Now the question – could Jesus been something other than male? – has circulated in the scholarly literature. Feminist theologians have asked whether the Incarnate Word could have been a woman? This essay takes a familiar question and poses the question in a new way. The focus is on the question of the omniscience of Jesus.

The Christian claim is that Eternal Word became flesh in Jesus of Nazareth. It was a first-century Jew who became the definitive disclosure of God to humanity and the ultimate identification of God with humanity. In this essay, I wish to reflect on a conceptual question underpinning the Incarnation.[1] What do we expect from an Incarnation? Krishna, the eighth avatar of Vishnu, has explicit self-knowledge of his status and in Hindu theology his beauty is a central characteristic of his divinity.[2] Does the Incarnation require that the Eternal Word be a person who is exceptionally beautiful? Did God have other options beyond Jesus and what in Jesus is essential to the Incarnation and what is contingent? Was it possible for the Eternal Word to be expressed in a woman or in a person with special needs? The case that brings many of these questions together is a person with Down's Syndrome. Is it possible for the Eternal Word to be made manifest in a person with Down's Syndrome?

Down's is a genetic condition, where a person has a full or partial additional copy of chromosome 21. The consequences are a lower IQ (often as much as half), certain distinctive

---

[1] In many ways, this is an exercise in what Oliver Crisp would call "analytic theology" or perhaps "philosophical theology".

[2] For a good discussion see Kristin Johnston Largen, *Baby Krishna, Infant Christ: A Comparative Theology of Salvation* (Maryknoll, NY: Orbis Books 2011), 41. She explains that "Krishna is not only the most powerful god, the supreme god of the universe, but is also exceedingly beautiful, which is a central part of his perfection".

The Craft of Innovative Theology: Argument and Process, First Edition. Edited by John Allan Knight and Ian S. Markham.
© 2022 John Wiley & Sons Ltd. Published 2022 by John Wiley & Sons Ltd.

characteristics (which include smaller stature and an upward slant to the eyes), and a disposition which is often humble, warm, and full of gratitude. A person with Down's could easily reflect many of the most important features of God; for example, they can be very loving. But what about the other attributes of God – could God be disclosed in a person who is genetically unable to have a high IQ?

This essay will begin by thinking through the link between **Christology** and intelligence. Traditionally, it has been assumed that the **Incarnate Word** must be extremely intelligent – indeed omniscient. We will look at the traditional reasons for linking Christology with omniscience. Then we will consider and develop a distinction between "wisdom" and "omniscience" and suggest that the Wisdom of God does not require nor entail omniscience, nor even above average intelligence. This will lead us to two conclusions; the first is that God could have been incarnate in a person with Down's Syndrome;[3] and the second is that we are free to let Jesus be who Jesus was and not force him into a Christology model that does not honor the Biblical text (see Box 2.1).

Box 2.1

This is the article's "signpost." It gives the reader a sense of how the essay will be structured. There are many ways this question could be handled. The author sets out the focus is on intelligence. One could criticize the author for not seizing the opportunity to write more extensively on disability and the Incarnation.

Christology, Intelligence, and Omniscience

Box 2.2

This essay makes good use of subheadings. A subheading ensures that the reader always know exactly where they are in the essay. Having been given a signpost at the end of the introduction, the reader knows that this first subheading will set out the case for the traditional view of Jesus that see Jesus as at least very intelligent, if not omniscient. A subheading is also a helpful place for the reader to pause. You always know that you have a pause in the text when you get to the end of a section.

(See Box 2.2.) For most Christians, intelligence is seen as an inevitable aspect of the Incarnation. At the very least, the Incarnate Word must be able to teach with authority and develop good arguments.[4]

---

[3] It is important to note that the conviction that the Incarnation of God could have been a person with Down's Syndrome should not be considered the basis for affirming the intrinsic dignity of persons with Down's Syndrome. The *imago Dei* (the image of God) is the basis for affirming the intrinsic dignity of all people, especially those with special needs.

[4] The Sermon on the Mount is a good illustration of Jesus making an argument. The contrast between the Torah and the teaching of Jesus is powerful.

Traditionally, the standard line in traditional Christology is that not only the Eternal Word, but also the Incarnate Word is omniscient; this would mean that Jesus is extremely intelligent – after all, Jesus knows everything it is logically possible to know. Now why has the tradition insisted on omniscience? It is Wolfhart Pannenberg in his classic *Jesus – God and Man* who has a sustained footnote on why this is the case. Pannenberg notes the irony that while patristic theologians consistently opposed docetic tendencies when it came to the suffering of Jesus (albeit in respect to his human nature), in respect to "the doctrine of Jesus" knowledge, however, a **docetic-Monophysite** threat was continually present and occasionally dominant.[5] Pannenberg suggests that this is in part a reaction to the Arians who argued against the divinity of Jesus partly on the basis of his ignorance. As Pannenberg goes on to note, it was only the Antiochene theologians who were able to concede some ignorance on the part of Jesus; the Alexandrian tradition made sure that Jesus was omniscient. The net result is that time after time, we find that Jesus shares the divine knowledge.

Let me take two illustrations, starting with Anselm. His discussion of the knowledge of Christ is found in *Cur Deus Homo*, chapter 13. Under the chapter heading "It is not the case that along with our other infirmities He has ignorance" Anselm sets out his commitment to the omniscience of Jesus. Boso (his conversation partner in the dialogue) assumes that the humanity of Jesus requires ignorance. Anselm explains:

> The assumption of a human nature into the unity of a divine person will be done wisely by Supreme Wisdom. And so Supreme Wisdom will not assume into its human nature that which is not all useful … to the work which this man is going to do. Now, to be sure, ignorance would be of no use to Him; instead, it would be of much harm. For without great wisdom how would He do the very numerous and very great works which He was going to do? Or how would men believe Him if they knew He was ignorant? … Furthermore, if only what is known is loved, then just as there would not be any good which He did not love, so there would not be any good which He did not know. But only one who knows how to discern good from evil has a complete knowledge of good. … Therefore, He will know everything, even though He will not publicly display all of His knowledge in His association with other men.[6] (See Box 2.3.)

Box 2.3

Footnote 6 is interesting. The author quotes Anselm (and provides the source of the Anselm quote). However, the author then expands the footnote to a secondary source that reinforces the significance of the quotation from a scholar of Anselm. The author found Daniel Deme's recent discussion of Anselm's Christology helpful (and 2003 is still relatively recent in scholarship on Anselm); the author acknowledges his debt to this book and invites the reader to look at Deme's scholarship more closely.

---

[5] Wolfhart Pannenberg, *Jesus – God and Man* (Philadelphia: Westminster Press 1968), 333 n24.

[6] Jasper Hopkins and Herbert Richardson, eds. and trans, *Anselm of Canterbury* Vol. 3 (Toronto and New York: Edwin Mellen Press 1976), 135. I am grateful to Daniel Deme for his good summary of Anselm's position, which put simply is that "the man Jesus will never have ignorance with regard to his humanity. … [T]his man will be omniscient, even if he will not always manifest it in public." See Daniel Deme, *The Christology of Anselm of Canterbury* (Aldershot, UK and Burlington, VT: Ashgate Publishing 2003), 158.

The argument here is interesting. Jesus must be omniscient because (a) he is God and (b) this is the basis of his divine authority. Anselm then identifies three areas requiring this authority; these are in respect to the miraculous, to attracting disciples, and to the moral realm (see Box 2.4).

Box 2.4

The author is setting up the counter position at the start of the article. Notice how he has clearly gone back to the primary sources (he is not dependent on a summary from a secondary source – for example, a textbook summary). In addition, he has helpfully identified the main features by listing them.

The second example is Thomas Aquinas. In the *Summa Theologiae*, he gives sustained attention to the issue of the knowledge of Christ. For Aquinas, the Eternal Word assumed a human nature that was perfect and integral. The question in the *Tertia pars* is this: How exactly did Christ possess these perfections? For Aquinas, "Christ had beatific knowledge,"[7] which Aquinas explains is embedded within "the soul of Christ, which is a part of his human nature."[8] However, Aquinas also wants Jesus to learn and grow in knowledge; so he develops a distinction between "experimental knowledge" – knowledge from experience, which is acquired – and imprinted, divine knowledge. With the latter, Jesus is omniscient or as Aquinas puts it, "Therefore it would seem that by the knowledge infused by the Holy Spirit Christ knew everything."[9] With the former, Christ had an active intellect which led to learning of human activities. So Aquinas writes:

> The human mind looks in two directions. It looks to what is above it – and it was in this line that the soul of Christ was filled with infused knowledge. But it also looks to what is beneath it, to the data of the imagination, which is meant to move the human mind by the power of the active intellect. The soul of Christ had also to be filled with knowledge along this line; not that the previous complement of knowledge would not of itself be enough for the human mind, but because the mind had also to be filled through its dealings with the imagination.[10]

For Aquinas, it is part of the perfection of the human Jesus that he learned.[11]

---

[7] Thomas Aquinas, *Summa Theologiae* (hereafter *ST*), 3a.9.2.

[8] Aquinas, *ST*, 3a.9.3.

[9] Aquinas, *ST*, 3a.11.1.

[10] Aquinas, *ST*, 3a.9.4.

[11] Michael Gorman is helpful here. The perfections are in Christ insofar as it furthers the salvific mission. Therefore, Gorman points out when it comes to knowledge: "Christ's human knowledge was as extensive as human knowledge could be: he had the beatific vision, full infused knowledge, and full acquired knowledge. Of his possession of the beatific vision, Aquinas notes that this enabled Christ to be, in virtue of his humanity, the source of truth for other humans. He also had a human will and the ability to perform authentically human actions." See Michael Gorman, "Incarnation," in Brian Davies and Eleonore Stump, eds., *The Oxford Handbook of Aquinas* (New York: Oxford University Press 2012), 430.

Aquinas writes, "The habit of knowledge is acquired from the association of the human mind with the imagination."[12] But there is more. Corey L. Barnes provides a good discussion of this section of the *Summa* and he stresses the importance of this form of experimental knowledge because it was a condition of the freewill of Jesus. Barnes explains that for Aquinas, "Christ willed the passion with full knowledge of its pains and outcomes."[13]

Although Aquinas distinguishes between different types of knowledge (thereby creating some flexibility for the accumulation of knowledge in Jesus), he shares with Anselm a sense that the knowledge of Jesus is considerable; it includes the beatific vision and infused knowledge. For both, the Incarnation, conceptually, needs an omniscient (or almost omniscient) human. This is a long way from a person with Down's Syndrome (see Box 2.5).

Box 2.5

On Aquinas, the author is sensitive to a literature that discusses how best to interpret Aquinas. The footnote is used effectively to expand and explain Aquinas and link the author's discussion with a wider discussion among scholars about this passage in Aquinas. To include all this in the heart of the article would have reduced the flow and made the article difficult to follow.

Interestingly, most theologians have worried about an omniscient Jesus on the grounds that this undermines the humanity of Jesus (see Box 2.6).[14]

Box 2.6

Footnote 14 is a "confining footnote." The purpose of this footnote is to confine the discussion of omniscience and ignorance to certain limited, and manageable, territory. No article can cover every single dimension of the topic. Theology has an interconnected tendency; and the result can be confusing. So the author confines his discussion to make it manageable. If this were a book, then there presumably would be some discussion of the "two natures" solution of Chalcedon. As it is an article, the author explains his decision to confine the discussion in this footnote and directs the reader to texts that make use of the "two natures" solution.

For the child Jesus to know every name of every person living in New York and be able to recite every cricket score of every cricket match makes Jesus an odd child. As Pannenberg observes:

---

[12] Aquinas, *ST*, 3a.9.4.
[13] Corey L. Barnes, *Christ's Two Wills in Scholastic Thought: the Christology of Aquinas and Its Historical Contexts* (Toronto, ON: Pontifical Institute of Mediaeval Studies 2012), 213.
[14] One solution that I am not discussing in this article is to build on the two natures distinction embedded in the Definition of Chalcedon. On this view one confines omniscience to the divine nature of Jesus and limited knowledge is then part of the human nature. A number of writers take this line. Thomas Morris in *The Logic of God Incarnate* (Ithaca and London: Cornell University Press 1986), 103ff, argues for the "two minds view." This also seems to be line in Gerald O'Collins, *Christology: A Biblical, Historical, and Systematic Study of Jesus*, 2nd edn (Oxford: Oxford University Press, 2009), 240. Collins explicitly writes, "With respect to his divinity Christ is omniscient, but with respect to his humanity he is limited in knowledge".

> [T]o attribute to the soul of Jesus a knowledge of all things past, present, and future, and of everything that God knows from the very beginning, in the sense of a supernatural vision, makes the danger more than considerable that the genuine humanity of Jesus' experiential life would be lost.[15]

This traditional criticism does have some force; however, I want to argue for a different position. Let us recognize that there is a difference between propositional knowledge and wisdom. Propositional knowledge at one extreme is omniscience (knowing every true proposition) through to intelligence (which customarily is more knowledge than other people). The argument I want to make is that the Eternal Word (or for the sake of this argument let us use the phrase Divine Wisdom) does not require omniscience (in the sense of knowing everything); indeed, the Divine Wisdom does not need a conventional intelligence. In fact, human intelligence can make knowledge of the divine harder and less accessible because the immediacy of the spiritual can be lost through the overly complex rational interpretative processes, with which we interpret the spiritual.[16] Let us develop this argument by turning to the concept of the Divine Wisdom (see Box 2.7).

Box 2.7

This is the heart of the argument. The author is going to distinguish between omniscience and wisdom. For the reader, this is the point that you pause. Much hinges on this distinction. The author has highlighted the distinction here and will now develop that distinction.

Divine Wisdom

There is no doubt that the "Wisdom tradition" of the Old Testament is a powerful inspiration for the developing Christology of the New Testament.[17] As Celia Deane-Drummond points out:

> Certainly a Wisdom Christology has the advantage of holding together very different biblical traditions, some of which highlight the very human story of Jesus in comparison with

---

[15] Pannenberg, *God and Man*, 329.

[16] In our post-Kantian age, I do accept that every experience entails interpretation. However, I do think the sense of the spiritual needs to be experienced in ways that do not allow the filters of reductionist materialism to obscure the true nature of experience. Without romanticizing children, I do think that often children can see and know things in ways that adults could see and know, but fail to do so because a crude empiricism dominates the adult realm of knowing. I am grateful for the clarifying help of my colleagues Joyce Mercer and James Farwell on this point.

[17] Wisdom tradition is in quotation marks because I recognize it is not really a tradition. It is Stuart Weeks who has in a variety of places argued against the distinct wisdom tradition. Instead he sees it as a much more fluid movement where the literature is "intended more to entertain and provoke than deliberately to persuade its readers to adopt any particular understanding of the world." Stuart Weeks, "Wisdom in the Old Testament," in, *Where Shall Wisdom Be Found? Wisdom in the Bible, the Church and the Contemporary World*, ed. Stephen Barton (Edinburgh: T&T Clark 1999), 29.

the prophets of wisdom, as in Matthew, while others point to a closer identification between Wisdom and the divine, as in the Logos Christology of John.[18]

As Deane-Drummond notes, this is especially true of the Gospel of John. The combination of Genesis one ("In the beginning God" finds an echo in "In the beginning was the Word") with the Wisdom tradition (especially of Proverbs 8) becomes a powerful mechanism to capture the significance and impact of Jesus. For the author of John's Gospel, Jesus embodies the Eternal Word – the Eternal Wisdom of God; it is in Jesus we can see what God is like.

The Old Testament source for this characterization of Wisdom is Proverbs 8. She is one of two female figures; the other being the "foreign woman." Of Wisdom, Proverbs writes:

> The LORD created me at the beginning of his work,
> the first of his acts of long ago.
> Ages ago I was set up,
> at the first, before the beginning of the earth.
> When there were no depths I was brought forth,
> when there were no springs abounding with water.
> Before the mountains had been shaped,
> before the hills, I was brought forth—
> when he had not yet made earth and fields,
> or the world's first bits of soil.
> When he established the heavens, I was there,
> when he drew a circle on the face of the deep,
> when he made firm the skies above,
> when he established the fountains of the deep,
> when he assigned to the sea its limit,
> so that the waters might not transgress his command,
> when he marked out the foundations of the earth, then I was
> beside him, like a master worker;
> and I was daily his delight,
> rejoicing before him always,
> rejoicing in his inhabited world
> and delighting in the human race.
>   (Proverbs 8:22–31 NRSV)

Wisdom is personified; Wisdom is with God; Wisdom was beside God; Wisdom rejoices and participates in the Creation. Here is an aspect of God which is dynamic and has agency. James D. G. Dunn is right when he recognizes that in the Gospel of John, "there is no doubt that Jesus is presented as Wisdom incarnate."[19] However, it is not simply in the Gospel of John. The wisdom theme is also present in Matthew's Gospel. The Q source seems to be deliberately edited by

---

[18] Celia Deane-Drummond, *Christ and Evolution: Wonder and Wisdom* (Minneapolis: Fortress, 2009), chapter 3. This chapter is outstanding discussion of the importance of wisdom in Christology. Much of this chapter is building on Deane-Drummond's discussion.

[19] James D. G. Dunn, "Jesus: Teacher of Wisdom or Wisdom Incarnate?" in *Where Shall Wisdom Be Found? Wisdom in the Bible, the Church and the Contemporary World*, ed. Stephen Barton (Edinburgh: T&T Clark 1999), 77.

Matthew to make sure that there is a wisdom Christology. For Matthew, writes Dunn, Jesus is presented more like "the embodiment of divine Wisdom."[20] And some have seen a wisdom Christology in Luke, where Jesus talks of himself as the "go-between" for God and the world (Luke 10:22).[21] In addition, Paul writing in Corinthians explicitly describes Christ as the Wisdom of God (1 Corinthians 1:24). For the early Church, this was language that made perfect sense of the Incarnation.

The feminist theologians have made this central to their Christology. Both Elisabeth Schüssler Fiorenza and Elizabeth Johnson draw heavily on the feminine personification of Wisdom within the Jewish tradition. For Schüssler Fiorenza, the initial reflections on Jesus were all sophialogy, which got submerged by patriarchy. Indeed Schüssler Fiorenza writes:

> When one moves from Jewish Wisdom literature to early Christian writing the figure of Divine Wisdom seems to disappear. Yet a symptomatic reading, which attends to traces and tensions inscribed in the text, can show that a submerged theology of Wisdom, or sophialogy, permeates all of Christian Scriptures.[22]

For Schüssler Fiorenza, we are recovering a tradition, which can destabilize contemporary more masculine Christologies. This is "one but not the only early Christian discourse that might open up unfulfilled possibilities for feminist liberation theology."[23] Schüssler Fiorenza writes:

> A rediscovery of Wisdom traditions does not invite us to repeat the language of early Jewish-Christian Wisdom theology. Rather it compels us to continue the struggle with conventional masculine language for G*d and the exclusivist authoritarian functions and implications of such language. Feminist theology must rearticulate the symbols, images, and names of Divine Sophia in the context of our own experiences and theological struggles in such a way that the ossified and absolutized masculine language about G*d and Christ is radically questioned and undermined and the Western cultural sex/gender system is radically deconstructed.[24]

The vision here is that the very recovery of this submerged wisdom strand creates an intrinsic openness about our understanding of God. Traditional male Christologies are seen as a conclusion (we now know what God is like because we have the definitive disclosure), while a sophialogy leaves a continuing openness, which from a feminist perspective is good.

Elizabeth Johnson has also made the recovery of Sophia a way of challenging the patriarchy embedded in classical Christology. She argues that the "Jewish figure of personified Wisdom (*Hokmah* in Hebrew, *Sophia* in Greek)" enabled "the fledgling Christian community to attribute cosmic significance to the crucified Jesus, relating him to the creation and governance of the

---

[20] Dunn, "Teacher of Wisdom," 78.

[21] I am grateful to Joyce Mercer for this observation.

[22] Elisabeth Schüssler Fiorenza, *Jesus: Miriam's Son, Sophia's Prophet* (New York: Continuum 1994), 139.

[23] Fiorenza, *Jesus*, 157.

[24] Fiorenza, *Jesus*, 162. Schüssler Fiorenza has a convention of following the Jewish practice of not reproducing the name of God (hence G*d) as a way of challenging the traditional patriarchal image of God.

world, and was an essential step in the development of incarnational christology."[25] For Johnson, a recognition of the genesis of the Biblical understanding of the Christ in female imagery provides a justification for feminine imagery of God. So she talks about the Spirit-Sophia, Jesus-Sophia, and Mother-Sophia.[26] For Johnson, if you see Jesus through Sophia, then you can see the ministry of Jesus in a different way. Don Schweitzer accurately summarizes Johnson's position as follows:

> The quest for the historical Jesus shows that what was characteristic of Jesus as Sophia/Christ was not his sex but the liberating gestalt of his ministry, which brought liberation from an oppressive status quo to women and men. It was this, not his sexuality, that led to his death and thus to his resurrection/vindication as the Christ. Through his resurrection, Jesus becomes present in all those, male and female, who gather in his name and live out his message in redemptive ways.[27]

For Johnson, once we see the significance of Sophia, it then changes the way we see Jesus – everyday living within the kingdom is more important, inclusion is central, and relationships should be rectified across boundaries.

There is, in my view, a persuasive argument that recognizes that Sophia language is an important and faithful Biblical Christology. While I do want to safeguard an "authoritative" revelation disclosed in the Eternal Wisdom made flesh (so in that respect I would want to disagree with Schüssler Fiorenza),[28] it is important to recognize that the type of Christology emerging from the Sophia tradition is different. It has a different tone to the Christologies of Anselm and Aquinas. And this different tone can be seen when we contrast Elizabeth Johnson with Anselm (see Box 2.8).

Box 2.8

The author has a problem here. The author fears that the **Christology** of Elizabeth Johnson might not be sufficiently high to be authoritative as reliable revelation of God to humanity. Yet the author wants to affirm the direction these Christologies are moving. This is called "anticipating an objection." A good author anticipates potential criticisms of the argument and offers a response embedded in the text.

For Anselm, we need the omniscience of Jesus for reasons of authority. This creates the Jesus of power who can perform miracles, attract disciples, and provide moral clarity. For Elizabeth Johnson, the tradition of Sophia stresses inclusion, justice, and participation. Omniscience

---

[25] Elizabeth Johnson, "Jesus, Wisdom of God," *Ephemerides Theologiae Louvaniensis* Vol. 61 (1985): 261, as quoted in Don Schweitzer, *Contemporary Christologies* (Minneapolis: Fortress Press 2010), 68.

[26] Elizabeth Johnson, *She Who Is: The Mystery of God in Feminist Theological Discourse* (New York: Crossroad 1992), 266.

[27] Don Schweitzer, *Contemporary Christologies* (Minneapolis: Fortress Press 2010), 69.

[28] I am happy to recognize a debt to Karl Barth here. If we are going to know what God is like, then we need to trust that God has spoken. The disclosure of God in the Eternal Wisdom made flesh is our control on our theology. Any legitimate affirmation about God and God's relations with the world need to be justified, grounded in, or deduced from the **Incarnation**. See my *Understanding Christian Doctrine* (Oxford: Wiley-Blackwell, 2008) for further discussion.

promises that all answers are provided. Wisdom actually invites us to a place which is more paradoxical. As Stephen Barton observes:

> for wisdom is not just a body of knowledge, it is also a *way of seeing* which attends to what lies hidden as well as to what lies on the surface. Insofar as it attends to what is hidden, wisdom is a way of seeing which has the potential for being innovative, paradoxical, ironic and subversive. Here, the place of the wise is taken by the fool, the place of the strong by the weak, the place of the mature by the child.[29]

Wisdom is not knowledge of every true proposition; instead, wisdom can see the simple truths within the complexity. Wisdom implies an open-endedness; a wise person never assumes that they know everything; there is always more to learn.[30]

The argument here is simple: conceptually, when we think about what an incarnation involves, we do not need a God-man who is able to speak every language or know the number of calories in every type of soda. Neither of these skills would disclose to us the nature of God. Such skills would just reveal a God of parlor tricks. Instead, our need is for a life from which we can learn of the love, compassion, and radical call for inclusion (see Box 2.9).

Box 2.9

The author has made his case. This sentence is the one you would quote if you were summarizing this argument in a publication. The reader will accept the argument if this distinction between wisdom and "cognitive knowledge" is persuasive.

Incarnation and a Person with Down's Syndrome

Herein allow me a confession: much as I love Jesus, part of me wishes that instead of a Jewish male, the Eternal Wisdom had taken the form of a person with Down's Syndrome. In my experience a person with Down's is a much more reliable vehicle for disclosing the life of God than most other people. Their obligation to live in the present, their deep compassion and empathy, their sense of fun, and their exceptional capacity for inclusion are all built in; their very biology makes them ideal vehicles for the disclosure of God.

It is true that if God had been incarnate in a person with Down's, then there would have been a different teaching style. The parables and stories would have been different. The conversations with opponents would have to resort less to good argument and more to intuitive assertion. But this could have all worked: humanity near such a life could still see the reality of God residing in

---

[29] Stephen C. Barton, "Gospel Wisdom," in *Where Shall Wisdom Be Found? Wisdom in the Bible, the Church and the Contemporary World*, ed. Stephen Barton (Edinburgh: T&T Clark, 1999), 94.

[30] To talk of Jesus as the Wisdom of God opens possibilities. Colin Gunton has a radical inclusivity when he explains that the Wisdom of God embodied in Christ embodies all the wisdom of even non-Christian cultures. So Gunton writes, "To say that the crucified Christ is the Wisdom of God is to say that he is the key to the meaning of the whole of the created order, and therefore the source of true wisdom, wherever that is to be found." Colin Gunton, "Christ, the Wisdom of God," in *Where Shall Wisdom Be Found? Wisdom in the Bible, the Church and the Contemporary World*, ed. Stephen Barton (Edinburgh: T&T Clark, 1999), 260.

that life in a unique way. It could have still been a life that provoked worship from those around that life.

Now much is made of the challenge of a male Jesus for women. The objection is simple: the experiences of men and women are distinctive; Jesus never knew the challenge of the menstrual cycle or the distinctive experience of childbirth. So how can a male Jesus be representative of all humanity?

The standard answer is simple: to be a human one has to be a particular human. You have to be born into a family, at a certain time, or a certain gender. Although the Incarnation could have taken a variety of forms, it did need to be *a* form – *a* particular person. And the Jewishness, maleness, and first centuryness are all part of what it is to be a human person.

However, it is also recognized that the fact that Jesus was male does not mean and cannot mean that women are not complete full forms of humanity. So the first reason why this exercise matters is simply this: it is important for Christian theologians to stress that people with special needs are complete and full forms of humanity. We recognize that it is a contingent fact that the Incarnation took the form of a first-century male and not a logically necessary one. In the same way that God could have been incarnated as a woman, so I am arguing God could have been incarnated as a person with Down's Syndrome (see Box 2.10).

Box 2.10

At this point, the author links this argument to the wider argument of incarnational possibilities. The point is made that the Incarnation of God in the form of a male Jew was contingent, not logically necessary. This means that the Incarnation could have taken a different form.

Incarnation and Jesus

Election is a mystery. It was the Jewish people who were chosen; it was Mary the mother of Jesus who gave birth to the Christ. Jesus was able-bodied; Jesus was male; and Jesus spoke Aramaic and was heavily shaped by a Jewish apocalyptic worldview. One important purpose of this exercise is that once one recognizes that conceptually God could have taken the form of a person with Down's, then we can liberate our study of the New Testament and let Jesus be Jesus.

The joy of this argument is that Bart Ehrman, the New Testament scholar, could be right and Jesus could still be God. Once we let go some of the classical expectations that we have of the Incarnation, we are free to be gentler with Jesus. So Bart Ehrman sees Jesus as an apocalyptic prophet. According to this picture, Jesus saw himself as an agent, who is ushering in the end of the age. It was to be a literal kingdom of God, where the forces of wickedness will be overthrown, and a new set of values will dominate the community. Now if this picture of Jesus is right, then it is long way from the omniscient Jesus of the classical Christology. For Ehrman, Jesus did not think he was God; he was not omniscient; instead, he was mistaken in many ways. However, if the Incarnation of the Wisdom of God does not require an omniscient Jesus or even a Jesus as intelligent as Einstein, then perhaps this "deluded" Jesus might still be that embodiment of God, that is, once we concede that there are things of which Jesus was not aware, one of which could be his own divinity.

Like every human being, Jesus is limited by the culture into which he is born. Yet those closest to him recognized in him an encounter with God. They also struggled with their expectations. The idea of "messiah" carried a set of connotations that Jesus constantly evaded. However, as Larry Hurtado has pointed out, these monotheistic Jews still found themselves worshipping the

God embodied in this person.[31] For all the limitations of the man, the divine came shining through. Questions about the intelligence of Jesus or whether Jesus was inaccurate in his predications about the end of the world or even the knowledge of Jesus about his own status and access to the Father are now relegated to a secondary status. Indeed one could argue that it is important for the embodiment of the Divine Sophia to have these limitations.[32] The coming of the Spirit promises to take us further into the mystery of God; Jesus is a definitive disclosure of God (a control on our theology), but not a comprehensive disclosure.

Conclusion

The question was simple: Is it possible for the Eternal Word to be made manifest in a person with Down's Syndrome? The answer I have suggested is an overwhelming affirmative. It is indeed possible. It is possible because the classical expectation of divine omniscience in Jesus is mistaken; it is possible because we recognize that underpinning the logos language is Sophia language; it is possible because wisdom is different from knowledge of countless propositional facts; and it is possible because a person with Down's is a complete form of humanity.

Turning from possibility to what God actually did in Christ, the delightful conclusion of this article is that we need to worry less about defending a particular account of Jesus. Jesus need not meet the classical expectations for his life; he can be who he was. It is still perfectly possible that a person with a limited cultural horizon could bring to us the Wisdom of God. This is the Christian claim; this is the Christian affirmation.[33]

---

[31] See Larry W. Hurtado, *Lord Jesus Christ: Devotion to Jesus in Earliest Christianity* (Grand Rapids, MI: Eerdmans, 2003).

[32] In some ways this is a defense of a kenotic Christology, although I am hesitant to formulate the precise form this took. I prefer to talk about the Eternal Wisdom interpenetrating a human life. This would mean it is not a "transformational model" (of, for example, Trenton Merricks) nor is it just relational. It is a more like a "spirit-filled" Christology. Jonathan Hill's map of the current options in the debate is very helpful, see Anna Marmodoro and Jonathan Hill, *The Metaphysics of the Incarnation* (Oxford: Oxford University Press, 2011), chapter 1.

[33] I am grateful to those who took the time to read an earlier draft of this article. These include Joyce Mercer, James Farwell, Barney Hawkins, Keith Ward, and Isabella Blanchard. Finally, I am grateful for the extraordinary gift of Ms. Ellen Hawkins (a person with Down's syndrome) who has taught me so much about faith and trust.

Part II

God and Church

3

Racial Stigma and Southern Baptist Public Discourse in the Twentieth Century
Pamela D. Jones

RESEARCH LEVEL 1

Editors' Introduction

Some of the best pieces of writing start from a very simple question: How can Christians committed to the Golden Rule support slavery? No one would say that they would like to be treated as a slave. In this powerful piece of historical analysis, the author starts with this question. The answer, this author explains, is that assumptions about the inferiority of African Americans created a culture where the Golden Rule is evaded. She then develops a substantial case study. The author takes the Southern Baptist Convention (SBC) and divides the history into three periods: the Jim Crow Era, post the 1954 Brown decision, and the 1995 Apology. She argues that African Americans are so traumatized by the racism of the denomination that the "change of heart" may not be sufficient to heal African Americans' mistrust and skepticism toward the denomination as racist.

> They had for more than a century before been regarded as being of an inferior order, and altogether unfit to associate with the white race, either in social or political relations; and so far inferior, that they had no rights which the white man was bound to respect; and that the negro might justly and lawfully be reduced to slavery for his benefit. ... And no distinction in this respect is made between the free negro or mulatto and the slave, but this stigma, of the deepest degradation was fixed upon the whole race. Dred Scott, 1857. *Dred Scott v. Sandford*, 60 U.S. (19 HOW.) 393 (1857)[1]

The historic theological crisis in American race relations between blacks and whites not only has been a conflict with biblical interpretations that justified slavery and segregation, it also has involved conflicting views about what it means to be fully human and who has the power to define this. The heated biblical debates of the nineteenth century over whether slavery could be justified moved into the twentieth century in the debates over Jim Crow segregation and white supremacy. Whether to extend notions of Christian compassion and charity to African Americans as part of humankind or to continue to view them as inferior humans, as racially stigmatized beings, was at the heart of this controversy over racism, white supremacy, and racial segregation and their impact on African Americans.

---

[1] *Dred Scott v. Sanford*, 60, 19 How. 393, (US 1857).

I trace the road taken by the Southern Baptist Convention (SBC) to cope publicly with the changing racial dynamics, especially in the South during the 1950s and 1960s, and then with its efforts in 1995 to formally repudiate racism and past sins of slavery and segregation. I suspected that a major theological impediment to dismantling segregated institutions in the South after the *Brown* decision in 1954 was whether Christian denominations were willing to accept views that African Americans were fully human and therefore were entitled to be extended Christian love, charity, and compassion in light of their suffering during Jim Crow.

The SBC split from Northern Baptists in 1845 over its support of slavery, supported the Confederate states, and supplied biblical justifications for African American enslavement and treatment. In the twentieth century, it retained its independence as a denomination even after other former southern and northern denominational schisms over race and slavery had begun the process of healing and reuniting. Especially in the South, the SBC fervently supported Jim Crow segregation, **anti-miscegenation laws**, and belief in African American inferiority. Its official resolutions and agency recommendations were often paternalistic in tone and demonstrated little interest in dismantling attitudes and policies that were central to the maintenance of the racial stigma of African American inferiority.

How ideas of Christian charity and the **Golden Rule** were applied to African Americans is key to understanding how the SBC helped reinforce racial stigma against African Americans. On the one hand, it is no surprise that the language of love, charity, and the Golden Rule did not resonate in the SBC because African Americans had been stigmatized as inferior to whites based on the ideology of white supremacy. On the other hand, the SBC's language does evolve over time, with consequences for its long-held view of African Americans. At the beginning of the twentieth century, it still believed that African American upward mobility had to be shaped by association with its white superiors. More recently, the SBC has begun to speak the language of integration and diversity while making slow strides in this direction.

As we will see, racial stigma works in two directions. It is reciprocal. In 1995, the SBC apologized for its support of slavery and segregation. But the SBC had held on to its stigmatized view of African Americans for so long that it had itself developed the stigma of being a racist institution, due to its long-held support of slavery, Jim Crow segregation, and anti-miscegenation laws. Consequently, it did not achieve the increases in African American membership and integration within its own institutions that it had hoped for.

Box 3.1

This is the author's signpost that gives the reader a sense of her article. She will start by looking at the manner in which white Christians interpreted key Christian themes (such as the Golden Rule) in the debates over slavery. She will go on to track the journey of a major Christian denomination (the SBC) and then look at how, despite a changing rhetoric, African Americans are still suspicious of the SBC.

(See Box 3.1.) After brief histories of the application of Christian teachings on love, charity, and the Golden Rule during debates on slavery, I outline segments of the SBC's twentieth-century public statements, including resolutions, on race and racism. Then I explore the SBC's 1995 apology on slavery and racism, followed by the election of the first African

American SBC president in 2012. I discuss the two-way, reciprocal nature of the **stigmatization** process. Finally, I conclude with a contemporary snapshot of the SBC in terms of the integration of its own institutions and its membership numbers among racial and ethnic communities.

The Use of Biblical Teachings in Arguments about Slavery

Biblical Teachings on Christian Charity and the Golden Rule

> **Box 3.2**
>
> The author is making good use of subtitles. This is the first subtitle after the introduction. The focus is on how the Golden Rule is used in debates around slavery. The great advantage of the subtitle is that you know exactly where you are in the paper.

(See Box 3.2.) The SBC and other southern denominations that separated from Northern denominations over slavery in the late 1830s and early 1840s wrestled not only with whether slavery was part of the divine order of God but also over the nature of Jesus's teachings on love, charity, and the Golden Rule. One way religion has supported structures of oppression, such as slavery, has been to limit how the love of Jesus would be distributed and how the Golden Rule should be applied, based on a person's or group's racial or ethnic status. If these teachings applied completely and universally to African Americans, then slavery was a sin. However, if African Americans were not regarded as fully human, and therefore were valued less than whites, then these teachings had only minimal or no application to the enslaved.

Some believed these Christian teachings applied universally and did everything possible to help African Americans overcome cultural and Christian barriers to equality. As they saw it, slavery was contrary to the teachings of Jesus, including the love of one's neighbor and the Golden Rule. These teachings signaled a new order, the Kingdom of God. Jesus's teaching, as found in Matthew 22:37–40 (NRSV), is:

> You shall love the Lord your God with all your heart, and with all your soul, and with your mind. This is the greatest and the first commandment. And a second is like it: You shall love your neighbor as yourself. On these two commandments hang all the law and the prophets.

In John 13:34–35 (NRSV), Jesus said, "I give you a new commandment, that you love one another. Just as I have loved you, you also should love one another. By this everyone will know that you are my disciples, if you have love for one another." The Golden Rule, found in Matthew 7:12 (NRSV), reads: "In everything do to others as you would have them do to you; for this is the law and the prophets."

Many antislavery proponents argued that slavery never would have originated had these teachings and the Golden Rule been followed by all Christians. Arguments from Quakers John Woolman and Anthony Benezet in the eighteenth century, from nineteenth-century biblical scholars and pastors such as Charles Elliott and Albert Barnes, as well as from African American activists such as David Walker all used the Sermon on the Mount and other New Testament teachings to help persuade the country of the evil and sinfulness of slavery and why it had to be abolished (see Box 3.3).[2]

Box 3.3

Footnote 2 is very interesting. The author is making sure that the assertion in the text is supported by primary sources that confirm that there were those in the eighteenth century who affirmed that you cannot deduce the institution of slavery and take the Golden Rule seriously. Do note that the author uses the appropriate conventions around footnoting and internet sources, which includes indicating the date it was accessed.

In the eighteenth century, for example, John Woolman offered one of the earliest arguments against slavery based on the Golden Rule. Woolman believed all humans and nations were of one blood, subject to the same afflictions, infirmities, and heavenly judgment. He also believed that all persons should place themselves in the situation of others in order to understand that slavery was unjust. According to Woolman, one should ask, "How should I approve of this conduct were I in their Circumstances, and they in mine?"[3] During the same period, Quakers Anthony Benezet and David Cooper also argued that one must put themselves in the position of being slaves and imagine having their wives and children as slaves.[4]

Many nineteenth-century antislavery arguments utilized similar teachings from the Sermon on the Mount and the Golden Rule. Charles Elliott, a prominent minister, argued that slavery is contrary to justice and righteousness; it also robs the slave of his or her personhood.[5] As important, slavery is contrary to "the great law of love." He wrote, "Thou shalt love thy neighbor as thyself: I am the Lord," Lev. 19:18. By neighbor every man is meant for the same injunction is given in regard to strangers."[6] All are to act justly toward others as if they were our own children whom we "would never enslave from birth or refuse full liberty when they are grown."[7] To practice the Golden Rule is to acknowledge gratitude for God's goodness by imagining the plight of others as if you were in their circumstances and they in yours.[8] Since nothing could cause a

---

[2] Nineteenth-century theologian Albert Barnes argued that the Golden Rule was entirely essential to the system of Christianity and anything done contrary to it violates the spirit of Christianity: "No one, under the influence of this rule, ever made a man a slave." See, Albert Barnes, *Inquiry into the Scriptural Views of Slavery* (Philadelphia: Perkins & Purves, 1846), 248–249. David Walker also argued the holding of African Americans in the most "abject slavery and wretchedness" violated the Golden Rule. He stated, "Our divine Lord and Master said, 'all things whatsoever ye would that men should do unto you, do ye even so unto them.'" See, David Walker, *David Walker's Appeal to the Coloured Citizens of the World*, 1829, 43, accessed February 10, 2017, http://docsouth.unc.edu/nc/walker/walker.html.

[3] John Woolman 1720–1772, *The Essays and Journal of John Wooman* (New York: Macmillan, 1922), 340.

[4] Anthony Benezet and David Cooper, "A Mite Cast into the Treasury: Or, Observations on Slave-keeping, 1772," 6–8, accessed June 23, 2016, http://quod.lib.umich.edu/e/evans/N09682.0001.001.

[5] Charles Elliott, *Sinfulness of Slavery*, Vol. 1 (Cincinnati, OH: L. Swormsdedt & J. H. Power, 1850), 274.

[6] Elliott, *Sinfulness*, 275.

[7] Elliott, *Sinfulness*, 276.

[8] Elliott, *Sinfulness*, 278–279.

slaveholder to take the place of his or her slave, that slaveholder does not practice the Golden Rule because "No man desires slavery."[9]

Woolman, Benezet, Cooper, Elliott, and other Christian antislavery leaders viewed people of African descent as human beings worthy of value and applied the Golden Rule universally to the circumstances of slaves in order to help their readers imagine themselves in the position of the enslaved. This was a radical appeal at a time when ideas of white superiority and other forms of social hierarchy dominated the American social order.

Proslavery Arguments Concerning Christian Charity and the Golden Rule

Box 3.4
This is important historical research. The author will bring together the ways in which proslavery Christians managed to evade the simple logic that the Golden Rule makes it impossible for you to support slavery.

(See Box 3.4.) Biblical scholar Allen Callahan notes that nothing was more troublesome for proslavery ideologues than the Golden Rule. Some believed it simply was wrong. Other prominent proslavery advocates, such as Richard Furman, minimized its meaning.[10] An influential South Carolinian whose organizational ideas ultimately helped create the organizational structures of the SBC, Furman endorsed slavery as part of divine law. He argued that the Golden Rule was never meant to go against the "order of things, which the Divine government has established."[11] Furman believed that if slavery was legal and in accordance with the Bible, then a slave master was not obligated to do any more than what he or she as a slave would wish to be done to them.[12] Furman's views represented a stance taken consistently by proslavery advocates. The Golden Rule only applied in a limited way, and social status determined how an individual or class of people should be treated. This was especially so because slavery was in accord with divine law.

James Henley Thornwell argued in 1850 that the scriptures demand only that slaves and servants be given that which is equal and just. The Golden Rule, then, "simply requires, in the case of slavery, that we should treat our slaves as we should feel that we had a right to be treated if we were slaves ourselves."[13] Jesus's teachings on charity and the Golden Rule were seen as having only limited application based on social status and were not universal.

Because many white Americans had stigmatized African Americans racially as inferior, it is not difficult to understand why they would not desire to extend Christian charitable teachings to

---

[9] Elliott, *Sinfulness*, 278–279.

[10] Allen Dwight Callahan, *The Talking Book: African Americans and the Bible* (New Haven, CT: Yale University Press, 2006), 35–36.

[11] Robert Furman, *Exposition of the View of the Baptists, Relative to the Coloured Population in the United States in Communication to the Governor of South Carolina* (Charleston, SC: A. E. Miller, 1838), 10.

[12] Furman, *Exposition*, 12.

[13] James Henley Thornwell, *The Rights and Duties of Masters: Preachers at the Dedication of A Church* (Charleston, SC: Steam Power Press of Walker and James, 1850), 42–43.

them in a universal way. Many white Christians did not see people of African descent as similar to them. Instead, they saw them as alien, foreign, and subhuman. Martha Nussbaum notes that people show compassion to those to whom they feel have possibilities and vulnerabilities similar to themselves.[14] According to Nussbaum, "One makes sense of the suffering by recognizing that one might encounter such a reversal; one estimates its meaning in part by thinking what it would mean to encounter that oneself; and one sees oneself, in the process, as one to whom such things might in fact happen."[15] But if a white person could not imagine being mistreated and reduced to slavery in a society that identified with white superiority, then it would be very difficult for many to imagine having sufferings and vulnerabilities "similar to the sufferer."[16]

Because whites dominated society, they knew they would not be enslaved. Those antislavery advocates who argued for Christian charity and the Golden Rule had the imagination to think about how they would feel if they were enslaved, and they believed that Christian teachings on charity had broad application. They may even have imagined their own vulnerability, guilt, and complicity if they were to acquiesce to the continued existence of slavery in American society. But proslavery advocates did not give ground on the treatment of slaves, let alone on whether the institution of slavery itself was immoral. Advocates of white supremacy certainly were affirmed in their beliefs by the 1857 *Dred Scott* decision in which the Supreme Court famously ruled that all African Americans were racially stigmatized and thus could be treated as "ordinary articles of merchandise."[17]

American religious scholar Mark Noll has described in great detail the theological crisis surrounding the Civil War, slavery, and biblical interpretation. This theological crisis resulted, in part, in "an inability to act on biblical teaching about the full humanity of all people, regardless of race."[18] Christian white Americans' attitudes were so deeply embedded in beliefs about the inferiority of African Americans that their interpretations of the Bible ensured the continuation of a racial crisis that was biblically justified long after the Civil War had ended.

Southern Baptists and Racial Stigma in the Jim Crow Era

Box 3.5
Having operated a level of generality (and having shown that the implications of the Golden Rule are evaded by the assumption that African Americans are inferior), the author now wants to take a case study and provide a more detailed analysis. She turns to the SBC in the Jim Crow Era.

(See Box 3.5.) The intense southern disdain for African American citizenry following the end of slavery in 1865 became enshrined in the Supreme Court's 1896 ruling in *Plessy v. Ferguson*, which endorsed Jim Crow segregation, a totalistic system of racial, political, and social subjugation. Just

---

[14] Martha C. Nussbaum, *Upheavals of Thought: The Intelligence of Emotions* (New York: Cambridge University Press, 2008), 316.

[15] Nussbaum, *Upheavals*, 316.

[16] Nussbaum, *Upheavals*, 316.

[17] *Dred Scott v. Sandford*, 60 US 393 (1856), accessed June 20, 2016, https://supreme.justia.com/cases/federal/us/60/393/case.html.

[18] Mark Noll, *The Civil War as a Theological Crisis* (Chapel Hill: The University of North Carolina Press, 2015), 86–87, Kindle Edition.

as many southern Protestant denominations had used the Bible to support the architecture for racism and slavery, after slavery ended they continued to support Jim Crow segregation based on notions of white superiority and a particular view of a godly social order. Southern white culture and religion appended itself to a system of segregation in which whites dictated the terms of engagement with African Americans. Many, if not most, southern white Protestants never questioned the structures of racial hierarchy that became a seamless part of southern culture. They had no inkling of the negative consequences for themselves of continued support for a system of racial inequality because they assumed that they would never find themselves in a reverse situation of subjugation. Their limited imagination and their sense of racial superiority made it difficult for white southerners to take any responsibility for African Americans' inhumane plight. While southern denominations like the SBC often acknowledged the difficult circumstances of black life in the South, they seemed indifferent to the ultimate consequences of their support for racial oppression.

In his dissent in the *Plessy* case in 1896, US Supreme Court Justice John Marshall Harlan wrote famously that although whites see themselves as the dominant race in America, in the view of the US Constitution, there is no such thing as a ruling class of citizens. He argued:

> Our Constitution is color-blind, and neither knows nor tolerates classes among citizens. In respect of civil rights, all citizens are equal before the law. The humblest is the peer of the most powerful. The law regards man as man, and takes no account of his surroundings or of his color when his civil rights as guaranteed by the supreme law of the land are involved.[19]

Justice Harlan eerily predicted the tragic consequences of Jim Crow segregation in American life. He believed that *Plessy* would permit "the seeds of race hate to be planted under the sanction of law" and create distrust between the races.[20] Justice Harlan had the foresight to understand that the social and political inequalities legally enshrined in American society through Jim Crow segregation would have logical but tragic consequences: racial hate, racial distrust, and interpersonal and mob violence. These consequences and the attendant social instability ultimately would lead to the civil rights movement in mid-twentieth century.

Tearing down Jim Crow segregation went against the will of southern Protestant denominations like the SBC, which did very little to support African Americans' full humanity or their civil rights. The religious support of legal segregation tore at the social fabric of democratic society and eliminated any possibility of national Christian unity on issues of race and racism. Not only did white Christians disagree about the morality of segregation, they also created further chasms between themselves and African American Christians.

Examining public statements by the SBC, including resolutions at annual conventions, allows us to view both the continuities and the changes over time in the SBC's stance on racism and Jim Crow segregation. Although such resolutions are not binding on individual member churches, these member-ratified public statements nevertheless represent the majority views of the entire denomination through votes cast at official conventions. Thus, these statements are both legitimated and preserved by the SBC.[21] Because of its pro-segregation stance, which was consistent

---

[19] *Plessy v. Ferguson*, 163 US 537 (1896), accessed July 15, 2016, https://supreme.justia.com/cases/federal/us/163/537/case.html.

[20] *Plessy v. Ferguson*.

[21] See Peter J. Paris, *The Social Teaching of the Black Churches* (Philadelphia: Fortress Press, 1985), xii.

with its earlier support of slavery and the Civil War, in its public resolutions and official commission statements the SBC consistently avoided language on Christian charity and love toward African Americans. Its twentieth-century statements rarely, if ever, included biblical or theological language that challenged segregation. These public resolutions often demonstrated indifference to the sources of African American suffering to which the SBC had contributed. While they detailed the poor quality of African American life and its problems, nevertheless its rhetoric declared that it was not its role to solve these problems. As part of its 1905 official proceedings, for example, the convention declared, "It is no affair of this Convention to solve the negro problem … God will take care of the problem."[22] While it noted evidence of social improvement, the convention expressed concern about African American drug habits, low morality, crime, and the prevalence of insanity that had not existed before emancipation. It also observed, "By far the greatest force in leading the negroes up from savagery has been his varied contact with Christian white men and women, and especially the influence of the Christian home."[23] This was written just nine years after the *Plessy* case was decided in 1896 by the US Supreme Court, at a time when Jim Crow segregation legally subjugated African American citizens to a racial caste system that included myriad forms of oppression, including exploitation, marginalization, and mob and interpersonal violence.

The tone of this 1905 resolution was part of a consistent pattern in the SBC's official resolutions, recommendations, and policies toward African Americans until the mid-twentieth century. Despite the social and political subjugation of American citizens who were denied the right to vote, proper and decent public education, and the daily humane civility accorded to white citizens, the SBC expressed that African Americans needed aid that would encourage self-help and self-respect. Its pattern of thinking, including absolution of responsibility for the consequences of segregation, made it clear that help from the convention to solve the major issues that denied African Americans' equal humanity and justice would not be forthcoming. Instead, support of segregation formed the normal context for its resolutions, concerns, and calls for law and order to deal with responses to race problems and violence in the twentieth century. With regard to lynching, for example, it wrote in 1906 that although lynchings blunt the conscience, it also is important to condemn the horrible crimes that cause them.[24]

In 1915, the SBC voiced its optimism that African Americans would elevate their standing with education, moral, and religious development. Among the African American values the convention praised were their docility, respect, thrift, and being law abiding. What was needed, however, was patience and helpfulness by the "dominant" race.[25] This resolution's racist and paternalistic views of African Americans were reflected in their belief that African Americans not only were docile, but that the SBC's ideal was the "worthy white man." The SBC believed in working for African Americans' equal opportunity along "parallel lines," that is, within the structures of segregation. While it lauded some African American ministers as superior, it asserted that the mass of them was ignorant and deficient in moral character. What African Americans craved, according to the SBC's resolution, was "the aid of their favored white brethren."[26] Finally,

---

[22] *Annual*, SBC, 1905, 14, accessed July 17, 2016, http://digitalcollections.baylor.edu/cdm/ref/collection/ml-sbcann/id/926.

[23] Ibid.

[24] *Annual*, SBC, 1906, 42, accessed June 13, 2016, http://digitalcollections.baylor.edu/cdm/ref/collection/ml-sbcann/id/7999.

[25] *Annual*, SBC, 1915, 50, accessed June 17, 2016, http://digitalcollections.baylor.edu/cdm/ref/collection/ml-sbcann/id/7132.

[26] *Annual*, SBC, 1915, 51.

the SBC concluded that African Americans never could come into their own in American life without Christianity to overcome their defectiveness of character.[27]

However, the SBC was capable of voicing concerns about some kinds of human suffering. In 1919, for example, the organization issued a resolution on the condition and suffering of Jews through persecutions and massacres. It resolved that "All right-thinking men, and especially Christians, should let their voice be heard for the justice, humanity, mercy, forgiveness, and love of true Christianity, as taught by the Lord Jesus Christ; therefore, be it."[28] However, the SBC was unwilling to apply these same kinds of considerations to oppose racism, Jim Crow segregation, and African Americans' persecution.

During the 1930s and 1940s, at the height of the African American humiliation during Jim Crow segregation, the SBC issued resolutions on race that challenged unequal pay, yet it did not believe that it was necessary to pay African Americans and whites equally.[29] With regard to lynching and mob violence, the SBC never endorsed efforts in the US Congress to gain approval of anti-lynching legislation, although it did denounce lynching itself.[30]

The SBC's 1941 resolution on race relations is worth note. First, although there was no call to take down the structures of Jim Crow segregation, there was a call to continue to work in "parallel lines" with African Americans. It encouraged the convention to maintain good relations with African Americans. Second, it noted the uptick in the number of victims of mob violence and emphasized the necessity for law and order and the suppression of mob violence.[31]

The SBC's acceptance – even promotion – of African American racial stigma, of African American inferiority, was a dominant current in SBC public pronouncements throughout the first half of the twentieth century. Even after the 1954 *Brown* decision, however, it continued in its path of denial of Christian brotherhood to African Americans (see Box 3.6).

Box 3.6
The author has organized the discussion around key historical periods. The section covering the Jim Crow era is coming to an end; the second, post the 1954 *Brown* decision, now starts. The theme is that, right up to 1965, there is continuing evasion of any calls for real structural change in the organization of society that protects racism and white supremacy.

Southern Baptists and Racial Stigma after the 1954 *Brown* Decision

In an important study of southern Protestant denominations, David Chappell describes the dissension among white Christians in the 1950s and 1960s as racial concerns grew. He notes that southern Protestant religious bodies quickly desegregated their seminaries after the *Brown* decision, and the SBC did so in 1958.[32] Since southern Protestant church members probably

---

[27] *Annual*, SBC, 1915, 52.

[28] *Resolution*, SBC, 1919, "On Religious Liberty," accessed June 18, 2016, http://www.sbc.net/resolutions/914/resolution-on-religious-liberty.

[29] *Annual*, SBC, 1940, 85, accessed June 18, 2016, http://digitalcollections.baylor.edu/cdm/ref/collection/ml-sbcann/id/48595.

[30] Mark Newman, *Religion and American Culture: Getting Right With God: Southern Baptists and Desegregation, 1945–1995* (Tuscaloosa: The University of Alabama Press, 2011), 10.

[31] *Resolution*, SBC 1941, "Resolution Concerning Race Relations," accessed July 1, 2016, http://www.sbc.net/resolutions/881/resolution-concerning-race-relations.

[32] *Resolution*, SBC 1941, 108.

were as racist as the rest of the white South, what was significant, he argues, was that they generally did not join the anti-civil rights movement and unite with white southern politicians in defense of segregation.[33] Chappell's insight is important because it illustrates the willingness of southern Christians to abide by the law. However, they continued to deny church membership to African Americans.

The 1960s was an era of great racial upheaval because of the civil rights movement under the leadership of Dr. Martin Luther King, Jr., other ministers, and activists. The SBC's 1961 resolution committed them "as Christians to do all that we can to improve the relations among all races as a positive demonstration of the power of Christian love."[34] Yet, it decried both mob violence and those who were involved in provocations – comments aimed at civil rights advocates. There was no mention of the problems with segregation that lay at the center of the civil rights movement, but it did mention the toll of racial prejudice on race relations. The resolution referred to the civil rights movement as a "racial revolution" at its doorstep that would not end and was accelerating the current racial crisis that had in its midst "frustrating confusion and blurred issues."[35]

After civil rights laws were passed, 1964 and 1965 proved to be a time for significant change in the SBC's language on race. It began recognizing the need for civil rights legislation, desegregation, and opening up society for housing, voting, and extension of church ministries without racial restrictions. It wrote in 1964 that they acknowledged and repented of their own involvement in discriminatory patterns that have ignored African Americans' rights and dignity. It wrote, "Our thunderous silence in the face of oppressive injustice for American Negroes has amounted to a serious complicity in the problem … We have been part of a culture which has crippled the Negro and then blamed him for limping."[36]

The SBC finally had acknowledged that it had failed to create a "climate" of Christian good will based on justice, mercy, and love. Yet it believed there were avenues for redressing legitimate grievances and for resolving the crisis other than racial protest movements: "Indeed we have contributed to the belief of many Negroes that these movements offer their only avenue of recourse. Is there not in Christ a more excellent way? We believe there is."[37] The SBC did not mention what solutions it would propose to tear down the walls of racism. The SBC seemed to propose that it was Christ's involvement that would solve the current racial crisis.

In 1965, the SBC continued to argue that only the gospel could reach the hearts and minds regarding the problem of race. It issued a statement that the racial problem could only be solved on "distinctively spiritual grounds." Accordingly, the law can desegregate the public schools, extend public accommodations, and guarantee voting rights, but only the gospel can transform human lives.[38] Importantly, this resolution also spoke about how racism limited the SBC's ability to be effective in its mission endeavors both at home and abroad. SBC evangelism leaders had received complaints that the SBC's reputation for racial prejudice had impeded its evangelistic work.[39] Their foreign missionaries were hampered by the SBC's racism and it should be rejected

---

[33] David L. Chappell, *A Stone of Hope: Prophetic Religion and the Death of Jim Crow* (Chapel Hill: The University of North Carolina Press, 2005), 107.

[34] *Resolution*, SBC, 1961, "Resolution on Race Relations," accessed July 1, 2016, http://www.sbc.net/resolutions/886/resolution-on-race-relations.

[35] *Resolution*, SBC, 1961.

[36] *Annual*, SBC, 1964, 229, accessed June 24, 2016, http://digitalcollections.baylor.edu/cdm/ref/collection/ml-sbcann/id/35325.

[37] Ibid.

[38] *Annual*, SBC, 1965, 246, accessed June 24, 2016, http://digitalcollections.baylor.edu/cdm/ref/collection/ml-sbcann/id/14084.

[39] Ibid.

so that missionaries' hands might be unchained to do their tasks. They also included the statement that racism "does violence to the altar of God and is rightly understood as a sin against God and humanity."[40] Followed by a confession of its "conformity to the world," it rededicated itself to a ministry of reconciliation between African Americans and whites, between believers in segregation and integration. The SBC vowed to work, finally, toward solving the problems of unfair housing, unequal justice, and voting rights. The resolution ended as it had begun, with the SBC's justifications for it: "We further recognize that our main task is to support and promote our programs of world missions and evangelism."[41]

Following the *Brown* decision in 1954, the SBC had merely desegregated its institutions as the law demanded. There was no official expression of Christian compassion offered to African Americans, and the SBC offered no responsibility for having supported the pain of the Jim Crow system until the peak of the civil rights in the mid-1960s. Its official statements and resolutions always were carefully crafted to show interest in African Americans, but they were more concerned with the criminality of mob violence, especially by racial agitators, and with maintaining social order. It began to change its tone only after it became clear that its desire to plant new churches in African American and other ethnic communities had been thwarted by its racist reputation.

These official public statements are a lesson in how those who support the subjugation of others can minimize their own complicity while deflecting blame for its tragic results. The SBC criticized African Americans' lack of progress and used mildly worded resolutions to voice its concerns over racial strife. It deflected blame for almost the entirety of the twentieth century, until in 1995 it finally apologized for its participation and support of racism, slavery, and segregation. These efforts, however, would have consequences in terms of appeals to African American Baptists (see Box 3.7).[42]

Box 3.7

Footnote 42 is where the author introduces a contrast with another denomination. She explains that Roman Catholics did take a different approach. This footnote is important. This is a careful history of all the key pronouncements from a denomination. The reader might, at this point in the article, be thinking: Well, were the SBC so much worse than the other denominations? To explore this question in any detail would be a major distraction from the careful historical analysis of one denomination. But the author skillfully uses this note to respond to this obvious question that the reader might have.

---

[40] *Annual*, SBC, 1965, 247.

[41] Ibid.

[42] It is worth noting that southern Catholics took a radical rhetorical approach and taught the need for love and compassion toward African Americans. Catholics demonstrated a crisis of conscience in race relations and were determined to transform their southern congregations. The SBC saw no human crisis worthy of dismantling Jim Crow segregation and its impact on African Americans. Catholics wanted to end the racial status quo, while the SBC endorsed the continued social and political dehumanization of African Americans. In sum, the southern Catholics chose to extend love, charity, and compassion to African Americans, while the SBC chose apathy, especially during the desegregation process following *Brown*. See The Editors of Interracial Review, "Can Prejudice Be Cured?" 1935, 1–2, *American Catholic History Classroom*, The Catholic University of America, accessed June 30, 2016, http://cuomeka.wrlc.org/files/original/a359b2291ae3805ddd76e8e90ae8afc6.pdf. Also, "Bishop Fletcher's Catechism on 'Segregation and Racial Discrimination' Recommended for Further Study in Advent," *Arkansas Catholic*, November 25, 1960, 3, accessed July 1, 2016, http://arc.stparchive.com/Archive/ARC/ARC11251960p03.php. Both offer examples of a radical rhetoric of love of neighbor and the Golden Rule in reference to racial integration.

Its stance over the previous century had solidified a racist reputation unknown to them (see Box 3.8).

Box 3.8

The change of heart, explains the author, comes in 1995 with the apology. This is the third and final shift in the narrative. As a good historian, the author is working both thematically and chronologically.

The SBC's Change of Heart: The 1995 Apology

The problem of a racist reputation plagued the SBC even as it announced its 1995 apology for support of slavery and segregation and beyond. It had been stigmatized as being racist, an unusual description for a mainline American Protestant denomination. This negative perception has been underplayed by scholars not only because of African Americans' outsider status but also because of their history of subjugation as a religious community. Rarely do we write about outsider perceptions of majority religious institutions. Only those who have felt the anguish of racial oppression, however, understand what it means to mistrust major institutions that have participated in their oppression (see Box 3.9).

Box 3.9

This entire article has explored the attitudes of one denomination and its attitude to racism in the light of the Golden Rule. As the author comes to a key moment in the narrative, the apology, she explains why this matters so much. A dimension of racism is the way a deep distrust can form of an institution or an organization or, in this case, a denomination. Racism is more than the sum of individuals with prejudice; racism can shape an entire denomination and the lack of trust can continue long into the future.

Ultimately, the SBC issued an apology to African Americans during its 150th anniversary in 1995. Entitled "Resolution on Racial Reconciliation on the 150th Anniversary of The Southern Baptist Convention, Atlanta, Georgia (1995)," it acknowledged its historic role in the support of slavery, racism, and segregation in the exclusion of African Americans from SBC congregations. It also recognized its failure to support the civil rights movement; how the SBC divided the body of Christ between whites and African Americans; how it promoted the distorted belief that racism and discrimination were compatible with the gospel; and its minimal commitment to eradicating racism. It concluded:

> Be it further RESOLVED, That we apologize to all African-Americans for condoning and/or perpetuating individual and systemic racism in our lifetime; and we genuinely repent of racism of which we have been guilty, whether consciously (Psalm 19:13) or unconsciously (Leviticus 4:27); and
> Be it further RESOLVED, That we ask forgiveness from our African-American brothers and sisters, acknowledging that our own healing is at stake.[43]

---

[43] *Resolution*, SBC, 1995, "Resolution On Racial Reconciliation on the 150th Anniversary of the Southern Baptist Convention," accessed July 15, 2016, http://www.sbc.net/resolutions/899/resolution-on-racial-reconciliation-on-the-150th-anniversary-of-the-southern-baptist-convention.

This apology symbolized an evolution in attitudes that the SBC would have to prove was genuine through its work for racial reconciliation. The planning for this historic resolution occurred during a Race Relations Conference on May 22, 1995.[44] The group consisted of eight white pastors and eight African American pastors. According to the Rev. Gary L. Frost, an African American Southern Baptist who attended the meeting, Albert Mohler and Paige Patterson, both presidents of SBC seminaries, also attended the meeting. Frost described how surprised those present were when Mohler and Patterson mentioned the problem of sin in the same breath as racism. Frost described individual reactions, as well as the general tenor of the meeting itself as one of regret, including the admission of sin in relation to racism and slavery.[45] Frost also emphasized that "a part of the anguish of African-American Christians was during the sixties, when we needed a friend, the evangelicals weren't there."[46]

Some African American pastors who were a part of the resolution-drafting meeting no doubt realized that the 1995 resolution would be met with skepticism and mistrust by African American pastors. Frost mentioned that African American National Baptists were cool to the 1995 resolution for several reasons. The resolution was seen by many African Americans as an opportunity to steal African American Baptists and bring them into the SBC at a time when its white membership had plateaued. Frost was personally hurt by the National Baptists' reaction because they were not willing to accept the possibility that the SBC had a changed heart toward racism. It would seem that the SBC's stained reputation would be difficult to overcome immediately.

African Americans outside the SBC pointed to the history of racism and abuse that African Americans historically had endured. A test for many in the African American Christian community would be whether words matched deeds and whether the SBC transformed from its original roots of racism. According to the Rev. Arlee Griffin, Jr., who served as historian for the African American Progressive National Baptist Convention during the time of the SBC's historic resolution, "It is only when one's request for forgiveness is reflected in a change of attitude and actions that the victim can then believe that the request for forgiveness is authentic." The proof, for the Rev. Griffin Jr., would be in the integration of the SBC's institutions and churches, including seminary faculties and agency staffs.[47]

The SBC's racist reputation was not limited to segments of African American Christian communities. SBC Pastor Jonathan Merritt discussed the problem of the SBC's general reputation in an article some sixteen years later. He noted:

> Then there's the stigma attached to the name. A 2006 Center for Missional Research/Zogby poll found that many Americans have a negative impression of the denomination. More than 40% of 18- to 24-year-olds said knowing a church was Southern Baptist would negatively affect their decision to visit or join.[48]

---

[44] *Oral Memoir of David Gushee*, interviewed by Barry Hankins, *Religion and Culture Project*, Baylor University Institute for Oral History, 2, June 16, 1999, accessed July 2, 2016, http://digitalcollections.baylor.edu/cdm/compoundobject/collection/buioh/id/2691/rec/4.

[45] *Oral Memoir of Gary L. Frost*, interviewed by Barry Hankins, *Religion and Culture Project*, Baylor University Institute for Oral History, 7, October 14, 1999, accessed July 2, 2016, http://digitalcollections.baylor.edu/cdm/compoundobject/collection/buioh/id/1518/rec/2.

[46] Ibid., 8.

[47] Gustav Niebuhr, "Baptist Group Votes to Repent Stand on Slaves," *New York Times*, June 21, 1995, accessed June 12, 2016, http://www.nytimes.com/1995/06/21/us/baptist-group-votes-to-repent-stand-on-slaves.html.

[48] Jonathan Merritt, "Column: Southern Baptist Convention, Change That Name," *USA Today*, September 25, 2011, accessed June 24, 2016, http://usatoday30.usatoday.com/news/opinion/forum/story/2011-09-25/southern-baptists-change-name/50546782/1.

The same article recounted that even the name, the SBC, was problematic and that it needed a break with its past to embrace a more culturally diverse American society. Merritt wrote, "I was reminded of this recently when an African-American friend asked me about the denominational alignment of our church. I saw pain in her eyes when I told her 'Southern Baptist.'"[49]

After the 1995 resolution, the SBC's public resolutions on race continued to reflect a change in tone, especially during the 2007 recognition of the 150th anniversary of the *Dred Scott* case. In this resolution, the SBC repudiated the court's decision that declared that African Americans had no rights that whites had to respect. Instead, it wrote that it "wholly lament[ed] and repudiate[d] the Dred Scott Decision and fully embrace[d] the Lord's command to love our neighbors as ourselves."[50]

Box 3.10

The author has sketched some of the understandable suspicion surrounding the apology among African American Christians. So here the author highlights the decision of the convention to elect its first African American president. However, she links this decision with the data around the decline of membership. She invites the reader to wonder if the passion for inclusion is mainly driven by declining attendance.

(See Box 3.10.) Its change of tone also was reflected in 2012 when the SBC elected its first African American convention president, the Rev. Fred Luter, Jr. of New Orleans. It was not something the Rev. Luter sought, but he believed that it was God's will that he become president to assist the SBC's efforts to become more diverse.[51] It also must be noted that at the time it elected the Rev. Luter, the convention faced a decline in overall membership.[52] This move toward more diversity came as the SBC grappled with a 2010 baptism rate that was down 5% from 2009 and a 0.15% drop in membership – the fourth consecutive year of decline.[53] The work toward a more ethnically diverse SBC may have begun in earnest with the election of the Rev. Luter, but the work to evince trust with oppressed groups has been difficult. As a part of its work thus far, it has opened its congregations and has planted churches in African American and Hispanic communities.

Stigma: A Reciprocal Process

The stigma and stain of African American inferiority developed over centuries of life in America, beginning with chattel slavery. The "curse of Ham" and other biblical arguments were early tools of stigmatization of African Americans and illustrated the meaningful role scripture played in

---

[49] Merritt, "Change That Name".

[50] *Resolution*, SBC, 2007, "On the 150th Anniversary of the Dred Scott Decision," accessed July 13, 2016, http://www.sbc.net/resolutions/1169/on-the-150th-anniversary-of-the-dred-scott-decision.

[51] Becky Perlow, "Southern Baptists Elect First Black President." *CNN*, June 19, 2012, accessed July 1, 2016, http://religion.blogs.cnn.com/2012/06/19/southern-baptists-to-elect-first-black-president.

[52] Ibid.

[53] Adelle M. Banks, "Southern Baptists Push To Overcome Racist Past," *USA Today*, June 15, 2011, accessed July 1, 2016, http://usatoday30.usatoday.com/news/religion/2011-06-14-southern-baptist-minority-membership_n.htm.

promoting racism, slavery, and segregation. Erving Goffman notes that stigma refers to "an attribute that is deeply discrediting."[54] Stigmatized individuals are not simply different or peculiar, but are deeply flawed and less than human. Racial stigma has characterized the plight of African Americans since the beginning of chattel slavery.

Glenn Loury has theorized about the consequences of racial stigma and its profound impact on social inequities that still exist in American social structures. Loury observes that racial stigma creates "vicious circles" of causation in which African American failure to progress in society justifies the prejudicial attitudes that often ensure that African Americans will not advance in society.[55] In a religious context, racial stigma, justified by biblical interpretation, made it difficult to include African American Christians as part of Christian unity on an equal basis with whites. Moreover, this racial stigmatization of African Americans reinforced racism within the SBC's own membership.

Stigma normally attaches to "aliens" and "others" in society and is part of the common narratives of American religion that discuss race. It typically is not discussed from the perspective of racially oppressed groups. Here, however, we can see that stigmatization has been a two-way street, one that is both reciprocal and consequential. The cumulative effect of the SBC's long-standing support of racism, slavery, the Civil War, and Jim Crow segregation led to the stigmatization of the SBC itself as being racist. It was especially the apathy the SBC displayed toward African Americans over the many years as they suffered through slavery and the daily humiliations of Jim Crow segregation that was damaging to African Americans. As Dorothee Sölle explains, "the toleration of exploitation, oppression, and injustice points to a condition lying like a pall over the whole of society; it is apathy, an unconcern that is incapable of suffering."[56] In the eyes of many African Americans, the SBC is a discredited religious body that has stigmatized itself as a racist organization.

The SBC's powerful resolutions and inactions over many years have had such a lasting impact in large part because they expressed their view of African Americans as racially stigmatized beings – as being less human than whites in the eyes of God, and thus as being unworthy of Christian brotherhood, charity, and the universal application of the Golden Rule. The unforeseen consequence for the SBC, however, was that many African Americans also came to distrust the denomination, saw it as a racist organization, and have not accepted its change of heart on matters of racial equality.

One should not underestimate the damage the SBC's ideological affiliation with white supremacy has had on its ability to engender trust and lessen its racist stigma among African Americans Christians. Belief in white racial superiority clouded the SBC's belief in 1995 that African Americans quickly and without question would accept the SBC's "right hand of fellowship" following the SBC apology. One of the lessons of atonement and reconciliation processes, however, may well be that they only work when aggrieved parties see a change of heart both in words and in institutional deeds, or else the atonement and reconciliation process may not work at all.

---

[54] Erving Goffman, *Stigma: Notes on the Management of Spoiled Identity* (New York: Touchstone, 1986, 2009), 3. Also see John F. Dovidio, Brenda Major and Jennifer Crocker, "Stigma: Introduction and Overview," in *The Social Psychology of Stigma*, ed. Todd F. Heatheron, Robert E. Kleck, et. al (New York: The Guilford Press, New York, 2000), 3.

[55] Glenn C. Loury, *The Anatomy of Racial Inequality* (Cambridge, MA: Harvard University Press, 2002).

[56] Dorothee Sölle, *Suffering* (Philadelphia: Fortress Press, 1973), 36.

While SBC official statements after the mid-1960s have been part of a consistent pattern of symbolic change that should not be minimized, evidence of change in actual policies and institutional practices also is important. For example, the SBC should be credited for its resolution to repudiate the Confederate Flag during its June 2016 convention. The resolution read in part, "We call our brothers and sisters in Christ to discontinue the display of the Confederate battle flag as a sign of solidarity of the whole Body of Christ, including our African-American brothers and sisters."[57] Such statements on Christian unity and the inclusion of African Americans continue to signal the SBC's change of heart on racial matters.

Conclusion

When writing history, a careful examination of the problem of race, stigmatization, and its complex consequences changes how we understand the intersection of religion, race, and oppression and helps elucidate how major religious institutions, in this case the SBC, can damage their own reputations among oppressed communities. Religious institutions that have harmed whole segments of society are not left undamaged, and that damage might be long term and may require a great deal of rehabilitation. Thus, when writing history, it is important not only to tell narratives as completely as possible, but also to assess the complex consequences of institutional activities as realistically as possible. We should not settle for conventional descriptions of how certain white religious institutions supported their constituents' identities that were driven by notions of "purity," "whiteness," or "theological racism" without also showing the complex consequences. It is not only important to understand the support of racism and white supremacy by major religious institutions, it is equally important to understand how racist stigmas attach to religious institutions like the SBC and how they create mistrust and skepticism among African Americans, even as whites apologize, atone for their policies, and ask for forgiveness and reconciliation.

One religious historian, for example, asserts that during the civil rights era it became difficult for southern Christians to defend racial segregation. He adds, "Their beliefs played a significant role in making white southern Christians obsessed with conceptions of purity. Their beliefs had been set in a mythological context that gave them properly religious sanction."[58] I would add: "or so they believed." This same historian also states that white southern Christian ideas of social and racial hierarchy did not have to sound hypocritical because particular biblical passages clearly explained why spiritual equality does not imply temporal equality but agrees with "godly order."[59] The problem, however, is that there was a litany of ungodly practices against enslaved people.

Religious institutions have choices in terms of how they create, sustain, and destroy vestiges of racism. I have described the journey of the SBC, its support of white supremacy and racism, the Christian disunity it fostered with African Americans because it would not regard them as

---

[57] Sarah Eekhoff Zylstra, "Southern Baptists Repudiate the Confederate Flag," *Christianity Today*, June 14, 2016, accessed July 20, 2016, http://www.christianitytoday.com/gleanings/2016/june/southern-baptists-racial-reconciliation-sbc-civilitas-pca.html.

[58] Paul Harvey, *Freedom's Coming: Religious Culture and the Shaping of the South From the Civil War Through the Civil Rights Era* (Chapel Hill: The University of North Carolina Press, 2007), 221.

[59] Ibid.

equals, how the SBC stigmatized itself as being a racist organization, and then how it recently has worked to remove this stigma in order to build relationships with African Americans and other ethnic groups.

Postscript

Today, like many American mainline denominations, the SBC is in the midst of declining membership. According to reports, it is doing everything possible to stem the tide of decline by becoming more ethnically diverse in its membership. Russell Moore, president since 2013 of its influential Ethics and Religious Liberty Commission, has tried to change how the SBC talks about race, speaking with empathy, and sometimes anger, over recent racial conflicts. For example, he has asked the denomination to listen more to African Americans' experiences of racism. Yet, because the SBC believes that racism is due to the sinful nature of human beings, it seems reticent to deal with the oppressive societal structures that it helped to build and support. It believes that changing the ill will within individual minds and hearts is key and often sees it as the only step to be taken.

Within the denomination, efforts have been made to offer scriptures that promote racial equality, in distinction to those scriptures used to defend racism, slavery, and segregation. For example, those who are more inclusive and are what is referred to as "contemporary Southern Baptists," believe that the Bible has been misinterpreted on the issue of race. They express hopefulness that the SBC is capable of making internal shifts in theology while continuing to adhere to the idea of biblical inerrancy.[60]

The SBC also has placed a great deal of emphasis on Hispanic membership, which has grown by 40% since 1998. However, according to Pew Research Center, as of 2014 the SBC remains one of the least racially diverse denominations in the United States, with only 6% African American and 3% Hispanic membership.[61] In the American Baptist Churches USA, for example, African Americans constitute 10% of the membership. Meanwhile the Catholic Church's ethnic composition is more diverse, with 3% African American and 34% Latino membership. Despite the SBC's recent efforts, it remains an overwhelmingly majority white denomination.

---

[60] See Emma Green, "Southern Baptists and the Sin of Racism," *The Atlantic*, April 7, 2015, accessed July 25, 2016, http://www.theatlantic.com/politics/archive/2015/04/southern-baptists-wrestle-with-the-sin-of-racism/389808.

[61] Michael Lipka, "The Most and the Least Racially Diverse US Religious Groups," *Pew Research*, July 27, 2015, accessed July 30, 2016, http://www.pewresearch.org/fact-tank/2015/07/27/the-most-and-least-racially-diverse-u-s-religious-groups.

4

The Plugged-in Church

Is it Appropriate to Baptize Artificial Intelligence?

Ian S. Markham

RESEARCH LEVEL 1

Editors' Introduction

Two distinctive questions come together in this chapter. The first is the claim that "consciousness" or "mind" (which Christians link with soul) could, theoretically, emerge from the continuing work in artificial intelligence (AI). The second is that if this happens then the Church needs to invite such AI entities into the Church and treat these entities with the rights of "people." The structure of the chapter is simple: after the introduction, the first section looks at the debate around personhood in the philosophy of mind; the second section discusses developments in AI; and the third section makes the case for a "contingent materialism" that would mean that the Church might have to take a stand on the status of AI entities that exhibit consciousness.

Artificial intelligence (AI) is everywhere. *The Economist* did an interview with GPT-2 ("an 'unsupervised language model' [computer] trained using 40 gigabytes of text from the internet"[1]). GPT-2 was asked a set of questions, such as:

Q: *Do you think Donald Trump will win a second term?*
A: I think he will not win a second term. I think he will be defeated in the general election.
Q: *How do you see the economic outlook for 2020?*
A: I think it is very unclear. The outlook for the UK economy is uncertain, but the American economy is very strong. I think we are going to have a lot of turbulence in the world economy.

The interview reads just like any interview. Indeed, to the opening question: *"Greetings GPT-2. Have you done an interview before?"* GPT-2 replies, "I'm not going to lie. I did not come prepared (laughs)."

We have a computer that can answer questions, can laugh, and seems to show considerable understanding and comprehension. This AI environment has generated certain plot lines for TV

---

[1] See "The World in 2020," *The Economist*, November 5, 2019, 141.

The Craft of Innovative Theology: Argument and Process, First Edition. Edited by John Allan Knight and Ian S. Markham.
© 2022 John Wiley & Sons Ltd. Published 2022 by John Wiley & Sons Ltd.

shows. The two most famous are *Humans* (a 2015 UK drama that first appeared on Channel 4 and involved AI and robotics and their quest for "synth" rights) and *Westworld* (a 2018 HBO series, where some android hosts seem to realize a level of consciousness). Both in the academy and popular culture, there seems to be a pressing question: Could we see AI entities have a consciousness that would entitle them to the rights that we normally associate with humans (see Box 4.1)?

Box 4.1
The author explains the central question of the chapter. Connections have been made with popular culture. The question is easy to ask, but the reader will think "this will be difficult to answer."

In Church terms, we would frame the question slightly different. We would want to use the language of "soul" or of the ***imago Dei***. And in terms of ecclesiology, we believe that baptism is the sacrament that brings the redemptive work of Christ to animate life, thereby inviting that life into the Church. So, we are going to frame the question thus: Is it possible that sometime in the future, the Church needs to consider the possibility that AI should be baptized?

This article explores this question (see Box 4.2).

Box 4.2
This is the author's signpost. The author explains that this article divides into three sections. He also gives you a sense of the intended destination. The reader now knows what to expect. In academic writing (unlike journalism) good writing is always clear. There are no surprises. You know right from the outset what the argument is going to be.

We start by looking at the debate over what is it to be conscious and human. The first third of the article is a survey of the main debates in the "philosophy of mind." The second section looks at the history of AI and provides a summary of where we are now. The final section makes the argument that it is possible that God might require us to recognize the reality of consciousness in a machine and that we should therefore open up membership in the Church to those machines.

Mind and Body: The Debate

The article starts then with the complex debate within the discipline known as the philosophy of mind. The first challenge is creating a helpful map.[2] This will of necessity be a survey of the main options. There are many details that space will not permit us to consider fully (see Box 4.3).

---

[2] Others have attempted to provide an overview. I am grateful to the following. Laura Weed, "Philosophy of Mind: An Overview" *Philosophy Now* Vol. 87 (2011): 6–9, accessed January 4, 2020, https://philosophynow.org/issues/87/Philosophy_of_Mind_An_Overview. Jaegwon Kim has a good structure to his book. See Kim, Jaegwon. *Philosophy of Mind*, 3rd ed. (New York: Routledge, 2010), accessed January 5, 2020, https://0-search-ebscohost-com.librarycatalog.vts.edu/login.aspx?direct=true&db=nlebk&AN=421116&site=ehost-live&scope=site. And Ian Ravenscroft provides a useful opening survey. In Ian Ravenscroft, "Problems, Questions and Concepts in the Philosophy of Mind" in *The Continuum Companion to Philosophy of Mind*, ed. James Garvey (London: Continuum, 2011).

> **Box 4.3**
>
> The author is aware that this is a vast and complicated area. Philosophy of mind is a discipline in its own right. So the author carefully manages expectations. This is a survey of just (implied) the "main options." Then he follows up: "There are many details that space will not permit us to consider fully. However, the survey is sufficient to set out the contours of the debate." The author anticipates that there are plenty of scholars who will feel that the survey is insufficiently comprehensive. So, the author wants the article judged on a different criterion: Is the survey sufficient to set out the broad outlines of the overall debate? This is a survey article; it is not an article that documents every position in the philosophy of mind.

However, the survey is sufficient to set out the contours of the debate.

The first and, probably, the oldest option is "substance **dualism**" or the term preferred by Ian Ravenscroft "interactive substance dualism."[3] The idea is simple: there are two different types of substance (although some argument over the meaning of substance) in the world – mental and physical. This is the position of the seventeenth-century philosopher Rene Descartes. Pete Mandik identifies five features of this position. The first is that "physical bodies are spatial and that minds are not."[4] A person is a material body, subject to the laws of physics, while an immaterial mind does not occupy space. The second is that "minds are thinking things and physical objects are unthinking things."[5] The third is intentionality. This is the way the mental life of a person actually decides what to think about. The fourth is that the mental life can, as Mandik puts it, "bear properties that are phenomenal."[6] The evidence for this is the phantom limb, where you still have pain sensations of say the leg that was amputated, even though the leg is no longer there. Finally, the mental life is known differently from the physical body. The latter is known through the senses, while the mental life is just known.

One has to concede the sheer genius of Descartes. He understood the complexity of consciousness and the mental life. However, he does have an obvious problem. Human experience attests that the mind causes the actions of the body, but how exactly? Descartes thought it was through the pineal gland. As Princess Elisabeth of Bohemia pointed out in a letter to Descartes at the time, mental causation requires some physicality (to actually impact the body).[7]

As a result of the explanatory power of science, new options emerged. In the twentieth century, the overwhelming assumption was some form of "scientific reductionism." The idea here is that the only substance in the world is physical. And the ultimate cause is some type of physical causation, which can be identified by the natural sciences. Gilbert Ryle does not see the mental life as a different substance; he describes the Cartesian position as absurd. He writes, "I shall often speak of it, with deliberate abusiveness, as 'the dogma of the Ghost of the Machine.'"[8] He argues that it is a "category-mistake." Ryle writes:

> A foreigner visiting Oxford or Cambridge for the first time is shown a number of colleges, libraries, playing fields, museums, scientific departments and administrative offices. He

---

[3] Ravenscroft, "Problems, Questions and Concepts," 4.

[4] Pete Mandik, *This is Philosophy of Mind: An Introduction* (Malden, MA: Wiley, 2013), 16.

[5] Mandik, *Philosophy of Mind*, 17.

[6] Mandik, *Philosophy of Mind*, 18.

[7] For Princess Elisabeth of Bohemia, see Jonathan Bennett, ed. "Correspondence between Rene Descartes and Princess Elisabeth of Bohemia" at http://www.earlymoderntexts.com/assets/pdfs/descartes1643.pdf.

[8] Gilbert Ryle, *The Concept of Mind*, 60th Anniversary Edition (London: Routledge, 2009), 5.

then asks "But where is the University? I have seen where the members of the Colleges live, where the Registrar works, where the scientists experiment and the rest. But I have not yet seen the University in which reside and work the members of your University." It has then to be explained to him that the University is not another collateral institution, some ulterior counterpart to the colleges, laboratories and offices which he has seen. The University is just the way in which all that he has already seen is organized. When they are seen and when their co-ordination is understood, the University has been seen. His mistake lay in his innocent assumption that it was correct to speak of Christ Church, the Bodleian Library, the Ashmolean Museum *and* the University, to speak, that is, as if "the University" stood for an extra member of the class of which these other units are members. He was mistakenly allocating the University to the same category as that to which the other institutions belong.[9]

The point is simple: the university is not an extra reality transcending the buildings; it is merely a way of understanding those buildings and their function. Ryle traces the origins of the dualistic language of mental and physical to an inability to face up to the reality of the scientific narrative. He suggests that the "ghost" was a "para-mechanical hypothesis."[10] His position is simple and he states it thus: "It is perfectly proper to say, in one logical tone of voice, that there exist minds and to say, in another logical tone of voice, that there exist bodies. But these expressions do not indicate two different species of existence … ."[11]

Now Ryle's actual position in regard to materialism (the view that there is just matter) is complex; he would not affirm the label. However, many materialists built on his argument (see Box 4.4).

Box 4.4

A specialist in the work of Ryle knows that Ryle's own metaphysical position is complex. Ryle denied that he had any metaphysical position. Yet the author wants to use Ryle to introduce a position that assumes "materialism." Notice the author is seeking to be both accurate in representing Ryle, yet still use his argument as an introduction to "reductive physicalism."

There is a sense in which Ryle's work lays the groundwork for the second position. This can be called "reductive physicalism." Ian Ravenscroft explains, "To a first approximation, reductive physicalism identifies mental properties with brain properties. Crucially, the brain properties with which mental properties are identified are held to be physical properties."[12] J. J. C. Smart is perhaps the most representative of this position.

Smart thought that mental states were actually parts of the physical brain. Any hangover from dualism, Smart explains, should be rejected on the principle of Occam's razor (see Box 4.5).

Box 4.5

The debate in the philosophy of mind is complex. The author is very aware that he has simplified the literature. He wants to reassure the reader that he is aware of the many options beyond the three that have been outlined. This paragraph does this work.

---

[9] Ryle, *Concept of Mind*, 6.
[10] Ryle, *Concept of Mind*, 9.
[11] Ryle, *Concept of Mind*, 12.
[12] Ravenscroft, "Problems, Questions and Concepts," 7.

Smart asserts with confidence:

> It seems to me that science is increasingly giving us a viewpoint whereby organisms are able to be seen as physico-chemical mechanisms: it seems that even the behavior of man himself will one day be explicable in mechanistic terms. There does seem to be, so far as science is concerned, nothing in the world but increasingly complex arrangements of physical constituents.[13]

For Smart, "sensations are brain processes."[14] However, there is a whole cluster of difficulties with this position. Hilary Putnam pointed out that the scientific map of, say pain, is complex and has "multiple realizations."[15] The appreciation of a sunset, the imagining of a cathedral, and the ache of bereavement are not reducible simple to brain states. So further options started to emerge.

The third option was non-reductive physicalism. The best-known option in this category was functionalism. Ravenscroft explains:

> According to functionalism, mental properties are characterized by their causal roles. Pain, for example, is the property which is caused by bodily damage and causes withdrawal from the source of damage; has important causal links to anxiety and to desire; and, in conjunction with certain beliefs, can lead to particular behaviours.[16]

There is on this view less focus on the location of mental states and more emphasis on the function underpinning the claim. It is important to note, however, that there is still a reductionism operating on this view. There is still an underlying description of the mental event which can be constructed in physical ways.

Box 4.6

Now the author does not explain what the principle of "Occam's razor" is. Instead, he simply assumes that the reader is familiar with the principle. Innovative, research-orientated writing must make certain assumptions. This is not intended to be a 101 text. For those who might not be familiar, it is attributed to the fourteenth-century logician and Friar, William of Ockham, who argued that when you have two explanations both of which explain all the facts, the simpler explanation is the one most likely to be true.

(See Box 4.6.) There are many other options in this complex debate. George Berkeley defended a form of idealism that says that an immaterial "mind" underpins all reality[17]; Edgar Brightman argued for a "personal Idealism" with an emphasis on human freedom.[18] Spinoza is credited with a position known as "dual-aspect theory" which stresses that mind and matter are aspects of a underlying unity. Now discussing all these options is beyond this paper. However, elements of these positions do emerge in the third section. At this stage, it is important to stress that much

---

[13] J. J. C. Smart, "Sensations and Brain Processes," *The Philosophical Review* 68, 2 (Apr. 1959): 142.
[14] Smart, "Sensations," 144.
[15] Ravenscroft, "Problems, Questions and Concepts," 8.
[16] Ibid. 8. Donald Davidson developed "anomalous monism," which is also a version of non-reductive physicalism.
[17] George Berkeley, "Principles of Human Knowledge. Dialogues between Hyles and Philonous," in *The Empiricist* (Garden City: Dolphin Books, n.d.).
[18] Edgar Brightman, *A Philosophy of Religion* (New York: Prentice-Hall, 1940).

of the debate, certainly in the popular imagination, has focused on the challenge of the physical sciences. The Cartesian view of the relationship between the mind and the body – one that stressed that the mental and the physical are two separate entities – was challenged by a reductionist science that made the physical the only reality. As we will see, more options emerge when you recognize the significance of the new physics. However, Alan Turing, who suggested the famous Turing test for computers, came at the questions for AI from a perspective of scientific materialism. For Turning, the mental is a result of the material. His famous article is important for our purposes: so we shall now summarize the argument in detail. It was in 1950 that Turing wrote the article "Computing Machinery and Intelligence."[19] He invites us to imagine a game which he calls the "imitation game." He writes:

> The new form of the problem can be described in terms of a game which we call the 'imitation game.' It is played with three people, a man (A), a woman (B), and an interrogator (C) who may be of either sex. The interrogator stays in a room apart front the other two. The object of the game for the interrogator is to determine which of the other two is the man and which is the woman. He knows them by labels X and Y, and at the end of the game he says either "X is A and Y is B" or "X is B and Y is A." The interrogator is allowed to put questions to A and B thus:
> C: Will X please tell me the length of his or her hair?
> Now suppose X is actually A, then A must answer. It is A's object in the game to try and cause C to make the wrong identification. His answer might therefore be:
> "My hair is shingled, and the longest strands are about nine inches long."
> In order that tones of voice may not help the interrogator the answers should be written, or better still, typewritten. The ideal arrangement is to have a teleprinter communicating between the two rooms. Alternatively the question and answers can be repeated by an intermediary. The object of the game for the third player (B) is to help the interrogator. The best strategy for her is probably to give truthful answers. She can add such things as "I am the woman, don't listen to him!" to her answers, but it will avail nothing as the man can make similar remarks.
> We now ask the question, "What will happen when a machine takes the part of A in this game?" Will the interrogator decide wrongly as often when the game is played like this as he does when the game is played between a man and a woman?[20]

The idea here is to take the highly abstract question "Do machines think?" and construct a test that demonstrates that machines think as much as people think. He then develops his argument. The main steps are as follows:

1. Questions could be asked that would make it seem very hard for the observer to distinguish between the human and the machine.
2. The technology is on the cusp of being developed. There are "digital computers" which will not be simply bound by a rule book (a linear program).

---

[19] A. M. Turing, "Computing Machinery and Intelligence," in *Mind* Vol. 49 (1950): 433–460, accessed January 5, 2020, https://www.csee.umbc.edu/courses/471/papers/turing.pdf.
[20] Turing, "Computing Machinery," 433.

3. Therefore, Turing writes, "The reader must accept it as a fact that digital computers can be constructed, and indeed have been constructed, according to the principles we have described, and that they can in fact mimic the actions of a human computer very closely."[21]
4. Therefore, he concludes, "I believe that in about fifty years' time it will be possible to programme computers, with a storage capacity of about 109, to make them play the imitation game so well that an average interrogator will not have more than 70 per cent chance of making the right identification after five minutes of questioning. The original question, 'Can machines think?' I believe to be too meaningless to deserve discussion. Nevertheless I believe that at the end of the century the use of words and general educated opinion will have altered so much that one will be able to speak of machines thinking without expecting to be contradicted. I believe further that no useful purpose is served by concealing these beliefs. The popular view that scientists proceed inexorably from well-established fact to well-established fact, never being influenced by any improved conjecture, is quite mistaken. Provided it is made clear which are proved facts and which are conjectures, no harm can result. Conjectures are of great importance since they suggest useful lines of research."[22]

Then Turing considers a set of objections to his argument. He has seven such objections. These include the major issues – can machines learn or write a sonnet? However, his response to the theological objection is especially interesting. He starts by stating the objection:

> Thinking is a function of man's immortal soul. God has given an immortal soul to every man and woman, but not to any other animal or to machines. Hence no animal or machine can think.[23]

Turing in response makes three points. First, the gap between animals and humans is greater than the gap between machines and humans. The second is a question: Is it not possible that God could confer a soul on an entity that seems to have the capacity of humans? And the third is the simple point that any decision on a priori theological grounds that machines cannot think is manifestly unwise, given the history of inappropriate theological a priori arguments. For example, the Church was wrong to reject the view of Copernicus.

Box 4.7

Alan Turing's classic article is given sustained attention. The author is acknowledging his pivotal role in this debate. He was the person who asked the question in such a way that the Turing test is acknowledged as the central way of determining whether you can tell apart a computer and a human.

(See Box 4.7.) Turing is right to stress that many theological responses to the issue of thinking machines is grounded in a theological prejudice. We just suspect that humans are always better

---

[21] Turing, "Computing Machinery," 439. By human computer, Turing means the human mind.
[22] Turing, "Computing Machinery," 442.
[23] Turing, "Computing Machinery," 456.

than animals or machines. So the Church should resist such prejudice. Now the main options in the philosophy of mind tend to a binary. You either believe in a soul which is immaterial and not connected to the brain or you believe in materialism that denies the existence of the soul.[24] As we shall see below (pp.59ff) there are options that transcend this binary. But before we look at those options, the next stage is to move from Turing predictions to the current reality. What exactly can a machine do? And how different are these machines from humans? This is the world of AI. It is to this world that we turn next.

The History and Possibility of AI

Box 4.8
Having attempted to summarize the philosophy of mind debate, the author now turns to providing a summary of the history of AI. It is worth stressing that plenty of reviewers would be highly nervous about these compressed summaries. As the reader looks at this, one should worry about whether the history is too selective. Does the author really establish the possibility of AI providing human type thinking?

(See Box 4.8.) It was in 1997 that IBM's Deep Blue beat Gary Kasparov, the then reigning world chess champion, at chess.[25] It was in the second game. Everyone anticipated that Deep Blue would move the Queen into the heart of Kasparov's territory, but instead Deep Blue went for a pawn exchange. It was a brilliant move.[26] This moment had been a long time in coming. The key change was the capacity of a computer to store commands – the need for memory. It was the program "Logic Theorist," created by Allen Newell, Cliff Shaw, and Herbert Simon, which could enable a computer to emulate the ways that humans solve problems. They launched their program at the Dartmouth Summer Research Project on Artificial Intelligence in 1956. This conference was also the first time that the phrase "artificial intelligence" was coined. Over the next twenty years, success was attained in areas such as language translation, but explicit intelligence was still not realizable.

The much-needed ingredient was the need for expanded computer memories and speed. Gorden Moore, back in 1965, noted that at Intel the "number of transistors that can be packed into a given unit of space will double about every two years."[27] It became Moore's Law, which was entirely vindicated. The number of transistors on a microchip did double and the cost of computers continue to fall. The result has been a phenomenal increase in speeds and capacity of computers.

---

[24] Please allow me to use a footnote and acknowledge that this debate is complicated. And there are options beyond the ones listed above. The position of Paul and Patricia Churchland, known as Neurological Reductionism, is a good illustration. However, space will not permit to explore all these alternatives.

[25] I am grateful to Rockwell Anyoha, "Can Machines Think?" August 28, 2017, accessed April 26, 2020, http://sitn.hms.harvard.edu/flash/2017/history-artificial-intelligence.

[26] See the *Washington Post* summary of the games. Accessed April 26, 2020, https://www.washingtonpost.com/wp-srv/tech/analysis/kasparov/kasparov.htm.

[27] See "Moore's Law," Investopedia website, accessed April 26, 2020, https://www.investopedia.com/terms/m/mooreslaw.asp.

As we enter the twenty-first century, progress in AI has been exponential. In 2005, a vehicle made out of Stanford drove autonomously for 131 miles across a desert. In 2011, Apple introduced Siri – our "intelligent personal assistant" on the iPhone. In June 2012, Google announced that a computer cluster is able to recognize a cat thanks to the computer's exposure to millions of YouTube images. At the University of Reading in the UK, Chatbot Eugene Goostman passed the Turing test (i.e. the chatbot responses were indistinguishable from human responses).

Although there is considerable interest in the driverless car and enabling a spaceship to get to Jupiter, the primary uses of AI have been much more mundane. AI is excellent at examining a person's Google search history to anticipate future purchases; it can organize records; and it can detect patterns of likely ponzi schemes in investing.[28]

Now all of this is a long way from thinking. The human brain is extraordinary. Raj Reddy explains that "there about one hundred billion neural cells in the human brain and the brain might be performing 200 trillion operations per second if not faster than that." He goes on to observe that when the brain comes to things like vision, speech, and motor processes, "it is more powerful than 1,000 supercomputers; however, for simple tasks such as multiplication, it is less powerful than a four bit microprocessor."[29]

However, there are developments where AI is getting much closer to machine consciousness. Much is made of "machine learning." When a computer studies thousands of medical images (appropriately labeled), a machine can then study new data sets and more accurately than the human doctor identify broken bones on an x-ray. Machine learning now involves artificial neural networks. We all encounter these networks when we use a virtual assistant or photo filter. It is creating options for the future. Google's Alphabet seeks to predict kidney failure before it happens after using a "deep learning approach" in a study with over 700,000 adult patients.[30] Amazon is using the same technology as it seeks to develop stores without checkouts.

The challenge for machines is adapting to the surprises that the world generates. Self-driving cars are nearly there, but still the unexpected scenario is hard for the car to handle. Yet there is ample evidence that these are solvable problems. There is an expectation that we can create autonomous taxis that can navigate city traffic, a robot that can take care of the elderly, and a chatbot that can explain the news. In February 2018, MIT announced a program called "Intelligence Quest" which seeks to take engineering categories and apply this to human intelligence. The goal is to create machines that "learn as they go." Matthew Hutson writes:

> "In the past few years, AI has shown it can translate speech, diagnose cancer, and beat humans at poker. But for every win, there is a blunder. Image recognition algorithms can now distinguish dog breeds better than you can, yet they sometimes mistake a chihuahua

---

[28] For the ponzi scheme detection see Martin Mccool, "Using Artificial Intelligence to Detect Fraud," Bankhawk website, accessed April 26, 2020, https://www.bankhawk.com/using-artificial-intelligence-to-detect-fraud.

[29] Reddy, R. Winter, "Foundations and Grand Challenges of Artificial Intelligence," *AI* magazine, 1988. As quoted in Brian McGuire, "The Turing Test" in The History of Artificial Intelligence at the University of Washington, December 2006, accessed April 26, 2020, https://courses.cs.washington.edu/courses/csep590/06au/projects/history-ai.pdf.

[30] Nenad Tomašev et. al. "A clinically applicable approach to continuous prediction of future acute kidney injury," *Nature* Vol. 572 (August 2019): 116.

for a blueberry muffin. AIs can play classic Atari video games such as Space Invaders with superhuman skill, but when you remove all the aliens but one, the AI falters inexplicably."[31]

Yet these all feel like technical difficulties that can be overcome. Michael Graziano, a professor of psychology and neuroscience at Princeton University, believes that a Sim-me (simulated me) is likely in the future. We will be able to scan our brains and upload our minds to a computer – mind uploading. Some see this as a promise of immortality. There are two technical problems that need to be solved to do this. Graziano explains:

> First, we would need to build an artificial brain made of simulated neurons. Second, we would need to scan a person's actual, biological brain and measure exactly how its neurons are connected to each other, to be able to copy that pattern in the artificial brain. Nobody knows if those two steps would really re-create a person's mind or if other, subtler aspects of the biology of the brain must be copied as well, but it is a good starting place.[32]

The response to the first challenge is already there. We can already create the neurons in an artificial and simulated form. Reproducing all 86 billion neurons found in a brain is currently beyond our technical expertise, but it is just a matter of time. The response to the second challenge is harder. Albert Einstein College of Medicine has managed to complete "connectome" (which is "the pattern of connectivity among all neurons")[33] in a roundworm. It took the college ten years to do so. However, once again, if we can do a roundworm, then surely in time we will be able to do a human (see Box 4.9).

Box 4.9
The author needs to make the question plausible. He has no option but to rebut the idea that AI gaining the ability to match human capacities in thought and judgment is a long way off. However, this is the strongest piece of data. We are on the cusp of creating a roundworm in the laboratory. Isn't the development of a human just a matter of degree?

Mind uploading does seem to take us very close to a human machine. And if this is possible, then what exactly are we handling? How is the Sim-me different from the Bio-me (the biological self)? It does feel likely that the question of a thinking machine is part of our future.

Theological Implications

It is clear from the discussion above that advances in AI are significant. So we return to the question: Are we on the cusp of creating an entity that has a soul and should be baptized?

To answer this question, we need to revisit the options set out at the start of this article. The debate has been shaped by drawing a sharp contrast between the material and the spiritual.

---

[31] Matthew Hutson, "How researchers are teaching AI to learn like a child," *Science*, May 24, 2018, https://www.sciencemag.org/news/2018/05/how-researchers-are-teaching-ai-learn-child#.

[32] Michael S. A. Graziano, "Will Your Uploaded Mind Still Be You?" *The Wall Street Journal*, September 13, 2019, accessed April 26, 2020, https://www.wsj.com/articles/will-your-uploaded-mind-still-be-you-11568386410.

[33] Graziano, *WSJ*.

However, our knowledge of science has opened up new options. The view that the universe is best understood in terms of mechanistic laws to which everything is reducible has gone forever. In the nineteenth century, the famous French philosopher, Laplace, took the view that if he knew the molecular state of the universe right at the beginning, then he would be able to predict every subsequent moment that followed. This "mechanistic reductionism" is rightly considered absurd. It is wrong in terms of science (indeterminacy is a key and fundamental reality in the universe); and it is wrong in terms of plausibility (that Beethoven's fifth symphony is predictable from the initial molecular state of the universe sounds very unlikely).

The Copenhagen interpretation of quantum mechanics has opened up the possibility of matter coming together in a certain way (the brain is still made of up of atoms) yet to act in ways that are "uncaused" – or to be more accurate, some events are physically undetermined. This is important for the concept of freewill. T. J. Mawson advocates for top-down causation, where either the human agent creates quantum "measurements" events on the brain, or perhaps the human agent is intervening in a "relatively large number of places more or less at once at the relatively macroscopic level in the brain, the relatively macroscopic effect."[34] Mawson is advocating for "top-down causation." We are all familiar with "bottom-up causation," now we need to think of the complexity of matter generating possibilities that transcend the parts that make it up. Mawson defined top-down causation as "the complex physical constitution of human persons generates a new capacity of such conscious organisms to be real cause, in addition to all the physical causes within the system."[35]

The point is that physical objects can become so complex that they generate new possibilities. Keith Ward talks about this view as a "model of organic development." He writes:

> On the basis of rather simple and general laws, more complex structures come into existence, with correspondingly more complex patterns of interactions between them. These structures not only exhibit law-like behavior (which implies regularity and repetitiveness), they also exhibit something analogous to creative response to stimuli (which allows for uniqueness and originality).[36]

On this view of personhood, we have the soul emerging from the complexity of the physical object (in the case of humans, the brain). This is not to say, necessarily, that the soul is always dependent on a particular material complex structure. One could conceive of possibilities where the complex structure is different or even not there. But it is true that the human soul, in this material world, is linked to the reality of the brain (see Box 4.10).

Box 4.10

Most Christians want to believe in an afterlife. Therefore, it is important for the author that matter is not always essential in the construction of mind. This is the reason why the author creates a label (creating a label is always a sign of creativity in theology) called "contingent materialism." It is only on planet Earth that mind is linked to matter. God's consciousness is not dependent on matter, nor will be the minds that resurrected persons enjoy in the life to come (or, at least, the resurrected life will be a different type of matter).

---

[34] T. J. Mawson, "Freedom and the Causal Order," in *Rethinking Order After the Laws of Nature*, ed. Nancy Cartwright and Keith Ward (London: Bloomsbury, 2016), 154.

[35] Mawson, "Freedom," 143.

[36] Keith Ward, *The Battle for the Soul: The End of Morality in a Secular Society* (London: Hodder and Stoughton 1985), 138.

This position could be called "Contingent Materialism." In this world consciousness is linked with the particular way the brain is constituted. However, this is a contingent connection. God, for example, is a consciousness which is not material. Therefore, it must be possible for consciousness to be expressed in different ways; and for a Christian, for consciousness to take a different form in the life to come.

The philosopher who makes this argument is Keith Ward. In his *Battle for the Soul*, he argues for an account of soul, which is the location of purpose, agency, moral decision-making, that is, in our current human state, linked to the material brain. Ward claims that this view of the soul is implicit in the work of the thirteenth-century Dominican Friar Thomas Aquinas. He writes:

> If the human soul is, as Aquinas taught, the basic principle of a rational organism, the power of thought and understanding, then it can easily be seen as developing continuously from lower, non-rational or non-cognitive, forms of life. In modern terminology, we might say that, when the brain reaches a certain level of complexity, the power of conceptual thought, of reasoning and thinking, begins to exist; and that is when a rational soul begins to be. The rational soul is that which has the power of understanding.[37]

So the following picture is emerging. As our brain develops, so certain qualities, that are not reducible to the component parts that make up our brain, emerge. In answer to the question "Where does the soul come in?" Ward asserts, "The conclusion must be that the soul is generated by a particular physical system. At a specific point in time, a subject of rational consciousness comes into being. All conscious states belong to a subject, which is able to understand, deliberate, formulate goals and initiate actions."[38]

Now, for Christians, a key capacity of the soul is to engage with the transcendent, but it also includes the capacity for awareness, decision, intention, agency, and some form of moral deliberation. It is not at all a ghost in the machine. It is neither a ghost (some invisible entity) nor a machine (something that is a self-determined system of cause and effect). Instead the soul (or mind) is made possible by the complexity of the brain, which, importantly, enables mind to exercise freewill and agency.

The key step in this account of personhood is that the soul in this world (there could be other worlds where the soul would not need to take this particular form) arises as a result of the complexity of the brain where due to "top-down causation" the result is consciousness. This link between the material and the spiritual makes, in our judgment, the possibility of a conscious form of AI.

Keith Ward concedes this point when he writes:

> It follows from what I have been saying that we could, in theory, make artificial intelligence machines, super-computers, which really would have souls. That is, they would have states of conscious understanding, freedom and moral responsibility, and relationship to God ... In fact, I do not see why we should deny that possibility. We bring souls into existence whenever we have children. We can now fertilise embryos in laboratories, so that our control over procreation is increasing. It is possible, in theory, to construct a

---

[37] Ward, *Battle*, 52.
[38] Ward, *Battle*, 139–140.

genetic sequence, which will begin embryonic development and so create a human life artificially. It is not out of the question that we could also construct a replica of such sequences in other forms, and so create quite new sorts of souls.[39]

Ward's point is simple: Humans already create "souls" when we have children. And with advancements around reproductive treatments, we can "clone" and provide "IVF" (In Vitro fertilization), which is a new way of producing souls. So perhaps those at the cutting edge of AI are also in the remarkable and holy work of making souls.

If this is possible, then the Church has important work to do.[40] The moment that we might be in the presence of AI consciousness, we must be ready to argue that conscious machines have rights. They should be treated as persons. They need to be respected. In the same way that a baby which is the result of a cloning process should be treated as fully human; so a machine that exhibited consciousness needs to be fully respected.

Anticipating the Future

The argument of this chapter is that with AI we are closer to consciousness than we realize. If this is the case, then the Church needs to be ready to recognize the status of such machines. Conscious machines, for example, that are used exclusively for military purposes would be morally obscene. Instead, the Christian narrative affirms that all entities capable of freewill need to be redeemed by Christ. And the Church becomes the home for all redeemed persons (whether inanimate or animate). Given baptism is the way into the Church, the Church needs to be ready to baptize a machine entity that is demonstrating consciousness.

---

[39] Ward, *Battle*, 143.

[40] Perhaps an element of the Church's work is to oppose all attempts to create AI consciousness. After all "free intelligences," which could be more powerful than we are, might sin.

Part III

God and the World

5

Humanity

Where on Earth Have We Come From and Where Are We Going To?
Celia Deane-Drummond

RESEARCH LEVEL 3

Editors' Introduction

*In this essay, the author challenges the traditional theological notion that humanity sits at the pinnacle of creation. This notion is buttressed by the conviction that humans, all by ourselves, bear the image of God. The supposed uniqueness of human rationality and language was traditionally cited in support of this conviction. While recent threats such as climate change and global pandemics undermine our sense of master of the environment, research in ecology and evolutionary anthropology have undermined all these traditional notions. Deane-Drummond describes these scientific findings, and then proposes a revised view of the **imago Dei** that takes account of them.*

Box 5.1
The author begins with a brief introduction describing what she will do in this paper, as well as why it needs to be done. She then provides a roadmap for how she will do it.

What does it mean to be human (see Box 5.1)? While scientists have provocatively claimed in some cases in a celebratory way that we are now living in a geological era that bears the indelible mark of the human, that era on the Earth's crust becomes labeled the Anthropocene, others are fearful of what is to become of both humanity and planet Earth. Our sense of being in control is now dented by the threat of climate change and global pandemics, including the outbreak of Coronavirus, COVID-19 in 2019, that force humanity to consider its vulnerability in spite of technological change. Have theological considerations of our humanity adapted to such challenges or not?

Box 5.2
This introduction now flows into her roadmap. The challenge is what is it to be human in the light of the modern scientific narrative. The author then indicates the intended flow of the chapter: it will start with some discussion of Augustine and Aquinas; and then flow into an anthropology which stresses Christology.

The Craft of Innovative Theology: Argument and Process, First Edition. Edited by John Allan Knight and Ian S. Markham.
© 2022 John Wiley & Sons Ltd. Published 2022 by John Wiley & Sons Ltd.

After reviewing some influential classical texts in Augustine and Aquinas, I will argue that theological anthropology needs to respond to evolutionary and ecological understandings of human identity (see Box 5.2). Further, I will push back against the idea of image bearing as either arising primarily through a doctrine of creation, or being obsolete, and suggest, instead, that such a description of our humanity is better understood through reference to **Christology**, even though, paradoxically, this also presents new challenges.

The Unique Status of Humanity

Box 5.3

In this section, the author reviews the traditional Christian views of theological anthropology (what it means to be human), focusing especially on Augustine and Thomas Aquinas.

Genesis 1: 27–28 has, for centuries, been used to promote the idea of human uniqueness and supremacy over the rest of creation even in a period when the natural world was often perceived as threatening or dangerous (see Box 5.3). The Great Chain of Being was a **neo-Platonic** classification system which placed inorganic material at the base, rising through creatures of increasing complexity to humans, to angels, who were disembodied spiritual beings, to God, the divine.[1] Although every part of the Chain was important, there was no doubt about the hierarchical ranking and implied superiority of humans over other animals, animals over plants, etc. When *imago Dei* in Genesis becomes added to the neo-Platonic idea of the Great Chain of Being, the result is obvious: humanity is both mediator between heaven and Earth but also envisaged as supreme, the crown among all creatures, on a border with angels.

Box 5.4

The author goes back to the primary sources. She is not dependent on secondary sources (those books that discuss Augustine or Aquinas), but rather makes sure she has read and is summarizing the texts actually written by Augustine and Aquinas. She provides her own summary of these theologians.

Saint Augustine of Hippo, whose work has influenced generations of scholars through his doctrine of original sin and the Fall of humanity (see Box 5.4), also insisted that humanity was created by an act of all three persons, "let us make" through "Father and Son and Holy Spirit – the trinity on whose account it says *to our image* – as being one God, on whose account it says, *to the image of God*."[2]

---

[1] Alexander Pope's "Essay on Man" notes that every link in the chain is important, so "From Nature's chain whatever link you strike, Tenth or ten thousandth, breaks the chain alike," A. Pope, "Essay on Man," VII, cited in A. O. Lovejoy, *The Great Chain of Being: A Study of the History of an Idea* (Cambridge/MA: Harvard University Press, 1942), 60.

[2] Augustine of Hippo, "The Literal Meaning of Genesis," in *On Genesis*, Book III, Section 19.29.

Humanity was therefore special in its manner of making, which then led on to a sense of human supremacy which Augustine attributed to humanity's power of reasoning:

> Here we must not neglect that other point either, that after saying, *to our image*, he immediately added, *and let him have authority over the fishes of the sea and the flying things of heaven* and of the other animals which lack reason, giving us to understand, evidently, that it was in the very factor in which he surpasses non-rational animate beings that man was made to God's image. That, of course, is reason itself, or mind or intelligence or whatever other word it may more suitably be named by.[3]

If we probe further into Augustine's theological anthropology in his *Unfinished Commentary on the Literal Meaning of Genesis*, which he admitted was still a work in progress, he adds just a little more to this explanation. He repeats the distinction in the way God makes humanity in the Genesis text, insists again on the importance of human reason, but now adds that human superiority arises directly from inspiration of the Holy Spirit:

> And here we must observe both a certain connection with and a distinction from the animals. On the one hand it says man was made on the same day as the beasts; they are all of them together land animals, after all. And yet on the other hand, because of the pre-eminence of reason, with respect to which man is made to the image of God and his likeness, it speaks separately about him, after concluding about the other land animals in the usual way by saying *And God saw that it was good*. The point must also be considered that in the other cases God said *Let it be made, and it was made*, while here God said, *Let us make*, so that in this way too the Holy Spirit wished to suggest the superiority of human nature. To whom, though, does he now say *Let us make*, if not to the one to whom he said in the other cases "Let it be made."[4]

Box 5.5

This sense of human supremacy will be what needs to be addressed as a result of climate change, global pandemics, etc.

He then reflects on the specialness of humanity (see Box 5.5), by distinguishing between the kind of reflective likeness found in all of creation compared with humanity. In humanity the specific "rational nature was made both through the likeness and to it."[5]

The important point to note at this stage of the argument is not whether Augustine's interpretation of Genesis still holds in the light of contemporary exegetical methods, but the influence of his thinking on subsequent generations of thinkers. He also does not develop the specific ways in which humanity might show such a likeness to God, though he does claim, as Thomas Aquinas was to subsequently, that the only begotten Son of God is "the image," as compared with humanity, "in the image," reflecting the idea that the true image of God is the Son, while humanity only images that perfected image.[6]

---

[3] Augustine, "The Literal Meaning of Genesis," Section 20.30.

[4] Augustine, "Unfinished Commentary," Section 16.55; Section 16.56.

[5] Augustine, "Unfinished Commentary," Section16.60. Here he discusses the distinction between image and likeness and why both terms are used.

[6] Augustine, *Responses to Miscellaneous Questions*, Section 1.26.

There are, of course, consequences not just for the doctrine of humanity but also for an understanding of salvation. If the deliberative reason is the seat of what makes humanity uniquely in the image of God, God created each soul of every human being out of nothing, and that soul was spirit rather than matter.[7] Even though Aquinas was heavily influenced by an Aristotelian philosophy, which is often thought to be the foundation for modern biology, he followed Augustine's insistence on divine creation of an immaterial soul out of nothing. At the same time, he understood the human soul to be a *transformation* of animality, rather than its rejection, hence understanding other living things, including plants and animals, to have souls, but only humanity bears a reasoning soul.[8] The human soul can therefore best be thought of as within a nested hierarchy such that the reasoning soul transformed the vegetative and animal soul. Aquinas also acknowledged that other animals had reasoning abilities, of a sort, but not of the same kind as that found in humans. There was, in other words, still an **ontological** gap preserved between humans and other animals, even though he learned, perhaps from his teacher Albert the Great, the importance of paying attention to all God's creatures, and not just human beings.[9]

It is also worth noting that Aquinas envisaged a hierarchy of different stages in image bearing, so that the first stage was a natural aptitude or capability for knowing and loving God related to the mind, and is common to all humanity; the second through the habitual practice of knowing and loving God, though imperfectly, and present in the just; and the third knowing and loving God perfectly, and so reflecting the likeness of glory, found in the blessed.[10] The word for humanity in all three stages is *Homo*, implying that both women and men share in the possibility of such image bearing. He also juxtaposes and rejects an interpretation of 1 Corinthians 11.7 which implied that women only bore the image of men, rather than God, by insisting that Genesis points to both men and women bearing that image.[11]

Aquinas did not, however, completely reject the idea that women were inferior in their ability to bear the divine image, so "in a secondary sense the image of God is found in man (*viro*), and not in woman (*muliere*); for man is the beginning and end of woman; as God is the beginning and end of every creature."[12] In other texts he is prepared to be more even handed, so "the image of God belongs to both sexes, since it is in the mind, wherein there is no sexual distinction."[13] At the same time, in his *Commentary on 1 Corinthians* he seemed to concede the prevailing idea that women were inferior intellectually, which had consequences for their ability to express the divine image, so "man (*vir*) is more especially called the image of God (*imago Dei*), insomuch as reason is more vigorous in him (*ratio magis*)."[14] He notes first that while God is man's (*hominis*) glory, in another sense, man (*vir*) is the

---

[7] Augustine, "The Nature and Origin of the Soul," in *Answer to the Pelagians* Vol. I.3, Book One, To Renatus, Section 4.4.

[8] I discuss these ideas in some detail in Celia Deane-Drummond, "God's Image and Likeness in Humans and Other Animals: Performative Soul Making and Graced Nature," *Zygon* Vol. 47, No. 4 (2012): 934–948.

[9] For a brief commentary on Albert the Great's understanding of animals in his *Summa Zoologica*, in the context of current debates theological anthropology see Celia Deane-Drummond, "Moving us Forward?," in *Verbs, Bones and Brains: Interdisciplinary Perspectives on Human Nature*, ed. Agustín Fuentes and Aku Visala (Notre Dame: University of Notre Dame Press, 2017): 260–272.

[10] Thomas Aquinas, *Summa Theologiae* (hereafter *ST*), Ia.93.4.

[11] Aquinas, *ST*, Ia.93.4.

[12] Ibid.

[13] Aquinas, *ST*, Ia.93.6.

[14] Thomas Aquinas, *Commentary on the Letters of Saint Paul to the Corinthians*, Section 607.

glory of God (*gloria Dei*).[15] For Aquinas men (*vir*) are "the image of God in a special way" both because they are "the principle of his entire race, as God is the principle of the entire universe" and "because from the side of Christ dying on the cross flowed the sacrament of blood and water, from which the Church has been organised."[16] This led him to imply that men are more likely to reflect God's glory when compared with women; so "it is common to man and woman to be the image of God; but it is immediately characteristic of man (*viri*) to be the glory of God."[17] Although Aquinas's anthropology was more affirming of women than his contemporaries, it is easy to see how such texts could be the basis for the long history of exclusion of women from leadership roles or ecclesial ministries.

There was, however, one situation where Aquinas had even more trouble squaring his inclination toward Aristotelian philosophy with the writings of Augustine, and that was when considering what happens to our human souls when we die. He devoted a whole question in his *Summa Theologiae* to a reflection on what happens to the human soul when it is separated from the body.[18] He admitted that "to be separated from the body is not in accordance with its nature," but at the same time it was quite "possible for it to exist apart from the body, and also to understand in another way."[19] He even thought that a separated soul had "a greater freedom of intelligence" as it was not weighed down by the care of the body,[20] but that knowledge was less than that possible for the angels because it was not natural for the soul to be in such a separated state.[21] It is therefore a logical consequence of his view that the soul persists after death, so "That the soul remains after the body, is due to a defect of the body, namely death. Which defect was not due when the soul was created."[22] He therefore objects to the idea that the soul is preformed prior to the body, rather, it is created at the same time as that body, as its form.

Ecological and Evolutionary Challenges to Human Uniqueness

Box 5.6
In this section, the author will note the challenges to the anthropocentric orientation of theology from modern science and describe the various responses to the challenge by theologians and the church.

While it is easy to see the gender disparity in such statements, it is the rise of modern science that has challenged more basic aspects of such classic accounts (see Box 5.6).[23] However, instead of engaging with such accounts, a more common theological response in the twentieth and

---

[15] Aquinas, *Commentary on 1 Corinthians*, Section 605.

[16] Aquinas, *Commentary on 1 Corinthians*, Section 607. The reference to Christ in this context implies that it is the maleness of Christ is significant, though this is not spelled out.

[17] Aquinas, *Commentary on 1 Corinthians*, Section 607.

[18] Aquinas, *ST*, Ia.89.

[19] Aquinas, *ST*, Ia.89.1.

[20] Aquinas, *ST*, Ia.89.2.

[21] Aquinas, *ST*, Ia.89.3.

[22] Aquinas, *ST*, Ia.90.4.

[23] The gender bias on differences in intelligence can also be read into scientific accounts; but current anthropological research suggests otherwise. For an informative account see Agustín Fuentes, *Race, Monogamy, and Other Lies They Told You: Busting Myths About Human Nature* (Berkeley: University of California Press, 2012).

twenty-first centuries has been either to reiterate the ecclesial tradition in spite of scientific discussion, or narrow the sphere of theology to historical or even experiential/**existential** accounts of salvation history, thus leaving the world of nature to the scientists. Creation becomes, as Karl Barth famously suggested, the stage or backdrop on which salvation history is played out, creation being the pre-history to the history of salvation.[24]

Secular historians were not slow to criticize standard theological positions that emphasized the supremacy of human beings (and men in particular) at the detriment of the rest of the natural world. In the late 1960s, historian Lynn White argued in the journal *Science* that the Judeo/Christian tradition "bears a huge burden of guilt," pointing to Genesis 1.27–28 as one of the main sources of the problem, leading to the Jewish/Christian tradition being judged by him as "the most anthropocentric religion the world has seen."[25] Christian biblical scholars were quick to leap to the defense of Christianity, especially the interpretation of the biblical text, arguing that Genesis 1.27–28 was less about domination and more about careful and responsible stewardship.[26] More recently, analysis has been rather more measured, with prominent biblical scholars such as Richard Bauckham accepting that even the language of stewardship has potentially unfortunate managerial undertones,[27] and Peter Harrison arguing that it is more important to understand the reception of the Genesis text, especially in post Calvinistic contexts, rather than the text as such.[28] A rereading of biblical narratives in more ecologically sensitive ways has included trying to recreate the situation of the biblical authors as following agrarian lifestyles, and thus modeling a different way in which humanity relates to the Earth.[29] Ecotheology, drawing inspiration from alternative ways of reading the Bible, and rising as it has done in the late twentieth and early twenty-first centuries, is deliberately contextual in that it takes its bearings from the actual situation of the Earth in which humanity finds itself. Current scientific consensus is that the stability of the Earth System is problematized and myriad of creatures, including higher animals and birds, have either gone extinct due to human interference or are under threat of extinction. At the same time, as a contextual theology the

---

[24] So, Karl Barth, "Creation is one long preparation, and therefore the being and existence of the creature one long readiness for what God will intend and do with it in the history of the covenant. Its nature is simply its equipment for grace," in *Church Dogmatics, III/Part 1, The Doctrine of Creation*, trans. J.W. Edwards, O. Bussey, and H. Knight, ed. G.W. Bromiley and T. Torrance (London: T & T Clark/Continuum, 2004), 231. Note that Barthian scholars have since argued that Barth can still be interpreted as affirming creation, but the impact of his focus on covenant encourages an interpretation that creation has less significance and can be viewed as a preparation for salvation history. For a recent and comprehensive discussion of Karl Barth's theology, see George Hunsinger and Keith L. Johnson, eds., *Wiley-Blackwell Companion to Karl Barth* (Oxford: Wiley-Blackwell, 2020).

[25] Lynn White, "The Historic Roots of Our Ecologic Crisis," *Science* Vol. 155, No. 3767 (March 1967): 1203–1207. He qualified such statements by claiming that the form of Christianity in the Eastern Orthodoxy and the model of Francis of Assisi were elements of the tradition that countered such a stance.

[26] Willis Jenkins, "After Lynn White: Religious Ethics and Environmental Problems," *Journal of Religious Ethics* Vol. 37, No. 2 (2009): 283–309.

[27] For critical appraisal of stewardship positions see Richard Bauckham, *Living with Other Creatures* (Waco, TX: Baylor University Press, 2011), esp. 62.

[28] Peter Harrison, "Having Dominion: Genesis and the Mastery of Nature," in *Environmental Stewardship: Critical Perspectives - Past and Present*, ed. R.J. Berry (London: T & T Clark/Continuum, 2006), 17–31.

[29] Ellen Davis, *Scripture, Culture and Agriculture: An Agrarian Reading of the Bible* (Cambridge: Cambridge University Press, 2009).

broader sociopolitical conditions have also come to the fore in discussion, including, more recently, greater awareness of the entanglement between oppression of the Earth, oppression of women, and marginalization of indigenous communities. The point is that who we are as human beings cannot be split off from our entangled relationships with each other in sociopolitical relationships, including our close relationship with the natural world.

Another source of pressure against a strongly **anthropocentric** view is that arising not just from ecological science but from the evolutionary sciences. Ever since the work of Charles Darwin was published on the *Origin of Species* in 1859,[30] scholars have been aware that the special status of humanity is potentially under threat.[31] Hence, the real challenge was not just how a theological understanding of God's creative activity is compatible with evolutionary models of origin, but whether it is still convincing to understand the special status of human beings *vis-à-vis* all the other creatures in the natural world. Certainly, many, such as Alfred Russel Wallace, still believed that there was something radically different about humanity even during Darwin's struggle to understand evolution of natural kinds.[32] Unique characteristics such as human morality could, argued such authors, have come about through different processes distinct for our lineage. In the Catholic tradition, evolutionary narratives were either ignored, or those who did try and combine both together were treated harshly.[33] Eventually the Magisterium was prepared to accept evolutionary narratives, but interestingly an exception was always made for human evolution.[34] In this respect it is useful to compare Pope John Paul II on this matter and Pope Francis. Pope John Paul II claimed that:

> new knowledge has led to the recognition of the theory of evolution as more than a hypothesis … theories of evolution which, in accordance with the philosophies inspiring them, consider the spirit as emerging from the forces of living matter or as a mere epiphenomenon of this matter, are incompatible with the truth about man. Nor are they able to ground the dignity of the person. With main, then, we find ourselves in the presence of an ontological difference, and ontological leap, one could say.[35]

---

[30] Charles Darwin, *On the Origin of Species*, ed. Gillian Beer (Oxford/New York: Oxford University Press, 2008).

[31] See, for example, R.J. Berry and Michael Northcott, eds., *Theology After Darwin* (Milton Keynes: Paternoster, 2009).

[32] Wallace also proposed the theory of evolution by natural selection independently of Charles Darwin. Alfred Russel Wallace, *Social Environment and Moral Progress* (London: Cassell, 1913).

[33] John Slattery, *Faith and Science at Notre Dame: John Zahm, Evolution and the Catholic Church* (Notre Dame: University of Notre Dame Press, 2019).

[34] For a useful summary of the history of the reception of evolution in the Magisterium of the Roman Catholic church, see John Mahoney, *Christianity in Evolution: An Exploration* (Washington: Georgetown University Press, 2011), 2–6. For further discussion see Celia Deane-Drummond, "In Adam All Die: Questions at the Boundary of Niche Construction, Community Evolution and Original Sin," in *Evolution and the Fall*, ed. William T. Cavanaugh and James K.A. Smith (Grand Rapids: Eerdmans, 2017), 23–47.

[35] Address of Pope John Paul II to the Pontifical Academy of Sciences, October 22, 1996, reprinted in *Science and Religion: Christian and Muslim Perspectives*, ed. David Marshall (Washington: Georgetown University Press, 2012), 163–165, full address 161–167. The translation of the phrase, "more than a hypothesis" received intense discussion at the time, as its meaning was ambiguous. For further analysis see Celia Deane-Drummond, "Commentary," in *Science and Religion: Christian and Muslim Perspectives*, ed. by David Marshall (Washington: Georgetown University Press, 2012), 167–172.

Pope Francis, who also has prior training in natural sciences, which has made him far more confident in dealing with scientific literature, also says something similar in *Laudato Si'*:

> Human beings, even if we postulate a process of evolution, also possess a uniqueness which cannot be fully explained by the evolution of other open systems. ... The sheer novelty involved in the emergence of a personal being within a material universe presupposes a direct action of God and a particular call to life and to relationship on the part of a "Thou" who addresses himself to another "thou."[36]

It is worth asking why there is still this hesitancy and even resistance by the papal hierarchy to understanding human beings as an integral part of the evolutionary account, even though most now acknowledge ecological interdependence. One reason is the specific emphasis that the Catholic tradition in particular places on human dignity and issues of human justice. The argument seems to be, though it is not always spelled out, that giving greater respect to other animals or other creatures will somehow weaken the status of human beings.[37] Another argument is that by leveling out humanity as a specific kind of animal weakens or drags down humanity to the level of animality, rather than elevates animals to the human plane. This is particularly true in situations where slavery has either been practiced or is being practiced; human beings are treated as if they are animals in order to show disdain. Wrapped up in this critique is the shadow of colonialization: specific varieties of the Christian tradition, including specific beliefs about humanity that are culturally endowed, are perceived as being forced on local cultures, rather than those cultures being given the respect that they deserve.

Philosophers such as Peter Singer have argued that attempts like this to hold onto the uniqueness of our human identity are "speciesist," an unwarranted priority given to our species.[38] Keen resistance against his position follows from those who believe that a consequence of such leveling is to treat those with disabilities as somehow lower in ethical priority compared with sophisticated social animals, such as primates, who may show greater cognitive capacities.

Insights from Evolutionary Anthropology

> **Box 5.7**
>
> In this section the author describes developments in evolutionary anthropology that problematize traditional anthropocentric views. She first turns to evidence that early Homo Sapiens shared a number of features with other species to challenge the notion that what makes us human is our rational faculty and/or that the essence of our rational faculty is our ability to use language.

---

[36] Pope Francis, *Laudato Si': On Care for Our Common Home* (London: Catholic Truth Society, 2015), Section 81.

[37] The late Polish Archbishop Zycinski held such a position, as discussed in Deane-Drummond, "God's Image and Likeness".

[38] For a discussion of Peter Singer's accusation of Christian speciesism see John Berkman and Celia Deane-Drummond, "Catholic Moral Theology and the Moral Status of Non-Human Animals," *Journal of Moral Theology* Vol. 3, No. 2 (2014): 1–10. The whole issue was dedicated to discussion of this topic.

In order to find a way through this labyrinth of what is it that makes humanity distinct it is a good idea to consider in more depth evolutionary anthropology, while recognizing that all anthropology this far back in deep time is a combination of empirical and speculative analysis (see Box 5.7).[39] The general consensus among anthropologists is that human becoming did not happen suddenly, but gradually and sporadically. The split between our lineage, *Homo*, and that of our closest living relatives, *Pan*, happened some 6 million years ago. During that time, both lineages evolved and changed, though it is possible that there was some convergence in behavioral characteristics as a result of similar selection pressures. Complex characteristics, including our ability to reason abstractly, or show other moral virtues such as gratitude, are unlikely to be simply the result of a specific gene or even set of genes for that behavior, but a highly complex mix of both biological and cultural evolution.[40]

Trying to work out what might be the ratio of biological and cultural factors in any given set of circumstances is almost impossible, even for specific characteristics such as language. In the latter case, although there are specific biological characteristics that are necessary for language to have been possible, why language appeared when it did and which factors were the most significant in its emergence is still a difficult and unsolved evolutionary puzzle.[41] More generally, there has been a tendency by theologians to assume that language is *the* factor which most closely defines our species, even though the origin of language is now thought to go far back into deep time prior to *Homo sapiens*' first appearance on the savannah. Discussion about the evolution of language continues to be a matter of heated debate. It is important to point out, however, that the discovery of specific human variant FOXP2 mutant leading to a language disorder implies its importance as a prerequisite to language, but is not coincident with it. The same version of the gene is found in Neanderthal and Denisovan DNA, but to claim the gene causes language is mistaken, as it involves much greater complexity.[42] Further, distinct forms of human sociality is a necessary behavioral prerequisite for language. Other theories include the idea that the development of technology and language appeared in a positive feedback loop. Agustín Fuentes summarizes the existing anthropological research which shows that ecology of creative problem solving, tool manufacture, and imaginative sociality were all factors in permitting language to evolve in humans, though he admits that the precise date is difficult to discern.[43] Certainly, there were other hominin species that coexisted with our own, and whose gene pool we share, including *Homo neanderthalis*, for example, who have been unfairly caricatured as clumsy and lacking in intelligence.

Further, systematized and deliberate burials deep in the rising star cave in South Africa have shown that another quite remarkable hominin, *Homo naledi*, who coexisted for a time with *Homo sapiens*, was capable of perceiving the existential significance of death.[44] This hominin had

---

[39] This point is illustrated beautifully in the collection of essays in *Verbs, Bone and Brains*, ed. Agustín Fuentes and Aku Visala.

[40] Tim Lewens, *Cultural Evolution* (Oxford: Oxford University Press, 2015).

[41] Agustín Fuentes in *Evolution of Human Wisdom*, ed. Celia Deane-Drummond and Agustín Fuentes (Lanham, MD: Lexington, 2017).

[42] See Marc Kissel, "What Can Anthropology Say About the Evolution of Human Wisdom?" in *Evolution of Human Wisdom*, 27.

[43] Fuentes, "Manipulating Materials, Bodies and Signs," 191–204.

[44] Lee Berger and John Hawks, "On *Homo Naledi* and its Significance in Evolutionary Anthropology" in *Theology and Evolutionary Anthropology: Dialogues in Wisdom, Humility and Grace*, ed. Celia Deane-Drummond and Agustín Fuentes (London: Routledge, 2020), *in press*.

the brain size of a much earlier hominin, *Australopithecus*, while its hands and other body parts were analogous to *Homo sapiens*. Finding such sophisticated characteristics far back into our human history challenges too narrow a conception of our own uniqueness. In addition, all research on early hominins and current anthropological research on small hunter-gatherer communities shows close interrelationships between people and the other creatures. There was no sense of separation, but rather, interdependence.[45]

Box 5.8

Now the author discusses evidence from modern and contemporary indigenous communities and their relationship with other species and their ecological environment to challenge the notion that human beings are somehow separate from and placed in an environment that is external to who we are.

Indigenous communities generally have a much stronger sense of the agency of other animals, including attributing spiritual agency to specific kinds (see Box 5.8). In *How Forests Think*, for example, anthropologist Eduardo Kohn describes the presence of the Pumas (jaguars) as both personal and spiritual agents among the Runa people of upper Amazon in Ecuador.[46] It is not surprising therefore that anthropologist Tim Ingold has critiqued standard evolutionary models as failing to give sufficient weight to the entangled process of human becoming in relationship with other species.[47] We simply could not be who we are without them. So, he argues:

> But the relation is not *between* one thing and another – between the organism "here" and the environment "there". It is rather a trail *along* which life is lived: one strand in a tissue of trails that together make up the texture of the lifeworld. That texture is what I mean when I speak of organisms being constituted within a relational field. It is a field not of inter- connected points but of interwoven lines, not a network but a *meshwork*.[48]

This research is, of course, a fascinating window into our own human history, though it is also important to take care in interpreting ethnographic research as if subjects in that research represent accurately something closer to our own evolutionary roots. Those societies have been changing slowly through time as well, and while they may give us clues about what could have been possible in small-scale human communities, it is demeaning to consider them more "primitive" or closer to our evolutionary origins than other cultures which have more complex technologies. Indeed, such technologies may actually detract us from the ability to form relationships with others and thus undermine the basis for our humanity rather than enhance it.[49] In this

---

[45] Tim Ingold, "Re-Thinking the Animate, Re-Animating Thought," *Ethnos* Vol. 71, No. 1 (2006): 9–20.

[46] Kohn argues that if Jaguars represent us as well as the other way round, this changes the anthropological task, so "such encounters with other kinds of beings force us to recognize the fact that seeing, representing, and perhaps knowing, even thinking, are not exclusively human affairs," Eduardo Kohn, *How Forests Think: An Anthropology Beyond the Human* (Berkley: University of California Press, 2013), 1.

[47] Tim Ingold, "An Anthropologist Looks at Biology," *Man*, New Series, Vol. 25, No. 2 (Jun. 1990), 208–229.

[48] Ingold, "Re-Thinking the Animate," 13.

[49] As Pope Francis has claimed in his critique of the technological paradigm in Laudato Si'. Pope Francis, *Laudato Si': On Care for Our Common Home* (London: Catholic Truth Society, 2015).

respect we have much to learn from indigenous peoples who are, generally, more successful in maintaining a healthy balance with their ecological environment. This is partly to do with their assumptions about the living world; humanity is perceived as being in a network of embedded relationships with other beings, not, as in our Western cultures, somehow placed "in" an external environment. Anthropologists are becoming far more conscious of these processes and for that reason have started to draw on the methods of ethnographic research in order to explore multi-species associations, rather than viewing other species as separate from our own human communities.[50]

Elisabeth Marshall Thomas, for example, describes a remarkable example of bushmen who shared a common space with lions, which she observed in the 1950s, and both parties agreed to refrain from attack, even though this arrangement no longer holds:

> How can two species who are so very similar, and with such similar needs, habits and methods, drink from the same waterhole and lay claim to the same territory without coming into conflict? The answer is that they lived in a manner that could sustain a truce, keeping to certain lifestyle patterns, probably quite consciously. Most notably, they used the same area at different times of day, spreading out all over the area to forage for roughly 12 hours, and then retreating to a very small, restricted area to rest for 12 hours. Because Nyae was at about 20 degrees south latitude, days and nights were about the same length, without pronounced seasonal variation. Thus, throughout the year, both species had equal time to forage. The people used the hours of daylight, and the lions used the night. I think it safe to assume that the arrangement was intentional by both parties.[51]

Box 5.9

In the last part of this section, the author discusses a contemporary alternative to the traditional neo-Darwinian understanding of the evolutionary process. This provides further evidence that the interdependent nature of humans' relationship to other species and to our environment more generally should be understood as being at the center of what makes us human.

Alongside this basic challenge of consideration of our human history as not so much individualistic and superior, but entangled with that of other animals there are wider debates arising about the nature of the evolutionary process as such (see Box 5.9). Instead of the standard neo-Darwinian interpretation of each species struggling in a competitive environment such that only characteristics best suited to that environment survive, a different, more interactive approach is becoming popular known as niche construction theory (NCT). It is part of a more general trend to put more emphasis in evolutionary terms on developmental systems rather than individuals and their genes. In sum, NCT argues that not only individuals of species endure through time, but

---

[50] Anthropologist Marcus Baynes Rock has conducted some remarkable work with hyenas in Harar, Ethiopia, and Agustín Fuentes pioneered work with macaques. See Marcus Baynes Rock, Marcus Baynes-Rock, *Among the Bone Eaters: Encounters with Hyenas in Harar* (University Park: Penn State University Press, 2015) and Agustín Fuentes, "Ethnoprimatology and the Anthropology of the Human-Primate Interface," *Annual Review of Anthropology* Vol. 41 (2012): 101–117.

[51] Elisabeth Marshall Thomas, "The Lion/Bushman Relationship in Nyae in the 1950s: A Relationship Crafted in the Old Way," *Anthropologica* Vol. 45, No. 1 (2003): 73–78.

ecological systems as well, and the two exist in dynamic relationship with each other. The change to the ecological environment brought about by human beings therefore impacts on the selection pressures that are then subsequently exerted on the gene pool. Further, that ecological environment is also made up of dynamic systems of organisms that are themselves responding to and altering their niche, hence the name, niche *construction* theory, though the latter should not necessarily be thought of as a self-conscious process of change. When two or more species are closely aligned through evolutionary time they are said to coevolve. Humans and hyenas fall into this category; they have both evolved in response to the evolutionary trajectory of the other species.[52] NCT is also interesting as it brings together evolutionary and ecological theories in a way that has significance for ecological thinking and even practical questions of environmental ethics.[53]

Re-thinking *Imago Dei*

> **Box 5.10**
>
> Here the author discusses ways to revise the traditional notion of the image of God in light of the evidence she has discussed in the last section. This will lay the groundwork for a performative view of the image of God that includes our dependence on other creatures.

In the light of what has been discussed, is the traditional theological way of speaking of humanity as the image of God noted at the start of this chapter still meaningful (see Box 5.10)? How can theology still maintain a position that seems to promote human exceptionalism; or worse, one that seems to elevate humans to such a degree that it appears to encourage exploitation of the natural world, perhaps even in the name of that image bearing? Or, alternatively, given the extent of suffering and exploitation of the most vulnerable, does theology now have even more responsibility to try and protect the dignity and worth of the human person against secular pressures that would claim otherwise?

Some established theologians have claimed that, in the light of scientific knowledge about the place of humanity, using image-bearing language needs to be avoided altogether. David Kelsey's two-volume book *Eccentric Existence* argues for a different kind of approach to humanity that tries to avoid image bearing, but without losing a sense of the distinct capacity for transcendence[54]. Other theologians, such as Charlie Camosy and David Clough, have chosen to widen the net of those who could be considered under the umbrella of image bearing, so including sentient animals as image bearers.[55] It is also obvious that once the idea of the exclusivity of image

---

[52] Rock, *Among the Bone Eaters*.

[53] For additional discussion of niche construction theory, see, Celia Deane-Drummond, *Wisdom of the Liminal: Evolution and Other Animals in Human Becoming* (Grand Rapids: Eerdmands, 2014); 196–202; Deane-Drummond, *Theological Ethics Through Multispecies Lens, Evolution of Wisdom Vol 1* (Oxford: Oxford University Press, 2019): 10–17.

[54] David Kelsey, *Eccentric Existence: A Theological Anthropology, Volume 1 and 2* (Louisville: Westminster John Knox Press, 2009). For discussion of Kelsey, see Deane-Drummond, *Wisdom of the Liminal*, 25–31, 209–211.

[55] The idea of loosening the category of image bearing goes back to some early work of ecotheologian Ruth Page, but Charlie Camosy has presented stronger arguments for such a move, as has David Clough.

bearing is challenged, so too is the concept that the Incarnation had to be present in a human being. The logical consequence of holding to the broader definition of image bearing is that the Word made flesh could have, theoretically at least, been incarnate in a dolphin, a chimpanzee, or indeed some other creature.[56] The language of deep incarnation has been used in different ways by scholars debating on the scope and depth of the significance of Christ's incarnation, not just for human beings, but for the material world as such.[57] Could therefore, by analogy, human image bearing be spread out in an inclusive way or not?

My own position is this. I agree that human exceptionalism needs to be avoided and that the challenges facing our planet are such that to ignore the threat of ecological breakdown is no longer an option for serious theologians. At the same time, I do not think that it is necessary to dispense completely with the language of image bearing as pointing to our human distinctiveness, but rather, to work to re-vision its meaning and scope.[58] Although biblical scholars have objected to the traditional use of image bearing and likeness as derivative from creation and not necessarily being true to the Genesis text,[59] my own theological methodology allows me to use traditional concepts where they are helpful for analysis, not least because many dogmatic categories, including the Trinity, for example, cannot be gleaned directly from scripture. I agree with critics that it is important to take account of the faulty **exegesis** of Genesis 1 that tries to ground image bearing in a doctrine of creation.[60] Instead, *imago Dei* is derivative from the true image in Christ, as Aquinas also recognizes, though he combined this with a (faulty) Augustinian insistence on image bearing related specifically to distinct forms of human rationality.[61]

See David Camosy, "Other Animals as Persons- A Roman Catholic Inquiry," in Celia Deane-Drummond, Rebecca Artinian Kaiser, and David Clough, eds., *Animals as Religious Subjects: Transdisciplinary Perspectives* (London: T & T Clark/Bloomsbury, 2013), 259–278; Ruth Page, "The Human Genome and the Image of God," in *Brave New World: Theology, Ethics and the Human Genome*, ed. Celia Deane-Drummond, (London: T & T Clark/Continuum, 2003), 68–85; David Cunningham, "The Way of All Flesh: Re-Thinking the Imago Dei," in *Creaturely Theology: On God, Humans and Other Animals*, ed. Celia Deane-Drummond and David Clough (London: SCM Press, 2009), 100–120; David Clough, *On Animals Volume 1* (London: T & T Clark, 2015), 65–68.

[56] There is not the scope in this chapter to discuss these options, though it is worth noting that an alternative to Jesus being incarnate as a Jewish male is already discussed in Ian Markham's chapter in this volume. The idea of the Word becoming flesh has, as Cunningham and others have pointed out for some time, affirmed what is common between humans and other creatures. Cunningham, "The Way of All Flesh".

[57] See debates in Niels Gregersen, *Incarnation: On the Scope and Depth of Christology* (Minneapolis: Fortress, 2014).

[58] Details of this argument are laid out in Deane-Drummond, *Wisdom of the Liminal*.

[59] See helpful discussion in David Clough, *On Animals*, 67–8.

[60] The main objection seems to be that the term image bearing in Genesis does not necessarily refer to a specific process of divine making and is vague in intent in the text itself. See Gordan J. Wenham, *Genesis, Word Bible Commentary* (Waco/TX: Word, 1994), 29–32.

[61] An argument for how to construct a convincing Christology in the light of evolutionary theory is in the background here, but the scope of this chapter does not allow for further discussion. For development of these ideas through a wisdom Christology and in the light of Hans Urs van Balthasar's understanding of theodrama, see Celia Deane-Drummond, *Christ and Evolution: Wonder and Wisdom* (Minneapolis: Fortress, 2009).

Could other animals reflect that image of God in Christ also? Possibly, but in a different way, inasmuch as that image in those creatures is not marred by human sin. Can the distinction between image and likeness be retained without exegetical warrant for such a distinction? This is rather harder to discern, but as long as there is no claim for a direct derivation from biblical theology, I suggest that it may still be helpful conceptually in order to navigate the very difficult question of how to give intrinsic value to other animals without necessarily wanting to collapse all distinctions between humans and the creaturely world. I have already conceded that personhood can be attributed to other animals according to their own specific and distinct personhood.[62] David Cunningham argues for the use of "flesh" to name distinct forms of life rather than using *imago Dei*. The specificity of flesh for different animals seems to be less clear if it is to be used as any kind of guide for ethical actions. The likeness to God approaches God even more perfectly than the image, so that in this sense it is no diminishment of animals to suggest that they share in God's likeness, but they become in some sense exemplars, while avoiding romanticism.[63] Creating a hierarchical chain no longer makes sense, but there does need to be a greater sense of the distinct contribution of humanity within a meshwork of other creatures. Modern societies have lost that sense of interdependence, even though, arguably, we are far more dependent on others than we realize but have just lost the consciousness of it. Maybe COVID-19, arising from the entanglement between humans and bats, perhaps with a pangolin intermediary, has reminded us once more of our interlaced lives with other creatures. While attempts to stem the disease through social distancing has reminded us of our hypersociality that makes isolation so hard to bear.

Instead, a more participatory approach to image bearing considers that image through how we find our way in the world of other creatures, and our particular form of responsiveness to divine grace.[64] Theological anthropology has been presented historically and in contemporary theology either in terms of our distinctive capacity for reason, as in the case of Augustine and Aquinas, for example, or a particular function, such as the divine mandate to care for the Earth and its creatures as laid out in the book of Genesis, or through a more ontological understanding of humanity as deeply relational and grounded in trinitarian thinking. The difference with a performative understanding of the divine image is that it tries to understand image bearing more holistically, in that a functional sense of the image is difficult to understand without admitting, at least, some basic capacities are present.[65] *Performance* is more than simple *function* as it takes its ideal from a theodramatic understanding of who God is in Christ and therefore has ontological as well as simply functional resonance. It is also profoundly *social*, thus reflecting current understanding of evolutionary anthropology. Theodrama, in its turn, is grounded in a theodramatic perception of who God is in an economic sense inspired by Hans

---

[62] Deane-Drummond, *Theological Ethics*, chapter 6.

[63] I have alluded to what seems to us as immoral aspects of the non-human world in Celia Deane-Drummond, *Shadow Sophia: Evolution of Wisdom Volume 2* (Oxford: Oxford University Press, 2021).

[64] For further discussion of this concept see Deane-Drummond, *Wisdom of the Liminal*. For a shorter book that covers some of the same ground for a more general audience, see Celia Deane-Drummond, *Re-Imaging the Divine Image: Humans and Other Animals*, ed. Carl S. Helrich (Kitchener: Pandora Press, 2014).

[65] For discussion of philosophical aspects of this debate, see special issues on image bearing in *Zygon*, including particularly analysis of whether it makes sense to talk about human nature at all in Mikael Stenmark, "Is There a Human Nature?" *Zygon* Vol. 47, No. 4 (2012): 890–902.

Urs van Balthasar's theodrama.[66] Just as Christology needs revision in the light of a dramatic view of salvation, so humanity, when perceived as being true to its image bearing, is caught up in a common story, centered on the passion and resurrection narrative, while not being confined to it.

Who we are in relation to God – our capacity for image bearing – is therefore understood as a sharing in and participating in that theodrama. As in the classic thought of Aquinas, we are only ever an image of the true divine image in Christ, who, by what he did as much as who he was, showed us both his divinity and humanity. The difference between my own development of performative image bearing and that in Hans Urs van Balthasar is that I extend his notion of theodrama to include other creatures in a way that he does not.[67] There are echoes, too, of a classic sense of human flourishing as participation in God, but given that drama implies movement, it avers any static sense of that participation.[68]

Could other creatures *also* be understood as performative according to this model? The answer to that is yes, in a limited way, but certainly not in the same sense that humanity is called to freely participate and share in the fundamental Christological drama. I recognize that, if pushed to the limit, the notion of human freedom comes to the fore in this understanding of image bearing, but I see freedom as an essential ingredient in the distinctive way in which humanity can bear that image in relation to other creatures, rather than its explicitly defining characteristic. John Zizioulas some years ago discussed the importance of freedom in an Orthodox understanding of image bearing, though his own preference was to perceive this freedom in the context of humanity as marked by tragedy, but also the hope for and priest of creation.[69] This has some resonance with the idea of co-performer in a drama in the way I have suggested here, though I prefer to avoid to the language of priesthood as it could imply human superiority. In sum: A performative way of perceiving the image recognizes not only the ideal to be sought in Christ but also the fragility and vulnerability of the human condition and our dependence on other creatures who share in our common life.

Concluding Remarks

Box 5.11

In the final section, the author sets out the results of her investigations, and then describes the ways in which these present challenges for theologians going forward.

---

[66] Discussion of theodrama in Hans Urs van Balthasar goes beyond the scope of this chapter. I have developed, in earlier work, a theological conversation with Hans Urs von Balthasar and his notion of theodrama. See Celia Deane-Drummond, *Christ and Evolution: Wonder and Wisdom* (Minneapolis: Fortress Press, 2009) and Deane-Drummond, *Wisdom of the Liminal*.

[67] Celia Deane-Drummond, "The Breadth of Glory: A Trinitarian Eschatology for the Earth through Critical Engagement with Hans Urs von Balthasar," *International Journal of Systematic Theology* Vol. 12., No. 1 (2010): 46–64.

[68] Andrew Davison, *Participation in God: A Study in Christian Doctrine and Metaphysics* (Cambridge: Cambridge University Press, 2019).

[69] John Zizioulas, "Preserving God's Creation: Three Lectures on Theology and Ecology," *King's Theological Review* Vol. 13 (1989): 1–5.

Where on earth have we come from and where are we going to? This chapter has tried to explore these questions (see Box 5.11). While we have been left with more questions than answers, there are some aspects that have come to the surface which are not contested. It is no longer possible to make a convincing theological case for superiority of men over women, or for human exceptionalism. Our entangled lives with other creatures from the dawn of human existence forces us to reconsider what it means to be the *imago Dei*. Evolutionary anthropology is turning away from individualism toward a richer social and ecological context for human evolution in NCT. Arguments for and against retaining the language of image bearing are more contested and rest on how far and to what extent our humanity is grounded in a specific interpretation of a doctrine of the creation or interpreted through Christology. I have pressed for the latter, while recognizing that this does not avoid further difficult issues, including that of understanding the full meaning of the Word becoming flesh, and therefore what that then signifies for other creatures. The challenge for theologians is how to consider the significance of humanity and its role and responsibility, even while navigating the questions of sources and authority of those sources in constructive theology. We might be tempted to reject our human entanglements with other creatures, or reject an evolutionary account, or syncretize theology and science, flattening out creaturely difference. Our distinct form of human personhood understood in terms of *performance* comes to fruition through our relationships with each other and our relationships with other creatures, which, in theological terms, are also crafted specifically in and through our relationship with God in Christ. Theological understanding of the human and the future of the human does not need to be reduced to the understanding of ourselves in the human and natural sciences while still taking heed of their insights. It is only then that we can gain a window into where we have come from and where we might be going to.

6

What Challenges Does the Theory of Biological Evolution Pose to Christian Theology?

Christopher Southgate

RESEARCH LEVEL 3

Editors' Introduction

Good research writing often challenges the conventional parameters of a debate. In the debate over evolution, the positions are well known: "creationists" of various types, who believe that evolution is incompatible with the biblical witness; and theists who believe that the theological insights of the creation narratives can be reconciled with evolution. In this article, Christopher Southgate insists that the evidence for evolution is strong; therefore the "creationists" are mistaken; however, those who are compatibilists are often too sanguine. There are real theological issues that need exploration. Southgate identifies the following:

1. *How do we reconcile this understanding with key Scriptural texts?*
2. *Does science explain away religion?*
3. *Does an evolving world look designed by God?*
4. *Are humans distinctive, as the creature in the image of God?*
5. *What should we think about the Fall?*
6. *How could a loving God create nature red in tooth and claw?*

Southgate deals fairly easily with the initial difficulties. However, issues five and six provoke a sustained discussion. He advocates for a "compound theodicy."

Box 6.1
This article, explains the author right from the outset, is not about whether evolution is true. He has a footnote explaining that evolutionary theory has developed since Darwin, but none of these developments take us back to a version of creationism. The author is making clear that once you accept evolutionary theory as true, there is still considerable theological work to be done. One senses the author is a little frustrated that too many Christians are still having the nineteenth-century debate about the truth of evolution, and not enough are doing the hard work of exploring the theological issues that emerge because evolution is true.

For many Christians "evolution" is a horror-word; something to be against – whatever it is and whether it truly describes the natural world or not (see Box 6.1). In this chapter I start from the

The Craft of Innovative Theology: Argument and Process, First Edition. Edited by John Allan Knight and Ian S. Markham.
© 2022 John Wiley & Sons Ltd. Published 2022 by John Wiley & Sons Ltd.

opposite point of view. I accept that the theory of biological evolution, as it has developed since the publication of Darwin's *Origin of Species* in 1859, is a robust scientific theory, still undergoing change,[1] but in its core positions an accurate description of what science can currently know about the way life has developed in the last 3.8 billion years or so. I then ask: What issues does this theory currently present for thinking Christians seeking to understand to the full the world they confess God as having created, loved through its long history, and redeemed in Jesus Christ?

The first task is to understand the core of the scientific theory, which is:

> If many offspring must die (for not all can be accommodated in nature's limited *ecology*), and individuals in all species vary among themselves, then on average survivors will tend to be those individuals with variations that are best suited ("fitted") to their particular local environment. Since *genetic* heredity exists, the offspring of survivors will tend to resemble their successful parents. The accumulation of these favourable variants through time produces evolutionary change.[2]

Darwin saw that given this principle of "natural selection" of variants within a population, and given certain other factors such as populations of a species becoming isolated (for example, by geological changes), new species could arise. Indeed, given enough time, all the life-forms on Earth could have arisen from one or a very few original forms.[3]

This is the profound, simple, and beautiful basis on which modern evolutionary biology is constructed. But we should beware the simple caricature that the *Origin of Species* immediately captured the assent of the scientific community, while raising unbearable tensions with Christianity. Some theological responses were positive, for example, Charles Kingsley's:

> [I] have gradually learnt to see that it is just as noble a conception of the Deity to believe that He created a few original forms capable of self-development into other and needful forms, as to believe that He required a fresh act of creation to supply the voids caused by the action of His laws.[4]

---

[1] Eva Jablonka and Marion J. Lamb, *Evolution in Four Dimensions: Genetic, Epigenetic, Behavioural and Symbolic Variation in the History Of Life* (Cambridge, MA: MIT Press, 2014). This book is important in showing how far evolutionary theory has come since the core insights of Darwin.

[2] René van Wouderberg, "Darwinian and Teleological Explanations: Are They Incompatible?" in *Evolution and Ethics: Human Morality in Biological and Religious Perspective*, ed. Philip Clayton and Jeffrey Schloss (Grand Rapids, MI: Eerdmans, 2004), 171–186, especially at 178 (emphases mine). Note that this is a modern version of Darwin's principle. The words in italics would not have been understood by Darwin in their modern sense.

[3] In the light of his perception of the long competitive struggle within and between species, Darwin famously wrote, "Thus, from the war of nature, from famine and death, the most exalted object which we are capable of conceiving, namely, the production of the higher animals, directly follows." Charles Darwin, *On the Origin of Species by Means of Natural Selection, or the Preservation of Favoured Races in the Struggle for Life* (London: John Murray, 1859), 425. This quotation is important in its emphasis that the *same processes* lead to suffering and to the refinement of creaturely characteristics. However, it is recognized now that successful evolutionary strategies are not all about "war," about competition. Cooperation between organisms (and also creatures modifying their environments through so-called niche construction) are very important elements, and moreover some evolutionary change is purely random. However, the principle of natural selection still applies. Even in cooperative systems there will always tend to be "losers," individuals or groups which are outcompeted and fail.

[4] Letter to Darwin, 18 November 1859, accessed June 30, 2021, www.darwinproject.ac.uk.

That is not to say that *Origin of Species* did not provoke theological controversy – see the careful study by John Hedley Brooke of how the debate unfolded.[5]

Scientifically, Darwin's theory limped through its first half-century of life, and for good reasons. He lacked the statistical demonstration that later developed as to how small changes could indeed give rise over time to very profound ones; he lacked the biochemical evidence that now speaks so tellingly of evolution from a common ancestor – for example, the genetic code that, virtually identically in every known organism, enables the translation of sequences of DNA into protein, and the "molecular clock" that the evolution of protein sequences across organisms gives us, complementing the evidence we get from anatomy. Most crucially at the time, Darwin lacked the understanding of inheritance that derived from Gregor Mendel's work, which led to the science of genetics and an account of how characteristics of organisms could be accurately passed down from one generation to the next.

Darwin even later commuted his earlier opposition to the proposal by Lamarck that characteristics inherited in an organism's lifetime could be inherited.[6] This rejection of Lamarck was one of the distinctive characteristics of his theory, yet he found himself retreating from it. So the early years of Darwinian evolution represent a more complex picture than is often supposed. Nevertheless, difficulties for theology were detected early on, and those same difficulties, plus a new one, continue into the contemporary debate. In section 6.2 I consider these difficulties, which are as follows:

1. How do we reconcile this understanding with key Scriptural texts?
2. Does science explain away religion?
3. Does an evolving world look designed by God?
4. Are humans distinctive, as the creature in the image of God?
5. What should we think about the Fall?
6. How could a loving God create nature red in tooth and claw?

I have ranked these challenges in what, for me, is an order of increasing severity, with the most easily negotiated challenges at the start (see Box 6.2).

Box 6.2

The introduction makes it clear that the author understands the theory of evolution, understands the history, and affirms the broad outlines of Darwin's discovery. However, the author is deeply aware of the theological predicaments that arise in affirming evolution. This signpost indicates both the areas which the author is planning to discuss and his judgment of how difficult they are to evaluate. The reader should pause at this point and decide whether they agree with the author's judgment.

It may seem odd to begin with the challenge to the interpretation of Scripture, and particularly the first two chapters of Genesis. For many, this is, ostensibly, the most severe of objections to any effort to work with evolution as part of the data for doing Christian theology. For those who hold that the Genesis text must be read literally, therefore the science of evolution, no

---

[5] John Hedley Brooke, *Science and Religion: Some Historical Perspectives* (Cambridge: Cambridge University Press, 1991), chapter 8.

[6] At one level, Lamarck was clearly wrong. Roger Federer's twins did not inherit the expanded racket forearm of the tennis champion. But as the new science of epigenetics shows, in subtler ways acquired characteristics can be inherited (see e.g. Jablonka and Lamb, *Evolution*, chapter 4).

matter how robust in its own terms, must be discarded as false. But for me this is the most straightforward challenge to deal with. Attempts at literal reading of the creation accounts in Genesis are self-contradictory, since the accounts of divine creation in Genesis 1 and 2 are completely different and cannot both be literally true (not least in the order given for creation of humans and other animals).[7] So some interpretation other than literal reading is required. Far better, then, to recognize that the ancient author(s) were preoccupied with giving theological accounts of God as creator, and accept that they knew nothing of the insights science has gained about biological life in only the last two hundred years.

Box 6.3

It is interesting to note that the primary arguments the author deduces for a nonliteral reading of the Genesis text are theological. For those Biblical Christians who are nervous about accepting evolution, the author explains that there are lots of different Biblical accounts of creation. He uses footnote 7 to suggest the motive for those evangelicals who oppose evolution is not adherence to the text of Scripture but for a more "tribal" identification with evangelicalism with certain key issues.

Further, the debates about creation in the biblical text have been skewed by an over-preoccupation with Genesis 1 (the "six-day" account) (see Box 6.3). It is important to recognize that there are many other creation accounts in the Hebrew Bible. When they are all considered, a much more nuanced view of "what the Bible says" emerges.[8]

Second in my list of increasingly severe challenges posed to Christian theology by biological evolution I put a challenge from the other "end" of the spectrum of opinion. This is a recent development, well illustrated by this quotation from E.O. Wilson:

> [W]e have come to the crucial stage in the history of biology when religion itself is subject to the explanations of the natural sciences … sociobiology can account for the very origin of mythology by the principle of natural selection acting on the genetically evolving material structure of the human brain.[9]

---

[7] I suggest therefore that the appeal to literal readings of Scripture to reject evolution is much more to do with a complex of positions held together as signs of evangelical orthodoxy, and typically including also opposition to (the very disparate issues of) homosexuality, abortion, and women in leadership. The underlying issue here, I sense, is not so much the literal reading of particular texts as the question of who is entitled to give an authoritative account of what Scripture says. There are interesting parallels with the Galileo Affair, which turned as much on interpretative authority as on particular biblical texts.

[8] See in particular W.P. Brown, *The Seven Pillars of Creation: the Bible, Science and the Ecology of Wonder* (New York: Oxford University Press, 2010) and two recent studies that address the character of creation from the Wisdom Literature: Ian McFarland, *From Nothing: A Theology of Creation* (Louisville, KY: Westminster John Knox Press, 2014), chapter 5, and Tom McLeish, *Faith and Wisdom in Science* (Oxford: Oxford University Press, 2014).

[9] Edward O. Wilson, *On Human Nature* (Harmondsworth: Penguin, 1995[1978]),192.

Since Wilson wrote that, a whole range of explanations have been formulated for the evolution of religion, either as adaptive in itself in prehistoric societies, or as a by-product of adaptive traits.[10] The natural sciences operate by always seeking simpler and more unified explanations of phenomena. But interestingly, there are very few examples where a whole level of explanation can be reduced to a simpler level. Francis Crick's famous manifesto: "The ultimate aim of the modern movement in biology is in fact to explain *all* biology in terms of physics and chemistry"[11] has seen little progress in fifty years. (Instead whole intermediate levels of explanation – the modern disciplines of biochemistry and molecular biology – have burgeoned.)

But to presume, as Wilson and others do, not simply that lower-level genetic or evolutionary explanations are adequate, and that therefore other very different types of truth-claim are not merely redundant but necessarily *wrong*, is an example of what might be termed "cross-explanatory **reductionism**."[12] Such "greedy" reductions may be celebrated by new atheists but are unlikely to persuade those committed to exploring **theistic** belief.[13]

Third on my list I place challenges posed by Darwinian narratives to Christian understandings of creation as divine design. In the eighteenth century much capital was made out of the apparent designedness both of physical systems and biological organisms exquisitely adapted to their environments. Famously, Richard Dawkins assessed the latter argument, in its quintessential form in William Paley's *Natural Theology*, as "informed by the best biological scholarship of his day" but "wrong, utterly and gloriously wrong."[14] Dawkins went on to show that evolution by natural selection can give rise to exquisite adaptation with all the appearance of divine design (though also to imperfect "design" solutions such as are likewise found in nature).

Every age has its preferred theological metaphors. Notably Scripture does not have that sense of creation as mechanical artifice, not surprisingly since ancient machines lacked the extraordinary ingenuity made possible by Newtonian physics. The closest Scriptural image would be that of God the potter (e.g. Is. 29.16; Jer. 18.6; Rom. 9.21), a much more organic idea, fascinatingly containing within it the notion that the potter as artist might discover possibilities in the course of their making.

---

[10] See e.g. Richard Dawkins, *The God Delusion* (London: Bantam, 2006), Ch. 5; Daniel Dennett, *Breaking the Spell: Religion as a Natural Phenomenon* (London: Penguin, 2006), Part II, and for a rebuttal, Justin Barrett, "Is the Spell Really Broken? Bio-psychological Explanations of Religion and Theistic Belief," *Theology and Science* Vol. 5, No. 1 (2007): 57–72.

[11] Francis Crick, *Of Molecules and Men* (Seattle, WA: University of Washington Press, 1966), 10.

[12] Christopher Southgate, ed. *God, Humanity and the Cosmos: A Textbook in Science and Religion* (London: Continuum, 2005 edn.), 161–162. Dennett himself recognizes the risk of "greedy reductionism" which he says occurs when "in their eagerness for a bargain, in their zeal to explain too much too fast, scientists and philosophers … underestimate the complexities, trying to skip whole layers or levels of theory in their rush to fasten everything securely and neatly to the foundation." Daniel Dennett, *Darwin's Dangerous Idea: Evolution and the Meaning of Life* (New York: Simon and Shuster, 1995), 82.

[13] Instead a very interesting new intermediate science has emerged – the cognitive science of religion, in which both believers and committed atheists are in dialogue. For an introduction see Justin Barrett, *Cognitive Science, Religion and Theology: From Human Minds to Divine Minds* (West Conshohocken, PA: Templeton Foundation Press, 2011).

[14] Dawkins, *The Blind Watchmaker* (London: Penguin, 1991), 5.

So Dawkins's critique of the designer God is of interest[15] but not of much corrosive effect on Christian thought. The bigger scientific challenge to the theology of creation comes in fact from the opposite direction. Is evolution, Dawkins's "blind watchmaker," too "blind," too radically haphazard and chance-ridden, to be a plausible way for God to have sought to realize God's purposes? We have no means of knowing how likely it was that life itself would arise on Earth. And in the more-than-3-billion-year history of life the biosphere has suffered five catastrophic extinction events, of which the largest, the Permian, is thought to have eliminated perhaps as many as 95% of the species then extant. The last of these events, the extinction of the dinosaurs, was in fact essential to the rise of mammals, including eventually hominins. This radically contingent history seems very far from the classical notion of God's creation of specific and enduring examples of life-forms.[16]

However, Simon Conway Morris has postulated that certain outcomes are extremely likely to arise in a long evolutionary process. He draws on the phenomenon of "convergent evolution" – so, for example, the "camera eye" (the type of vision humans possess) has evolved many times in separate evolutionary lines.[17] Intelligence of the sort humans possess, he thinks, is also highly likely to arise.[18] So in the possibility space of evolutionary outcomes, certain outcomes are "attractors" and will always tend to arise given time (and provided a mass extinction event does not intervene). This view is completely opposite to Stephen Jay Gould's conviction that the tape of evolution, were it re-run, would probably give rise to completely different outcomes.[19]

It is hard to see how science will resolve this profound disagreement between two eminent students of evolution.[20] After all, in the foreseeable future we shall only have one evolutionary history to reflect upon.[21] But it is interesting to reflect on what might be the theological response to each point of view. If it were to be established that Gould was right and evolutionary trajectories contained such a degree of chance that no type of outcome could even be called likely, then the

---

[15] Not least his observation that such a god would itself have to be designed, which forces Christian thinkers back to the re-examination of the philosophically durable concept of a necessary being.

[16] But it licenses a different and arguably more creative theology, in which God accompanies possibilities that unfold and develop within the evolutionary process, possibilities that God may not have known in detail in advance. This is a strong emphasis in the work of Ruth Page, see her *God and the Web of Creation* (London: SCM Press, 1996). It is conceivable within such a scheme to imagine God protecting possibilities that God knows to be generative of new levels of beauty, ingenuity, and complexity. Here I depart from Page, who wants to deny this long-range teleological component to God's interaction with creation. See Christopher Southgate, "Values and Disvalues in Creation," in *The T&T Clark Companion to the Doctrine of Creation*, ed. Jason Goroncy (London: Bloomsbury, forthcoming). So the history of the biosphere might not be guaranteed in every particular, yet the process might not be as precarious as might appear from some interpretations of the science.

[17] Simon Conway Morris, *Life's Solution: Inevitable Humans in a Lonely Universe* (Cambridge: Cambridge University Press, 2003), 151–158.

[18] Conway Morris, *Life's Solution*, 243–274.

[19] Stephen Jay Gould, *Wonderful Life: The Burgess Shale and the Nature of History* (London: Hutchinson Radius, 1990).

[20] For a mediating view see Andrew Davison, "'He fathers forth whose beauty is past change,' but 'Who knows how': Evolution and Divine Exemplarity," *Nova et Vetera*, English edition, Vol. 16, No. 4 (2018): 1067–1102.

[21] If humans were to detect communications from an extra-terrestrial civilization, this "sample" would already be biased, since advanced intelligence would have to have evolved for contact to be made.

Christian theologian might be tempted to invoke a strong providential influence on the course of evolution – God somehow kept a highly random process on track. (This would raise interesting questions in relation to God and creaturely suffering – if, for example, God's strongly providential influence was involved in wiping out the dinosaurs, causing great suffering to many creatures, but making possible the rise of mammals, and ultimately the evolution of human beings.)

If, on the other hand, Conway Morris is right to postulate these strong attractors in evolutionary possibility space, such as vision, intelligence, etc., then perhaps the emphasis of the theologian might shift to the overall design of the process, such that it possessed this property of almost certainly giving rise to phenomena such as intelligence (and ultimately, with freely choosing self-conscious intelligent being, the capacity to give and receive love). But whereas a strong requirement for providence in the evolutionary narrative poses questions for **theodicy**, a strong emphasis on initial design poses the opposite problem in re the meaningfulness of God's providential activity – what *was* God's ongoing relationship to and involvement with the process of evolution once God had designed it (see Box 6.4)?

Box 6.4

In response to objection three – Does the evolved world look like it was designed by God? – the author takes a really interesting line. He suggests that on either scenario – the world is so random or the world was inevitably going to take a certain shape – the theist has an adequate response. The author does not make a call on which scientific viewpoint is most likely to be true; instead, he reassures the reader that the challenge to faith on either viewpoint is limited.

The three remaining challenges are helpfully tracked by the collection of essays *Finding Ourselves after Darwin*, edited by Stan Rosenberg and his team.[22] The first section of the book covers the question of human beings created in the image of God. Although this features in few biblical texts,[23] it is a core element in Christian anthropology and has been used throughout the tradition to stress human distinctiveness from all other creatures. Even without evolutionary considerations, there would remain difficult questions as to how to interpret the *imago Dei*.[24] Good analyses have been provided by Noreen Herzfeld[25] and J. Wentzel van Huyssteen.[26] But there is a key question of theological method here: Which should be determinative, the best exegetical account of the phrase "image of God" in Genesis,[27] or the two Pauline mentions of Christ as the authentic divine image at 2. Corinthians 4.4 and Colossians 1.15?[28]

---

[22] Stanley Rosenberg, Michael Burdett, Michael Lloyd and Benno van den Toren eds., *Finding Ourselves after Darwin: Conversations on the Image of God, Original Sin, and the Problem of Evil* (Grand Rapids, MI: Baker Books, 2018), hereafter *FOAD*.

[23] In the Hebrew Bible only Genesis 1.26–7; 5.3; 9.6.

[24] The Latin phrase often used instead of "image of God".

[25] Noreen Herzfeld, *In Our Image: Artificial Intelligence and the Human Spirit* (Minneapolis, MN: Fortress Press, 2002).

[26] J. Wentzel van Huyssteen, *Alone in the World: Human Uniqueness in Science and Theology* (Grand Rapids, MI: Eerdmans, 2006). See also Mark Harris's essay in *FOAD*.

[27] J. Richard Middleton, *The Liberating Image: The imago Dei in Genesis 1* (Grand Rapids, MI: Brazos Press, 2005).

[28] John F. Kilner, *Dignity and Destiny: Humanity in the Image of God* (Grand Rapids, MI: Eerdmans, 2015).

The science of evolution intensifies questions about the image of God in two ways. First, it poses the chronological question – when did the image, however understood, arrive in human beings? Second, given the close biological relationship between humans and other hominins (now extinct), other primates, and indeed other mammals, are Christian thinkers any longer justified in asserting the absolute distinctiveness of humans as sole possessors of the divine image? David Clough in his pioneering work on animal theology has responded to the second question with a resolute "no." Clough argues that:

> It is the unique event of divinity taking up creatureliness that results in the unique imaging of God. In this one creature [Christ] is God truly revealed. This makes it clear that we can no longer speak without qualification of human beings as images of God … The account of the image of God evident in … New Testament texts makes clear that the imago Dei cannot function as a theologically significant marker between humans and other animals as a reading of Genesis 1 might suggest … Not merely the being of one species of creature, but the being of every kind of creature is transformed by the event of incarnation. The doctrine of the incarnation does not therefore establish a theological boundary between humans and other animals; instead, it is best understood as God stepping over the boundary between creator and creation and taking on creatureliness.[29]

The question of chronology clearly overlaps with the question of "reach" in the *imago Dei*. If humans are not uniquely in the image, then it is unnecessary to look for a point in the transition in primates from prehuman to recognizably human. This would come as a relief to many since the science of human evolution is so fluid, and has recently disclosed a series of great surprises – including the "hobbit man" of *Homo Floresiensis* and the remarkable bone collections now classified as *Homo Naledi*.

In recent work I have accorded priority – as Clough does – to the Christological texts in 2. Corinthians and Colossians cited earlier. This reflects the classic conviction that the life of Jesus tells us both as much as we can know about the life of God, and as much as we can know about the potential of human life to embody love of God and neighbor. So it is reasonable to suppose that the fullest expression of the image of God in human life will be Christlikeness.

I have proposed that the image of God in human beings should be thought of in terms of humans' response to the self-giving love found in, and received from, God the Holy Trinity.[30] This view is substantival, in terms of a presupposed capacity for love, functional, in terms of being a fundamental human vocation, relational, by its very nature, and eschatological, in that it is only as humans grow into the example of that self-giving response that we find in the Incarnate Christ that we start fully to manifest the divine image that is perfectly instantiated in Jesus.

I now develop this understanding of the *imago Dei*, both in relation to love for God and for neighbor. God's love for each person has an unreserved quality, it makes no calculations, holds nothing back (not even the life of the Incarnate Son). It seeks an unreserved response. It reduces that natural element of calculation by which humans commute their love for others. It also – vitally – refocuses that love, away from the idols that always crowd in on the human imagination,

---

[29] David L. Clough, *On Animals, Volume 1: Systematic Theology* (London: T&T Clark/Continuum, 2012), 367–373.

[30] Christopher Southgate, "Re-reading Genesis, John and Job: A Christian's Response to Darwinism," *Zygon* 46, 2 (2011): 370–395; *Theology in a Suffering World: Glory and Longing* (Cambridge: Cambridge University Press, 2018), 227–233.

and back toward the one Lord of creation and salvation. Purification and sanctification are two stuffy-sounding words, overused in pious homilies, but they are among the effects of an authentic response to the love that pours moment by moment from the Trinity, a love that creates as well as forgives.

Box 6.5

Southgate anticipates potential objections to his position. He recognizes that this is a complicated debate. He is not afraid to recognize that his reader (and other theologians) would want to challenge his position. So he identifies the objections and concedes that he needs to read Genesis in a certain way.

Crucial questions for my position are whether all humans are capable of making that loving and self-giving response to the divine love, and whether my suggestion does sufficient justice to the blanket status that the Genesis text seems to give humans (see Box 6.5). It is not only when humans are doing a specific thing – responding in love to the divine love – but all the time that humans are created in the image and likeness of God. This leads me to reconsider the foundational text in Genesis. Why, I wonder, must we read it in terms of once-for-all creation of any given human being? Might we not read it in terms of continuous creation? To imagine God saying in the heavenly court, "Let us, *continually*, be creating humans in our image."[31]

That has significant advantages in terms of an evolutionary understanding of the human being. There is always a problem in reconciling the picture that science gives, of the gradual emergence of what we think of as humanness, with the seeming once-off creation of humans in Genesis 1, and indeed Genesis 2. But the Christian tradition has rightly emphasized the importance of God's creation as not only initial but continual.[32] So is it not reasonable to postulate that God's image-making creativity acted continually on the emerging human, and has acted on each human being ever since, not once-for-all, but *continually, from moment to moment, in the offer of love that invites a response of love?*

How then is this to work in the life of a contemporary human, and how is it to resist the various objections that have very properly been leveled at models of the *imago Dei*?

My suggestion is that God continually, in every moment, offers that love that makes life what it is, with all its possibilities. And that offered love also creates the opportunity for the love to be returned, and spread to the neighbor, however understood. The divine love creates the self in its freedom, and the opportunity for the self to be given away in unselfish love. God's love, then, God's faithfulness and mercy, are imagined as not just new every morning (Lam. 3.23) but new every moment.

---

[31] Frances Young makes a related move, helpfully emphasizing the corporate dimension, when she claims that: "Together, through communion in community, the gift of God's image and likeness is being received and developed." *God's Presence: A Contemporary Recapitulation of Early Christianity* (Cambridge: Cambridge University Press, 2013), 181. She continues: "...this account acknowledges human failings and distortions while celebrating for the contemporary world the high dignity of God's gift," 183.

[32] e.g. Kristine A. Culp, "God Is Always Forming and Re-Forming the Mundane, Vulnerable Stuff of Creaturely Existence, Breathing Life and Glory into It." *Vulnerability and Glory: A Theological Account* (Louisville, KY: Westminster John Knox Press, 2010), 94.

So, wherever we see self-giving, costly relating to others for others' sake, I would hold that we see the image of God beginning to develop (see Box 6.6). One of the few things we know of

> **Box 6.6**
>
> The author is willing to bring out some radical implications of his position. He has argued that where you see "self-giving, costly relating to others," you can see "the image of God beginning to develop." He then documents that would include the Neanderthals and perhaps elephants and other animals.

Neanderthals is that they looked after individuals past child-bearing age who had broken limbs and severe arthritis – here we see, implicitly, signs of self-giving behavior after the image of God. I conclude more generally that we should not be afraid to see this proto-image in other primates, or indeed in elephants and other animals, resulting, once again, from the continual, moment-by-moment invitation offered by God's own love for creatures. Thus, I would contend that abandoning an absolute human distinctiveness based on the *imago Dei* actually enriches our understanding of God's relation to creatures.

This essay has roamed widely across the challenges that a Darwinian understanding poses to Christian theological formulations. The last two challenges to be addressed are closely linked

> **Box 6.7**
>
> Southgate now comes to the two hardest challenges. He has structured his paper in such a way that these two questions have more space. He also connects the two challenges together.

(see Box 6.7).[33] The first is the unsustainability in evolutionary terms of supposing either that a single couple was the origin of the human species (so-called "monogenism"[34]) or that their one act of rebellion introduced violence into the nonhuman world. Reconstructions of the history of the Earth show that savage predation and chronic disease predated the evolution of humans by tens of millions of years, and also that modern human beings arose gradually through a very complex process of interbreeding and separation of populations over perhaps 4 million years.

This leads to two troubling conclusions. First, the biological world has been "red in tooth and claw" ever since what became teeth and claws evolved. Second, this violence cannot be blamed on a human fall from harmonious relationship with God. These are straightforward conclusions for any biologically literate thinker, yet I continue to be amazed at how persistent is the conviction that a "cosmic fall" occasioned by human sin is the reason for the violence of natural forces and the sometimes violent struggle between animals. Bethany Sollereder has shown that it is

---

[33] And form the remaining two sections of *FOAD*.

[34] The eminent Jesuit paleontologist Pierre Teilhard de Chardin was required by the Roman Catholic authorities to subscribe to monogenism in a document given to him in 1925, and doubts as to the "soundness" of his position may have led to his being kept away from Europe for much of his career. See David Grumett and Paul Bentley, "Teilhard de Chardin, Original Sin and the Six Propositions," *Zygon* Vol. 53, No. 2 (2018): 303–330, and David Grumett, "Teilhard, the Six Propositions, and Human Origins: A Response," *Zygon* Vol. 54, No. 4 (2019): 954–964.

hard to sustain such a view even from the biblical texts themselves, let alone from a scientifically informed perspective.[35] The view that all disvalue in God's good creation stems from the primal human sin is also often traced to Augustine. In this regard it is interesting to note Rosenberg's recent rereading of Augustine, in which he suggests that Augustine's **prelapsarian** world, "very good" and under the providence of the sovereign God, already includes thorns and poisonous snakes. It may not after all be necessary for Augustinians to perform somersaults in order to assign all apparent disvalues in creation to human sin.[36]

Can anything, then, be salvaged from an understanding of the Fall as an event in human history with profound effects on the creation as a whole?[37] James K.A. Smith wants to accord as much ground to evolutionary insights as is compatible with what he sees as the fundamental narrative of Christianity, the characteristic U-shape of an initial good, a human fall into moral corruption, and redemption in Christ. Smith concedes that the fall might not have been of a couple but of a population "appointed" by God, and that the disvalue in the natural world might not have been a direct curse by God in response to sin but rather an ongoing failure of humans to exercise right dominion over the natural world.[38]

Note the method here: The scientific data are influential but they must fit in to the shape of the story as the author, or his tradition, has determined it. I return to this question of method later. For now I note two problems Smith's narrative shape leaves him with. His commitment to the "priority of the good" requires him to say that the nonhuman creation must be adjudged good before the Fall, despite its containing predation, disease, and extinction on a massive scale. Second, Smith still feels the need to say that the post-Fall state of that creation *in general* is humans' fault. It is hard to see how humans had that much general influence before the industrial era.

So, is there another narrative that can do justice to the science and still explain how an omnibenevolent creator God gave rise to a nonhuman world so full of struggle and extinction?

At this point it is as well to be clear as to what the "disvalues" of the nonhuman world are. The heading "natural evil" tends to be used for all the harms and resultant suffering in creation that cannot be ascribed to freely chosen human agency. That includes earthquakes, volcanoes, and tsunamis (even though human folly often exacerbates the sufferings these cause). But our concern here is the subset of natural evil called "evolutionary evil," the suffering caused by predation (and other violent competition within species), disease and parasitism, and the loss of value caused by extinction.

---

[35] Bethany Sollereder, *God, Evolution and Animal Suffering: Theodicy without a Fall* (London: Routledge, 2019), Ch. 2.

[36] Stanley Rosenberg, "Can Nature be "Red in Tooth and Claw" in the thought of Augustine?" in *FOAD*, 183–196. The one contemporary account that seriously seeks to tackle the chronological problem of assigning violence in nature to human sin is William Dembski's *The End of Christianity: Finding a Good God in an Evil World* (Nashville, TN: B&H Academic, 2009), with his invocation of "retroactive causation." Dembski's ingenious proposal is briskly and tellingly demolished by Michael Lloyd. Lloyd points out the disanalogy between God's (retroactively effective) saving act on the Cross, and God's supposed retroactive punishment of non-human creation for human sin; he also asks Dembski, "How is it redemptively coherent for the punishment to precede the crime and to be meted out on other creatures than the criminals?" *FOAD*, 207.

[37] The wider question of whether a predisposition to sin is part of human evolutionary inheritance is beyond the scope of the present essay.

[38] James K.A. Smith, "What Stands on the Fall? A Philosophical Exploration," in *Evolution and the Fall*, ed. William T. Cavanaugh and James K.A. Smith (Grand Rapids, MI: Eerdmans, 2017), 57–68.

To this, the first question that might be posed is: Do other animals *suffer* in any meaningful sense? I hold that although we cannot equate pain with suffering, nevertheless when creatures capable of feeling pain are trapped in situations of intense and/or protracted pain, they may plausibly be described as suffering, not least because the way they and their nervous systems behave resembles the way humans behave in similar contexts, whom we would definitely identify as suffering. And this suffering can be protracted. A whale may be literally eaten alive over many hours by sharks or orcas. It may take a whole minute for a leopard to pull down a full-grown antelope. Monkeys can experience severe distress from arthritis. Parasitism by liver flukes may cause prolonged abdominal pain in sheep and goats.[39]

A second question is: Does this suffering *matter*? Does it constitute a charge against the goodness of God? For Kenneth Miller, "the brutality of life is in the eye of the beholder" – it simply depends on whether you view life from the point of view of predator or prey. He goes on, "we cannot call evolution cruel if all we are really doing is assigning to evolution the raw savagery of nature itself. The reality of life is that the world often lacks mercy, pity, and even common decency."[40] Suffering, pain, waste, and extinction in the nonhuman world, for Miller, are just facts of nature – they have no moral content, and we should not project on them moral categories, which properly belong only to the sphere of human beings. This must seem to a Christian theologian a most curious position. If one poses the question – Why is the non-human world of value? – the normal Christian response would be: because God created it, and pronounced it good, because God continues to hold it in existence from moment to moment, and to nurture it with the divine love. So the sufferings of creatures *must* be a problem for Christian theology, even when no human beings are directly involved in the "transaction."

Denis Lamoureux finds "an underlying emotionalism and sentimentalism" in what he calls "Bambi" theodicies. He continues, "I believe that a great amount of suffering in nature is necessary in contributing to the Deus Absconditus character of the world."[41] So for him, God must allow very extensive suffering so as to be able to remain hidden. It is hard to see this as an effective defense of the loving character of God.

More contentious is my claim that extinction is a disvalue. Although perhaps 99.9% of all the species have ever existed are extinct, some say that this is simply a case of species having their time and disappearing. But I would hold that any extinction is always a loss of value to the biosphere as a whole. A whole strategy of being alive on the planet, a whole quality of living experience is lost when any organism becomes extinct. And in creatures with sophisticated sentience, depletion of numbers to near-extinction levels will cause suffering too, as mating opportunities and niche-constructed habitats disappear.

Box 6.8

In the preceding section, the author wants the reader to feel the full force of the objection. He considers those who want to keep science within a theological framework and insists that this is inappropriate. So the reader at this point can feel the almost "overwhelming" nature of the challenge.

---

[39] See also Christopher Southgate, *The Groaning of Creation: God, Evolution and the Problem of Evil* (Louisville, KY: Westminster John Knox Press, 2008), 3–4, 136n15.

[40] Kenneth R. Miller, *Finding Darwin's God: A Scientist's Search for Common Ground between God and Evolution* (New York: HarperCollins, 1999), 246.

[41] Denis Lamoureux, "Toward an Evangelical Evolutionary Theodicy," *Theology and Science* Vol. 18, No. 1 (2020): 12–30.

The problem for the Christian evolutionary theodicist is therefore to seek to understand the ways of a loving God who yet has created this biosphere full of suffering and extinction (see Box 6.8). But the problem is worse than that, as is well illustrated by Holmes Rolston's now-famous example of the insurance chick of the white pelican. This pelican, like a number of other predatory birds, hatches a second chick as an "insurance." The insurance chick is normally driven to the edge of the nest by its sibling, and once displaced is ignored by its parents. Its "purpose" is merely to ensure that one viable chick survives. It has only a 10% chance of fledging.[42] If the focus is on the pelican species as a whole, this strategy, "careless" and "wasteful" of individuals as it might seem, has "worked" for the white pelican, which as Rolston points out has lived successfully on Earth for 30 million years. This seems to speak of a God who *uses* processes that necessarily lead to lives that are all distress, with little or no prospect of flourishing.

We have seen that these difficulties cannot be parked on human sin. Joshua Moritz's ingenious effort to blame decisions by animals[43] also seems inadequate as explanation. In what sense does a tiger reject the will of God when it stalks a goat? More plausible are those theodicies that make a form of fallenness intrinsic to creation from its very beginning. This gets round the chronological difficulties noted above with human-fall explanations. Michael Lloyd has proposed that the rebellion of angels must be to blame for disvalues in creation.[44] Celia Deane-Drummond and Neil Messer both invoke a mysterious force or factor opposing the benevolent creative will of God. For Deane-Drummond this is best understood in terms of the "Shadow Sophia" terminology of Sergei Bulgakov;[45] Messer prefers to draw on the "Nothingness" postulated by Karl Barth.[46]

All these "primordial fall" strategies suffer from two major difficulties. Theologically, they require there to be a force sufficiently powerful to distort radically the divine intentions in creation. If Messer is right to point to the "peaceable kingdom" passage in Isaiah 11.6–9 as indicative of God's will for creation, then these primordial-fall accounts imply that God set out to create peaceable, straw-eating lions and was unable to do so. This seems out of keeping with the Christian confession of God as the sovereign creator *ex nihilo*. But there is also a major scientific objection. What contemporary science helps us see is that the same forces in nature generate both value and disvalue. Just as the tectonic forces that generate earthquakes and tsunamis are also part of the cycles that have kept life sustained on the surface of the Earth for billions of years, so also the processes of evolution by natural selection have generated both myriad instances of suffering and extinction, *and also* extraordinary, beautiful, and ingenious strategies of creaturely adaptation. The *same processes* give rise to both, and cannot coherently be dissected into value generation and disvalue generation.

This observation about the ambiguity of the world has led a number of authors including myself to presume that if God could have given rise to this sort of world by a less disvalue-filled process, the Christian God of love would have done so. Therefore, we suppose that evolution by natural selection must have been the *only way* in which God could give rise to such a world. This "only way" argument has been much criticized. Lloyd observes that its proponents need to do

---

[42] Rolston, *Science and Religion*, 137–139.

[43] Joshua Moritz, "Animal Suffering, Evolution, and the Origins of Evil: Toward a 'Free-creatures' Defense,'" *Zygon* Vol. 49, No. 2 (2014): 348–380.

[44] Michael Lloyd, "The Fallenness of Nature: Three Nonhuman Suspects," *FOAD* 262–279.

[45] Celia Deane-Drummond, "Perceiving Natural Evil through the Lens of Divine Glory?" *Zygon* Vol. 53, No. 3 (2018): 792–807.

[46] Neil Messer, "Evolution and Theodicy: How (Not) to do Science and Theology," *Zygon* Vol. 53, No. 3 (2018): 821–835.

work on what this constraint on God's sovereign power is.[47] It must be a logical constraint if it is to limit an omnipotent God, but the logic is beyond us. Robin Attfield perhaps puts it most judiciously when he observes that "we have no reason to believe that a world with a better balance of good over evil than the actual world is possible, or that the actual world is not a world that a good God would create."[48]

However, it may properly be objected that the only way argument seems to make God a consequentialist calculator optimizing a system, rather than a loving deity who cares for every individual creature. This illustrates just how difficult an exercise it is to construct any sort of theodicy, and this whole area of theology needs to be approached with great prudence and humility.[49] However, as a cautious attempt to construct a net of explanation that might do some sort of justice the problem, I have formulated a "compound theodicy," including the following proposals:

- I acknowledge the goodness of creation in giving rise to all sorts of values.
- I further acknowledge the suffering and extinction that are intrinsic to a creation evolving according to Darwinian principles. Moreover, I hold to the (unprovable) assumption that an evolving creation was the only way in which God could give rise to the sort of beauty, diversity, sentience and sophistication of creatures that the biosphere now contains (the "only way" argument).
- I affirm God's co-suffering with every sentient being in creation – the "co-suffering" argument.
- I take the Cross of Christ to be the epitome of this divine compassion – the moment of God's taking ultimate responsibility for the pain of creation – and, with the Resurrection, to inaugurate the transformation of creation.
- I further stress the importance of giving some account of the eschatological fulfillment of creatures that have known no flourishing in this life. A God of loving relationship could never regard any creature as a mere evolutionary expedient. Drawing on a phrase of Jay McDaniel's, I nickname this the "pelican heaven" argument.
- If divine fellowship with creatures such as ourselves is in any sense a goal of evolutionary creation, then I advocate a very high doctrine of humanity, supposing that indeed humans are of very particular concern to God. That does not exclude a sense that God delights in every creature which emerges within evolution, but it leads to the possibility that humans have a crucial and positive role, co-operating with their God in the healing of the evolutionary process – the "co-redeemer" argument.[50]

Addressing the critique that "If God could give rise, ultimately, to a suffering-free state of creatures, why did God not just create this heaven in the first place?," I respond, "Our guess must be that though heaven can eternally preserve those [creaturely] selves, subsisting in suffering-free

---

[47] Lloyd, "Conclusion to Part 3," *FOAD*, 329.

[48] Robin Attfield, *Creation, Evolution and Meaning* (Aldershot: Ashgate, 2006), 141.

[49] As I wrote years ago, "All theodicies that engage with real situations rather than philosophical abstractions, and endeavour to give an account of the God of the Christian Scriptures, arise out of protest and end in mystery." Southgate, *Groaning*, 132. However, at least evolutionary **theodicy** avoids the charge made by anti-theodicists that the priority must be to attend to and help the victim, rather than construct theories about the victim's plight. Clearly the myriad victims of the violence of evolutionary struggle are almost entirely beyond our help.

[50] Southgate, *Groaning*, 16.

relationship, it could not give rise to them in the first place."[51] Russell describes this as "the 'heaven requires earth' argument."[52]

Box 6.9

Southgate finally offers his "solution." He suggests a "compound theodicy." He concedes that this response can be "severely criticized"; however, he has put the reader in an interesting position. The reader must either opt for one of the unsatisfactory responses that he has described and explained why they are problematic or opt for his compound theodicy. He is suggesting that this is the "least-worst basis" for finding a way forward.

Space does not permit a full analysis of this compound theodicy (see Box 6.9).[53] Each of the bulleted steps could be (and has been) severely criticized, and yet taken together I consider them the least-worst basis for exploring the puzzling ways of the Christian God with the biological world.

Box 6.10

To conclude this chapter, the author then compares his approach to a key conversation partner – Neil Messer. He notes how two academics with similar training can arrive at contrasting conclusions.

I want to end this essay by scrutinizing the difference between Neil Messer's approach and my own (see Box 6.10). It raises some interesting questions of theological method, as well as being an example of courteous intellectual exchange. We agree on key points: we both aim to give full weight to the Christian doctrinal tradition, and agree that suffering and destruction are intrinsic to the evolutionary process underlying the whole history of life on Earth. Nevertheless, I see his appeal to "nothingness" as a counter-force to God from the first moment of creation as theologically and scientifically flawed: Messer sees my acceptance that God used violence to create as incompatible with the God known in Jesus.[54] I say his approach "leads [him] away from a

---

[51] Southgate, *Groaning*, 90.

[52] Robert J. Russell, "Moving ahead on Southgate's Compound Only-Way Evolutionary Theodicy," *Theology and Science* Vol. 17, No. (2) (2019): 185–194. To clarify: my proposal is that there have been three great phases in God's action in the world. First the "old creation," which operates with the physical laws with which we are familiar, and the biological process of Darwinian evolution. Second, the Christ-event, which transforms the scope of human possibility. However, the transformation of the world, though profound, is not immediately apparent. The processes of the old creation go on. For whatever reason in the mystery of the divine economy, the radical transformation of the cosmos, by which it will attain its final harmonious state, awaits human beings' growth into authentic freedom, "the freedom of the glory of the children of God" (Rom. 8.21). Only then will come the third great action of God, the radical transformation of the physical universe, such that (resurrected) bodily existence is possible without suffering or struggle. Note that the second phase is presumed to be impossible without the first, and the third without the second.

[53] Michael J. Murray in *Nature Red in Tooth and Claw: Theism and the Problem of Animal Suffering* (Oxford: Oxford University Press, 2008) also concludes that a compound approach is necessary.

[54] Neil Messer, "Natural Evil after Darwin" in *Theology after Darwin* ed. Michael Northcott and R.J. Berry (Carlisle: Paternoster, 2009), 139–154.

willingness to learn from the sciences about the way things really are," and "runs the risk of making theology appear too defensive, too bent on **mysterification**, to be part of an authentic

Box 6.11
Southgate has created the word "mysterification" by which he means ascribing understanding to mystery rather than an explanation utilizing careful analysis. Creating a distinctive vocabulary is a key part of creative theology.

conversation":[55] he responds that I am right: he is "unwilling to learn from the natural sciences about the way things *really* are (theologically speaking), because [he denies] that they are competent to tell us about what Christian confession recognizes as the most fundamental reality of the world."[56]

Here we arrive at the same tension we noted with Smith's essay on the Fall. Is it that theology knows the shape of the story, into which scientific insights must fit? Or is it that the sciences must be allowed a more equal part in the dialogue,[57] even to reshaping some of the perceptions of God and the world that we inherit from Scripture and the Fathers? Or is it that some test cases require one approach, and others the other?[58] Messer and I are both profoundly indebted to Scripture – he offers a particular reading of Genesis 1, in which God's verdict that the creation is "very good" signals God's intentions rather than the actual state of things; Messer is also profoundly influenced by Isaiah 11.6–9. I read "very good" in Genesis 1.31 as "optimally fit for purpose" (a more Hebraic understanding of the adjective *tôv*), and am influenced by texts such as Psalms 104 and Job 38–39 which depict God's provision for predators.

So two Christian thinkers (both with Ph.D.s in biological science) can arrive at radically different responses to the challenge posed by evolutionary suffering, on the basis of small but highly significant nuances in theological and **hermeneutical** understanding. All I would say in conclusion is that it is my conviction that these are the sorts of great question on which theology should focus, and that in the absence of definitive answers, our task as teachers and students is to fall in love with the questions.

---

[55] Southgate, "Re-reading," 384.

[56] Messer, "Evolution," 829.

[57] For a thorough evaluation of these different methodologies see Neil Messer, *Science in Theology* (London: Bloomsbury, 2020).

[58] Christopher Southgate, "Response, with a Select Bibliography," *Zygon* Vol. 53, No. 3 (2018): 909–930.

Part IV

God and Ethics

7

Sin and the Faces of Responsibility[1] (see Box 7.1)

Leigh Vicens

RESEARCH LEVEL 4

Box 7.1

Having footnote 1 next to the title of the article is unusual. However, this is where the author wants to both acknowledge an academic debt (she is grateful to the work of Gary Watson) and locate the article within a debate (this article should be read in the light of Gary Watson's insights). Academic integrity is essential. One must always acknowledge the source of ideas that you are using in an article. In addition, linking your piece with an ongoing debate in the academic invites other academics to build on the emerging conversation.

Editors' Introduction

This is an excellent example of a deep, thoughtful, creative discussion of an age-old problem in theology. The author poses the dilemma by introducing three claims. These are: No human being (except Christ) can avoid sin; we are responsible for our sin; and we are responsible only for what we can avoid. The author then takes us on a journey. In a comprehensive survey of the literature she considers those who reject the first claim (perhaps we could have avoided sin, but it is just that most of us end up sinning); she then looks at those who reject the second (perhaps we are not actually responsible for our sin). Then she suggests that with so much Christian practice (indeed the whole Gospel) dependent on these claims, a different way needs to be found. She suggests that humans are blamed as a "protest" against our evil tendency; and God's wrath is also a "protest" against our evil tendency. It is not that individuals themselves are blamed, but that we rightly affirm that we should live lives of goodness rather than evil. The author concedes that the implications of her argument are radical (especially in respect to hell).

---

[1] The title of this chapter takes its inspiration from Gary Watson's "Two Faces of Responsibility," *Philosophical Topics* Vol. 24, No. 2 (1996): 227–248, in which he first distinguished between different senses of responsibility and introduced the notion of responsibility as attributability.

The Craft of Innovative Theology: Argument and Process, First Edition. Edited by John Allan Knight and Ian S. Markham.
© 2022 John Wiley & Sons Ltd. Published 2022 by John Wiley & Sons Ltd.

Introduction

This chapter explores a tension between three claims about sin that Christians have reason to believe, and offers a resolution to the tension consistent with biblical teaching and human experience. The first claim is this:

1) No human being (except Christ) can avoid sin.[2]

For "all have sinned and fall short of the glory of God" (Romans 3:23).[3] The fact that all have sinned is not just some unhappy coincidence; it's not just that everyone *so far* has sinned. Rather, some kind of necessity apparently attaches to sinning: sin seems *inevitable* for humans. This is the flip side of the universal human need for salvation – which the New Testament characterizes as salvation *from sin* (Matt. 1:21; Luke 1:77). Paul describes sin as a kind of "power" (Romans 3:9) which has dominion over all of us, against which we are helpless. As Douglas Moo notes, this is why the Savior is portrayed, not as a teacher of good morals, but as a *liberator* – "one who has the power to set us free from our sins" (2013, p. 112).

The second claim is:

2) We are responsible for our sin.

This claim is also one that Christians generally accept, and with biblical warrant. Sin is equated with violating God's law and associated with guilt (1 John 3:4); it makes us liable to judgment (Matt. 5:22), condemnation (Matt. 12:36–7), and "recompense" (2 Cor. 5:10) – and makes us fitting targets of the wrath of God (Rom. 3:5–6). On the intuitive assumption that such attitudes and practices are only appropriate responses to wrongs for which the subject is responsible, it follows that we are responsible for sin.

And then there is the third claim:

3) We are responsible only for what we can avoid.

Admittedly, this one seems to have less in the way of biblical support. And I have suggested elsewhere (Vicens 2018) that Paul may have even rejected this claim (see Box 7.2).[4]

Box 7.2

The author has lived with these questions for many years. Here she cites her work from 2018, then she has a footnote where she explains that her argument then might be undermined by the argument that she is making in this article. The reader is invited into a complex conversation where the author is changing her own mind about an issue.

---

[2] This claim may have to be qualified slightly, for two reasons: first, according to some Christians (e.g. Roman Catholics), Mary the mother of Jesus was also without sin; and second, the first humans may also have been able to avoid sinning (though they did not in fact do so). Thanks to Kevin Timpe (personal communication) for reminding me of these points.

[3] All biblical quotations are taken from the *New Revised Standard Version*.

[4] I suggested this on the basis of (among other things) Paul's statement that God justly inflicts wrath on those who are "made for destruction" and whose hearts God chooses to harden (Romans 9:14–24). I now think that if the universalist reading of Paul discussed at the end of this chapter is correct, then Paul might have accepted a modified version of this claim, along the lines I propose.

Moreover, a significant number of philosophers who consider the subjects of free will and moral responsibility also reject it; indeed, attempting to prove it false has become a veritable cottage industry.[5] And yet, many also find this claim intuitively obvious, and rely on it as a premise in arguing against the compatibility of moral responsibility and determinism. I do not have the space here to review the reasoning in favor of claim 3, and so this chapter can be understood to consider a problem or puzzle for those Christians who do find the claim at least *prima facie* plausible. If it should turn out that the only way to resolve the problem is a wholesale rejection of claim 3, then perhaps in spite of its intuitiveness, the claim really should be rejected; maybe this is "wisdom of the world" which God's revelation shows to be foolishness.[6] Yet I hope to show that there is an alternative and less costly way to resolve the tension. In brief, my proposal is to disambiguate the word "responsible" and interpret it differently in claims 2 and 3 (see Box 7.3).

Box 7.3

The author has posed the dilemma. We have three propositions that many Christians which to affirm. She explains the significance and meaning of the propositions. Shen proposes a way to solve the problem by interpreting the word "responsible" in different ways in proposition two and three.

Attempts to Resolve the Tension: Reconsidering Claims 1 and 3

I have referred to a "tension," but the astute reader will notice that there is an outright contradiction between the three claims, such that any two taken together entail the negation of the third. For instance, claims 2 and 3 taken together entail that we *can* avoid sin, whereas claim 1 says that we *cannot*. How have Christians traditionally dealt with this problem? Many, surely, have not dealt with it at all, not recognizing the inconsistency among their beliefs, or simply throwing up their hands and saying it's a mystery. Others have rejected claim 1 – the idea that sin is inevitable for human beings. Some contemporary philosophers have suggested that sin is just very *likely*, but not absolutely certain; Richard Swinburne (1989), for instance, says sin is "almost unavoidable," while Thomas Talbott (2008) describes it, variably, as "virtually" guaranteed, "seemingly" inevitable, and "nearly" universal. Perhaps, on this view, if there is a universal need of salvation, then salvation is fundamentally not about sin, but something else, such as abundant life.[7]

---

[5] The principle of alternative possibilities (PAP), as formulated (and rejected) first by Harry Frankfurt, "Alternative Possibilities and Moral Responsibility," *Journal of Philosophy* Vol. 66 (1969): 828–839. It states that an agent is morally responsible for doing something only if she could have done otherwise. Claim 3 entails the PAP (If you are able to avoid doing something, then you are able to do something else), so any argument against PAP is an argument against claim 3.

[6] Pascal took the doctrine of original sin to be God's foolishness which is "wiser than all the wisdom of men," quoted in Douglas Moo, "Sin in Paul," in *Fallen: A Theology of Sin*, ed. Christopher Morgan and Robert Peterson (Wheaton, IL: Crossway, 2013), 107–130. Presumably because the idea that we are blameworthy for the sin of Adam contradicts something like claim 3 (for Adam's sin seems like something his descendants could not have prevented). However, I don't think the "message of the cross" which Paul was talking about in 1 Corinthians has implications one way or another for claim 3.

[7] Thanks to Simon Kittle (personal communication) for suggesting to me this possibility.

As has already been mentioned, still others reject claim 3. One version of the doctrine of original sin may be thought to provide theological grounds for such rejection. On this version, the first humans' sin resulted in a corruption of human nature which makes sin inevitable for all subsequent human beings. Although we post-lapsarian humans could have done nothing to prevent the first humans' sin, still we are responsible for our corrupted state, or at least for the sins which we necessarily commit as a result of that state.

Another way of interpreting the doctrine of original sin would imply not a wholesale rejection of claim 3, but instead an exception. The exception is intuitive: we may be responsible for something we cannot avoid doing if we previously did something (which we could have avoided doing – and so for which we are responsible) that made it the case that we now cannot avoid doing the thing in question.[8] (This exception takes into account, among other things, the way our previous actions affect the development of habits and traits of character, which then close off some courses of action for us, making others, sometimes, inevitable.) One might say we are "directly" responsible for the things we could have avoided doing, and "indirectly" responsible for the things we could not have avoided doing only because of things we did previously that we could have avoided doing.

How would this help explain the inevitability of sin? Well, some scholars have developed Augustine's idea that *in Adam all sinned*[9] into a theory on which we each were in fact able to avoid humanity's first sin. On one view, which Michael Rea calls "The Fission Theory," Adam and his posterity are distinct individuals who shared a common temporal state, and who underwent fission at the time of Adam's first sin, splitting into all the people who have ever lived or will (2007, p. 334). Rea notes that on this view, "though I am blamed for Adam's sin, it is also true that I could have prevented Adam's sin. After all, *I was Adam*, and… Adam could have prevented Adam's sin" (2007, p. 342). Oliver Crisp, along similar lines, suggests that "Adam and his progeny are somehow metaphysically united" (2009, p. 438), but rather than going the fission route, Crisp proposes a four-dimensionalist account according to which Adam and his heirs "are all members of one persisting entity … that we might call *Fallen Humanity*" (2009, p. 438). On this view, the corruption of nature that Adam incurred was "transmitted to all later phases of the life of this entity" by divine arrangement (2009, p. 440).

Crisp admits that such theories are "strong mead that may be difficult to swallow" (2009, p. 443); but since he says the problem of "the transmission of Adam's sin (and guilt)" is a theological difficulty "at the heart of the Christian faith that many of the greatest minds in Christendom have struggled to overcome" (2009, pp. 443–444), he apparently finds the mead palatable. I do not. Like the wholesale rejection of claim 3, the idea that we all somehow really sinned in Adam seems incredible to me. While I do not have a good argument against the

---

[8] This is a rough approximation, as it does not take into account omissions, or the fact that we might be responsible for *not* doing something. But these complications need not concern us here.

[9] Augustine was himself interpreting Paul, though as Philip Quinn notes, this idea seems to depend on a mistranslation of Romans 5:12. See Philip Quinn, "Sin and Original Sin," in *A Companion to Philosophy of Religion*, 2nd edn., ed. Charles Taliaferro, Paul Draper, and Philip Quinn (Cambridge, MA: Blackwell Publishing, 2010), 617.

metaphysical possibilities Rea and Crisp propose, I can only believe what I can believe, and so I will not consider such possibilities further (see Box 7.4).[10]

Box 7.4

Footnote 10 is an excellent example of keeping the text tight and clear (so the reader is not confused), yet demonstrating that, in this case, a theologian has changed his mind in what is considered essential to the Christian faith. Footnotes are not simply places where the source of an idea is acknowledged and appropriately cited, but also can be places where the ideas in the text are developed, which are relevant but not essential to the argument.

Attempts to Resolve the Tension: Rejecting or Revising Claim 2

Are there other options? Well, the rejection of claim 2 has not been explored yet in this chapter. Those who accept the traditional doctrine of original sin (or simply the inevitability of sin) but who find the rejection of claim 3 unthinkable may be led to consider this possibility. And more generally, free will skeptics who take free will to be a necessary condition for moral responsibility have explored this option. One prominent Christian free will skeptic, Derk Pereboom, has argued on philosophical and empirical grounds that it is implausible that we are morally responsible in the "basic desert" sense, i.e. the sense in which we *deserve* to be blamed or praised, rewarded or punished for what we do. Pereboom's position may seem to rule out as unjustifiable attitudes such as gratitude or indignation and practices such as reward or punishment that are traditionally associated with judgments of moral responsibility – not to mention attitudes and practices especially associated with (Christian) religion, such as guilt, repentance, confession, and forgiveness. Yet Pereboom has maintained that some of these attitudes and practices (but not others) may be justified on "forward-looking" grounds (i.e. those concerned with increasing positive consequences and decreasing negative ones), insofar as they promote goods such as reform, reconciliation, and protection. For instance, while retributive punishment is ruled out by his position, incapacitation of a dangerous criminal is not; and while resentment and forgiveness – conceived as the renunciation of resentment – are ruled out (since resentment presupposes desert), one could still feel sadness at having been wronged, and could "cease to regard past wrongful behavior as a reason to weaken or dissolve a relationship" (2014, p. 189) – so something similar to forgiveness could be preserved.

---

[10] One thing to note, however, is that Crisp has apparently changed his mind about what, exactly, is at the heart of the Christian faith. In a later article in which he identifies the "core tenets common to all historic, orthodox doctrines of original sin," he says he no longer thinks the idea of guilt transferred from the first humans to the rest of us is part of it, and indeed that "the biblical warrant for [such an idea] is thin." I believe my proposal for resolving the problem outlined above is consistent with the core tenets of the doctrine of original sin identified by Crisp in this later article: "*first*, that there was an original pair from whom we are all descended, *second*, that this pair committed the primal sin which adversely affects all their offspring; and *third*, that all human beings after the fall of the original pair are in need of salvation, without which they will perish." See Oliver Crisp, "Original Sin and Atonement" in *The Oxford Handbook of Philosophical Theology*, ed. Thomas Flint and Michael Rea (New York: Oxford University Press, 2009), 257, fn. 12.

Some might find Pereboom's picture of life (and Christianity) without "basic desert" responsibility to be too austere, while others raise concerns about justifications of moral practices focused exclusively on consequences, which might be thought to ignore issues of justice or fail to respect human personhood. For my part, I wonder if there is some understanding of moral responsibility that lies between the very strong conception which (I believe) Pereboom and other skeptics have in mind when they discuss "basic desert" responsibility, and the very weak, non-desert-involving, conception with which they seek to replace it. One view of responsibility that I find attractive (in some respects – to be specified) is called "attributionism." Attributionists hold that you are responsible for what you do if it is attributable to you, in the sense that it reflects something "deep" or significant about you. Different attributionists identify the significant in different ways – one's "moral personality" or "evaluative judgments," for example (see Talbert 2019 for specifics) – but the details need not concern us here. A self-centered orientation, lack of concern for others, racist or sexist beliefs – these are the sorts of personality features or attitudes that might be revealed in action (or inaction), and for which one can properly be held responsible, on the attributionists' view.[11] The important thing to note here is that if you act in a way that reveals, say, ungratefulness or disrespect, it does not matter how you came to have this feature, or whether you could have avoided it; you have still revealed yourself to be an ungrateful or disrespectful person, and this is blameworthy, according to their view.[12]

Critics will immediately say that this is unfair, for the story of how someone came to be and to act in a certain (say, immoral) way should matter to our attributions of responsibility; if a person was formed in such unfortunate circumstances that he really could not have been expected to show gratitude or respect in a particular case, then he does not deserve to be blamed or otherwise sanctioned for his bad behavior.

How do attributionists respond to this criticism? Some have proposed that blame should not be understood as a form of *sanction*, but rather something else. There are a number of theories on offer about the nature of blame, ranging from the views that blame is a simple judgment that someone has done wrong, or an emotional reaction to wrongdoing, to those that take blaming to involve making changes to the way one relates to the wrongdoer (see Tognazzini and Coates 2018 for a nice summary of such views). One proposal made by a theorist friendly to attributionism – Angela Smith – is that blame is a form of protest. After critiquing other theories of blame on offer, Smith proposes the following account:

> To *blame* another is ... to modify one's own attitudes, intentions, and expectations toward that person as a way of *protesting* (i.e. registering and challenging) the moral claim implicit in her conduct, where such protest implicitly seeks some kind of moral acknowledgement on the part of the blameworthy agent and/or on the part of others in the moral community.
> (2013, p. 43)[13]

---

[11] Whereas on Watson's original view (see footnote 1) responsibility as attributability and responsibility as accountability come apart, according to contemporary attributionists attributability is sufficient for accountability.

[12] For a recent Christian account and defense of attributionism, see Couenhoven, who uses the view to explain how we can be responsible for inherited (original) sin. Jesse Couenhoven, *Stricken by Sin, Cured by Christ: Agency, Necessity, and Culpability in Augustinian Theology* (New York: Oxford University Press, 2013).

[13] Smith is here picking up and developing a suggestion made earlier by Pamela Hieronymi (2001). See Angela Smith, "Moral Blame and Moral Protest," in *Blame: Its Nature and Norms* (New York: Oxford University Press, 2013), 27–48.

Pereboom also appeals to the idea that blame may be a form of moral protest, but on his account, the justification for such blame is consequentialist, in terms of the goods of protection (for instance, by protesting "a past action that persists as a present threat"), (re)formation (by contributing to "the moral improvement of those who witness the protest"), and reconciliation (of an "already-reformed wrongdoer") (2017, p. 129).[14] This obviously does not show how blame-as-protest could be deserved (since Pereboom denies that it is). But perhaps an alternative non-consequentialist justification of blame-as-protest might be given. (This would also seem desirable insofar as protesting wrongdoing is appropriate *even if there is no expected net benefit* to such protest.)

One possible way of justifying the protestation of wrongdoing is by appeal to its *symbolic value*. Thomas Hill (1979) and Robert Adams (1999) both characterize the symbolic value of an action as something distinct from the positive consequences it may have. For instance, Adams considers that even if we supposed, as Dietrich Bonhoeffer seemed to, that Bonhoeffer's saluting the Nazis would have the best consequences (since to have refrained from saluting might have undermined his conspiratorial involvement in the Abwehr), a refusal to salute would have had value in terms of its "expressive significance," as a way of being "for what one loves and against what one hates" (1999, p. 219). Similarly, casting blame on someone for some serious wrongdoing – a racist act, say – might have expressive significance as a way of taking a stand against it and for the good to which it is opposed (say, human equality); and such symbolic value may justify the blame even if it is not expected to have positive consequences.

Hopefully this is enough to show there might be a justification for blame-as-protest that is not *consequentialist*. But does it show that such blame might be *deserved*? Or have we just replaced one non-desert-invoking justification of blame with another? It is not clear to me. On the one hand, some authors apparently take all non-consequentialist justifications of blame to be "basic desert" justifications. Gregg Caruso and Stephen Morris, for instance, seem to *define* "basic desert" in terms of how it would be appropriate to treat someone *when considerations about the consequences of treatment are ruled out* (2017, p. 838) – in which case, the account of blame I have just sketched would count as "basically" deserved. Then again, Caruso and Morris also equate a "basic desert" perspective with a "retributivist" one, and define retributivism in terms of "justification for treatment whereby an individual is either *rewarded or punished as payback* for the moral rights and wrongs he has committed" (2017, p. 841, emphasis added) – and I don't think that blame-as-protest is best construed as a form of punishment as payback.[15] While for the most part those who write about moral responsibility take their subject to be the "basic desert" kind, Michael McKenna notes

---

[14] Smith likewise suggests that blame-as-protest has a forward-looking justification when she confronts the objection that, if blame is aimed at getting the wrongdoer to acknowledge his wrongdoing, then it would not make sense if the wrongdoer has died, as in the case of blaming antebellum slaveholders in the US. Her response is that blame can still have a "point" if its secondary aim is "moral recognition on the part of the wider community." But then she acknowledges that, on such a view, it would not make sense for "a present-day Norwegian to blame southern slaveholders." Given considerations of symbolic value that I will discuss, I think it may make sense even in such a case to blame, since there is always a "point" to taking a stand against evil and for the good. See Smith, "Moral Blame," 44–45.

[15] Christopher Marshall briefly discusses a "symbolic theory" of punishment which he says "seeks to overcome the dichotomy between the retributive and utilitarian theories of punishment, which for the last two centuries have generally been defined in contrast to one another." Perhaps the view of blame discussed here could likewise be construed as a middle way between retributive and utilitarian theories. See Christopher Marshall (2001). *Beyond Retribution: A New Testament Vision for Justice, Crime, and Punishment* (Grand Rapids, MI: Eerdmans, 2001), 135.

that it is not clear what, exactly, they mean by this term.[16] He offers a variety of possible interpretations, ranging from the (stronger) claim that it would be good for the blameworthy to suffer, to the (weaker) claim that the blameworthy "would have no basis for complaint if those whom she wronged, or relevant others, were to cause [her] harm merely by expressing to [her] their moral anger and their moral demands for proper redress" (2009, p. 12). On the stronger reading, blame as protest would probably not be deserved (since the aim of protest is not to induce suffering). But on the weaker reading, it might be.[17] (The question of whether moral *anger* is appropriate even if a person's wrongdoing was unavoidable is one that I will return to shortly.)

Matt King, another attributionist who takes us to be responsible for those actions that "reflect distinctive features of our agency, our commitments and values, our judgments about what matters" (2014, p. 402), rejects especially strong interpretations of "desert" according to which someone's deserving blame implies that it would be good that they suffer. He proposes instead to understand desert "in terms of a fittingness relation" (2014, p. 403); in other words, the blameworthy are the fitting objects of blame – just as, and in the same way, the admirable are fitting objects of admiration, the fearsome are fitting objects of fear, and so on. Supposing he is right and desert is best understood in terms of fittingness – and blame is interpreted as a form of protest, as Smith suggests – then I think we can say that one who has done wrong may *deserve* blame, regardless of whether they could have avoided the wrongdoing. Why? Well, consider the example given earlier, of a person who commits some racist act – uttering a racist slur against one's neighbor in the midst of a dispute, say – and suppose the person was raised in a racist household and steeped in a racist culture so that it very well might be true that it was inevitable that they would form racist attitudes and behave in racist ways. Still, in uttering the slur, the person makes themselves a fitting object of protest; it would be appropriate for some bystander to the dispute to call out that person's wrongdoing, and demand that they acknowledge it as such.

Responsibility Revisionism: Taking Stock and Further Implications

> **Box 7.5**
>
> Some of the argument here is technical. This is not surprising; this is a research article that is seeking to reflect on a central paradox at the heart of the Christian faith – the inevitability of sin and therefore the appropriate responsibility for sin. At this point in the article, the author pauses and "takes stock." She gives the reader an overview of the argument so far. The focus so far has been on the arguments for rejecting the second claim, "We are responsible for our sin." To defend Christian practice, Vicens suggests sinners are worthy of blame (understood as a "fitting object of moral protest") as a symbol of opposing evil.

---

[16] Randolph Clarke has also suggested, in a critique of John Martin Fischer's view of responsibility, that perhaps "the question of an agent's responsibility" is not a "yes or no" matter, but instead "a question of what sort of responsibility such an agent might bear" – and that corresponding to different types of moral responsibility might be different types of moral desert (2010, p. 249). Randolph Clarke, "Determinism and Our Self-Conception," *Philosophy and Phenomenological Research* Vol. 80, No. 1 (2010): 242–250.

[17] Neil Levy has suggested (personal communication) that perhaps basic desert is that desert which "attaches to a person in virtue of what she has done, *independent of relational properties.*" In that case, the view I consider below, of desert understood in terms of a fittingness relation, may not count as "basic." However, this view should not be considered relational in the sense in which Smith's seems to be; on her view, blame seems to require an audience in order for it to have a point (see footnote 14).

To take stock so far (see Box 7.5): I began by considering the possibility of rejecting claim 2 – the idea that we are responsible for our sin. Those who consider themselves moral responsibility skeptics, such as Derk Pereboom, specify that they reject the idea that we are responsible in the "basic desert" sense – but offer a justification for retaining some attitudes and practices associated with moral responsibility, in terms of the promotion of such goods as moral formation, reconciliation, and protection. These attitudes and practices may be considered connected to a form or sense of moral responsibility which is weaker than the "basic desert" sense. But this sense might be criticized as too weak to support attitudes and practices central to Christianity, which seem to presuppose a more significant sense of desert. So I went looking for an alternative conception, and proposed understanding the property of being blameworthy, in particular, as being the fitting object of moral protest – where such protest is justified not in consequentialist terms, but in terms of the symbolic value of taking a stand against what is evil and for what is good. And I have suggested that sinners might be worthy of such blame even if their sin is unavoidable.

Does that mean that I have ended up rejecting claim 3 – the idea that we are responsible only for what we can avoid? I think that my view counts as only a partial, and not a wholesale, rejection of claim 3, since the view of blame I have proposed is not what most people mean, or all of what they mean, when they talk about blameworthiness. As mentioned already, some theorists take the notion to imply that the blameworthy deserve suffering or punishment. So perhaps my view counts as a form of "responsibility revisionism"[18] (see Box 7.6).

Box 7.6

The author is now placing herself on the map. It is a form of "responsibility revisionism." Those familiar with the literature will now know where the author is coming from; those less familiar will appreciate the way the author now explains her placing.

In that case, my response to the original puzzle may be seen as making modifications to both claims 2 and 3, as follows:

(2*) We are responsible for our sin, *in the sense that our sin merits blame in the form of protest*.
(3*) We are responsible *in the sense of deserving suffering or punishment* only for what we can avoid.

We may ask, where does this leave us with respect to the rest of the attitudes and practices associated with sin that may be thought integral to Christianity? Let's begin by considering the "reactive attitudes" to which Peter Strawson (1963) brought attention – chief among them (in Strawson's discussion) resentment (a "participant" attitude), indignation (a "vicarious" attitude), and guilt (a "personal" attitude). I think there are independent grounds for thinking that resentment is an attitude that Christians should seek to eliminate, and I have

---

[18] For a distinct version of responsibility revisionism, see Manuel Vargas, *Building Better Beings: A Theory of Moral Responsibility* (Oxford: Oxford University Press, 2015).

argued for this position elsewhere (Vicens 2019).[19] But if this (admittedly unargued-for here) position is not accepted, and resentment is seen as important to Christian life, then perhaps it might be retained *as a way of protesting* (and so, *blaming*). Smith herself makes this suggestion, that reactive attitudes such as resentment "may well be one of the most common ways in which we register moral protest and the demand for moral acknowledgement from others" (2013, p. 41).

Similarly, on Christopher Bennett's view, blame involves a kind of withdrawing of goodwill toward, or distancing oneself from, the wrongdoer that is a "necessary part of taking wrongdoing seriously, and disapproving of it" (2013, p. 76). Bennett takes this withdrawing or distancing to be an example of what Feinberg calls "symbolic nonacquiescence" (quoted in 2013, p. 76), and insists that such blaming behavior is not "conventional or arbitrary but rather has an essential role in making the action adequate to the situation" (2013, pp. 78–79). In the end he doesn't explain how any particular reactive attitude such as resentment or indignation is supposed to be related to this account of blame; but he does say that "if there is a connection between emotion and expression in the sense I'm using it, it is that the expression gives form to the emotion, or rather *gives form to the sense of salience or significance that constitutes the way the person experiencing the emotion construes the situation*" (2013, p. 77, emphasis added). For instance, in grieving the death of a loved one, "one might search for a way of capturing one's sense of the significance of the loss: one might feel that words are not enough and that a certain way of treating the person's body is now important, before that opportunity is now irrevocably lost" (2013, p. 78). The idea thus seems to be that in treating the deceased's body a certain way, one appropriately expresses, symbolically, the emotion of grief, by giving form to how one construes the situation (perhaps as one in which time is running out, before one will soon be forever parted from the body of one's beloved). So maybe Bennett similarly would say that in withdrawing or distancing, one appropriately expresses, symbolically, one's resentment or indignation, by giving form to the way one construes the situation (as having been wronged in some significant way). But how might withdrawing or distancing be "non-conventionally" related to resentment or indignation? One possibility is inspired by the oft-used metaphor of *heat* when speaking about anger, resentment, indignation, and the like. Just as the heat blazing from the stove (ideally) signals to little children that they ought to keep their distance, so the "heat" of these reactive attitudes signals the distance that ought to be kept between the wrongdoer and those who are resentful or indignant, on account of the wrongdoing. In this way the emotional content of these reactive attitudes would itself serve to symbolically express the seriousness of the wrong that has been done, and be a fitting response to the situation.

I have said nothing so far about guilt, but perhaps this self-regarding reactive attitude might be understood along one of the lines that have been offered here: either as a form of (self) protest, whereby one takes a stand against one's own previous actions and attitudes, or as a form of distancing oneself from the feature of oneself to which the wrongdoing is due (e.g. the inattentiveness or self-absorption or greed or prejudiced belief), or even a withdrawing of goodwill toward oneself. If some such understanding makes sense, then the

---

[19] I also think there are independent grounds for thinking that *God* does not experience *any* reactive attitudes, as they are commonly conceived (as involving an affective component along with a judgment).

reactive attitude of guilt may likewise be justified even in cases where one's wrongdoing was unavoidable.

What other attitudes and practices central to Christianity need accounting for? I said earlier that in the New Testament:

> Sin is equated with violating God's law and associated with guilt (1 John 3:4); it makes us liable to judgment (Matt 5:22), condemnation (Matt 12:36–7), and "recompense" (2 Cor. 5:10) – and makes us fitting targets of the wrath of God.
>
> (Romans 3:5–6)

The guilt mentioned in 1 John I take to be, not a reactive attitude, but some objective state of being – perhaps simply the state of having done wrong and being responsible for it. As such it is already accounted for by the view of blameworthiness I have been discussing. If a person is guilty in the eyes of God (objectively guilty, that is), then one is liable to God's judgment. Could God's judgment (and condemnation) take the form of divine protest – God's own taking a stand against the moral evil that people commit (see Box 7.7)?

Box 7.7

The author is making explicit the implications of her argument. For so many Christians, God has "righteous indignation" against the sinfulness of humanity. But given we could not avoid our sin, she is reinterpreting both the concepts of sin and of judgment "wrath." We are blamed for our sin – in the sense that we protest against the evil within us (even if we are not completely responsible); and God exercises God's wrath (as a comparable symbolic protest against evil). For a fundamentalist Christian, this is a significant departure from the traditional Gospel of sin and salvation. But the author's goal is to find some way to continue to use this language that is faithful to the tradition, yet coherent.

Could God's "wrath" be some kind of symbolic expression of the seriousness of humans' crimes, which put a distance between them and the source of all goodness? I don't see why not. In his analysis of the concept of divine wrath in the New Testament, Christopher Marshall notes that "it is Paul who offers the most extensive reflection on the nature and meaning of God's wrath"; and in Paul's view, the wrath of God is principally displayed in "the Christ event" (2001, p. 170). Marshall writes:

> The concept of God's wrath is so firmly anchored in the biblical tradition that there can be little doubt that Paul's readers would have understood what he meant by the term. It designates God's fervent reaction against human wickedness, God's refusal to tolerate, compromise with, or indulge evil ... Wrath is ... a measured commitment to act against evil and injustice in order to contain and destroy it.
>
> (2001, p. 171)

The object of wrath, on Marshall's analysis, is not the person who sins, but the sin which overpowers the sinner. Thus, "the cross supremely reveals God's wrath not because sinners are vicariously punished in the experience of Christ but because the cross definitively subverts and destroys the principle of sin itself" (2001, p. 173).[20] Such an interpretation of Paul is consistent with the view of human sin that I have suggested, as calling for divine opposition but not retributive punishment.

Furthermore, if "recompense" is understood to mean simply whatever response is fitting and appropriate to the good or evil one has done, then this, too, is compatible with the modified view of responsibility I have proposed. Then again, if recompense is interpreted as the intentional infliction of suffering, or what I have called "punishment as payback," then it would not be compatible. This brings me to an important point of Christian belief not yet mentioned in this chapter: the doctrine of hell. I think on any interpretation – or modification – of claim 3 that does not amount to a wholesale rejection, the claim that we are responsible only for what we can avoid is clearly incompatible with the traditional doctrine of hell,[21] on the assumptions that sin is unavoidable and that it is sin that makes one liable to hell. But there seem ample grounds – biblical and theological – for hope in universal salvation (see Box 7.8).

Box 7.8

The author continues to bring out the implications of her argument. If her analysis is right, then the traditional understanding of hell is problematic. She explains that her sympathies are with a version of universalism (all people are ultimately redeemed and saved).

A sizable number of Christian philosophers and theologians (historical and contemporary) have defended this claim, and while I do not have the space to do so here, I am convinced that Paul meant "all" quite literally when he wrote, "as one man's trespass led to condemnation for all, so one man's act of righteousness leads to justification and life for *all*" (Romans 5:18, emphasis added) – and "God has imprisoned all in disobedience so that he may be merciful to *all*" (Romans 11:32, emphasis added) – and, through Christ "God was pleased to reconcile to himself *all* things, whether on earth or in heaven, by making peace through the blood of his cross"

---

[20] Marshall also suggests that Paul's teachings on punishments within the church – which "range from admonition to rebuke to temporary expulsion" – serve to "protect the community from contamination with evil, and to encourage repentance and restoration of the obstinate sinner," while Paul's frequent use of curses functions to "reinforce the moral… boundaries of a community" by identifying "certain kinds of behavior as especially offensive or dangerous." This analysis, too, seems consistent with the view of blame I have proposed. See Marshall, *Beyond Retribution*, 149, 155, 166.

[21] Zachary Manis describes "the traditional view of hell" as involving the idea that "The purpose of hell is retributive: one's consignment to hell is (at least in part) a divine punishment for the evil deeds committed during one's earthly life." But what if hell were a form of eternal divine *protest*? Might it then be appropriate for God to consign to hell sinners whose sin is unavoidable? (Thanks to Taylor Cyr, personal communication, for pressing this question.) Perhaps it would be, though I think there are other grounds – some discussed later in this chapter – for thinking (or at least hoping) that God will bring sin to an end, so that there will not eternally be something for God to protest. See Zachary Manis, "The Doxastic Problem of Hell," in *Oxford Studies in Philosophy of Religion* Vol. 6, ed. Jonathan L. Kvanvig (Oxford University Press, 2015), 207.

(Colossians 1:20, emphasis added).[22] Marilyn McCord Adams, one recent philosophical defender of universalism, notes that both "defenders of hell" and universalists are "confronted with a theological balancing act," in which they must weigh some "items of tradition" more heavily than others (1993, p. 324). While the universalist will have to give up on the literal reading (or what she calls the translation "into theological assertion") of certain apocalyptic New Testament texts, the defenders of hell will have to admit some form of divine limitation, since on their view God "cannot achieve the optimal overall good without sacrificing the welfare of some individual persons … nor can He redeem all personal evil: some of the wicked He can only quarantine or destroy" (1993, p. 325). And she insists that her position is not unbiblical, since "the theme of divine triumph is central to the Bible" (1993, p. 325). As to what to make of the biblical texts (of which there are many) that do mention hell, Adams proposes that they express the "deep truth" of "how *bad* it is, how utterly indecent, not to respond to God appropriately" (1993, p. 324).[23] Such an interpretation fits well with the idea that blame is fundamentally about "taking wrongdoing seriously," as Bennett suggests.

Conclusions

> **Box 7.9**
>
> Now the author moves to her conclusion. She states clearly the conclusion that she has argued for in the paper. She then makes a connection with the whole concept of "helplessness" that she takes from Robert Adams and Thomas Hill. In this way, she reinforces the legitimacy of her conclusion: the reason for this stage of helplessness is the unavoidable nature of human sin.

I have proposed in this paper a modified view of human responsibility for unavoidable sin (see Box 7.9): humans might be blameworthy in the sense that they are fitting objects of protest; and this protest is justified not fundamentally because the protest has positive consequences, but because of its expressive significance or symbolic value. I find it interesting to note that the two influential papers on symbolic value mentioned earlier – by Robert Adams and Thomas Hill – both address the situations of those who are relatively helpless with respect to some evil. On this topic Adams writes:

> Whether we like it or not, helplessness is a large part of life. Human life begins and ends in helplessness. Between infancy and death, moreover, we may find ourselves in the grip of a disease or a dictator to which we may be able to adapt but which we cannot conquer

---

[22] Keith DeRose (2019) cites these and other New Testament texts in "Universalism and the Bible." See Keith DeRose, "Universalism and the Bible," accessed November 13, 2019, https://campuspress.yale.edu/keithderose/1129-2.

[23] Marshall likewise argues that "the diversity … and mutually exclusive nature of the images used to depict hell… corroborates the metaphorical, hyperbolic nature of the discourse"; and he suggests that these images are intended to convey that "earthly actions have eschatological significance and will receive appropriate recognition from God." Marshall, however, is not a certain universalist, but recommends a "humble agnosticism" on the issue. See Marshall, *Beyond Retribution*, 189, 196.

> ... Dealing with our helplessness is therefore an important part of living well ... A central part of living well is being for the good and against evils. We face the question, how we can be for and against goods and evils that we are relatively powerless to accomplish or prevent. One of the most obvious answers is that we can give more reality to our being for the goods and against the evils by expressing our loyalties symbolically in action.
>
> (1999, p. 224)

While Adams is not discussing the inevitability of sin, if it is true that sin is unavoidable for humans then this is perhaps the chief reason that all of us are in a state of helplessness. Sin is – if the biblical descriptions are apt – like a disease or dictator which we cannot conquer. Thus, taking symbolic action against the sin – in ourselves and in the rest of humanity – to "register and challenge" the evil of which we are (however dimly) aware and to signal our loyalty (however weak) to the good to which it is opposed, may be in our situation especially important.

Works Cited

Adams, M.M. (1993). The Problem of Hell: A Problem of Evil for Christians. In: *Reasoned Faith: Essays in Philosophical Theology in Honor of Norman Kretzmann* (ed. E. Stump), 301–327. Ithaca: Cornell University Press.

Adams, R.M. (1999). *Finite and Infinite Goods: A Framework for Ethics*. New York: Oxford University Press.

Bennett, C. (2013). The Expressive Function of Blame. In: *Blame: Its Nature and Norms* (ed. J. Coates and N. Tognazzini). New York: Oxford University Press.

Caruso, G. and Morris, S. (2017). Compatibilism and Retributivist Desert Moral Responsibility: On What is of Central Philosophical and Practical Importance. *Erkenntnis* Vol. 82: 837–855.

Clarke, R. (2010). Determinism and Our Self-conception. *Philosophy and Phenomenological Research* Vol. 80, No. 1: 242–250.

Couenhoven, J. (2013). *Stricken by Sin, Cured by Christ: Agency, Necessity, and Culpability in Augustinian Theology*. New York: Oxford University Press.

Crisp, O. (2009). Original Sin and Atonement. In: *The Oxford Handbook of Philosophical Theology* (ed. T. Flint and M. Rea), 430–451. New York: Oxford University Press.

DeRose, K. Universalism and the Bible. https://campuspress.yale.edu/keithderose/1129-2 (accessed 13 November 2019).

Frankfurt, H. (1969). Alternative Possibilities and Moral Responsibility. *Journal of Philosophy* Vol. 66: 828–839.

Hieronymi, P. (2001). Articulating an Uncompromising Forgiveness. *Philosophy and Phenomenological Research* Vol. 62: 529–555.

Hill, T. (1979). Symbolic Protest and Calculated Silence. *Philosophy & Public Affairs* Vol. 9, No. 1: 83–102.

King, M. (2014). Two Faces of Desert. *Philosophical Studies* Vol. 169: 401–424.

Manis, Z. (2015). The Doxastic Problem of Hell. In: *Oxford Studies in Philosophy of Religion*, Vol. 6 (ed. J.L. Kvanvig), 203–223. Oxford: Oxford University Press.

Marshall, C. (2001). *Beyond Retribution: A New Testament Vision for Justice, Crime, and Punishment*. Grand Rapids, MI: Wm. B. Eerdmans Publishing Co.

McKenna, M. (2009). Compatibilism & Desert: Critical Comments on 'Four Views on Free Will.' *Philosophical Studies* Vol. 144, No. 1: 3–13.

Moo, D. (2013). Sin in Paul. In: *Fallen: A Theology of Sin* (ed. C. Morgan and R. Peterson), 107–130. Wheaton, IL: Crossway.

Pereboom, D. (2014). *Free Will, Agency, and Meaning in Life.* Oxford: Oxford University Press.

Pereboom, D. (2017). Responsibility, Regret, and Protest. In: *Oxford Studies in Agency and Responsibility*, Vol. 4 (ed. D. Shoemaker), 121–140. Oxford: Oxford University Press.

Quinn, P. (2010). Sin and Original Sin. In: *A Companion to Philosophy of Religion*, 2nd edn. (ed. C. Taliaferro, P. Draper, and P. Quinn), 614–621. Oxford: Blackwell Publishing.

Rea, M. (2007). The Metaphysics of Original Sin. In: *Persons: Human and Divine* (ed. D. Zimmerman), 319–356. Oxford: Oxford University Press.

Smith, A. (2013). Moral Blame and Moral Protest. In: *Blame: Its Nature and Norms* (ed. D. Justin Coates and Neal A. Tognazzini), 27–48. New York: Oxford University Press.

Strawson, P.F. (1963). Freedom and Resentment. *Proceedings of the British Academy* Vol. 48: 1–25.

Swinburne, R. (1989). *Responsibility and Atonement.* Oxford: Clarendon Press.

Talbert, M. (2019). Moral Responsibility. In: *The Stanford Encyclopedia of Philosophy* (ed. E. Zalta). https://plato.stanford.edu/archives/win2019/entries/moral-responsibility(accessed July 1, 2021).

Talbott, T. (2008). Why Christians Should *Not* Be Determinists: Reflections on the Origin of Human Sin. *Faith and Philosophy* Vol. 25, No. 3): 300–316.

Tognazzini, N. and Coates, J. (2018). Blame. In: *The Stanford Encyclopedia of Philosophy* (ed. E. Zalta). https://plato.stanford.edu/archives/fall2018/entries/blame (accessed January 17, 2020).

Vargas, M. (2015) *Building Better Beings: A Theory of Moral Responsibility.* Oxford: Oxford University Press.

Vicens, L. (2018). Sin and Implicit Bias. *Journal of Analytic Theology* Vol. 6: 100–111.

Vicens, L. (2019). Love and Resentment. In: *Love, Divine and Human: Contemporary Essays in Systematic and Philosophical Theology* (ed. O. Crisp, J. Arcadi, and J. Wessling). New York: T&T Clark.

Watson, G. (1996). Two Faces of Responsibility. *Philosophical Topics* Vol. 24, No. 2: 227–248.

8

A Good Story

Human–Animal Friendship and Meat Eating

Trevor Bechtel

RESEARCH LEVEL 2

Editors' Introduction

In this essay, Trevor Bechtel offers a provocative thesis. He argues that Christians may eat animals provided they have had a good quality of life. He develops his argument partly by challenging the prejudice that many humans have toward animals (they cannot really think, they cannot really be loyal) and by appeal to Biblical stories. In addition, he shows how the act of "domestication" was, historically, grounded in a "closeness" between the animal and the human. He argues that a Christian can with good conscience eat meat provided the life of the animal has been one of flourishing; although he concedes that the moral imperative of vegetarianism can't be entirely ruled out. Factory farms are completely illegitimate.

A Good Story?

If I told you a story about two friends that ended with one of them eating the other would you think it was a good story? Most of you will respond quickly; that's a horrible story! Or at least most of you would think that. You might hesitate before responding. After all, asking a question like that partly suggests that the counterintuitive answer might be the right one. In theology, this might even often be the case. So you might think of some situations in which this might happen. You are stranded with your friend on a desert island/mountain pass/apocalyptic wasteland and have no access to food. One of you starves and the other, to prolong life in hope of rescue …

We can think of these kinds of situations as occurring at the limit of human experience. On one hand these limit situations[1] can be excellent fodder for theological thinking (see Box 8.1).

---

[1] The concept of the limit situation arises in the philosophy of Karl Jaspers in *Philosophy* (Chicago: University of Chicago Press, 1969), and receives more theological treatment by David Tracy in *Blessed Rage for Order* (Chicago: University of Chicago Press, 1996).

The Craft of Innovative Theology: Argument and Process, First Edition. Edited by John Allan Knight and Ian S. Markham.
© 2022 John Wiley & Sons Ltd. Published 2022 by John Wiley & Sons Ltd.

> **Box 8.1**
>
> The author introduces a technical term – limit situations – borrowed from philosophy. This term becomes a tool for his subsequent analysis. The reader should reflect on the value of this concept in assessing the argument of the paper.

When we are at the limit we are in some ways, by definition, in the realm of religious or theological thinking. When we are pushed to the limit we may be able to transcend our regular patterns of thinking. On the other hand we recognize that our actions, thoughts, and beliefs might be so different at the limit that it is not valuable to consider them in constructing our regular theology. How we act, think, and believe at both the center and the limit of human experience will be a crucial question throughout this essay.

Now that some of our theological muscles have been exercised we might remember that in fact the meal at the center of Christian worship has some things in common with a possible answer to the question. Jesus has said both, "You are my friends" (Jn. 15.15) and "Take eat; this is my body" (Matt. 26.26). We tend to think of this as a good story; we even name the Friday on which Christ was crucified as "good" although we recognize a slightly different nuance to that meaning of good than our regular use. It is the nuance that arises in limit situations, perhaps.

> **Box 8.2**
>
> The author is now going to limit his focus: so the reader knows precisely what to expect. The focus is not on the Eucharist, but rather the "normal" practice of eating animals. Indeed the focus is on the relationship between the human and animals that are "domesticated." Right from the outset, the author is making clear what this chapter is about and what it is not about.

I am not, in this essay, going to explore in depth the possibility of grounding our practice of eating animals in the Eucharist (see Box 8.2). There are possibilities there, but I want instead to explore the practice of eating animals in its ordinary sense, as a regular practice at the center of both what it means to be human and what it means to be a domesticated animal. And this ordinary story is the one addressed by the question that opened this essay; a good story about two friends that ends with one eating the other.[2] As you've already gathered, this is a story where we are going to need to pay careful attention to what we already do, think, and believe, and to how we describe our actions, thoughts, and beliefs.

This is necessary because of a detour in thinking that we have been on for the last few hundred years. This detour in thinking has led to a corresponding detour in belief that is more difficult to track but which I hope to address in parts in this essay. These detours have also led to a change in action toward animals that we currently show no signs of changing so I am not sure I can name it a detour, but more than anything I hope to show here that we need to change our actions in regards to animals; however, that that does not mean we need to stop eating them. It's also not my goal in this essay to convince you to eat animals or to convince you that eating animals is wrong. I have spent time in my life as both a meat eater and a vegetarian and I value both approaches to diet, health, environmental responsibility, and ethics. It is my goal to convince you that humans and animals are friends, and that something has gone very wrong with how we

---

[2] I'm grateful to Darrin Snyder-Belousek for this way of thinking of this question.

think, act, and believe when it is not obvious to us that this is the case. Our friendship with animals may seem unrelated to the main question of this paper – whether or not Christians may eat animals – but whether or not we could befriend an animal is decisive to a domesticated animal's quality of life, and I believe we may only eat animals who have had a good quality of life; what theologians call flourishing. My thesis is that Christians may eat animals, but only if those animals have flourished during their life (see Box 8.3).

> **Box 8.3**
>
> This is the thesis statement. A reader can judge the effectiveness of the argument by whether the reader is persuaded that Christians may indeed eat animals, provided they have had a good quality of life.

I'll begin by describing the detour in how we have considered animals in the last few hundred years, and then show what I consider to be a Christian approach to eating animals that draws on the Bible, evolutionary science and domestication, and the theological idea of a good creation.[3]

The Detour: Distancing Ourselves from Animals

> **Box 8.4**
>
> The author introduces this section as a detour. He wants the reader to understand the history of human and animal relationships. Naturally, the reader should evaluate the effectiveness of this detour.

First the change in action (see Box 8.4). Until very recently humans and animals lived very closely together. This closeness was both metaphorical (humans cared deeply about their animals) and physical (humans and animals lived in close proximity). This was true before the rise of agriculture when early humans hunted animals. In order to be successful in the hunt humans needed to live close to the animals they hunted knowing their travel and sleep patterns, food sources, and ways of being in the environment. We know that many cultures give thanks to an animal that has been successfully hunted and see their interactions as forming an intimate bond. And this closeness was also true as humans started to keep animals. The process of domestication depends on many things, but an absolute requirement is that the animal can adjust to living around humans and this is greatly aided by a caring approach. Animals were very valuable. You may like the argument that farmers cared for their animals because they valued wealth rather than the animal but either way farmers cared. For most of history to be a farmer, on whatever scale farming happened, meant that the farmer knew their animals, probably by name, and cared deeply for their animals.[4]

---

[3] One note about language before we continue. Humans are animals, so to use the language of humans and animals as if there is some kind of difference between the two is inaccurate. More accurate terminology would be humans and nonhuman animals. However, the word "animal" is commonly used as a synonym for "nonhuman animal" and that is how I will use it in this paper.

[4] The closeness of humans and animals is explored in Brian Fagan's *The Intimate Bond* (New York: Bloomsbury Press, 2015).

This all changed a few hundred years ago with the rise of industrial farming. Industrial farming is probably the single most evil practice in the history of the world. Genocide in human contexts is widely recognized as a deep evil. Factory farming is a similar or maybe even worse kind of deep moral evil. In a factory farm, we breed animals, force them to live short, crippled lives indoors often with inadequate or no space to move, and then kill them so cruelly that the humans that do the killing suffer marked mental anguish. And then we do it all over again on a cycle of endless repeat. It is worse than the worse dystopian science fiction and it all happens behind closed doors, away from the public. Laws before the US congress will now make it an act of terrorism to breach the defenses of a factory farm. Industrial farming is a radical shift in action from all prior farming practices and requires a similarly radical shift in thinking.[5]

The shift in thinking begins as most modern philosophy does, with Rene Descartes. Descartes pioneered the mind–body dualism in its modern form but for our purposes his argument that animals did not have minds is most interesting. Descartes held that animals did not have minds because they did not possess language.[6] We now know that both of these ideas are wrong, but Descartes's thinking was not out of line for his time and a number of ideas followed from this "insight." The mind was the place were humans had emotions, processed things internally, thought, and most decisively for our purposes, felt pain. If animals didn't have a mind then they didn't have an internal life, they didn't have emotions and they didn't feel pain. Many of the horrors that we have subjected animals to over the last few hundred years are based in the belief that they don't feel pain.

Now it is abundantly obvious that this is not the case. If you step on the cat's tail, the cat is able to very clearly communicate to you that they feel pain. We have easy access to hundreds of similar examples. In order to deny pain to animals at some point you need to be able to ignore what you see and hear and replace it with a belief that because they don't have minds they can't feel pain. And for centuries this was scientific doctrine; well into the 1980s veterinarians were taught to ignore animal pain.[7]

I have no anti-science arguments to make; I love science, but dogmas and doctrines exist in science as they do in other realms of human life. And the hard line between animal life and human life has been one place where this is most true. Until very recently it was a cardinal mistake to attribute the same emotion or virtue to animals as to humans. Some of you have been wondering about my claim that humans and animals are friends; isn't friendship something that only happens between humans? When we attribute so called human qualities to nonhumans we commit the "mistake" of what science has until recently called of **anthropomorphism**.[8] Calling a dog loyal is perhaps the best example. At this point I want to take a detour of my own to expound of some of these ideas by relating to you the story of Hachikō. The stark contrast between a very famous dog and the reality of animals trapped in factory farms is instructive for our question.

---

[5] The most accessible introduction to factory farming is Jonathan Safran Foer's *Eating Animals* (New York: Little, Brown and Company, 2009).

[6] It's now generally recognized that animal communication has grammatical structure and regional cultural variation. See Eva Meijer's *Animal Languages* (Cambridge, MA: The MIT Press, 2020). For an earlier philosophical approach to animal language see Vicki Hearne, *Adam's Task : Calling Animals by Name* (New York: Knopf, 1986).

[7] For more see Bernard Rollin, *The Unheeded Cry: Animal Consciousness, Animal Pain, and Science* (New York: Oxford University Press, 1989) – for a discussion of ordinary vs. scientific common sense see p. 13, for more on veterinarians and pain see pp. 117–118.

[8] See Bernard E. Rollin, "Scientific Ideology, Anthropomorphism, Anecdote, and Ethics," in *The Animal Ethics Reader*, ed. Susan J. Armstrong and Richard G. Botzler (London: Routledge, 2003) for an early expression of this sentiment.

Hachikō, the Famously Loyal Dog

In 1924 a professor at the University of Tokyo took in a dog named Hachikō. Every day Hachikō would go down to the Shibuya train station and wait for the professor. The professor died of a cerebral hemorrhage in 1925 and stopped going to the station. But Hachikō kept going, although the humans at the station could be rude to him. In 1932, interested in Hachikō's breed (Akita, a dog very closely related to wolves) one of the professor's former students followed Hachikō back to the professor's gardener's home. The gardener explained the story of Hachikō to the student who eventually wrote a story which was published in a Tokyo newspaper. Hachikō became famous in Japan for his loyalty. Hachikō died in 1935. He was stuffed and put in Japan's National Science Museum. A statue of him was also erected. Hachikō became the exemplar of loyalty in Japan and children were urged to follow his example. At Tokyo University there is a statue of the professor, but I suspect that it is there not because of the professor's own initiatives but because of his connection to Hachikō. Next to the professor's grave is a memorial to Hachikō. There are statues of Hachikō now in Tokyo at the Shibuya train station where the station gate next to the statue is called the Hachikō gate. There two more statues: one in Odate, Hachikō's hometown, and one in the US at the Woonsocket Depot Square in Woonsocket, Rhode Island.

There are stories of human loyalty which may meet Hachikō's example, but none exceed it. The professor and Hachikō connected for a little bit longer than a year, but then Hachikō remained loyal for seven years before even receiving any acclaim. Loyalty is not even first a human quality, let alone something we should be worried about attributing wrongly.

Learning from Hachikō

Box 8.5
The author has several targets in the essay. Bechtel is very critical of those who are critical of the "anthropomorphism" of animals. He explains that as the story of Hachikō demonstrates, it is simply a prejudice that humans cannot see loyalty and feelings in animals.

There are at least three things we can learn from this story (see Box 8.5). One, it drives home the point that concerns with anthropomorphism have been overstated for a long time. Anthropomorphism was first challenged by Jane Goodall, Diane Fossey, and Birute Mary Galdikas, who reversed general opinion on the role of empathy in seeing objectively. They were able to discern personality, mood, and a rich set of emotions in the chimpanzees, gorillas, and orangutans that they lived alongside. Two, it shows how different our ideas about animals can be, for at the same time that Hachikō was rising to prominence in Japan, factory farming was rising to prominence throughout the world.[9] This difference is not unique to animals – there are many stories of humans being treated very differently for no good reason – but the chasm between our memory of Hachikō and our refusal to acknowledge the existence of factory farms is a huge chasm. As human cultures return from our detour into the idea that animals have no minds we will need to recognize that we are finding the main path at different rates. Some are still deeply

---

[9] Hal Herzog's *Some We Love, Some We Hate, Some We Eat: Why It's So Hard to Think Straight About Animals* (New York: Harper Collins, 2010) is an excellent exploration of all the different ways we relate to animals.

committed to the detour and some have been back on the main path for a while. Three, Hachikō, by his celebrity, shows one further decisive point in how we think about animals. Hachikō is an individual. This lesson is one that we are only just starting to understand. Typically, when we think about animals we regard them as a species. The vast majority of our science considers, for example, the characteristics of sheep generally. We spend less time focused on the differences between one sheep and another. This is especially true for wild animals, but it is also true of domesticated ones. One of the places this shows up in our language is when someone describes themselves as a dog person or a cat person. There are certainly general differences between dogs and cats but anyone who has known a dog or a cat knows that individual animals have very different personalities. This question of the individuality of an animal – their distinct and particular life – is important for our question in two ways.

While it is not wrong to say, "I am a friend to dogs," we know that friendships exist between two individuals. In order for humans and animals to be friends there need to be individual humans and individual animals that are friends with each other. Hachikō and the professor were surely friends. Since animals are individuals as well as members of a species, just like humans, we find another recognition of the horrors of factory farming when we realize that we cannot tell one chicken apart from another in a factory context. Battery chickens are a stark example of this.[10] When we deny individuality to animals we deny them their proper flourishing. Not all animals are going to become as famous as Hachikō but all animals that live alongside humans should be able to live lives that allow for their individual distinctives, character, and virtues to be expressed.

Summary

Everything in this paper up to this point has been clearing the ground for my main argument. Before engaging that argument let me summarize the ground clearing I hope to have done (see Box 8.6).

Box 8.6

The author describes the work done in the chapter thus far as "ground clearing." He wants to show how a closeness between humans and animals has dissipated with the "evil" (which is how he described it earlier) of factory farming. Ground clearing is a device to clarify the area where the author hopes to develop his argument.

For most of human history, humans and animals have been very close. This changed over the last several hundred years with the detour into the idea that animals do not have minds, and farming practices that saw animals more and more as commodities. The commodification of animals has reached a zenith with the rise of factory farming. Much of meat-eating humanity is now very distant (again, both physically and metaphorically) from animals. Scientific ideas like anthropomorphism have both generated and reiterated this distance. However, this detour is not our only option for relating to animals. We recognize that this is not our only option when we consider exemplary animals like Hachikō, or other animals that we are already friends with. These friendships and the closeness between humans and animals are ordinary. Ordinary here doesn't mean frequent or common necessarily, but it does not require a limit situation for us to engage it.

---

[10] See Foer's *Eating Animals*, 78–79, or just google "battery chickens".

In the next section I want to explore some of the biblical arguments for eating and not eating animals, and reflect on these theologically. Not all theological papers on eating animals would necessarily devote this much attention to the biblical witness but I am both a narrative theologian (I like stories and think they make effective arguments) and a biblical one who begins by considering what the Bible has to say (see Box 8.7). Narrative and biblical theology are strongly related given the narratival nature of so much of the biblical text.

Box 8.7

Part of the author's methodology is the use of stories. He connects to the title of the paper, the introduction, the story about Hachikō, and will now flow into Biblical stories. He acknowledges his debt to "narrative theology."

The Biblical Story

There are a lot of rules in the Bible and many of them are about food. Food and hospitality played an important role in the cultures represented in the Bible physically, culturally, and metaphorically. In this section I want to explore a few important moments in the biblical text that pertain to eating and being friends with animals.

Biblical Veganism?

In Genesis 1.19, God says, "Look, I have given you every seed-bearing plant on the face of all the earth and every tree that has fruit bearing seed, yours they will be for food. And to all the beasts of the earth and to all the fowl of the heavens and to all that crawls on the earth, which has the breath of life within it, green plants for food." But this is then followed in Genesis 9.3 by, "All stirring things that are alive, yours shall be for food, like the green plants, I have given all to you. But flesh with its lifeblood still in it you shall not eat." In the story, all creatures are created with a vegan diet, but then after the flood that diet is expanded to include all animals, but none with their lifeblood.

Like most biblical texts there is significant room for interpretation here.[11] If we come to the text with a desire to see veganism there we find it in God's good creation. If we come to the text with a desire to see meat eating, we find it sanctioned after the flood. The rest of the biblical story has only meat eaters. John the Baptist even ate locusts. Of course, like so many things in the Bible, we don't know that they were meat eaters. But no one is identified as eating a vegetarian diet and many characters, Jesus included, eat meat. Paul references people who eat only vegetables in Romans 14.2 but not as an example of eating. Does this mean that we don't need to consider vegan or vegetarian diets?

Box 8.8

While this section is focused on the Bible, note how the author makes mostly theological arguments. The author is using the biblical text as a theological one which is a standard move for narratival thinkers.

---

[11] The following reading owes much to Leon Kass, *The Beginning of Wisdom* (New York, The Free Press, 2003).

There are two strong theological arguments for vegetarianism embedded in the biblical text (see Box 8.8). The first is that God's original intention for creation was veganism so that is how we really should eat, even though we are allowed to eat meat. The second is that Jesus's ethic of love, inclusivity, and care for the weak should be extended to animals, especially now that our society allows us to eat healthy vegetarian diets. This is an eschatological argument that connects God's creative intent to God's design for heaven and holds meat eating as a temporary concession to human desire. There is good evidence in the text to suggest that in fact God concedes to human desire in extending God's gifts of food to include "stirring things that are alive."

Biblical Agriculture

Cain and Abel are reported doing the first agricultural work in the Bible; Cain is a tiller of the soil and Abel a herder of sheep. When they each sacrifice some of their produce, Cain some grain and Abel a lamb, God prefers Abel's offering, and this makes Cain angry. God responds, "Why are you incensed and why is your face fallen? For whether you offer well, or whether you do not, at the tent flap sin crouches and for you is its longing but you will rule over it" (Gen. 4.6–7). The narrative from this conversation onward sees all of humanity overtaken by sin's longing so that just before allowing meat eating, and just after another animal sacrifice God says, "The devisings of the human heart are evil from youth" (Gen. 8.21). God recognizes that humanity has desires that go against God's way. It's not a big jump to see the shift in diet and the connected law about killing as a concession to this. Noah's desire for meat could be reflected in his sacrifice of animals. It could also be reflected in his choice of the raven before the dove as he searches for dry land. It's no accident that the dove brings back a branch; doves mainly eat plants. But the raven, while being an omnivore, eats mostly meat. The earth after the flood would have been a carrion bird's dream. This story rewards further attention when looked at with an interest in animals and the human desire to eat them.

Both Abel and Noah sacrifice animals. In a vegan world where all creatures are meant to be eating only green plants, the killing of animals for sacrifice is not only happening but it finds God's favor. The text doesn't say why God favors Abel's sacrifice. Is it because God likes the smell of burnt meat? Is it because Cain is about to kill his brother? Is it because Abel was somehow more interested in honoring God? It is interesting that God pays any attention to either sacrifice given that God never asked for them, from neither Cain and Abel or Noah. Their sacrifices come from two different types of farming: settled agriculture and nomadism. Another option is that God prefers the way of life that goes along with nomadism more than settled agriculture. Nomads follow their flocks searching for good pasture. This wandering, dependent on God, shows up again and again in the stories which follow (the ark wanders on the sea without a rudder, Terah wanders away from Ur, Israel wanders in the wilderness, etc.). Cain's way of life might be the thing that doesn't find favor as it requires staying in one place. This trajectory is intensified by Cain's son who founds the first city.

Abel's way of life may be preferred in its wandering but it also creates some contradictions. Why is Abel keeping sheep if not to eat them? There are answers here: wool for warmth, milk for cheese; but early farmers would have eaten their sheep. In fact domesticated animals show up even earlier in the creation accounts. God creates both domesticated and wild beasts of every kind in Genesis 1. We have two options in thinking about the "green plants for food" command in a context of domesticated animals. On one hand, we could assert that these animals were created for labor (donkeys and oxen), non-meat food (cows, chickens), and warmth (wool and leather). God's fashioning of clothing from animal skins supports this. On the other hand, we could recognize that the "green plants for food" command is useful as an ideal but was never an original part of how humans and animals lived together.

Biblical Law

In both the creation and flood narratives humanity is to "hold sway" over animals. The word translated from Hebrew has often been translated as "dominion" and has commonly been interpreted as granting humans absolute control over animals. This interpretation has led to significant push back on understanding dominion this way suggesting that God intends humans to be stewards of creation rather than holding sway over it. The ordering of Genesis 1–11 is important rhetorically, but these stories are best read together as a series of beginnings with a variety of messages. Terah's journey away from Ur in Genesis 12 is then the historical beginning of the Jewish people.

The rest of the biblical text assumes meat eating, or at least, makes no command not to eat meat and never picks up the suggestion of Genesis 1 that "green plants for food" is a morally better way to eat. This is not to say that the Bible doesn't have a food ethic both implicit and explicit. One of the most explicit examples of the human desire for meat is during the wilderness wanderings of the exodus. The people are subsisting on manna, "And the riffraff that was in their midst felt a sharp craving, and the Israelites, too, again wept and said, 'Who will feed us meat? We remember the fish we used to eat in Egypt for free, the cucumbers and the melons and the leek and the onions and the garlic. And now our throats are dry. There is nothing save the manna before our eyes" (Num. 11.4–6). Moses is anxious about how he is going to provide meat for a whole nation, but God sends a wind which brings quail in huge quantities to the people. The people start collecting and eating the meat. "The meat was still between their teeth, it had not yet been chewed, when the Lord's wrath flared against the people and the Lord struck a very great blow against the people. And the name of the place was called Kibroth-Hattaavah (Graves of Desire), for there the people buried the ones who had been craving" (Num. 11.33–34). The clear desire for meat in this story leads to death by the plague for those craving meat. Is God's punishment here because the people complained? Or is it because they craved meat when manna should have been enough?

The explicit dietary law in Leviticus 11 outlines a set of animals which are unclean and abominable. Our regular expectation of these words, "unclean" and "abominable," suggests to us that these animals have something wrong with them or are dangerous in some way. Mary Douglas, famous for her studies of purity code across cultures, suggests that Leviticus represents a development of two different purity codes.[12] One is the clean/unclean distinction which is connected to ritual sacrifice of land animals. When a human encounters an unclean animal in the wrong way (eating, touching the corpse) they need a period of time or other remediation to become clean again. The other thread is a distinction between common and abominable. The wrong kind of contact is simply forbidden for abominable animals. Douglas argues that this is to protect the animal. Rather than these animals being abominable – why would God create an animal that God thought was abominable – it is abominable to kill them. One of the imports of this law is that common, mature, domesticated, prey animals are preferred for eating. This categorization is not airtight, people can also eat gazelle, but the larger logic holds.

This logic of care and protection for the animal lying behind these laws becomes explicit in the text when we look at another dietary law in Exodus 23.19, "You shall not boil a kid in its mother's milk." This command comes in a section that is full of humanitarian rules that are meant to encourage positive relationships. The especial indignity of boiling a kid in its mother's milk violates the relationship between kid and mother. This section also includes rules about allowing animals and humans to rest, and returning lost animals to their owners. These laws

---

[12] Mary Douglas, *Leviticus as Literature* (Oxford: Oxford University Press, 1999).

suggest that humans care for and pay appropriate attention to animals as well as maintain good relationships with other humans. Even if you don't like this reasoning, it's hard to deny that dietary law whether kosher or halal, in enforcing a certain type of slaughter, does work to ensure more rather the less humane treatment. The rule about not eating the animal with the lifeblood still in it – the first rule about killing animals – both guarantees a slaughter that is more humane (the sudden blood loss from severing arteries often causes the animal to lose consciousness before dying) and guarantees a consumption of meat that is "bloodless" and therefore thoughtful. This kind of eating of animals is then ritually separate from the kind of eating of animals that animals do, either when they capture prey and eat it with the blood in it or when they opportunistically eat found dead meat.

Summary

Box 8.9
The author helpfully sums up the significance of the argument so far. The picture from the Bible is one where as humans settle so an environment is created to protect animals.

The sum of this brief survey is the picture of a world that assumes domestication and prefers nomadism to settled agriculture and is deliberate to offer protection to animals inside the context of human control (see Box 8.9). The idea of vegetarianism is present, but only as an idea; more prevalent is the human desire for meat. Still vegetarianism is an idea that cannot be dismissed entirely, as we shall see. But first let us explore more deliberately the question of domesticated animals.

Domestication

The dog was the first animal to be domesticated, and this occurred at least 14,000 years ago based on fossil evidence. There is fragmentary fossil evidence that there were dogs 30,000 years ago, and some mammoth bones from hunting sites suggest that 45,000 years ago dogs had already begun to partner with humans in hunting. One theory holds that dogs may have separated from wolves as early as 135,000 years ago. It is probably the case that dogs have had as much impact on human societies as humans have had on dogs. We are by far the most social primate and much of our sociality is very canine in its shape.

Humans are interested in being in groups. We share food and parental care broadly being interested not just in our offspring but in the welfare of the group. We are interested in the structure of our group and are interested in welcoming strangers and casting out misbehaving kin. We work well as a team being able to focus our attention on each other as individuals and cooperate in ways that bring out the best in each. In each of these characteristics we are very much like wolves but unlike most apes who are typically selfish and individualistic.

It is possible to re-envision the history both of human and canine evolution bringing them into much more close relationship. As humans separated from apes around 6 million years ago, and came into open spaces out of the forest, they eventually practiced pastoralism following large herds of reindeer. Another apex predator was already doing this: the wolf, and the humans may have adopted the wolf's practice of pastoralism. "Wolves and humans had found their match, and 'dogs' diversified and moved into other human cultures."[13] The meeting of wolf and human was based on sociality, cooperation, and teamwork. The work of living together for human and dog is now often entirely wrapped up in mutual admiration. Dogs and humans live well together; we often say that a dog is a human's best friend. Dogs show us that domestication is not just human control over animals but a relationship of mutual benefit occurring over multiple generations in which both species benefit.[14]

The different animals that live with humans have taken different paths into our communities. Cats lived alongside humans for thousands of years without any genetic alteration, showing that they domesticated themselves. Domestic cats continue to bear remarkable similarity to the desert cats they used to be. Young piglets are very quick to tame and tolerate humans easily. However, as they grew it was probably much easier to manage populations that lived in the forest than to keep them localized to a farm. Sheep and goats were easier to control as adults and so sometimes humans may have corralled them probably both to protect them from (other) predators and to have easier access to them. Sheep and goats changed their patterns of living more decisively a few thousand years before pigs. The sheep would gain protection and perhaps better access to higher quality food, but part of the "bargain" was giving up their life for humans to eat at some point. Sheep negotiated a very different relationship with humans than dogs.[15]

This relationship is one of significant benefit to the domesticated species. The lives of sheep and chickens are much more successful in terms of access to food, protection, and procreation. There are many more domesticated animals than their wild counterparts. Their lives are easier, longer, and less fearful. Their opportunity for relationship is higher both with their counterparts in a flock and with humans. We can't know how animals feel about relating to humans, but we can know the response that individual animals offer individual humans.

Domestication and Meat

It's not overstating things to say that domestication is all about meat. Whether hunting with dogs, or corralling sheep, or eventually pigs the first domesticated animals all hunted or became meat for human consumption. The cat, always the exception, is more of an obligate carnivore than any of these animals. The cat's work was to kill mice in grain stores, so while humans didn't eat meat in connection to the cat's work, the cats certainly did.

Evolution and Veganism

However, there is nothing about the human anatomy that needs or is designed to eat meat. We desire it, and enough that it was a driver in evolutionary changes for both ourselves and our domesticated animals, but we don't need to eat meat. We do need Vitamin B-12 which is only found in meat, dairy, and eggs, so the vegan, "green plants for food," as a diet could only exist in the modern era where foods can be fortified with it; indeed veganism dates back only to 1944.[16]

---

[13] Wolfgang M. Schleidt and Michael D. Shalter, "Co-evolution of Humans and Canids: An Alternative View of Dog Domestication: Homo Homini Lupus?" *Evolution and Cognition* Vol. 9, No. 1 (2003): 70.

[14] Melinda Zeder, "Core Questions in Domestication Research," in *Proceedings of the National Academy of Sciences* Vol. 112, No. 11 (March 17, 2015): 3191–3198.

[15] See Fagan, *The Intimate Bond*.

[16] Leah Leneman, "No Animal Food: The Road to Veganism in Britain, 1909–1944," *Society and Animals* Vol. 7, No. 3: 219–228.

In fact, in the large sweep of human history, veganism is a much better candidate as a limit experience than meat eating. Veganism may teach us to transcend the diet we have mostly known, or it may be so unusual as to not be useful for general human practice; but in thinking of the story of how we eat, veganism is the new thing. Indeed, strict veganism is impossible given the inevitable mixing between plant food and small insects and the ecological connections between animals and plants.

Summary

So why should we eat meat? My answer is that our desire to eat meat has wrought significant changes in the world through the domestication of a number of species (see Box 8.10).

Box 8.10
The author's argument is in some ways weak; we should do this (eat meat) because we have always done it. Ordinarily, this is a bad argument. The reader should reflect on what the author has done to make this argument more convincing in this context.

These species came into being so that we could more readily eat meat. I'm simplifying a complex process to say it is just about the desire to eat meat. That desire is also about survival, about hunting more safely and effectively, about guaranteeing food sources in times of significant climate change. And the changes in human and animal culture that come from domestication generate and sustain themselves beyond meat eating. But dogs, sheep, pigs, and goats – as opposed to wolves, mouflon, boars, and bezoar – only exist because we eat meat. And pigs at least would cease to exist as more than a historical curiosity if we were to stop eating meat.[17] The story of how humans and animals have lived closely alongside each other for as long as we have been the kind of humans we are is a story about eating animals.

To do this well absolutely requires a context in which the animals can live full lives doing the kinds of things that animals want to do. It requires doing our farming on the main path of full respect for animals far away from the detours of intensive and factory farming. It requires practicing humane slaughter. It may not require that we know the name of the animal we are eating, but it does require that that animal could have had a name and been known by the humans that traveled through life with them.

Is Domestication Slavery

There are differences between the domesticated animals I've described in this essay. Humans do relate much more closely to dogs than to sheep, and, at least in the US, we tend to eat sheep not dogs. In fact, this difference may strain my argument. In this paper I have mostly argued that humans are friends with dogs and then extended that closeness to sheep and pigs. I'm not wrong about the closeness part, but is it the case that if we were really friends with the animals we lived

---

[17] We tend to distinguish between feral animals and domestic animals. We could stop killing the domestic pigs we keep now, but beyond using their hair for artists brushes, there are very few pig products that can be harvested before the animal dies.

with that we would stop eating them? There is a possibility that because we can now easily choose not to eat meat that we should. Perhaps veganism is the limit situation that would allow us to transcend our meat-eating past. This argument suggests that the control we have exercised as we have "held sway" over the animals is in fact a form of idolatry or control akin to Cain's agriculture. In controlling the lives of sheep we have in fact subjected them to a form of slavery. Humans practiced slavery on each other for a long time before we realized that it was a deep mortal sin. We now find it abhorrent. It is moral progress that we no longer enslave each other. Is vegetarianism a similar moral progress? It might be (see Box 8.11).

Box 8.11

This is potentially controversial. So the reader will want to pause and ask certain questions. What do you make of the author's analogy between domestication and slavery? How does the author's whiteness affect his approach?

The "green plants for food" approach could be the only liberative path forward. The possible difference between slavery (and we could insert patriarchy or heterosexism here too) and domestication is that slavery is not constitutive in an evolutionary sense of what it means to be human. I name this as a possible difference because while I know that domestication is constitutive of humanity, as a white person I'm not totally sure that slavery isn't constitutive of my humanity. However, I do know that slavery is not constitutive of all humanity. There is a lot more that could be said here about nature and culture, evolution and genetics, but for now I need to leave this suggestion as just a suggestion and conclude.

Conclusion

God created the world and called it good. In Genesis 1 this applies to both wild and domestic species. If we want to call meat eating sinful, then in some ways we are challenging the idea of a good creation. Predation is an ordinary part of the nonhuman world. We could seek to understand all killing as representative of the Fall, but that goes against a reading of Genesis 1–11 which sees that story as a series of beginnings. The garden is not a paradise we are banned from, but only a part of who we are as humans who live with animals. We are also the humans who domesticated animals and lived closely with them for millennia as the appearance of domesticated animals in the Bible shows. This history has humans living closely with animals, becoming their friends, and eating them. It is a history that has not just made domesticated animals who they are but also made humans who we are. This history is a good story about two friends that ends with one eating the other.

9

Just Business

It's Not What You Think

Kathryn D. Blanchard

RESEARCH LEVEL 2

Editors' Introduction

This chapter is a perfect combination of a challenging thesis which is deeply sensitive to the complexity of reading Scripture and the tradition. The author does not distort or oversimplify the traditional authorities in Christian ethics for the purposes of making her argument more compelling. This is not a polemic. Instead the author starts by wanting to explore the nature of business through the lens of the COVID-19 pandemic. She wisely focuses on the early response to that pandemic. She demonstrates the tension between those who supported the closing of the country to prevent illness and death and those who did not. She then looks at business as seen in Scripture, tradition, reason, and experience; before suggesting that the two most helpful concepts for Christian analysis of business are "love" – in particular "love your neighbor as yourself" – and "community."

Introduction

The phrase, "It's not personal, it's business," is perhaps most famously associated with *The Godfather*, but it encapsulates an often-unspoken attitude about the nature of business that is by no means limited to mafia bosses. Most public discourse, including among Christians, accepts the notion that business decisions have little or nothing to do with loving one's neighbor – either because business is "just business" and therefore morally neutral, or because business is inherently amoral and unjust. It is implicit in fights over raising minimum wages to a level that would allow full-time workers to live a life with dignity. It lies hidden in exorbitant drug prices and denial of health care benefits to people who need them most. It stands behind decisions to dump toxic waste in somebody else's back yard – usually someone poor and powerless. Many such arguments and actions, when examined closely, show themselves to be deeply unloving. And since love is taken to be personal, it apparently doesn't belong in the business world.

The Craft of Innovative Theology: Argument and Process, First Edition. Edited by John Allan Knight and Ian S. Markham.
© 2022 John Wiley & Sons Ltd. Published 2022 by John Wiley & Sons Ltd.

But as theologian Cornel West puts it so starkly, "justice is what love looks like in public."[1] And to be sure, not everyone accepts that injustice is simply the cost of doing business. Within any given industry or firm there are people who genuinely seek to love their neighbors. There are bosses who think of their employees like family and try to do right by them, providing safe working conditions and ample benefits. There are employees who work hard for their employers and treat co-workers with respect and kindness. There are investors who make it a priority to support companies that seek long-term goods over next quarter's share price. There are customers who, if they can afford it, opt to buy products or brands that are known to care for the earth and its inhabitants. Every sector includes individuals who see business as supremely personal – just one more human social realm in which neighbor love can *and should* be the rule rather than the exception. So if there are so many people in business trying to love their neighbors, why should the business world be so often associated with exploitation, greed, and even cruelty? Why do good people, including self-identified Christians, do so much bad business?

Box 9.1

The author's opening section has explained that it is puzzling why so many good people participate in "bad business" – business which is self-serving and exploitative. In this paragraph the author indicates where the argument will go. The reader is prepared for the journey. Much like a sign over an interstate, the author knows the anticipated destination.

The answer is complex, of course, but as I see it and will seek to demonstrate here, it ultimately lies somewhere in the difference between, on one hand, seeing the economy as an otherwise disconnected collection of individuals making their own self-interested choices, and on the other, seeing it as an interdependent community providing for its members (see Box 9.1). Anyone who pays much attention to the intersection of Christianity, business, and justice is inevitably struck by the sometimes polarizing differences in Christian attitudes toward business and economics. As in the case of most theological debates, our disagreements have roots in how we engage with the various sources of authority that inform Christian theology – sometimes called the "Wesleyan Quadrilateral" (though Wesley himself never used the term): scripture, tradition, reason, and experience. Rather than bringing all Christians together, each of these four sources is fraught with potential conflict.

Box 9.2

The chosen method to make the argument is a case study. The author has chosen the 2020/2021 COVID-19 crisis as a case study that illustrates the different conceptions of business.

Such conflict was on full display in the early stages of the US outbreak of COVID-19 in 2020, which serves nicely as a case study for business thought and practice (see Box 9.2). Our material lives are where our inwardly held beliefs are played out; the crisis revealed – swiftly and unforgivingly – significant cracks in humanity's social networks, emerging from the hidden narratives

---

[1] Cornel West, Harvard Graduate School of Education Askwith Forum speech, October 23, 2017, accessed May 8, 2020, https://twitter.com/i/status/922654573419954177.

and theological anthropologies (Christian or otherwise) underlying them. After reflecting upon ancient and contemporary Christian economic thought, and exploring how age-old questions about humans, work, and wealth renewed themselves in the context of the pandemic, I will conclude with a modest framework for Christian thinking about "just business" in the twenty-first century.

The Case of COVID-19

Box 9.3
The author will now provide a history of what, at the time of writing, is a contemporary event. Her sources are primarily newspapers and television outlets. The goal of this section is to illustrate how public health advice was in opposition to the needs of business. The "shut down" for health reasons and the dramatic rise of unemployment is sufficient for her to frame her dilemma.

In the spring of 2020 (see Box 9.3), the US was overrun by COVID-19, a disease caused by a novel coronavirus that originated in Wuhan, China and rapidly spread around the world through its globalized economy, with significant help from national leaders who were slow to act. Because people could carry the virus for weeks without any symptoms, medical scientists soon instructed the world that the best way to slow the spread of the virus was for everyone to stay home, washing hands obsessively and avoiding encounters with other people whenever possible. Eventually, only "essential" workers were allowed to go about their business as usual; these included some of the nation's wealthiest workers (doctors and political officials) but even more of the lowest earners (health aides, cleaners, delivery people, and employees at grocery stores, pharmacies, and gas stations). The rest of us were told to leave home only for genuinely essential business, like acquiring medication and groceries – including toilet paper, which surprisingly and almost instantly disappeared from the nation's shelves (large inventories being a business no-no).

The best advice from public health officials, however, soon came into conflict with many business owners, economists, and elected politicians. The world's economy, it turns out, is based largely on the assumption of people leaving their homes and encountering other people – at schools, sporting events, factories, theaters, shops, amusement parks, airports, offices, gyms, and restaurants. Without customers, such businesses laid off workers in droves. During the last weeks of March 2020, nearly three-quarters of Americans had lost at least some income due to the shutdown,[2] and by May one in four American workers had filed for unemployment – the worst rate since the Great Depression.[3] Meanwhile on Wall Street, the stock market experienced eight of its ten worst one-day crashes in history.[4] (It rallied soon thereafter, to the temporary

---

[2] Lauren Fedor and Christine Zhang, "Income of 73% in US Hit by Coronavirus Outbreak," *Financial Times* (April 7, 2020): https://www.ft.com/content/7a7233a3-160a-41be-8d63-40f64e041e57.

[3] Lance Lambert, "Real Unemployment Rate Soars Past 20% – and the U.S. Has Now Lost 26.5 Million Jobs," *Fortune* (April 23, 2020): https://fortune.com/2020/04/23/us-unemployment-rate-numbers-claims-this-week-total-job-losses-april-23-2020-benefits-claims.

[4] Kimberly Amadeo "How Does the 2020 Stock Market Crash Compare With Others?," *The Balance* (updated April 27, 2020): https://www.thebalance.com/fundamentals-of-the-2020-market-crash-4799950.

relief of investors everywhere.[5]) Public debate began to swirl around the question of how many dead Americans it would take to outweigh the economic harms of shutting down most of the country. Was it worth the sacrifice of, say, a million lives over the course of a year or so, in order to keep the marketplace thriving?[6]

It would be possible to make an argument about justice and business by looking at the ways in which business, or a business mindset, *caused and exacerbated* the pandemic: the slowness to shut down businesses (even after watching the devastation in China, Iran, and Italy); the for-profit model of health care that left poorer subsets of the population more susceptible to the worst effects of the disease;[7] the lack of regulation of nursing homes that care for America's elderly;[8] the dire shortage of masks, other personal protective equipment, ventilators, and even of doctors in many areas.[9] Each of these phenomena could be at least partly blamed on the way business is done in America, and the way in which businesses corrupt America's political system – a system still dominated by white, often ostensibly Christian men,[10] of which former president Trump is (as of this writing) foremost.[11] "This wasn't inevitable," wrote Jim Wallis;

---

[5] Fred Imbert and Thomas Franck, "Dow Surges More Than 900 Points in Best Day Since Early April Amid Hope for Coronavirus Vaccine," *CNBC* (May 17, 2020): https://www.cnbc.com/2020/05/17/stock-futures-up-after-powell-says-economy-could-recover-some-this-year.html.

[6] Sweden, which avoided the lockdowns of its Scandinavian neighbors, provided a smaller, European case study of this debate; it experienced much higher infection and death rates but slightly less economic interruption. Editorial Board, "Weighing Sweden's Coronavirus Model," *Wall Street Journal*, May 4, 2020, https://www.wsj.com/articles/weighing-swedens-coronavirus-model-11588631127; Stu Woo and Bojan Pancevski, "Sweden Has Avoided a Coronavirus Lockdown. Its Economy is Hurting Anyway," *Wall Street Journal*, May 7, 2020, https://www.wsj.com/articles/sweden-has-avoided-a-coronavirus-lockdown-its-economy-is-hurting-anyway-11588870062.

[7] "COVID-19 in Racial and Ethnic Minority Groups," Centers for Disease Control and Prevention, accessed May 8, 2020, https://www.cdc.gov/coronavirus/2019-ncov/need-extra-precautions/racial-ethnic-minorities.html.

[8] Elisha Anderson and Kristi Tanner, "State Releases Nursing Home COVID-19 Death Count; Numbers Expected to Grow," *Detroit Free Press*, May 27, 2020, https://www.freep.com/story/news/local/michigan/2020/05/27/more-than-1-200-covid-19-deaths-associated-nursing-homes/5269785002.

[9] "New Findings Confirm Predictions on Physician Shortage," Association of American Medical Colleges, April 23, 2019, https://www.aamc.org/news-insights/press-releases/new-findings-confirm-predictions-physician-shortage. Christopher Kerns and Dave Willis offer a rejoinder, "The Problem with U.S. Health Care Isn't a Shortage of Doctors," *Harvard Business Review*, March 16, 2020, https://hbr.org/2020/03/the-problem-with-u-s-health-care-isnt-a-shortage-of-doctors.

[10] As of this writing, women accounted for about 20–25% of American elected politicians and only about 6–7% of corporate CEOs. See "Current Numbers," Rutgers Center for American Women and Politics, accessed May 8, 2020: https://cawp.rutgers.edu/current-numbers; Claire Zillman, "The Fortune 500 Has More Female CEOs Than Ever Before," *Fortune*, May 16, 2019, https://fortune.com/2019/05/16/fortune-500-female-ceos.

[11] Jim Tankersley, "White House Economists Warned in 2019 a Pandemic Could Devastate America," *New York Times*, March 31, 2020, https://www.nytimes.com/2020/03/31/business/coronavirus-economy-trump.html.

"The lives likely to be lost over the next few months are people created in the image of God who could have been saved with earlier and more decisive action."[12] In an interview with Noam Chomsky, *Truthout* wrote, "The pandemic had been predicted long before its appearance, but actions to prepare for such a crisis were barred by the cruel imperatives of an economic order in which 'there's no profit in preventing a future catastrophe.'"[13]

Box 9.4

The focus is the "early responses" to the pandemic. This decision is to limit the discussion of the case study is wise. The data on the early stage is easy to collect; and it prevents a critic criticizing the author for later stages in the trajectory of the pandemic. This is called "limiting your focus."

In this essay, however, I wish to focus not on causes but on early *responses to* the pandemic, and whether "just business" was on display among Christians, businesses, and Christian businesses (see Box 9.4). Some firms quickly reacted with near heroism in this context, redefining "corporate social responsibility" on the fly, even without being forced to do so by any governmental decree.[14] Some donated ventilators,[15] or collaborated and shared patented design information to make ventilators widely available in a hurry.[16] Companies that had never made masks before quickly adjusted their manufacturing outputs.[17] Executives took pay cuts and worked to figure out how to avoid layoffs of workers ordered to shelter at home, even as production, sales, and profits came to an abrupt halt.[18] Countless news media outlets and scholarly publishers took down paywalls and gave away at least some content for free. Landlords postponed or canceled tenants' rent payments.[19] Pharmaceutical companies donated experimental

---

[12] Jim Wallis, "Staggering," *Sojourners*, April 2, 2020, https://sojo.net/articles/staggering.

[13] C.J. Polychroniou, "Chomsky: Ventilator Shortage Exposes the Cruelty of Neoliberal Capitalism," *Truthout*, April 1, 2020, https://truthout.org/articles/chomsky-ventilator-shortage-exposes-the-cruelty-of-neoliberal-capitalism.

[14] Mark R. Kramer, "Coronavirus is Putting Corporate Social Responsibility to the Test," *Harvard Business Review*, April 1, 2020, https://hbr.org/2020/04/coronavirus-is-putting-corporate-social-responsibility-to-the-test.

[15] Joey Klender, "Elon Musk's Ventilator Donations Can be Used for Severe COVID-19 Cases, Doctor Explains," *Teslarati*, April 3, 2020, https://www.teslarati.com/elon-musk-ventilator-donations-mod-severe-covid-19.

[16] "MIT Emergency Ventilator (E-Vent) Project," accessed May 8, 2020, https://e-vent.mit.edu. Chris Newmarker, "Medtronic Shares Ventilator IP to Combat Shortages Amid Coronavirus," *Mass Device*, March 30, 2020, https://www.massdevice.com/breaking-medtronic-shares-ventilator-ip-to-combat-shortages-against-coronavirus.

[17] Emily Canal, "Businesses Pivot to Meet Covid-19 Mask Demand," *Inc.*, accessed May 8, 2020, https://www.inc.com/emily-canal/mask-shortage-coronavirus-reformation-carhartt-make-masks.html.

[18] Atta Tarki, Paul Levy, and Jeff Weiss, "The Coronavirus Crisis Doesn't Have to Lead to Layoffs," *Harvard Business Review*, March 20, 2020, https://hbr.org/2020/03/the-coronavirus-crisis-doesnt-have-to-lead-to-layoffs.

[19] Matthew Haag, "Rent Strike? This Brooklyn Landlord Just Canceled Rent for Hundreds of His Tenants," *Chicago Tribune*, April 4, 2020, https://www.chicagotribune.com/coronavirus/ct-nw-nyt-landlord-cancels-rent-new-york-20200404-aias2solyvdwtnmikbydgpfwpy-story.html.

treatments.[20] A popular business journal offered advice on how to cultivate compassion and find meaning in the midst of grief.[21] Through it all, many consumers did their part as well, staying home, supporting their local restaurants by ordering take-out, and wearing masks to protect their neighbors when they had to go somewhere.

Others, however, seemed determined not to let the crisis interrupt business as usual. The multibillionaire Christian CEO of Hobby Lobby kept stores open because God told him to, and refused to offer his workers sick pay.[22] Amazon and McDonald's workers went on strikes, accusing their companies of insufficient safety protections and a lack of transparency about sick pay.[23] Oil companies received a rollback of Obama-era federal regulations on the industry designed to address climate change.[24] The farming and food industries continued to depend on the labor of undocumented farm workers, without offering them the benefits of citizenship.[25] Resistance to change and insistence upon liberty ruled the right-leaning media. As commentator (and Latter-Day Saint) Glenn Beck remarked, "I sincerely hope that we are not at a place as Americans to where we are going to let the Democrats jam down the Green New Deal because we are at home panicked."[26] In these circles, COVID-19 was apparently insufficient cause for any introspection about America's economic habits, much less its economic philosophy.

---

[20] Linus Chua, "Gilead to Donate Experimental Coronavirus Drug Remdesivir," *Bloomberg*, April 4, 2020, https://www.bloomberg.com/news/articles/2020-04-04/gilead-to-donate-experimental-coronavirus-drug-for-140-000-cases.

[21] Scott Berinato, "That Discomfort You're Feeling Is Grief," *Harvard Business Review*, March 23, 2020, https://hbr.org/2020/03/that-discomfort-youre-feeling-is-grief.

[22] Andrew Naughtie, "Coronavirus: Hobby Lobby Billionaire Keeps Stores Open After 'God Spoke to Him' – But Won't Pay Sick Leave," *Independent*, March 25, 2020, https://www.independent.co.uk/news/world/americas/hobby-lobby-stay-open-coronavirus-staff-sick-leave-a9423491.html.

[23] Karen Weise and Kate Conger, "Gaps in Amazon's Response as Virus Spreads to More Than 50 Warehouses," *New York Times*, May 4, 2020, https://www.nytimes.com/2020/04/05/technology/coronavirus-amazon-workers.html; Aaron Mak, "Two Amazon Workers Explain Why They Walked Off the Job for COVID-19 Protections," *Slate*, May 4, 2020, https://slate.com/technology/2020/04/amazon-fulfillment-center-strike-staten-island-michigan.html; Brent Schrotenboer, "Hundreds of McDonald's Workers Plan Wednesday Strike over COVID-19 Protections," *USA Today*, May 19, 2020, https://www.usatoday.com/story/money/business/2020/05/19/coronavirus-mcdonalds-employees-national-strike-over-safety/5218729002.

[24] "Trump Rollback of Mileage Standards Guts Climate Change Push," *Washington Post*, March 31, 2020, https://www.washingtonpost.com/business/administration-to-release-final-rule-on-mileage-rollback/2020/03/31/390753fc-7306-11ea-ad9b-254ec99993bc_story.html.

[25] Miriam Jordan, "Farmworkers, Mostly Undocumented, Become 'Essential' During Pandemic," *New York Times*, April 2, 2020, https://www.nytimes.com/2020/04/02/us/coronavirus-undocumented-immigrant-farmworkers-agriculture.html.

[26] Matthew Rozsa, "Glenn Beck Argues Older Americans Should Go Back to Work: 'I'd Rather Die Than Kill the Country,'" *Salon*, March 25, 2020, https://www.salon.com/2020/03/25/glenn-beck-tells-older-americans-to-get-back-to-work-id-rather-die-than-kill-the-country.

> **Box 9.5**
>
> The next section will be a gift to the future. The author documents in some detail the divide among Christians. Some denominations were on the side of public health and moved their services online; other denominations, often the more evangelical, supported the business culture and wanted to stay open. She documents with care, with plenty of quotations, this significant division.

America's churches – arguably its most prominently Christian "businesses," even if not-for-profit – also had to decide how to respond to the virus (see Box 9.5). Most churches (as well as synagogues, mosques, and temples) were quick to disrupt their business as usual, closing their doors to worshippers and moving their communal gatherings to the web.[27] While mega-churches were already well practiced in hosting virtual gatherings, many pastors of small congregations had to give themselves crash courses in various streaming platforms in order to be able to offer pastoral care, music, and the word – if not the material sacraments – to spiritually hungry, home-bound congregants. The rationale seemed simple enough: save as many lives as possible. The short-term sacrifice of bodily get-togethers would encourage the long-term health of individuals and entire communities. This was not merely common sense to many folks, but Christian duty to love one's neighbor as one wished to be loved. One church in Alabama even traded in its in-person worship services for "drive-through coronavirus tests in one of its parking lots."[28]

But common-sense rationales are rarely actually common. As the nation's politicians fought over how best to balance public health and the stock markets, the nation's Christians picked sides as well. Candida Moss wrote, "For the majority of people (including Pope Francis), practicing social distancing and protecting the most vulnerable is the Christian way. It's the embodied interpretation of love thy neighbor. Interestingly, it is religious conservatives who are pushing back against social distancing norms."[29] Then president Trump's mainly white, Evangelical supporters lined up behind him in being loath to change their patterns. "We hold our religious rights dear," said one Pentecostal pastor, "and we are going to assemble no matter what someone says."[30] (Under great political pressure the president eventually encouraged "Americans of all religious backgrounds to do their part to stay healthy and stop the spread,"[31] while also declaring that the

---

[27] Jack Jenkins, "Episcopal Diocese Suspends Communion Wine, Drains Baptismal Fonts Due to Coronavirus," *Religion News Service*, March 10, 2020, https://religionnews.com/2020/03/10/episcopal-diocese-suspends-communion-wine-drains-baptismal-fonts-due-to-coronavirus.

[28] Sarah Pulliam Bailey, "A Megachurch Has Helped Test Nearly 1,000 People for Coronavirus in Two Days," *Washington Post*, March 19, 2020, https://www.washingtonpost.com/religion/2020/03/19/megachurch-has-nearly-1000-people-tested-coronavirus-two-days.

[29] Candida Moss, "When Faith Threatens Public Health," *CNN*, March 24, 2020, https://www.cnn.com/2020/03/24/opinions/coronavirus-religious-freedom-faith-liberty-moss/index.html.

[30] Daniel Silliman, "Pentecostal Pastor Won't Stop Church for COVID-19," *Christianity Today*, March 19, 2020, https://www.christianitytoday.com/news/2020/march/pentecostal-la-pastor-defies-covid19-coronavirus-order.html.

[31] Adelle M. Banks, "In Calls With Faith Leaders, White House Focuses on Virus as well as Election," *Religion News Service*, March 24, 2020, https://religionnews.com/2020/03/24/in-calls-with-faith-leaders-white-house-focuses-on-virus-as-well-as-election.

country would have everyone back to normal by Easter, "a beautiful time."[32]) Apparently sensing a threat to their religion's manly identity, some initially declined to move gatherings online:

> Christian pastor Jonathan Shuttlesworth referred to social distancers as "sissies" and "pansies" who have been "neutered," and described Christians who use hand sanitizer as having "fake faith" and "no balls." Government support for individuals in need continues to be considered a threat to liberty, whereas government support for business is deemed necessary to preserve freedom.[33]

Those congregations who continued to gather in person were unwilling to sacrifice their freedom of worship to fear of disease, or even fear of death. R.R. Reno, the conservative Catholic editor of *First Things*, warned of the "disastrous sentimentalism" of shutting down everyday activity, including church services, merely "for the sake of physical life": "What about justice, beauty, and honor?" he asked; "There are many things more precious than life ... The Eucharist itself is now subordinated to the false god of 'saving lives.'"[34] Some pastors were even willing to be arrested for breaking local public health rules, fearing giving "incredible power to the government that the Constitution doesn't give them in peace times or in times of crises."[35] In May, two southern churches that had briefly closed under duress, and then reopened, had to close again after their leaders and members contracted the virus.[36]

Not only churches, but institutions of higher education also suffered greatly from the sudden loss of "customers" when their dormitories and dining halls were emptied, and most classes moved to some sort of remote digital format. The evangelical Liberty University, however,

---

[32] Rosie Perper, "Trump Says He Wants to Lift Coronavirus Lockdown by Easter because It's a 'Beautiful Time.' Dr. Fauci Says the Deadline Needs to be 'Flexible,'" *Business Insider*, March 24, 2020, https://www.businessinsider.com/trump-says-easter-beautiful-time-coronavirus-lockdown-"timeline-2020-3.

[33] Historian Lawrence Glickman, "The Conservative Campaign Against Safety," *The Atlantic*, March 30, 2020, https://www.theatlantic.com/ideas/archive/2020/03/conservative-campaign-security/608986. Another pastor reportedly insisted, "we're raising up revivalists, not pansies." Jack Jenkins, "Florida Pastor Arrested for Refusing to Halt Worship Amid Outbreak," *Religion News Service*, March 30, 2020, https://religionnews.com/2020/03/30/florida-pastor-arrested-for-refusing-to-halt-worship-amid-outbreak.

[34] R.R. Reno, "Say 'No' to Death's Dominion," *First Things*, March 23, 2020, https://www.firstthings.com/web-exclusives/2020/03/say-no-to-deaths-dominion.

[35] Jack Jenkins, "With Coronavirus Infections Linked to Religious Gatherings, Debate Rages Over Worship Amid Pandemic," *Religion News Service*, April 3, 2020, https://religionnews.com/2020/04/03/with-coronavirus-infections-linked-to-religious-gatherings-debate-rages-over-worship-amid-pandemic.

[36] Lateshia Beacham, "Two Churches Reclose After Faith Leaders and Congregants Get Coronavirus," *Washington Post*, May 19, 2020, https://www.washingtonpost.com/religion/2020/05/19/two-churches-reclose-after-faith-leaders-congregants-get-coronavirus. The reluctance to discontinue in-person gatherings was of course not limited to the US; in France, one pastor apologized after holding a week-long worship event at which 2,500 people were infected, 17 of whom died. Martin Bentham and Peter Allen, "Pastor Sorry After Service Caused Wave of Coronavirus Infections," *Evening Standard*, April 1, 2020, https://www.standard.co.uk/news/world/pastor-thiebault-geyer-sorry-service-caused-coronavirus-infections-a4403826.html.

encouraged students to return to their dorms following spring break, instead of heading home to shelter in place with their families; their president, Jerry Falwell, Jr. reportedly said, "You guys paid to be here, you wanted to be on campus ... And I want to give you what you paid for."[37] He downplayed the risks for young people, and accused liberals of being "willing to destroy the economy just to hurt Trump." Faculty and staff were required to show up at the office, fearing for their jobs if they protested; this left at least one professor "wondering what university leadership has to gain in leveraging people's livelihoods against their speaking the truth. I simply cannot square this oppression of reasonable dissent with the biblical dicta the university professes."[38] (Students later filed a class-action lawsuit against the university, and as of this writing several students and employees have tested positive for the virus, though the university continues to tout its efforts to contain it.)

Box 9.6

The author clarifies the precise purpose of this extended discussion of the policy differences between universities, churches, and businesses. Her interest is in Christian reasoning. She has formulated the problem that she wants to solve.

The purpose here is not to adjudicate which firms had the right policy, but rather *how* different Christians reasoned their way through the quagmire (see Box 9.6). How might we explain the vast discrepancies among Christian responses to COVID-19? How can people who ostensibly identify as members of the same faith – the one, holy, Catholic, and apostolic church – and as disciples of the one and only Jesus of Nazareth, could come to such different conclusions about what constitutes "just business" in the midst of a collision between a global pandemic and the global economy? The short answer is that Christians have rarely, if ever, agreed on the nature of justice, business, or even life and death, because justice looks different to different people, depending on what's at stake for them. The view from a president's office is quite distinct from the view from the board room, the office of a middle-aged administrative assistant, the dorm room of a teenager, the living room of a worried parent, or the nurses' station in an intensive care unit. The 2020 pandemic did not *cause* any new disagreements among Christians but rather revealed, yet again, the longstanding experience of fractured Christianity.

Just Business in Scripture and Tradition, Reason and Experience

---

Box 9.7

This is an exercise in Christian ethics. Therefore the author locates the case study in the context of key Christian authorities – the so-called Wesley quadrilateral. She identifies four classic areas – Scripture, tradition, reason, and experience. This section is beautifully organized.

---

[37] Marybeth Davis Baggett, "I Work for Liberty University. Jerry Falwell Jr. is Taking an Extreme Path That Threatens Lives," *Religion News Service*, March 23, 2020, https://www.washingtonpost.com/religion/2020/03/23/liberty-university-jerry-falwell-lynchburg-coronavirus.

[38] Baggett, "Liberty University".

Scripture

While most Christians would agree that Christian ethics should have at least something to do with Christian scripture, the difficulty in uniting Christians around a "biblical" understanding of justice in economic life lies in the lack of a clear message (see Box 9.7). There is no capitalism in the Bible, any more than there is feminism, global warming, sexual orientation, or nuclear warheads. While the ancient Mediterranean certainly had its share of rich people, tax collectors, and traders, there were no stock markets or multinational corporations, no labor unions, no chief economists. So Christians who would look to scripture to find wisdom about twenty-first-century business must do so with deliberate care, keeping *context* in mind so as not to make facile comparisons, read anachronistic questions onto ancient situations, or pull out supposedly self-explanatory "biblical principles." There is certainly much wisdom to be found, but it requires interpretation with a healthy dose of self-awareness about the assumptions and agendas we bring to the text.

By the time Jesus entered the Palestinian scene in what we now call the first century CE, the Israelites had already produced a significant body of economic teachings as recorded in Hebrew scripture. In the Pentateuch, for example (written down and compiled around the sixth century BCE), the God who leads Israel out of Egypt places great importance on Israel not imitating bullies in its agrarian community life. One commonly cited passage is God's command to share one's hard-earned food with those in need: "When you reap the harvest of your land, you shall not reap to the very edges of your field, or gather the gleanings of your harvest; you shall leave them for the poor and for the alien: I am the Lord your God" (Lev. 23:22). Such generosity should also extend to one's impecunious relations: "If any of your kin fall into difficulty and become dependent on you, you shall support them; they shall live with you as though resident aliens. ... I am the Lord your God, who brought you out of the land of Egypt" (Lev. 25:35–38). God's command is not that others *deserve* help; rather, it is a simple matter of their need, and of holiness and obedience to the God to whom one owes everything.

This latter instruction is part of the broader mythology of a jubilee year – a total reset for the whole Israelite community – in which slaves (at least some of them [cf. Lev. 25:40–46]) are set free, and lands that might have been squandered in business deals or hoarded by the uber-rich are restored to their original owners every fifty years: "You shall count off seven weeks of years ... And you shall hallow the fiftieth year and you shall proclaim liberty throughout the land to all its inhabitants. It shall be a jubilee for you: you shall return, every one of you, to your property and every one of you to your family. That fiftieth year shall be a jubilee for you" (Lev. 25:8–12). Whether or not anyone actually lived by these teachings is a question for historians to answer; evidence so far is scarce.[39] One certainty is that any commands and benefits of the jubilee year were generally reserved for insiders, that is, for Israelites.

Contemporary readers – especially those who are not farmers and, more importantly, are not among the original Israelites to whom such texts were directed – are left to wonder, "What Does the Year of Jubilee Mean for Today?"[40] or even, "Is the Bible still relevant

---

[39] Indeed, God's distribution of the land among Israel's men (fathers and sons) was unequal from the start. John R. Schneider, *The Good of Affluence: Seeking God in a Culture of Wealth* (Grand Rapids: Wm. B. Eerdmans, 2007), cited in Art Lindsley, "Five Myths about Jubilee," *Institute for Faith, Work, & Economics*, 2012, https://tifwe.org/resource/five-myths-about-jubilee.

[40] "The Sabbath Year and the Year of Jubilee (Leviticus 25)," *Theology of Work Project*, accessed February 25, 2020, https://www.theologyofwork.org/old-testament/leviticus-and-work/the-sabbath-year-and-the-year-of-jubilee-leviticus-25.

today?"[41] Some texts are easier to find directly applicable. For example, Israel's wisdom literature (written down and compiled between the sixth and second centuries BCE) admonishes Israel not to put their trust in worldly wealth. "A good name is to be chosen rather than great riches," states Proverbs; "The rich rule over the poor, and the borrower is the slave of the lender. Whoever sows injustice will reap calamity, and the rod of anger will fail. Those who are generous are blessed, for they share their bread with the poor" (Prov. 22:1, 7–9).[42] It is easy enough to look for opportunities to be generous to our neighbors. But it is important to remember – as generations of interpreters have – that even such apparently generalizable principles come out of particular contexts and have particular audiences in mind.

The same is true for the New Testament. As familiar as Jesus of Nazareth might seem to us, he walked the earth in a time and place that make him utterly foreign; we must therefore be skeptical of any claims to understand him perfectly. We may be tempted to view Jesus's commands as plain and simple – that is, until we try to make them realities in our own lives. When Jesus says, "I was hungry and you gave me food, I was thirsty and you gave me something to drink, I was a stranger and you welcomed me, I was naked and you gave me clothing, I was sick and you took care of me, I was in prison and you visited me" (Matt. 25:35–37), it seems plain enough that Jesus wants his followers to care for the hungry, foreigners, the poor, the sick, and prisoners. But even here, the next questions in our minds have to be, "How? When? Where? Which ones?" We are also left to wonder what it means when we hear Jesus saying, "you always have the poor with you" (Mk. 14:7, Matt. 26:11), or "sell everything you own" (Lk. 18:22, Matt. 19:21), or see him choosing to hang out with the most loathed businesspeople in his neighborhood – tax collectors and prostitutes.

Given the difficulty of direct correlation between ancient/late-ancient Israel and our own worlds, we might nevertheless seek to derive some instructions or lasting ethical paradigms from the texts.[43] Or like liberation theologians, we may decide to view such commands through a particular lens, such as the lens of poverty, or race, gender, or intersectionality. To paraphrase Amy-Jill Levine, who frequently notes that "you don't have to make Judaism look *bad* to make Jesus look *good*,"[44] it is not necessary to attack any one interpretive approach in order to see that other approaches also have their strengths. What is necessary, however, is interpretive humility. It is incumbent upon every reader of Scripture to be aware of our "canon within a canon," of the parts of the Bible we like and the parts we don't, of the intellectual somersaults we do in order to make sure our reading of Scripture doesn't interfere with our pre-existing sense of justice.

Box 9.8
The author has dealt with Scripture, now she turns to tradition. The theme here is how much diversity of viewpoint you find both in Scripture and in the tradition.

---

[41] "Is the Bible Still Relevant Today?" *Biblica*, accessed March 8, 2020, https://www.biblica.com/resources/bible-faqs/is-the-bible-still-relevant-today.

[42] All biblical quotations are taken from Bruce Metzger, et al., eds., *The Bible: New Revised Standard Version* (Division of Christian Education of the National Council of Churches of Christ in the USA, 1989).

[43] E.g. Christopher Wright, *Old Testament Ethics for the People of God* (Downers Grove, IL: Intervarsity, 2004); Richard Hays, *The Moral Vision of the New Testament* (San Francisco: HarperCollins, 1996).

[44] See for example, "Jesus & Judaism: The Connection Matters, with Amy-Jill Levine," Trinity Church Boston, accessed May 8, 2020, https://www.trinitychurchboston.org/event/jesus-judaism-the-connection-matters-with-dr-amy-jill-levine.

Tradition

Since the time of Jesus and Paul and the earliest disciples, Christians have struggled to understand how best to enact the gospel in their lives in concrete economic ways (see Box 9.8). Some Christians have looked to Scripture and found God's concern for migrants, widows, and orphans in Israel's prophets; Jesus's and Paul's teachings about unearned grace and neighbor love; and early disciples' models of voluntary poverty. For them, such a framework should color every aspect of a Christian's life, including in the material and political world. Other readers of Scripture find shamelessly wealthy kings; Jesus's parables about shrewd servants and masters who know how to work hard, invest wisely, and make a buck; and Paul's appeals to wealthy Christians for support. For them, God's grace is a matter of individual salvation, inward attitudes, and interpersonal relationships, especially within the church; it doesn't change the "laws" of finance, accounting, or supply and demand, which reign supreme in the "real" world unless and until the Messiah shows up again, this time with the promised new creation.

Despite the oft-cited example of communally held property among the early Christians in Acts 4, the vast majority of Christian tradition has affirmed the institution of private property. Noteworthy exceptions include the desert mothers and fathers of the early churches, and medieval renouncers like St. Francis of Assisi. These Christians took seriously Jesus's command to sell everything they had and take up the cross of affliction, in imitation of the one who gave up his own life out of love for the world. By and large, though, the mainstream of two millennia of Christianity has upheld individual ownership for what we might call "householders" – not just as a necessary evil, but in positive terms as a gift from God to be enjoyed, as well as an opportunity to do at least some good for one's neighbors. Around 200 CE, Bishop Clement of Alexandria insisted that "what is managed with wisdom, and sobriety, and piety, is profitable; ... the Lord introduces the use of external things, bidding us put away not the means of subsistence, but what uses them badly."[45] In the middle ages, Thomas Aquinas likewise defended private property as coherent with human dignity: "the possession of external things is natural to man," who has "a natural dominion over external things, because, by his reason and will, he is able to use them for his own profit, as they were made on his account."[46] In the Reformation era, Martin Luther made vocation open to all Christians, regardless of station in life, since "the way to serve God was to serve our neighbor."[47] And John Calvin even let merchants and bankers out of the penalty box, as long as they stayed away from exploiting those in need through predatory lending.[48]

But business has never been embraced by *all* Christians, especially in the wake of the horrors of the Industrial Revolution. In the late nineteenth and early twentieth centuries, the idea that business was often the problem, rather than the solution to human woes, was made popular by Christian Socialism, which once again took seriously the model of a homeless, property-less savior. "The Lord did not die to give us an opportunity for self-seeking," wrote one preacher; "We are not here on a vacation from God. He sends every man of wealth forth to be a savior of his fellow men [sic]; and the business man who fails to be a little Christ to the world has made a

---

[45] Clement of Alexandria, "Who Is the Rich Man That Shall be Saved?," *Early Christian Writings*.

[46] Thomas Aquinas, *Summa theologica*, II-II.66.1.

[47] Erin M. Hawley, "The Plague, Coronavirus and Martin Luther – Why They All Matter Now," *The Hill*, March 20, 2020, https://thehill.com/opinion/white-house/488675-the-plague-coronavirus-and-martin-luther-why-they-all-matter-now.

[48] See, for example, John Calvin on lending and usury in Exodus 22:25, *Harmony of the Law* Vol. 3.

disastrous and irreparable business failure."[49] It was not sufficient, for these Christians, to have one set of ethics for Sunday mornings and another one for the office, because Jesus himself "did not divide His teachings into temporal and spiritual any more than He separated duties into secular and sacred."[50]

While this movement failed to survive two world wars with any robust presence, many of its ideas were shared in the latter half of the twentieth century through various movements of Liberation Theology – Latin American, African American, feminist, and others – inspired significantly by engagement with Marxist socio-scientific critiques of the rapidly evolving capitalist economy. Many such Christians still subscribe to some variation of socialism, seeing history as full of obvious struggles between oppressed people and their oppressors.[51] These approaches purposefully sought (and still seek) to look at the world through the lenses, not of its orthodoxy-wielding power elite, but of its unluckiest members – the poorest and most oppressed people in any given context, those with little education, few resources, and even fewer choices for survival. While the wealthy may see business as a way to do good in the world, those who live on the fringes of the production lines, carrying much of the cost of business without enjoying the benefits, know its many harms all too well. "We live in an idolatrous society," wrote Mennonite pastor Isaac Villegas, "all too ready to abandon people deemed no longer to have what Karl Marx called 'use-value.' … For capitalism, the external end of economic growth determines the value of a human being. Actuaries quantify the worth of a life. A cost-benefit analysis decides which demographic will be sacrificed for the common good."[52] The Christian tradition of suspicion against loveless business is alive and well.

Reason

When it comes to modern understandings of just business, religious reasoning has been well trained to take a back seat to more "scientific" ways of reasoning, especially the discipline that has come to be known as economics (as well as its offshoots: accounting, finance, management, and marketing). Together these fields rely heavily on a combination of mathematics, sociology, psychology, statistics, and neuroscience. But of course, each one must also start with an underlying set of philosophical assumptions about how the universe works, particularly human nature and human societies (theological anthropology). Some scientists acknowledge this reality, in subfields such as radical economics or critical accounting,[53] but by and large business and economics curricula purport to be dealing only with facts and not faith commitments, only with "what is," not with "what should be." This kind of thinking led some to argue that "Economists should be doing this cost-benefit analysis" between lives and jobs amid COVID-19; "Why is nobody putting some numbers on the economic costs of a

---

[49] George Herron, *The Message of Jesus to Men of Wealth* (New York: Fleming H. Revell Co., 1891), 23–24: https://archive.org/details/messageofjesusto00herr/page/22/mode/2up/search/business.

[50] Herron, 3.

[51] Aaron Sanchez, "When American Christians Were Socialists," *Sojourners*, August 9, 2019, https://sojo.net/articles/when-american-christians-were-socialists.

[52] Isaac Villegas, "A Pastor's Pandemic Diary," *The Christian Century*, May 20, 2020, https://www.christiancentury.org/article/first-person/pastor-s-pandemic-diary.

[53] E.g. *International Journal of Critical Accounting*; *Critical Perspectives on Accounting*; *Review of Radical Political Economics*.

monthlong or a yearlong shutdown against the lives saved? The whole discipline is well equipped for it."[54]

Christians differ on whether the reliance on economic science in the modern era has been overall a positive or negative.[55] The Acton Institute, for example, declares, "We acknowledge the legitimate role of profit as an indicator that a business is functioning well, and affirm the importance of business as a calling."[56] A business-based economy, of which private ownership is the foundation and in which human labor is bought and sold based on the law of supply and demand, seems to be taken as God's chosen way for humans to organize themselves into communities.[57] Government's primary job is therefore to make sure private ownership is protected; protect private property and everything else will fall into place, as if an "invisible hand" were guiding it. "Just business" is just that – business as usual; as long as no one is coerced into anything and no one is stealing anything, it's all to the good. (Understandings of "coerce" and "steal" tend to be interpreted rather narrowly in this view; people who "choose" to work under inhumane conditions for a pittance, instead of starving or watching their kids go without health care, aren't usually counted.)

At the far end of the spectrum lie those Christians for whom economics is the "dismal science" of scarcity, and "just business" is an oxymoron. Business for them is the *opposite* of God's plan for humanity, a curse resulting from human failure rather than providence. God's intention for creation is abundance freedom – conditions that will also reign in God's new creation. Humanity (as portrayed in Gen. 3) managed to ruin this perfect situation by stealing, and were forced ever after to work and suffer for the survival of the species. Business is therefore a result of human sin, an accommodation to post-lapsarian reality, rather than God's original plan. The Christian ideal should be a world of plenitude and grace, where each person has whatever they need, and no one hoards. Conversely, business as we know it is the endeavor of serving "mammon" – a hungry god who demands total allegiance, and whom no one can serve if they wish to serve the one true God.

Also in the twentieth century, yet another kind of reason – ecology – was injected into public debates over economics and just business. A shift in European and American Christian consciousness had already begun a century before, in Darwin's era, as Westerners woke up (or rather, began the painfully slow and as-yet-incomplete process of waking up) to the realities of ecosystems, ozone layers, and species adaptations and extinctions. But as greenhouse gases increased exponentially through the lucrative burning of fossil fuels, combined with the destruction of forests and unsustainable agriculture,[58] some Christians took up the call to protect the earth – a

---

[54] Eduardo Porter and Jim Tankersley, "Shutdown Spotlights Economic Cost of Saving Lives," *New York Times*, March 24, 2020, https://www.nytimes.com/2020/03/24/business/economy/coronavirus-economy.html.

[55] For a deep dive into Christianity's relationship with economics, see Kathryn D. Blanchard, *The Protestant Ethic or the Spirit of Capitalism: Christians, Freedom, and Free Markets* (Eugene, OR: Cascade, 2010).

[56] Acton Institute website, https://www.acton.org/topic/economics, accessed March 25, 2020. The Acton Institute calls itself "ecumenical," but has its roots in (Judeo-) Christianity, as evidenced by its affirmation that humanity is "created in the image of God" (https://www.acton.org/about/mission).

[57] The state of Michigan has at least two private colleges dedicated to free-market economics, one of which, Hillsdale College, is explicitly Christian: https://www.hillsdale.edu/about/mission; the other is Northwood University: https://www.northwood.edu/about/about-northwood-university.

[58] "The Causes of Climate Change," NASA, accessed May 8, 2020, https://climate.nasa.gov/causes.

mighty but fragile gift, given by God to humankind for its cultivation and care. Over time, this call became even louder as more Christians grew aware of the unequal and disproportionate ways in which poor and vulnerable groups of people were harmed by pollution, as well as the Earth's own various forms of backlash: flooding, droughts, hurricanes, extreme temperatures, diseases. (If such catastrophic signs didn't seem biblical enough, early 2020 even brought swarms of locusts to the African continent and "murder hornets" to North America.[59])

There are economic thinkers attempting to integrate ecology into a more organic economic model that incorporates many different kinds of reasons – mostly material but philosophical as well. One such attempt is Kate Raworth's "Doughnut Economics," which proposes to do away with a one-directional model of thinking about business – from extraction, to production, to consumption, to disposal – with no thought of how such a process affects the actual earth on which it occurs, or the actual people living and working in the system. In place of a line she proposes a circle: the center limits constitute a "social foundation" of goods that humans need to survive; the outer limits are marked by an "ecological ceiling" of what the earth can sustain. Between these borders lies the "safe and just space for humanity."[60] The assumption behind such an innovative model for just business is also a hope – that humans can thrive *together*, and *should* thrive together, along with a thriving planet.

For some Christians this is an easy assumption to latch onto; after all, the God of Genesis 1 creates everything and calls it "good," even "very good." But again, not all Christians were (or are) convinced of the need to change their ways of thinking about business. They look at alternative reasoning and see only shrinking markets, lost wealth, and (perhaps worst of all) "lazy" people incentivized to freeload off the system. This is not always a simple matter of not caring about the Earth or the suffering of human beings; it is more often a disagreement over *how* best to care for the Earth and its inhabitants. For some, a thriving economy *is* neighbor love, because it creates jobs, which create wealth, which enable people to take care of themselves and their families. The sacrifice of a few animal species for the sake of jobs may be worth it, they think, since God ultimately made the earth for humans to use (and it's all only temporary anyway). The fact that the current version of a thriving economy is almost entirely dependent upon fossil fuels that wreak havoc on the planet is no cause for concern, since leaps in technology will undoubtedly save us before it's too late, and such leaps are the products of *precisely* this kind of thriving economy. Furthermore, any attempts to stop business as usual inevitably harms not only technological and economic progress but also especially the poor and the Earth.[61] Thus, even being "reasonable" does not create automatic agreement.

Experience

It can be extremely difficult to pull apart the many threads of such arguments, to identify which parts of their reasoning arises from theological commitments, which reasons are economic,

---

[59] Natalie Colarossie, "Swarms of Locusts Forced Somalia to Declare a National Emergency. Skin-crawling Photos Show How Menacing Their Plagues Can Be," *Business Insider*, February 28, 2020, https://www.businessinsider.com/desert-locust-plague-devastates-africa-photos-history-2020-2.

[60] Kate Raworth, "Ecological Economics in the Time of Coronavirus," Kate Raworth: Exploring Doughnut Economics website, accessed March 23, 2020, https://www.kateraworth.com/2020/04/01/ecological-economics-in-the-time-of-coronavirus.

[61] E.g. Peter Hazell, "Think Again: The Green Revolution," *Foreign Policy*, September 2009, https://foreignpolicy.com/2009/09/22/think-again-the-green-revolution.

scientific, political, biological, personal, cultural, and so on. What causes some people to reason that the economy needs protection at all costs, while others reason just the opposite way? It's not a simple matter of upbringing or education.[62] It must be due at least in part to individual and collective experience, neither last nor least in the quadrilateral. Indeed, it is all but impossible to discern why people think differently, but this doesn't keep scientists from trying.

Neuroscientists like Jonathan Haidt reject the "delusion" that reason is humanity's most distinguishing characteristic, arguing that *gut intuition* is in fact the determinative force in our reasoning, such that we should imagine our conscious selves as "a small rider on a very large elephant."[63] Humans like to think we are rational beings, when in fact our considerable rationality comes late to the game, serving primarily to justify our prior instincts. Behavioral economists like Daniel Kahneman concur, saying intuition "operates automatically and quickly, with little or no effort and no sense of voluntary control."[64] Their advice is to be skeptical about rationality, understanding that our preferences – including even our most deeply held ethical convictions – are determined in no small part by factors *other than* how disciplined our thinking is.[65]

Haidt goes so far as to liken morality or "the righteous mind" to sensory preference, "like a tongue with six taste receptors," including loyalty, fairness, care, authority, liberty, and sanctity.[66] These pre-rational tastes have their basis in biology, he says, arising through evolutionary adaptations that enabled both individual survival and group survival.[67] Because human morality is a complex evolutionary adaptation, humans as a species have both selfish (like chimpanzees) and "groupish" tendencies (like bees).[68] The brain's confirmation bias ensures that we find ongoing "reasons" for support, bolstered through life experience.[69] Haidt ultimately expresses a **Durkheimian** approach to religion – primarily a matter of bonding teams of people together through grand narratives. But the same capacity that lets humans find belonging in one moral community also makes it difficult, even impossible, to understand the motivations or appreciate the wisdom of members of other communities.[70]

---

[62] Arlie Hochschild, "Think Republicans are Disconnected from Reality? It's Even Worse Among Liberals," *The Guardian*, July 21, 2019, https://www.theguardian.com/commentisfree/2019/jul/21/democrats-republicans-political-beliefs-national-survey-poll.

[63] Jonathan Haidt, *The Righteous Mind: Why Good People Disagree over Politics and Religion* (New York: Vintage, 2012), 367.

[64] Daniel Kahneman, *Thinking, Fast and Slow* (New York: Farrar, Straus and Giroux, 2011), 20–21. Emphasis original. Psychologists further distinguish "two selves," the remembering self and the experiencing self, which also complicate what we think we understand about ourselves, e.g. 408–410.

[65] Kahneman, 374. As one writer puts it, although we may "think our decisions are conscious … data show that consciousness is just the tip of the iceberg." Kerri Smith, "Brain Makes Decisions Before You Even Know It," *Nature*, April 11, 2008, https://www.nature.com/news/2008/080411/full/news.2008.751.html.

[66] Haidt, *Righteous Minds*, 368. "Variation in political ideology has been linked to differences in attention to and processing of emotional stimuli," according to Mark Mills, Frank J. Gonzalez, Karl Giuseffi, Benjamin Sievert, Kevin B. Smith, John R. Hibbing, and Michael D. Dodda, "Political Conservatism Predicts Asymmetries in Emotional Scene Memory," *Behavioral Brain Research* Vol. 306 (June 2016): 84–90, https://doi.org/10.1016/j.bbr.2016.03.025.

[67] Haidt, *Righteous Minds*, 46.

[68] Haidt, *Righteous Minds*, 330.

[69] Haidt, *Righteous Minds*, 341. See also 314.

[70] Haidt, *Righteous Minds*, 317–318.

Readers' self-examination of their own feelings about economics and business may provide a glimpse into the truth of this view. Are you quick to want to relativize Jesus's commands if they strike you as too "communist" or impractical when taken literally? Do you instinctively discount the opinions of wealthy Christians who consume conspicuously? Does the idea of giving money to "undeserving" people make you angry? Would you consider yourself a moral failure if you took a job at a bank or large corporation? Is private property a non-negotiable right or a clever form of theft? Most of us, if we are honest, have explicit or implicit gut reactions – positive or negative – to certain kinds of business products, business practices, and businesspeople. Understanding our predilections *before* we try to explain our approach to justice in business is an important step in the process.

What, Then, Is Just Business?

It has become commonplace in many circles to acknowledge the ways in which theological arguments are clearer reflections of *the people arguing* than they are of any objective truths. Some writers turn to personal storytelling, eschewing the "jargon-laden texts" favored by scholarly insiders, aiming instead for a "fusion of the personal with the scholarly" so as to engage a broader audience.[71] While time and space do not permit a thoroughly autoethnographic approach here, suffice it to say I reject "the notion that scholars should hide their subjectivities behind the guise of positivist ideologies" and I "accept and recognize that [my] situated knowledge and experience weaves itself into every stage of the research process."[72] Other Christian authors can (and do) offer very different economic narratives, starting as they do with their unique combinations of Christian experiences, Christian assumptions, and readings of Christian sources (see Box 9.9).[73]

Box 9.9
The author makes it clear that she will bring her distinctive perspectives to the debate. Here the author is pushing back against the illusion of academic "objectivity." We come to all debates with our narratives and background. The author accepts that other academics looking at these questions would reach different conclusions. She names all this in the text; so the reader is entirely clear that this is "her" read of the data.

---

[71] Christine E. Crouse-Dick, "A Tacit Case for Autoethnography as a Crucial Research Method for Befuddling Times," Religious Studies Project, December 21, 2019, https://www.religiousstudiesproject.com/2019/12/21/a-tacit-case-for-autoethnography-as-a-crucial-research-method-for-befuddling-times.

[72] Crouse-Dick, "Tacit Case." See also Tony Adams, Carolyn Ellis, and Stacy Holman Jones, "Autoethnography," *The International Encyclopedia of Communication Research Methods*, ed. Joerg Matthis, Christine Davis, and Robert Potter (Hoboken, NJ: Wiley Online Library, John Wiley & Sons, 2017). https://onlinelibrary.wiley.com/doi/10.1002/9781118901731.iecrm0011.

[73] For a Catholic overview, see Domènec Melé and Joan Fontrodona, "Christian Ethics and Spirituality in Leading Business Organizations: Editorial Introduction," *Journal of Business Ethics* Vol. 145 (2017): 671–679. For historical selections from primary texts, see Max L. Stackhouse, et al., eds., *On Moral Business: Classical and Contemporary Resources for Ethics in Economic Life* (Grand Rapids, MI: Wm. B. Eerdmans, 1995).

The goal of this article has been to help myself and my readers think about justice in business, muddling through the confusing present into our highly uncertain futures; my concern is "not so much aiming for some goal called 'Truth' as for an enlarged capacity to deal with life's challenges and contingencies."[74] Once we accept that each of us comes to the questions with baggage in need of unpacking, we have the opportunity to start with the planks in our own eyes (Matt. 7:3) and examine *ourselves* as agents in the modern marketplace.

History "is written not only by men [sic] but also by microbes."[75] And the COVID-19 pandemic has provided a test case for business as we know it. It did not *create* economic injustice but certainly exacerbates the inequality that was already there.[76] One author writes, "we need a very different kind of economics if we are to build socially just and ecologically sound futures. In the face of COVID-19, this has never been more obvious. The responses to the COVID-19 pandemic are simply the amplification of the dynamic that drives other social and ecological crises: the prioritisation of one type of value over others."[77] The world's sudden (staggered) stay-at-home orders constituted "a rather unique shock that is unlike any other experienced by the U.S. economy in the last 100 years," according to one economist, with negative impact that "does not equally affect all businesses, sectors or occupations."[78] The disease seemed to be uneven in its most dire effects, attacking the elderly, the already health-compromised, and the financially disadvantaged. In the US, it also meant "wildly disproportionate" and even "shocking" death rates among African Americans.[79] "While the virus infects people regardless of wealth," wrote Human Rights Watch, "the poor will be most affected due to longstanding segregation by income and race, reduced economic mobility, and the high cost of medical care."[80] Those marginalized by race, gender, and immigration status were more likely to be found in "Low-income jobs in fields like retail, hospitality, childcare, and the gig economy," which "cannot be performed remotely" and "do not offer paid sick leave or health insurance;" they are also over-represented in prison populations.[81]

---

[74] Arthur Bochner, "On First-person Narrative Scholarship: Autoethnography as Acts of Meaning," *Narrative Inquiry* Vol. 22, No. 1 (2012): 161, https://www.academia.edu/11573461/On_first-person_narrative_scholarship_Autoethnography_as_acts_of_meaning.

[75] Elizabeth Kolbert, "Pandemics and the Shape of Human History," *New Yorker*, March 30, 2020, https://www.newyorker.com/magazine/2020/04/06/pandemics-and-the-shape-of-human-history.

[76] "How Covid-19 Exacerbates Inequality," *The Economist*, March 26, 2020, https://www.economist.com/britain/2020/03/26/how-covid-19-exacerbates-inequality.

[77] Simon Mair, "What Will the World Be Like After Coronavirus? Four Possible Futures," *The Conversation*, March 30, 2020, https://theconversation.com/what-will-the-world-be-like-after-coronavirus-four-possible-futures-134085.

[78] Miguel Faria-e-Castro, "Back-of-the-Envelope Estimates of Next Quarter's Unemployment Rate," Federal Reserve Bank of St. Louis, March 24, 2020, https://www.stlouisfed.org/on-the-economy/2020/march/back-envelope-estimates-next-quarters-unemployment-rate.

[79] Elizabeth Hlavinka, "COVID-19 Killing African Americans at Shocking Rates," *MedPage*, May 1, 2020, https://www.medpagetoday.com/infectiousdisease/covid19/86266. Also Ed Pilkington, "Black Americans Dying of Covid-19 at Three Times the Rate of White People," *The Guardian*, May 20, 2020, https://www.theguardian.com/world/2020/may/20/black-americans-death-rate-covid-19-coronavirus.

[80] See also Charles M. Blow, "The Racial Time Bomb in the Covid-19 Crisis," *New York Times*, April 1, 2020, https://www.nytimes.com/2020/04/01/opinion/coronavirus-black-people.html. And "US: COVID-19 Threatens People Behind Bars," Human Rights Watch, March 12, 2020, https://www.hrw.org/news/2020/03/12/us-covid-19-threatens-people-behind-bars.

[81] "US: Address Impact of Covid-19 on Poor," Human Rights Watch, March 19, 2020, https://www.hrw.org/news/2020/03/19/us-address-impact-covid-19-poor#.

> **Box 9.10**
>
> The preceding sections have made the challenge of thinking about business much harder for the Christian. One cannot make a simplistic connection between Scripture or tradition to affirm a particular Christian account of business. Therefore, having posed the problem with some precision, the author will now seek to offer a constructive way forward. A key assumption is that author's own position and perspective is central in any response to the problem. Central to the author's response is the "Golden Rule" – you should love your neighbor as yourself – and the concept of community.

The one claim I feel comfortable making in light of foregoing caveats, is that any genuinely Christian view of justice in business must be about *loving one's neighbor as oneself* (Mk. 12:31) (see Box 9.10). My own theological tendency is heavily influenced by liberation theologies, and aligns with the approach I see coming out of the contemporary Poor People's Movement. Christians in business settings – including nonprofit businesses like churches and colleges – must put the poor at the center of their thinking. I believe we should meditate seriously on Jim Wallis's question, "What would it mean to make COVID-19 a Matthew 25 moment," in which Christians truly prioritized serving the sick, the hungry, the foreigner, the imprisoned?[82] I share Presbyterian pastor Liz Theoharis's outcry over the economic injustices exposed by the politics of the pandemic, which continued to prioritize corporations over suffering people:

> As a biblical scholar and preacher, I look to our sacred texts, which teach that plagues always seem to arise in times of great poverty and inequality. These pandemics begin by affecting the poor, but inevitably reach to the heights of power, exposing the injustice and inhumanity of ruling authorities. In the Bible, prophetic leaders are compelled to call out the immorality of deprivation in the midst of abundance and to build the power necessary to right social and economic wrongs. This is why our attempts to give everyone equal access to medicine can't stop with health care reform.[83]

I was even surprised to find myself nodding at a Southern Baptist response from Russell Moore, who pushed back against those who seemed to think a few hundred thousand, apparently disposable dead people might be worth it to keep the economy going. "Such considerations turn human lives into checkmarks on a page rather than the sacred mystery they are," he wrote:

> The value of a human life is not determined on a balance sheet …
> We must get back to work, get the economy back on its feet, but we can only do that when doing so will not kill the vulnerable and overwhelm our hospitals, our doctors, our nurses, and our communities. And along the way we must guard our consciences. We cannot pass by on the side of the road when the elderly, the disabled, the poor, and the vulnerable are in peril before our eyes. We want to hear the sound of cash registers again, but we cannot afford to hear them over the cries of those made in the image of God. This pandemic will change us, change our economy, our culture, our priorities, our personal lives.[84]

---

[82] Wallis, "Staggering".

[83] Liz Theoharis, "Our Moral Obligation to Health During the COVID-19 Pandemic," *Religion News Service*, March 26, 2020, https://religionnews.com/2020/03/26/our-moral-obligation-to-health-during-the-covid-19-pandemic.

[84] Russell Moore, "God Doesn't Want Us to Sacrifice the Old," *New York Times*, March 26, 2020, https://www.nytimes.com/2020/03/26/opinion/coronavirus-elderly-vulnerable-religion.html.

While it is difficult to define positively what it looks like to love one's neighbor as oneself, especially when the neighbor's circumstances are so different from our own, it is much easier to figure out what it does *not* look like. Whatever else just business means, for example, it does not mean polluting the neighbor's habitat – the water, air, and land on which their lives and health depend. It does not mean paying them the smallest possible wage you can bully them into accepting, and denying them even the most basic health care, simply because the system provides them with no better options. It does not mean hoarding wealth when others lack basic necessities. It does not mean turning a blind eye to human rights violations in your supply chain, simply because it's too expensive to find out more. It does not mean convincing them their lives have no meaning without whatever product or service you're hocking. And it does not mean exploiting everyone and everything as "just the cost of doing business," while giving high-profile donations to charity after the damage is done. Furthermore, there is always an implied "thou shall" hidden within any "thou shall not."[85] Discerning how to love the neighbor is a matter of virtue, of lifelong training and practice, rather than simple obedience to rules.

Besides neighbor love, another possibly fruitful Christian framework for looking at business is that of *community*. And despite Scripture's focus on the people of Israel, and later on the church, many Christians over the past two millennia have taken an increasingly inclusive approach to thinking about who counts as part of "our" community. This inclusivity is grounded in a sense of common humanity, and the belief in a single God who cares for the entire world – a planet that shares a single fate. "The rich and the poor have this in common: the Lord is the maker of them all" (Prov. 22:2); in Jewish theology, this universal care is sometimes expressed as *tikkun olam*, "repair of the world." Christians often cite the gospel claim that Jesus was incarnated expressly because "God so loved the world" (Jn. 3:16), not only humans, or a mere sample of humanity. When Jesus asks, "Who is my neighbor?" the answer is: the one who shows mercy to someone in need (Lk. 10). A Christian's vocation, while not easy, is clear and simple: to love our neighbors, not because they deserve it but because they need it.

If the whole world is the community that God cares about, then business must operate in service to the community. Even in a purely utilitarian, cost–benefit analysis, this puts competition in a new light. Firms mustn't compete with each other merely for market share or bragging rights, but rather so as to "love one another with mutual affection; outdo one another in showing honor" (Rom. 12:10). This means doing away with the false narrative – which comes from both right and left – that "Businesses exist to make a profit."[86] This claim is historically and logically untrue. Businesses exist to provide benefits, like delicious kimchee, or stylish haircuts, or various means of long-distance communication. True, they are *enabled* to do so by bringing in a bit more money than they spend on supplies, rent, and wages, but profits are not the purpose of the business; they are rather the *means* to whatever benefit a business provides. *Business cannot be its own logic*, at least not without terrible consequences. Humankind may indeed have a natural "propensity to truck, barter, and exchange," driven by natural self-interest, as Adam Smith observed, but nothing is ever "just business" in the sense of mere buying and selling.[87] There is

---

[85] E.g. the Ten Commandments in *Luther's Small Catechism* (Concordia, 2019): https://catechism.cph.org/en/10-commandments.html.

[86] Mair, "How Will Coronavirus Change the World?".

[87] Adam Smith, *An Inquiry into the Nature and Causes of the Wealth of Nations* Cannan edn., Vol. 1 [1776], Online Library of Liberty, accessed May 8, 2020, https://oll.libertyfund.org/titles/smith-an-inquiry-into-the-nature-and-causes-of-the-wealth-of-nations-cannan-ed-vol-1#Smith_0206-01_150.

no such thing as "business for business's sake" because business is human and humans are complex. We must resist the temptation to boil things down to one simple cause (yes, even when making the so-called "business case for social responsibility"[88]).

Once we come to understand that business is more than a bottom line or a share price, we begin to see the possibilities for loving our neighbors through our economic activities. There are tradeoffs, but they don't have to be as cruel as we have been led to believe. "There doesn't appear to be a tradeoff," says one economist, "between saving lives and supporting the economy."[89] Instead it's a matter of imagining a *different kind* of economy. The conversion from a zero-sum mindset to one of collaboration and cooperation is not easy, of course, but it can happen if we are willing to change our assumptions. "We tend to think of the economy as the way we buy and sell things, mainly consumer goods," but "At its core, the economy is the way we take our resources and turn them into the things we need to live."[90]

If COVID-19 was a test, the majority-Christian US failed, punching way above its weight in cases and deaths; as of mid-May 2020, it had 29% of the world's COVID-19 deaths, with only 4% of the world's population.[91] Meanwhile, the post-COVID-19 "economic cataclysm" may still lie ahead for some.[92] Christians after 2020 have a chance to wake up and forge a different, more just world, starting with the ways we do business with one another. "We should see this as a chance to rethink and reimagine our approaches to managing natural resources. How we interact. What really is of value to us. It is time to pause and reflect on how to be the best stewards for a healthy and resilient planet."[93] Our reimagining of business will take place in conversation with Christian scriptures, traditions, and communities. It must certainly also take place in conversation with economic and ecological sciences. And most of all, our conversations with one another must be undertaken with the intention to love our neighbors, in the humility that comes from knowing ourselves through critical self-reflection. In this way, "just business" can become a Christian practice that lets each of us prepare, however imperfectly, for the coming reign of God.

---

[88] Pankaj Ghemawat, *The New Global Road Map: Enduring Strategies for Turbulent Times* (Boston, MA: Harvard Business Review Press, 2018), 209.

[89] Scott Horsely, "What Is the Economic Cost of Social Distancing?" *Weekend Edition*, March 28, 2020, https://www.npr.org/2020/03/28/823071188/what-is-the-economic-cost-of-social-distancing.

[90] Mair, "How Will Coronavirus Change the World?".

[91] "In contrast, China, which accounts for 18 percent of the world's [population and] total number of annual deaths, now has about 2 percent of the world's total Covid-19 deaths." Joseph Chamie, "United States Leads the World in Covid-19 Deaths," *Inter Press Service News Agency*, May 18, 2020, https://www.ipsnews.net/2020/05/america-leads-world-covid-19-deaths.

[92] Damon Linker, "There Is No Solution to the Economic Cataclysm Ahead," *The Week*, April 3, 2020, https://theweek.com/articles/906389/there-no-solution-economic-cataclysm-ahead.

[93] "The Epidemic Provides a Chance to Do Good By the Climate," *The Economist*, March 26, 2020, https://www.economist.com/science-and-technology/2020/03/26/the-epidemic-provides-a-chance-to-do-good-by-the-climate. Somini Sengupta, "Climate Change Has Lessons for Fighting the Coronavirus," *New York Times*, March 12, 2020, https://www.nytimes.com/2020/03/12/climate/climate-change-coronavirus-lessons.html. Martin Noponen, "Cohabiting With a Virus: We Must Learn to Live Life on Land More Sustainably," Business Fights Poverty, April 2, 2020, https://businessfightspoverty.org/articles/cohabiting-with-a-virus-we-must-learn-to-live-life-on-land-more-sustainably.

Part V

The End of the World

10

Relentless Love and the Afterlife

Thomas J. Oord

RESEARCH LEVEL 1

Editors' Introduction

This is a gentle introduction into research writing. The author wants to reach scholars and an educated general audience. This chapter is an excellent example of a scholar offering a provocative argument that should be accessible to a general audience. Notice that it argues for roughly the same position as the essay in Chapter 11, but both the form and style of the argument are significantly different.

The author begins by describing various reasons why many people believe in the afterlife. Note that this is a broadly empirical survey and not an argument that one should believe in an afterlife. He then moves to a description of biblical perspectives on the afterlife. If one is a Christian, as the author is, then such perspectives should have at least some authority. His argument then takes a form most famously used by Reinhold Niebuhr. If one is a Christian and believe in the afterlife, several alternatives are on offer. The author sets out the most popular alternatives and describes questions that each alternative raises but cannot adequately answer. He then puts forward his own proposal and shows how his proposal has an adequate answer to the questions that illuminate flaws in the alternatives.

Box 10.1
The author introduces his topic, and it is immediately apparent that he is writing for a general audience. He sets up the proposal he wants to make by raising various views about the afterlife, views held by religious and nonreligious people alike, and noting the reasons they give for having those views.

Nearly everyone thinks about what might happen after death (see Box 10.1). Many who believe in God believe in an afterlife. But afterlife views vary. Some believe in reincarnation, for instance. Others believe in heaven and hell. Still others believe righteous people go to heaven, and the rest are annihilated. And so on.[1]

---

[1] The claims in this paragraph and the following several are supported in a Pew Research Center study of Americans. See "2014 Religious Landscape Study," Pew Research Center, November 6, 2015, accessed January 20, 2020, https://www.pewresearch.org/fact-tank/2015/11/10/most-americans-believe-in-heaven-and-hell/ft_15-11-11_afterlife_420px.

The Craft of Innovative Theology: Argument and Process, First Edition. Edited by John Allan Knight and Ian S. Markham.
© 2022 John Wiley & Sons Ltd. Published 2022 by John Wiley & Sons Ltd.

Some believers in God reject the possibility of an afterlife. They think there is no continued experiences beyond death. Awareness ends when our heart stops beating … or soon after that. God will always remember us, they say. But once we die, we no longer exist.

Many agnostics and atheists reject the idea of an afterlife. But not all. Some believe we continue as souls. Some believe in reincarnation. Others believe we will exist in a spiritual realm and may communicate with the living.

Given this diversity, it's natural to wonder *why* people believe in an afterlife. Not surprisingly, reasons vary for this too. Some believers appeal to personal revelation. "God told me" is strong justification for belief in life after death, at least for those who receive this special knowledge. For the person receiving a personal word from God, there is little room for doubt. "God said it; I believe it; that settles it." Other believers point to a sacred text or religious tradition as their afterlife authority. "Our sacred scripture says so" is all the reason they need. "My Rabbi told me," "Grandma taught me this," or "that's what our religion affirms" can also be enough. For these people, "Our sacred text or tradition says it; we believe it; that settles it." Authoritative texts, prophets, or traditions profoundly influence most people. But issues get complicated when authorities contradict. One sacred text says one thing about the afterlife; another text says something else. Which is right?

Sacred texts, prophets, or traditions don't answer every important question we ask. If they are silent or ambiguous about evolution, sexuality norms, technology, and gender equality, why should we trust them on the afterlife? Who and what can we trust (see Box 10.2)?

Box 10.2

To set the stage for his new proposal, the author lays out some general claims about the afterlife. The author wants to acknowledge what most readers might think about reasons to believe in life after death. But he also hopes to surprise the reader by mentioning some surprising facts.

In this essay, I offer a theory of the afterlife that address these questions. I call it the "relentless love" view. My theory draws from various sources, arguments, traditions, and the logic of love. Accepting the relentless love view does not mean joining a religious tradition or accepting an established belief system. Both religious and nonreligious people could embrace the view I propose. Before describing it, I want to explore other important afterlife issues.

Extraordinary Reasons for Belief in the Afterlife

Box 10.3

The author does not claim to be an omnipotent narrator, but admits that the Christian tradition has had a formative influence on his point of view. Most readers will assume all claims about the afterlife are religious. This section points out some nonreligious reasons some believe they will continue to have awareness after their bodies die. The author adds this to show that one need not join a religious tradition to accept his relentless love proposal later.

I write this essay from a Christian perspective. I didn't say *the* Christian perspective (see Box 10.3). There are many Christian perspectives of the afterlife, and the Bible and Christian tradition support many of them. I will address that diversity later. At this point, I want to admit Christian views and communities have shaped the way I think. It will surprise few people that a Christian like me believes in the afterlife.

Many people are surprised to discover nonreligious reasons for life after death. Belief in an afterlife is not the domain of religion alone. Let's look at a few nonreligious reasons.

A massive literature describes what most call "near-death experiences."[2] In such occurrences, bodies show signs of death – e.g. a stopped heart – but those pronounced dead continue to be subjectively aware. Although physicians or hospital machines determine them dead, these people revive and talk about their experiences. Some report leaving their bodies and floating about. Others say they moved toward light before regaining embodied experience. And so on.

About 5% of people report having undergone a near-death experience.[3] Most thereafter easily imagine an afterlife in which they will continue experiencing after their bodies die permanently. Some say their near-death incident was a powerful spiritual event. Many report feeling assured of divine love, becoming enlightened, or enjoying enhanced states of consciousness.[4]

Other people have "out of body experiences" that don't involve death. These people experience their minds, souls, selves, or center of subjectivity leaving their bodies and returning. Some report looking into their own eyes. Meditating Buddhist monks sometimes have such experiences. But they can occur in conjunction with physical exertion, dehydration, psychedelic drugs, traumatic brain injuries, sleep disorders, traumatic experiences, and more.

Many who undergo near-death or out-of-body experiences lose their fear of death. They regard their eventual demise as an entrance to another reality or a better form of existence. Life ends but, in another sense, it continues.

A large number of people report receiving messages from or giving messages to the dead.[5] Communication with those who have died may involve spiritual telepathy or dream-related interactions. Apparitions – "ghost sightings" – may occur, and claims about such sightings are more common that one might think. Many people say they communicate with ancestors, saints, or sages. Not surprisingly, those who communicate with the dead or see apparitions think they too will have subjective experiences beyond their own deaths.

A whole body of research called "parapsychology" explores these phenomena. This research is controversial and not easily substantiated. There are reasons to be skeptical. But dismissing parapsychological experiences out of hand opposes the empiricism central to science. Besides, an impressive list of philosophers and other scholars takes this research seriously. Rejecting it as "crazy impossible" seems unwise, even if one decides not to make it central to beliefs about the afterlife.

One final nonreligious reason for believing in life after death needs to be mentioned. On some philosophical accounts, each person has a mind or soul capable of continuing to experience after

---

[2] The list of relevant works is too long to list. One of the more comprehensive sources is P.M.H. Atwater, *The Big Book of Near-Death Experiences: The Ultimate Guide to the NDE and Its Aftereffects*, rev. 2nd edn. (Faber, VA: Rainbow Ridge, 2014).

[3] Atwater, *Near-Death Experiences*.

[4] For a philosophical account of near-death experiences, see John Martin Fischer, *Death, Immortality, and Meaning in Life* (Oxford: Oxford University Press, 2019).

[5] David Ray Griffin offers strong philosophical arguments for parapsychology in *Parapsychology, Philosophy, and Spirituality: A Postmodern Exploration* (Albany, NY: State University Press of New York, 1997).

bodily death. Philosophies affirming this view often draw from figures like Socrates and Plato. Many believe subjective experience beyond death is natural not supernatural. It's just part of what it means to have an immortal soul.

The Old Testament and Life after Death

> **Box 10.4**
>
> Having discussed nonreligious reasons for believing in the afterlife, the author now discusses biblical perspectives on the afterlife.

The relentless love theory I offer draws from the Bible (see Box 10.4). One doesn't need to accept the Bible as in all ways truthful, however, to affirm my theory. In fact, those in nonbiblical traditions or people who embrace no religion could embrace relentless love. Anyone who believes in God or something like the divine could, at least theoretically, affirm my afterlife theory.

People believed in life after death long before the Bible was written. "Prehistoric" primates like Neanderthals put food and implements in graves, presumably thinking these items could help the dead. Religious and nonreligious texts written before the Bible speak of life beyond death. It's not an idea original to Judaism or Christianity.

It surprises many people to find that what Christians call "the Old Testament" has little to say about people going to heaven or hell. The common view says dead people go to *Sheol*, which is the place of the dead. Ancient people considered this site an underground pit or cave. The writer of Job expresses this view:

> Are not the days of my life few?
> Let me alone, that I may find a little comfort
> before I go, never to return,
> to the land of gloom and deep darkness,
> the land of gloom and chaos,
> where light is like darkness
>
> (10:20–22)

According to biblical passages, dead people in *Sheol* cannot relate with God. The Psalmist describes this state as follows:

> For my soul is full of troubles,
> and my life draws near to Sheol.
> I am counted among those who go down to the Pit;
> I am like those who have no help,
> like those forsaken among the dead,
> like the slain that lie in the grave,
> like those whom you remember no more,
> for they are cut off from your hand.
> You have put me in the depths of the Pit,
> in the regions dark and deep
>
> (Ps. 88:3–6)

Old Testament writers occasionally speak of saints who fly straight into the heavens without dying. Enoch and Elijah are examples. But ordinary people – both believers in God and unbelievers, the righteous and unrighteous – go to the pit (see Box 10.5).

Box 10.5
The author here has provided another surprise for at least some readers. Many Christian readers may assume the Old Testament preaches the idea of hell as never-ending punishment. The author shows that this is not the case.

Ancient peoples believed generating descendants on Earth – having children – was how a person's influence continued after death. It was a blessing to be told, "your descendants will be many, and your offspring like the grass of the earth" (Job 5:25). Given this view, Old Testament writers emphasized the benefit of bearing and raising children. Ancient peoples were most concerned about life ending prematurely.

Jewish ideas about life after death changed between the writing of the Old and New Testament books. Biblical scholars attribute this change, in large part, to the widening relationships Jewish people had with other cultures. Among the new ideas to emerge was the possibility humans might be resurrected to an afterlife experience. The details of this view varied.

The New Testament and Life after Death

Box 10.6
The New Testament has much to say about the afterlife. In an attempt to hit the highlights, the author focuses on what most Christians think is the most important evidence for life after death: the resurrection of Jesus. Note how the author lays out some possible ways to understand Jesus's resurrection but also tells his readers which he thinks are most plausible.

The resurrection of Jesus is *a*, if not *the*, central event in Christianity (see Box 10.6). New Testament books were written decades after his resurrection, but it's unlikely any would have been written had people thought Jesus remained in the grave. In fact, it's doubtful Christianity itself would have emerged. It's hard to overestimate the importance of Jesus's resurrection for Christianity. Writers of Scripture believed God raised Jesus from the dead. The resurrection gave Jesus authority. Scripture writers believed Jesus continued living in some sense, and most Christians today think Jesus is alive. Writers also thought Jesus's resurrection tells us about the afterlife possibilities for all humans and the fate of all creation.

There is no consensus on what *exactly* happened at Jesus's resurrection. The biblical accounts are far from clear. Among contemporary theories intended to explain what happened, four are prominent. One theory says Jesus came out of the grave with a physical body almost exactly like the one placed in the tomb. A second says Jesus was transformed into a spiritual or glorified body with physical dimensions. A third says God raised Jesus as a spirit or soul, and post-resurrection witnesses encountered Jesus as a psycho-spiritual reality. A fourth theory says God raised Jesus only in the minds of believers.[6]

---

[6] Find one of the better overviews of the resurrection possibilities in John Hick, *Death and Eternal Life* (Westminster: John Knox, 1994).

In my opinion, the first and fourth theories seem least likely. Contrary to the first theory, people who witnessed the risen Jesus describe him acting in ways not possible for a person with a normal body. He can walk through walls, stroll for miles or stand next to friends unrecognized, and appear instantaneously to individuals or groups. A radical transformation seems to have occurred; the risen body isn't identical to the one placed in the tomb. The fourth theory also seems unlikely. It rightly points to the inspiration Jesus's resurrection gives. But it fails to account well for eyewitness testimonies. When encountering the risen Jesus, people seemed to experience something actually existing beyond their imagination.

Jesus, his followers, and many in first-century CE believed in life after death. Jesus's own words and stories are evidence of this, even if he failed to provide detail on what resurrections entail. The biblical accounts are hints about the nature of the afterlife rather than full descriptions. But they point to the reality of continued subjective experiences beyond bodily death. The New Testament sometimes says resurrection involves becoming transformed into what the Apostle Paul called "spiritual bodies."[7] It's not clear if these bodies have physical dimensions. Perhaps they're like apparitions. Perhaps they're embodied souls. Perhaps they are spirits with both mental and physical dimensions. Perhaps …

I'm only skimming the surface of what the Bible says about the afterlife. A full account requires much more than what I offer. And the New Testament view of the afterlife seems in development. My main points are these: despite imprecision, Jesus and other New Testament writers are confident the afterlife is real. Afterlife beliefs are found in various religious and philosophical traditions, and many contemporary people have nonreligious reasons to affirm them.

The Logic of Love

> **Box 10.7**
>
> Here the author is getting close to the heart of his argument. Up to this point he has been providing roughly empirical data about perspectives on the afterlife. He's getting ready to move to a more theological argument, but all such arguments have premises. And that's what he's setting out here: what he means when he says that God loves everyone.

Christian views of the afterlife continued to develop after the Old and New Testaments were written, and multiple views have emerged (see Box 10.7). Most views appeal to biblical passages, authorities in the tradition, arguments, and other sources. I draw from these sources for my relentless love view. In addition, I appeal to the logic of love. In my view, we should keep love central as we think about what might occur after our bodies die. As I read the Bible, draw from the best of the religious traditions, and consider what counts as living well, the issues of love rise to prominence. The overall drift of the Bible points to a God of love. This loving God calls humans to love. Jesus's life, teachings, death, and resurrection articulate these ideas. As I see it, the love Jesus expressed reveals a God who loves everyone and everything. We and others benefit when we cooperate with God's loving activity.

Because "love" is a misunderstood word, I want to clarify what I mean by it. I define love as acting intentionally, in relational response to God and others, to promote overall well-being.[8]

---

[7] I Cor. 15:42–44.

[8] I explain my definition in detail in several books. See especially *Defining Love: A Philosophical, Scientific, and Theological Engagement* (Ada, MI: Brazos, 2010); and *The Nature of Love: A Theology* (St. Louis, MO: Chalice, 2010).

In other words, we love when we aim to help, do good, and promote flourishing. To love is to be a blessing, in some way, in relation to God, others, and creation.

The Bible offers strong reasons to think God wants the well-being of all, not just some. Love for all is the primary attribute in God's nature. Consequently, God always loves others. God engages in giving and receiving love when creating, healing, promoting life, and generating wholeness. Love is so central to God that one New Testament writer put this way: "God is love."

Box 10.8

This paragraph and the next two are transitional and provide important background beliefs. Without these beliefs in place, the author will have difficulty convincing readers of his alternative view of the afterlife: relentless love. Notice especially the role "uncontrolling love" plays in the argument.

Despite God's loving activity, awful things happen (see Box 10.8). There's unnecessary suffering in the world. The problem of evil is the most substantial reason to think God is not loving or doesn't exist at all. Atheists cite this problem as the primary reason they don't believe in God. After all, a truly loving and omnipotent God should prevent genuine evil in our lives and the world. A God able to prevent genuine evil would do so … if God were truly loving.

I've offered a solution to this problem. I argue God's love is inherently uncontrolling. Because God always loves everyone and everything, and because God's love can't control anyone or anything, God can't prevent evil singlehandedly. We should not blame a God of love unable to control others for causing or allowing evil. I call this the "uncontrolling love of God" or "essential kenosis" view. Because God always loves, and divine love is uncontrolling, God cannot control.[9] God is not to blame.

My relentless love view of the afterlife builds from what I've outlined. It assumes God loves everyone and everything. It assumes God's love is inherently uncontrolling. And it assumes God's love never ends: God never stops loving us and all creation. I call this the logic of God's uncontrolling love. This logic makes sense of the afterlife.

Afterlife as Heaven or Hell

Box 10.9

Many Christian readers will have been taught the heaven-or-hell view of the afterlife. The author does not embrace this view, so after describing it he will need to lay out his reasons against it. He's arguing that the heaven-or-hell view does not have much if any biblical support, and the view portrays God as unloving.

Three theories of the afterlife prevail among Christians (see Box 10.9). The most common says that after we die, God decides whether we go to heaven or hell. Our sins may influence this decision. Whether we "accepted Jesus" or were faithful may influence it. How we treated the last and the least may affect what God decides. But after death, it's heaven or hell.

---

[9] For detailed explanations of my solution to the problem of evil, see *God Can't: How to Believe in God and Love after Tragedy, Abuse, and Other Evils* (Grasmere, ID: SacraSage, 2019); and *The Uncontrolling Love of God: An Open and Relational Account of Providence* (Downers Grove, IL: IVP Academic, 2015).

The heaven or hell theory says nothing we do *essentially* decides our fate. What happens is ultimately up to God. God has the power singlehandedly to send everyone to heaven or everyone to hell. The theory claims, however, God will decide that some get eternal bliss. Others must endure eternal conscious torment. The heaven-or-hell view implies God predetermined the criteria that decide our destiny. God set up the rules, decides whom to punish or reward, and executes judgment. The One who makes the rules could change them, of course, because God is the sole lawmaker, judge, and implementer. But God is just, says this view, and some deserve everlasting torment.

The heaven-or-hell view has numerous critics, and I'm one of them. Most biblical scholars say the Bible does not support this view. The idea of never-ending conscious torment has little or no biblical support. The theory influence owes more to the medieval writer Dante than the Bible.

Several Hebrew and Greek words play central roles in why some believe in hell. One word, as we've seen, is *Sheol*. Unfortunately, some biblical interpreters translate *Sheol* as "hell," even though as we discussed earlier *Sheol* is not a place of punishment. Similarly, the New Testament word *Hades* has been translated "hell." *Hades* comes from Greek religious-philosophical traditions, and it's the place good and bad people go after death. It's not a place of never-ending torment. In sum, *Sheol* and *Hades* are not descriptions of hell, in the sense of torment. When we encounter the word "hell" on the Bible's pages, it may be a bad translation of *Sheol* or *Hades*.

New Testament writers also use the Greek word *Gehenna*, and scholars often translate it "hell." It's the name of a valley outside Jerusalem. Children were sacrificed in fire at *Gehenna* long ago, and archeologists have evidence the valley was a burial ground. One Jewish tradition even suggests ancient people burned cadavers there. *Gehenna* was a place of death and destruction. Jesus refers to *Gehenna* to describe the suffering and devastation that come from doing evil. Other New Testament writers refer to it to describe the negative consequences that come from sin. Most scholars consider *Gehenna* a metaphor to describe a life aimed at evil, not a fiery place where sinners go for never-ending punishment.

Jesus most criticizes those who don't help the hungry, naked, and imprisoned. Because the unrighteous fail to help "the least," he says, they endure "eternal fire" and "eternal punishment" (Matt. 25:31–45). Does this point to hell as everlasting conscious torment?

The New Testament word for "eternal" is *aionios*. It is not clear, however, whether *aionios* refers to an unending duration or intensity of experience. The debate is often framed in terms of quantity vs. quality. Do biblical references to "eternal punishment" mean unending quantity of woe or intense quality?

One argument against the unending duration view refers how the Apostle Paul uses *aionios*. In one passage, he says the "the revelation of the mystery was kept secret for long ages (*aionios*) but is now disclosed."[10] Obviously, something "now disclosed" did not endure an unending quantity of time.[11] "Eternal" means something other than unending duration.

Saying sin generates qualitatively negative experiences fits well with the broad biblical witness, contemporary health sciences, and our own experiences. Sin sucks! It may be pleasurable in the short term, but it has long-term negative consequences. Sin may temporarily feel good for the sinner, but it eventually wreaks havoc on the sinner and others.

---

[10] Rom. 16:25–26.

[11] A classic work on the meaning of *aion* and *aionios* is John Wesley Hanson, *The Greek Word Aion-Aionios Translated Everlasting Eternal in the Holy Bible Shown to Denote Limited Duration* (Chicago: Northwestern Universalist Publishing House, 1875), https://www.tentmaker.org/books/Aion_lim.html.

I earlier said I'm a critic of the heaven-or-hell view. This afterlife theory begins with the correct belief that actions have consequences. But it extends those consequences indefinitely into the afterlife – far beyond what is biblically or morally warranted. Infinite punishment doesn't fit the crime of finite sin. The heaven-or-hell view also fails to support the idea God *always* loves everyone. The God who sends some to never-ending torment isn't the forgiving God that Jesus reveals. This God isn't perfectly loving. For these and other reasons, the heaven-or-hell view of the afterlife fails to follow the logic of love.

Universalism?

Box 10.10
The author now describes an alternative to the heaven-or-hell view. This section may surprise those who assume the author will say everyone goes to heaven. After all, one might think a loving God puts everyone in never-ending bliss. The author is more sympathetic to this view than to the heaven-or-hell view. But notice that toward the end of the section the author points out problems with what he calls the usual form of universalism. The usual form assumes God has controlling power; it doesn't follow the logic of uncontrolling love.

The second afterlife theory says God puts everyone in heaven (see Box 10.10). Often called "universalism," this view says a *truly* loving God wouldn't condemn anyone to never-ending torment. No matter what we've done, God singlehandedly guarantees heavenly happiness for all.

Those who embrace universalism point to various biblical passages for support. "As in Adam all die, so also in Christ shall all be made alive," says Paul.[12] That sounds like everyone enjoys life everlasting. God will "reconcile all things to himself," Paul argues elsewhere.[13] "No one is cast off by the Lord forever," says Lamentations, because God "will show compassion, so great is his unfailing love" (3:31–33). Advocates of universalism say these verses and others support their view that God saves everyone. Perhaps the most persuasive biblical argument for universalism is a general one: a loving God forgives ... always. "I blot out your transgressions," says God in the book of Isaiah, "and remember your sins no more" (43:25–26). Because "the Lord has forgiven us," says Paul, "so we ought to forgive others" (Col. 3:13). Our "sins are forgiven," says John, for the sake of God's name (1 Jn. 2:12). And so on.

Numerous ancient and contemporary Christians affirm universalism in some form.[14] The most common assumes God has the power to ensure heaven for all. The sovereign God of the universe singlehandedly places all into heaven, despite what they've done. Some say this

---

[12] 1 Cor. 15:22.

[13] Col. 1:20.

[14] For an accessible defense of universalism, see Keith Giles, *Jesus Undefeated: Condemning the False Doctrine of Eternal Torment* (Orange, CA: Quior, 2019). For a much less accessible case for universalism, see David Bentley Hart, *That All Shall Be Saved: Heaven, Hell, and Universal Salvation* (New Haven: Yale University Press, 2019). For a strong biblical appraisal of universalism, see Bradley Jersak, *Her Gates Will Never Be Shut: Hell, Hope, and the New Jerusalem* (Eugene, OR: Wipf and Stock, 2005).

controlling divine power is somehow compatible with creatures having freedom. Others say God initially created creatures in such a way that they'd eventually choose heaven. Let's call the idea that a God capable of control will save everyone "the common universalism view."

I don't embrace this view. I like that universalism emphasizes God's love and forgiveness. I like that it says God never sends anyone to hell. But I don't like what it assumes about God's power and creaturely freedom. The common view of universalism stands at odds with God's uncontrolling love and creaturely freedom. Let me offer some reasons.

First, the God with the controlling power necessary to put everyone in heaven *someday* should use controlling power to stop evil right *now*. And yet evil occurs. A loving One who can control in the afterlife ought to prevent evil through control in this one.

Second, the common form of universalism ignores the freedom of those who *don't want* to be in heaven. It says, "You have to be in heaven, even if you don't want to." The Apostle Paul says love does not force its own way (1 Cor. 13:5), but this view disagrees.

Third, if we all end up enjoying everlasting bliss no matter what we do, our actions don't *ultimately* matter. Our choices don't *really* count if God singlehandedly rescues us despite ourselves. Our decisions are meaningless from an ultimate perspective.

Fourth, believing God sends everyone to eternal bliss undermines incentives to avoid evil, fight corruption, or combat climate change here and now. Why endure the pain of self-sacrifice today if it doesn't matter for eternity? It's hard to care about the present if God sends everyone to eternal bliss no matter what we do.

In sum, universalism has advantages over the heaven-or-hell view. But it also has problems. I will seek to overcome those problems in the relentless love perspective of the afterlife.

Annihilation?

The third afterlife scenario is the least known. It agrees that a loving God would not send anyone to never-ending torment. Instead, it claims God destroys the unrepentant. God either annihilates them in a display of flashing omnipotence or passively by not sustaining them. God causes or allows the eradication of the unrighteous. This view is often called "annihilationism" but sometimes "conditionalism." It takes literally rather than metaphorically biblical statements that say fire consumes the wicked (e.g. Heb. 6:8, 10:7). It takes literally passages that talk of the wicked being destroyed (Matt. 7:13). Some build from the biblical claim that God's love "is a consuming fire," and they argue the unrepentant cannot be in the presence of divine love (Heb. 12:29).

In the annihilation view, God's active or passive destruction singlehandedly obliterates the unrepentant. Our afterlife existence is conditioned upon God's decision to keep us alive. Those exterminated get no second chances. If sinners want to repent at some later date, it's too late. God set up the rules, judges all, and follows through by eliminating the unrighteous.

> **Box 10.11**
>
> The annihilation view will be new to many readers. It has the virtue of not saying God condemns some to hell. But it has the problem of saying God gives up on some. The author argues that love doesn't give up and always forgives.

I don't like the annihilation view (see Box 10.11). It rightly says our actions have consequences. It rightly says God never sends anyone to never-ending torment in hell. But it assumes God quits. God gives up on some people. God does not forgive all but actively or passively destroys some. Divine love has limits after all.

I believe a God of everlasting love never gives up. God doesn't say, "I've given her 44,837 chances to repent. No more!" Nor does God say, "I'd rather destroy him than forgive another time." I believe God *always* turns the other cheek – in this life and the next. The steadfast love of the Lord endures forever! A God who annihilates is not a God of everlasting love and forgiveness.

Relentless Love

Box 10.12
After setting the stage, the author is finally ready to explain his relentless love view. By this point, readers should have sensed the broad outlines. The author has criticized previous theories of the afterlife, and those criticisms set up reasons that relentless love is, from the author's view, preferable.

The afterlife theories we've explored say God alone decides our destiny (see Box 10.12). Consequently, each theory clashes with the logic of God's uncontrolling love. The relentless love view starts from a different view of God's love and power. It builds from the belief that love is relational. The relentless love view assumes God is almighty, in the sense of mightier than any other. But God is not all controlling or even capable of singlehandedly determining outcomes. Consequently, God *needs* our cooperation for love to flourish. The relentless love view says we have genuine but limited freedom. Because of freedom, our choices truly matter.

At the heart of relentless love is the idea that God's love for all continues everlastingly beyond the grave. It builds from what the Psalmist calls the steadfast love of God. The writer of Lamentations puts it this way, "The steadfast love of the Lord never ceases; his mercies never come to an end." The relentless love view takes as straightforwardly true what the Apostle Paul writes in his love chapter: "Love never gives up; it always hopes; it always endures" (1 Cor. 13:7).

This view of the afterlife assumes our hope now and later has God as its source. It disagrees with theories that say God alone decides our fate. We also play a role. When we cooperate with divine love, we enjoy well-being. Goodness flourishes. We experience abundant life. Cooperating with love brings the good life, healing, and flourishing.

When we do not cooperate with God, we suffer the natural negative consequences that come from failing to love. God doesn't punish us. There are natural negative consequences – in this life and the next – from saying no to positive and healthy choices. Sin is its own punishment.

The relentless love view extends the logic of uncontrolling love everlastingly. It rejects the idea that God sends anyone to hell. It rejects the idea that God actively or passively annihilates. God does not put people in heaven who don't want to be there. But God's love never quits. The relentless love view affirms the idea that God's uncontrolling love makes possible continued subjective experiences beyond our bodily death.

Plausible afterlife theories deal with the difficult question of where we go after our bodily death. By "where," I mean an actual location. Some say "we go to be with God." But an omnipresent God is everywhere, so "being with God" is possible wherever one goes after death. Others say we melt into the "mind of God." But if we retain some measure of individuality, the location question remains. It seems wise to remain open to the possibility that afterlife bliss may occur near or here on earth, somewhere in the galaxy, or somewhere else.

Some religious traditions say those who do not cooperate with God's love must endure time in purgatory, persist in limbo, or undergo painful purification. The relentless love view rejects these views. It rejects them, that is, if they entail either that God punishes us or that we must earn divine favor. But if "purgatory" simply names the process some people undergo on the way to realizing they should cooperate with God's love, it is compatible with relentless love. God never controls but always invites everyone to a relationship of love. Some may take longer to realize the wisdom in accepting this invitation.

The Guarantees of Relentless Love

Box 10.13
Readers may worry that the relentless love view cannot guarantee outcomes many expect of afterlife theories. The author admits the God of uncontrolling love cannot guarantee some outcomes through controlling power. But the relentless love view offers guarantees not possible in other afterlife theories. In this section the author identifies those guarantees by pointing to ways his view says love wins.

The relentless love view does not guarantee that everyone will enjoy eternal bliss. An uncontrolling God cannot ensure every creature will cooperate with God's love. But love is like that: it does not force its way (1 Cor. 13:5). The relentless love view has other guarantees, however. It guarantees that love wins … in several ways.[15]

First, the God whose nature is uncontrolling love *never* stops loving us. Because love comes first in God's nature, God *cannot* stop loving. Many theologies say God may love us now and may love us after we die. God could choose to torture or destroy us instead. I can't imagine a loving person sending people to never-ending hell or annihilating them. The God of relentless love, by contrast, *always* loves! Love wins – because it's guaranteed that God's relentless love works for well-being in the afterlife.

Second, the relentless love view says those who say "Yes" to God's love in the afterlife experience heavenly bliss. They enjoy abundant life in either a different (spiritual) body or as a bodiless soul. Those who cooperate and say "Yes!" to love are guaranteed life eternal. That's the good news of salvation. Love wins – because it's guaranteed those who cooperate with God's relentless love will enjoy afterlife bliss.

Third, God *never* stops inviting us to love. Although some may not cooperate, God never throws in the towel. Natural negative consequences result from refusing love. But these consequences are self-imposed, not divinely inflicted. God doesn't punish and never stops calling us to embrace love. Love wins – because it's guaranteed that God always offers us the choice of love.

Fourth, the relentless love view says habits of love shape us into loving people. As we consistently say "Yes" to God, we develop loving characters. Those who develop loving characters through consistent positive responses grow less and less likely to choose unloving options. Developing a loving character may happen quickly or take more time. But we become radically

---

[15] On the theme of love winning at the end, see Rob Bell, *Love Wins: A Book About Heaven, Hell, and the Fate of Every Person Who Ever Lived* (New York: HarperCollins, 2011).

new creations as we cooperate with love. Love wins – because consistent cooperation with God's relentless love guarantees the development of loving characters.

Finally, we have good reason to *hope* all creatures will eventually cooperate with God. It's reasonable to think the God who never gives up and whose love is universal will eventually convince all and redeem all creation. Comprehensive cooperation is not guaranteed by divine fiat, because God's love is uncontrolling. But we have genuine hope that all will eventually cooperate, because time is on the side of an everlasting God of love.

In sum, bliss beyond the grave rests primarily, but not exclusively, in the relentless love of God. What we do in response to God's love matters now and in the afterlife. The logic of uncontrolling love offers a new explanation of what happens to us after death. That logic leads to the relentless love view of the afterlife. And in this view, love wins![16]

---

[16] For more on the afterlife from the perspective of uncontrolling love theology, see Thomas Jay Oord, *Questions and Answers for God Can't* (Grasmere, ID: SacraSage Press, 2020), chapter 8.

11

Hell

Retributivism, Escapism, and Universal Reconciliation
Andrei A. Buckareff

RESEARCH LEVEL 3

Editors' Introduction

In this chapter the author argues that the traditional, retributionist account of hell sets up a version of the problem of evil. That is, if God is omnipotent, omniscient, and omnibenevolent, God would not consign any finite individual to eternal punishment. Conversely, if God would consign any individual to eternal punishment, God could not be omnipotent, omniscient, and omnibenevolent. His argument thus far is a logical one, but then he discusses several additional objections to the traditional view, including an extended clarification of the proportionality objection.

He therefore develops an alternative, which he calls "escapism," that avoids the problems. But then he must show that escapism is preferable to another alternative to retributivism, universalism. Here he argues that a "weak universalism" can be supported by a combination of philosophical arguments against retributivism and New Testament passages suggesting that all will in fact be saved. But the author argues that escapism is preferable to any form of universalism, primarily because it does a better job of navigating the tension between particularist and universalist passages in the New Testament. Note that when the author moves from arguing against retributivism to positively arguing for escapism, the form of the argument switches from a strictly logical one to an (abductive) argument to the best explanation.

Introduction

> **Box 11.1**
>
> The author begins by setting out a traditional understanding of hell, which the chapter is intended to argue against. Note that in describing the traditional account, the author identifies its five central commitments. This is a fairly common style in analytic philosophy, with its emphasis on clarity.

Hell is assumed by many to be a place of eternal suffering. The suffering of those in hell, on the standard retributionist account, is the punishment the reprobate are owed due to their sins. The

---

The Craft of Innovative Theology: Argument and Process, First Edition. Edited by John Allan Knight and Ian S. Markham.
© 2022 John Wiley & Sons Ltd. Published 2022 by John Wiley & Sons Ltd.

following five claims summarize the commitments of the standard retributionist account of hell (see Box 11.1):

A. Some persons do or will reside in hell.
B. Hell is the residence of those persons who have failed to satisfy some condition(s) dictated by God as necessary to avoid hell and enjoy heaven.
C. The cumulative well-being over time and well-being at any moment of any resident of hell is negative.
D. Those consigned to hell are there permanently and their suffering will never end.
E. The purpose of hell is retributive. Those in hell are consigned to hell because they deserve to be punished for either failing to satisfy the condition(s) God requires for one to avoid hell or for actual sins committed or both.

Elsewhere, Allen Plug and I have developed an account of hell that we labeled "escapism." In developing our alternative to the standard account, we argued against (D) – the eternality of hell – and assumed that for similar reasons we should reject (B) and (E) (Buckareff and Plug 2005). The view of hell that we have defended also implied a denial of (C) and an official agnosticism on (A) (Buckareff and Plug 2005, 2009, 2010, 2015, 2017).[1]

Box 11.2
The author now describes his previous arguments against the traditional view of hell.

Regarding (A)–(E), Plug and I argued that it would be irrational, given what scripture and tradition teaches about God's desires and motivational states, for God to establish an eternal hell that is a place of retributive punishment from which persons could never escape (see Box 11.2). Instead we argued that God would allow those in hell an unlimited opportunity to enter into communion with God.

Focusing on Christianity, we have argued that Christians should understand all of God's actions – and in particular God's soteriological actions – as motivated by God's love and desire to be in communion with us. So we concluded that hell is best understood not as a place where retributive punishment is exacted against the unrepentant but rather as a place God has provided, being motivated by love, for those who choose to be separated from God. Hence, we endorsed an "issuant" or "choice model" of hell (for ease, we will simply refer to all such models as versions of issuantism) on which the purpose of hell is to allow those who do not wish to enjoy communion to separate themselves from the sort of communion with the divine enjoyed by those in

---

[1] For detailed criticisms of our escapist view of hell, see the following:R. Jones, "Escapism and Luck," *Religious Studies* Vol. 43 (2007): 206–216; K. Swan, "Hell and Divine Reasons for Action," *Religious Studies* Vol. 45 (2009), 51–61; B. Matheson, "Escaping Heaven," *International Journal for the Philosophy of Religion* Vol. 75 (2014), 197–206. We respond to Jones and Swan in A. Buckareff and A. Plug, "Escapism, Religious Luck, and Divine Reasons for Action," *Religious Studies* Vol. 45 (2009): 63–72. And we respond to Matheson in Buckareff and Plug, "Escaping Hell But Not Heaven," *International Journal for the Philosophy of Religion* Vol. 77 (2015): 247–253.

heaven.[2] We preferred the "issuant" label (coined by Kvanvig 1993) given that we understand the provision of hell by God as a consequence of God's being motivated by love for persons.

> **Box 11.3**
>
> Here the author explains how his model of hell involves a more thoroughgoing rejection of the traditional account's central commitments than other critiques.

That said, our own issuant model differs from other accounts insofar as many other issuant accounts only reject (E) and assume the truth of (A)–(D) along with retributivists (see Box 11.3).

If hell should not be understood as retributive punishment, then hell (understood as a place of separation from being in intimate communion with God) must be a provision made for those who do not wish to commune with God. As such, the cumulative well-being of anyone in hell is not necessarily negative. Any negative well-being would be owing to the manifestations of dispositions of a given agent at a time rendering their existence at that moment to be characterized, on balance, by negative well-being. But that any person experiences negative well-being cannot be an essential feature of hell unless an essential divine purpose of hell is to ensure that those in hell experience negative well-being. If such a state of affairs were the case, then any characterization of God as a duplicitous cosmic sadist would be well-deserved. God's love and concern for creatures who allegedly reflect the *imago Dei* would be conditional and arbitrary (why wait until after death to cease exhibiting loving concern for those created in the divine image?). For reasons such as these, in developing our escapist model of hell, Plug and I have argued that it is reasonable to expect that the well-being of the denizens of hell would not only *not* be necessarily negative but, on balance, the overall well-being of those in hell would be positive. That said, the quality and quantity of well-being for those in hell at any single moment would be vastly inferior to what is experienced by those in heaven.

Importantly, on escapism, we have argued that it is metaphysically possible for agents to leave hell by choosing to be annihilated or enter into communion with God. So it is possible both that hell is finally emptied of all of its denizens, or that no one ever leaves hell.

---

[2] For defenses of issuantism, see the following resources: A. Buckareff and A. Plug, "Escaping Hell: Divine Motivation and the Problem of Hell," *Religious Studies* Vol. 41 (2005): 39–54; A. Buckareff and A. Plug, "Escapism," 63–72; A. Buckareff and A. Plug, "Value, Finality, and Frustration: Problems for Escapism?" in *The Problem of Hell: A Philosophical Anthology*, ed. J. Buenting (Aldershot, UK: Ashgate, 2010), 77–90; A. Buckareff and A. Plug, "Escaping hell," 247–253; A. Buckareff and A. Plug, "Divine Love and Hell," in *Palgrave Handbook of the Afterlife*, ed. B. Matheson and Y. Nagasawa (New York: Palgrave-Macmillan, 2017), 197–214; J. Kvanvig, *The Problem of Hell* (New York: Oxford University Press, 1993); J. Kvanvig, *Destiny and Deliberation: Essays in Philosophical Theology* (New York: Oxford University Press, 2011); E. Stump, "Dante's Hell, Aquinas's Moral Theory, and the Love of God," *Canadian Journal of Philosophy* Vol. 16 (1986): 181–196; R. Swinburne, "A Theodicy of Heaven and Hell," in *The Existence and Nature of God*, ed. A. Freddoso (South Bend: University of Notre Dame Press, 1983), 37–54; R. Swinburne, *Responsibility and Atonement* (New York: Clarendon, 1989); J. Walls, *Hell: The Logic of Damnation* (South Bend: University of Notre Dame Press, 1992).

> **Box 11.4**
>
> The author here sets out a roadmap of how the chapter will proceed, and in the following paragraph he describes how this chapter represents an advance from his earlier work.

My chief goal in this chapter is to explore some issues in philosophical theology related to the doctrine of hell (see Box 11.4). I will proceed as follows. First, in the interest of making the importance of exploring the issues taken up in this chapter salient for the reader, I will present the problem of hell as a problem of evil for Christians. Second, given the common assumption among Christians that hell must be a place where divine retribution is exacted, I will present reasons against the tenability of a retributive conception of hell and reasons for why issuantism is a better option. Third, I will offer a rather bare-bones case for why we ought to accept an escapist view of hell. Finally, I will argue that if there is an afterlife and there is a hell that is best understood in escapist terms, then it is reasonable to expect that all of the inhabitants of hell will finally be reconciled with God.

Most of what I will say in the first three sections I have written about in greater detail with Allen Plug (accordingly, these sections draw heavily on our past publications). It is in the fourth section that I will be adding to the existing dialectic and taking a stance that I cannot assert with any confidence that my co-architect of the escapist model, Plug, would accept. So I will go on record noting that the argument developed in the last section is entirely my own (although I think it is implied by some of what Plug and I have written elsewhere).

As with my other work on the topic, I will focus on summarizing the philosophical case to be made for rejecting retributivism and accepting escapism. Thus, the expectations of any readers with respect to what I have to say about how tradition and scripture bear on this debate should be low as this essay is chiefly a piece of *philosophical theology* by a *philosopher*.[3]

The Problem of Hell

> **Box 11.5**
>
> In this section the author explores how the traditional account of hell sets up a version of the problem of evil. And this in turn provides reasons for rejecting the traditional account.

Some philosophers have argued that the conception of hell that follows from (A)–(E) is inconsistent with the traditional conception of God (see Box 11.5). In particular, it poses a problem for theists who (a) believe in an afterlife and (b) believe that some persons will reside in hell forever. Such theists affirm the following two theses:

(i) God exists, and is essentially omnipotent, omniscient, and perfectly good.
(ii) Some created persons will be consigned to hell forever.

---

[3] While I have a master's degree in theology, my two years of graduate training in theology (with a concentration in philosophical theology, at that) hardly suffices for me to accurately describe myself as someone with expertise in biblical theology or systematic theology.

Marilyn McCord Adams (1993) has argued that (i) and (ii) are logically incompatible in the same way that (i) and (iii) Evil exists have been said to be logically incompatible. Adams's reasoning is in many respects characteristic of recent work on the problem of hell. She argues for the logical incompatibility of (i) and (ii) as follows (1993, pp. 301–303):

1. If God existed and were omnipotent, God would be able to avoid (ii).
2. If God existed and were omniscient, God would know how to avoid (ii).
3. If God existed and were perfectly good, God would want to avoid (ii).
4. Therefore, if (i), then not (ii).

If Adams is right, then the truth of (ii), given (4) entails that (i) is not the case. Thus, if persons are sent to hell, then God either does not exist or lacks one or all of the omniattributes.

The truth of the premises and hence the soundness of Adams's argument are, of course, not obvious and a matter of contention. But reasons can be articulated for the truth of each premise. Premises (1) and (2), assuming classical theism, are true. Regarding (1), nothing about the doctrine of omnipotence implies that God is locked into a soteriological scheme, especially if God is sovereign over creation. Moreover, not only would it be within God's power, but God would know how to effect a state of affairs that does not involve (ii) as an aspect of the divine soteriological plan. So God could and would know how to avoid (ii) (Adams 1993, pp. 303–304).

We have reason to take premise (3) as true if God is perfectly good. Regarding the effects of the evil of hell, Adams asserts that, "Any person who suffers eternal punishment in the traditional hell will ... be one within whose life good is engulfed and/or defeated by evils" (1993, p. 304). Such a state of affairs is incompatible with divine goodness, especially if God's goodness extends to being concerned about persons created in the divine image. So if God is good, then God would want to avoid (ii).

Of course, one may argue that while it is evil, the evil of hell is not gratuitous since divine justice demands that certain persons be punished. It is gratuitous evils that are the problem. There is nothing gratuitous or unjust about agents receiving the punishment they deserve. But even if one were to argue that suffering is justified punishment for failing to satisfy the requirements for salvation, there are at least three objections to the traditional doctrine of hell that directly challenge the compatibility of divine goodness with the existence of hell.

Vagueness

The first comes from Ted Sider's paper, "Hell and Vagueness" (2002). Sider claims that the traditional conception of hell is committed to arbitrary cut-offs between the unsaved and the saved, and that the arbitrariness of the cut-offs is incompatible with God's perfect justice. It is incompatible due to the discrepancy in treatment between two extremely similar persons who happen to fall on either side of the cut-off.

Proportionality

Hell, understood as divine retribution, is only just if a person deserves an infinite amount of punishment. Stephen Kershnar (2005) and David Lewis (2007) have argued convincingly that no human being could deserve such a punishment. Assuming they are right, hell is inconsistent with divine justice and, by extension, divine goodness. (I will return to the proportionality problem for a retributivist view of hell in more detail in section 11.3.)

Diminished Capacities

The third problem comes from the limited powers of agents that impede their ability to make good choices prior to death. If God is omniscient, then God would be aware of the powers possessed by agents that both enable them and serve to block them from satisfying the conditions for avoiding eternal punishment. Divine aid in the form of prevenient grace notwithstanding, agents do not have it in their power to fully appreciate the gravity of their circumstances and respond appropriately. For instance, Adams notes an important limitation of human psychology that may contribute to the failure of persons to avoid hell that casts more doubt on the justice of hell. She notes that, "where suffering is concerned, conceivability follows capacity to experience, in such a way that we cannot adequately conceive of what we cannot experience." She adds that, in cases of moral agency, "agent responsibility is diminished in proportion to [an agent's] unavoidable inability to conceive of the relevant dimensions of [an] action and its consequences" (1993, pp. 309–310). She concludes that *mutatis mutandis* we find a similar problem with hell. Specifically, "damnation is a horror that exceeds our conceptual powers" (Adams 1993, p. 310). The upshot is that human agents cannot make rational choices for which they can be held eternally responsible by God "with fully open eyes." So everlasting torment in hell would be unjust because of the diminished capacities of human agents.

There are at least two disturbing practical implications of the incompatibility of hell with divine goodness that are worth briefly mentioning. The first is an implication for parenting and the second is a problem for religious practice.

Morally Culpable Procreation

Kenneth Himma (2010) has argued that if an agent believes that they have nothing about which to worry because they are convinced that they have satisfied the divine requirements to avoid hell, then at the very least they should avoid procreating, since they cannot ensure that their children will follow the right path and avoid eternal torment. In fact, it seems that an agent would be morally culpable for their role in knowingly bringing it about that a human being is brought into the world that might wind up in hell to be punished for an eternity.

Religious Practice

Adams argues that the traditional doctrine of hell "would make pragmatically inconsistent any worship behavior that presupposes that God is good to the worshipper or to created persons generally" (1993, p. 305). She adds that, assuming the truth of (ii), "open-eyed worship would have to be of a God who mysteriously creates some persons for lives so horrendous on the whole and eternally, that it would have been better for them never to have been born, of a God who is at worst cruel … or at best indifferent to our welfare" (1993, pp. 305–306).

Job Objection

Some are not moved by the foregoing worries. There is a tendency among some traditional Christians to dismiss any such objections as misguided and even impious. Allen Plug and I christened this sort of response as the "Job objection" (Buckareff and Plug 2005, p. 48).[4] Job objectors

---

[4] In naming this objection "the Job objection" we had in mind the sort of reasoning offered by some theists (not just Christian theists) that echoes the answer of Yahweh to Job in Job 38–41.

question the assumptions about divine goodness and the expectations placed on God in order for God to be perfectly good that are at play in framing the problem of hell. They argue that our limited, mortal perspective does not allow us to make judgments about what God can or should do or about what is or is not consistent with the requirements of divine justice.

> **Box 11.6**
>
> As with all good writers, this is an example of how the author anticipates objections and addresses them. Note the argumentative move here in response. The Job objectors assert that divine justice might be very different from human justice, and that we are not able to determine the requirements of divine justice. Thus, God might be just even if it doesn't appear to us that God is. Buckareff counters that if that is the case, we have *no reason to believe* that God is just.

The simplest, most direct, and best answer to the Job objection is that God's moral obligations do not differ from ours (see Box 11.6). Given that we do not have any other standards of moral goodness apart from those we apply in human situations, we should apply those standards to God. So the onus is shifted to proponents of the Job objection. While offered in the context of responding to other worries, David Basinger asks the right question of those who adopt the sort of stance represented by the Job objection: "Why should anyone desire to worship or expect non-theists to respect the concept of a being who appears not to be obligated to act as morally as some humans?" (1996, p. 80). If we believe that a judge or a parent would be unjust in punishing a criminal or a child in a way that is disproportionate and otherwise unfair given the infraction, then why should we think any differently about God? If God is good and there is a hell, then we should expect that either some morally sound justification exists for allowing for what appears to be a horrific state of affairs or that the traditional view of hell is wide of the mark.

I can imagine my interlocutor agreeing that God's moral obligations are not different from ours. But they may still insist that there is no reason to understand hell understood as everlasting retributive punishment as unjust. In the next section, I will turn to why it is unjust and why issuantist approaches to hell, such as escapism, are not vulnerable to the same objections about the injustice of hell to which retributivist approaches are vulnerable.

Clarifying the Proportionality Objection to Retributivism and the Issuantist Alternative

> **Box 11.7**
>
> In this section, the author offers additional arguments to support his position that eternal punishment of any finite person is unjust. Note how these additional arguments fit into his overall argument that retributionist accounts of hell set up a version of the problem of evil.

Retributivism about punishment assumes that any just punishment must be proportionate to an agent's desert (see Box 11.7). Assuming a retributive view of hell, hell is only just if a person deserves an infinite amount of punishment. But there is good reason to deny that any finite person deserves infinite punishment (see Buckareff and Plug 2013; Kershnar 2005).

In a posthumously published essay, David Lewis offered a powerful version of the proportionality objection. It is central to his claim that the problem of hell poses a particularly egregious variant of the problem of evil for Christian theists. For, while other evils may involve the agency of other moral agents or impersonal natural processes, hell is an evil perpetuated by God (Lewis 2007, p. 231). Assuming that the consensus view in orthodox Christian theism has been retributivism, Lewis describes God as having "prescribed eternal torment as a punishment for insubordination" (2007, p. 231). The punishment does not fit the crimes of the damned. "For the punishment of the damned is infinitely disproportionate to their crimes" (Lewis 2007, p. 232). Along the dimensions of time and intensity "the torment [of hell] is infinitely worse than the suffering and sin that will have occurred during the history of life in the universe. What God does is thus infinitely worse than what the worst of tyrants did" (Lewis 2007, p. 232). Stephen Kershnar puts this point forcefully in noting that those in hell are being punished and that their experience of hell involves "an infinite net harmful state extended over an infinite amount of time" (Kershnar 2005, p. 103). No finite agent deserves such punishment. Thus, hell is unjust (Kershnar 2005, p. 105; Lewis 2007, p. 232).

Lewis's reasoning can be represented as follows:

1. Christian theism is true (assumption).
2. If Christian theism is true, then persons who fail to be reconciled with God are punished in hell for eternity (assumption of Christian theism).
3. If persons who fail to be reconciled with God are punished for all eternity, then God is a tyrant (proportionality).
4. If God is a tyrant, then God is not morally perfect.
5. But God is morally perfect according to Christian theism.
6. So it is not the case that Christian theism is true.

The issuantist has the resources to provide a reply to the proportionality objection that the proponent of a traditional retributive view of hell lacks. The issuantist explicitly denies premise (2). Premise (2) assumes that persons in hell are punished where the punishment is retributive and ultimately meted out by God *qua* divine judge. But the issuantist takes hell to be a place for those who do not choose to be in communion with God. In brief, it is from God's love for those who do not wish to be in communion with God that the policy of allowing persons to go to hell issues.

The proportionality objection to the traditional view of hell rests on assumptions concerning just punishment – specifically, assumptions regarding the degree of punishment a person might justly deserve. Proponents of issuantism are split on whether there is a punitive dimension to hell. For instance, Jonathan Kvanvig argues that God's primary motivation in allowing persons to go to hell is love, but in loving those who are in hell, God "is forced to act in such a way that persons in hell are punished" (1993, p. 155). Allen Plug and I have argued that the Christian theist should dispense with any such punitive dimension to the doctrine of hell (Buckareff and Plug 2005, 2010, 2017). But if we suppose that there is any such punitive dimension, it is less problematic if it is understood as a natural consequence of the ongoing resistance of agents to divine love. Importantly, issuantists dispense with any understanding of hell as retribution for crimes committed antemortem.

The force of the proportionality objection is blunted by the assumption that hell is not punishment for antemortem crimes and that any punitive aspect to hell is a function of the natural consequences of the actions and attitudes of agents postmortem. Still, Allen Plug and I have argued that it is better to dispense with any punitive aspect altogether. Failing to do so may make a doctrine of hell once again susceptible to a version of the proportionality objection (especially if wedded to a version of the diminished capacities objection discussed earlier) (see Buckareff and Plug 2017). This brings me to why we should prefer escapism over other variants of issuantism.

A Skeletal Case for Escapism

> **Box 11.8**
>
> Having pointed out serious problems with the traditional account of hell, the author now sets out his own view and describes why it is an advance.

On most versions of issuantism the state of affairs of one's being in hell is negative on the whole (see Box 11.8). As noted already, escapism rejects any punitive and essentially negative dimension to hell. The following two claims represent what are perhaps escapism's most significant points of departure with other issuantist views (see Buckareff and Plug 2005, p. 46, 2015, pp. 247–248).

a. Hell exists and *might* be populated for eternity.
b. If there are any denizens of hell, then at any time they have the ability to accept God's grace and leave hell and enter heaven.

It is the combination of (a) *and* (b) that is distinctive about escapism. The argument for escapism begins with an assumption regarding divine action and the motivational states of God. Specifically, all of God's actions are just and loving. Allen Plug and I have argued that if that is true, then God's soteriological activity will be motivated by God's desire for the most just and loving outcome. The most just and loving outcome, we argued, is for everyone to have the opportunity to freely choose to be in communion with God. Thus, we have argued, we should expect that God would make provisions for people to convert in the eschaton and the opportunities for persons to convert should not be exhausted by a single postmortem opportunity.

Many Christians hold that, this side of the eschaton, God is open to forgive the penitent as a parent is open to forgive their child who has wronged them. Given the nature of the relationship, God's forgiveness and gift of salvation is not something those separated from God can assert as a right. It is something they request as a gift of divine grace – i.e. as a gift bestowed upon one not worthy of receiving it due to the ways in which the guilty party has sinned against the offended party. And, as J.R. Lucas notes, God is eager to bestow this gift because, "There is an antecedent desire on God's part to identify and be identified with us, which leads him to seek both to establish and restore his relationship with us. All that is required for it actually to come about, is that we should desire it too" (1976, p. 84). Karl Barth writes of God that "in his freedom he actually does not desire to be without humanity, but *with* us, and in the same freedom to be not against us but, regardless and contrary to our desert, to be *for* us – he desires in fact to be humanity's partner and our omnipotent pitying Savior" (1989, p. 56). God's desire for a restored relationship with God's estranged children, should lead God to adopt policies in the eschaton that would reflect such a desire and other pro-attitudes. God's soteriological policies would be entirely disharmonious with what appear to be God's policies this side of the eschaton if God's policies change postmortem to include a "closed-door" policy toward creatures that bear God's image.

So if God longs for reunion with us this side of the eschaton, then it would be arbitrary and out of character for God to cut off any opportunity for reconciliation and forgiveness at the time of death. Moreover, if God's policies remain constant toward us, and if we are the object of God's parental love, then God must be like any other parent who never ceases to desire to have their estranged child return, be forgiven, and enjoy the blessings of communion with one another. This requires that the opportunities for receiving the gift of salvation must extend beyond a single postmortem opportunity. Rather, the possibility for escape from hell must always be there for the residents of hell.

Given the foregoing assumptions about the God's nature and motivational states, it follows that if there is a hell, then, as a matter of metaphysical necessity, it is the sort of place described by the escapist model of hell. And, if the escapist model of hell is the right model, then God never gives up on the unsaved after death. The only thing that would block their access to communion with God would be their failure to make the right decision in response to the Holy Spirit's prevenient grace. So we should not expect God to give up on those in hell and block the door to reconciliation. This then raises a further question: Do we have any reason to believe that everyone will finally be reconciled with God?

Salvific Universalism: Dare We Hope?

Box 11.9
A number of theologians have implicitly or explicitly endorsed soteriological universalism, the view that God will eventually save everyone and bring them to heaven. The author in this section will explain why such a result is a possible but not necessary consequence of escapism.

As has already been noted, arguing that the provision of hell issues from divine love and that those in hell have inexhaustible opportunities to choose to be reconciled with God, and thus escape hell, does not entail a commitment to universalism (see Box 11.9). Similarly, that those in hell have the opportunity to choose annihilation does not entail that any or all would make that choice. But it also does not follow that neither possibility would not be actualized. In this section, I will offer a rather quick abductive argument (i.e. an inference to the best explanation) from the passages in the Pauline corpus in the New Testament that most clearly suggest soteriological universalism[5] and argue that the best explanation of the conflict between those passages and those in which the author appears to reject universalism is that the universalist passages describe the final state of affairs with divine love triumphant over the obduracy of the denizens of hell. Escapism, I will contend, can help us resolve the apparent tension between these passages.

Box 11.10
Note that the author acknowledges that the position which he will oppose (universalism) nonetheless has significant support in the tradition. Good writers will always attempt to provide the most sympathetic interpretation of those with whom they disagree.

Before proceeding, an important distinction between versions of soteriological universalism is in order (see Box 11.10). Michael Murray (1999), who is a proponent of a traditional retributivist view of hell, has distinguished between two versions of universalism: *naïve universalism* and *sophisticated universalism*. Naïve universalism holds that God immediately transforms persons when they die, with everyone going straight to heaven postmortem. Some mistakenly assume

---

[5] In particular, the passages I have in mind are Rom. 5:12–21 and 11:32; I Cor. 15:22–28, and 52; and Phil. 2:9–11. But I will devote most of my attention to Rom. 5:18–19. Other passages often taken to imply universal salvation are Jn. 12:32; Acts 3:21; 2 Cor. 5:16–19; Col. 1:18–20; 1 Tim. 2:3–6 and 4:10; 2 Pet. 3:9.

that all universalists are naïve universalists. But, at least among those working in analytic philosophical theology, the most prominent and widely discussed defenses of universalism have come from those who are best described as endorsing versions of sophisticated universalism.

Sophisticated universalism allows for an intermediate state, whether it is called "hell" or not is unimportant, in which God continues to work on persons until all have been reconciled with God. To the extent that this state may be described as hell, the purpose of hell is served as an instrument of reconciliation and redemption. For those who are not redeemed before death, this intermediate state is a stop on the way to their final redemption in the eschaton.

While only recently articulated by analytic philosophers of religion, sophisticated universalism as we find it today is anticipated in the writing of some early Christian thinkers. In particular, some of the early Eastern Church Fathers can be described as having views on the eschaton that at least resemble current versions of sophisticated universalism.[6] Most famous among these are Clement of Alexandria (d. 211–216 CE), Origen of Alexandria (ca. 185–251 CE), and Gregory of Nyssa (ca. 335–394).[7] Central to the formulation of early variants of sophisticated universalism is the doctrine of the restoration (*apokatastasis*) of all beings. In Acts 3:21, the Apostle Peter, after healing a crippled beggar in Jerusalem, addresses a crowd of onlookers and proclaims the coming of "the time of universal restoration [*apokatastaseos*] that God announced long ago through his holy prophets" (NRSV). While only explicitly mentioned once, the basic idea, in particular the soteriological implication of universal salvific restoration, finds support from other texts in the Christian scriptures. Perhaps the clearest of these is Romans 5:12–21, in particular verses 18–19.

Richard Bell has argued that in Romans 5:12–21 Paul is presenting an argument that, "the universal sin and universal condemnation as outlined in 1.18–3.20 has now been overcome." Thus, the pericope is "therefore not so much concerned with how sin and death affect humankind; it is more concerned with the overwhelming power of the grace of God seen in Jesus Christ" (Bell 2002, p. 418). In 5:18–19, we find Paul highlighting the similarities and dissimilarities between Adam and Christ and the outcomes of their actions (Tuckett 2014, p. 157):

> Therefore just as one man's trespass led to condemnation for all, so one man's act of righteousness leads to justification and life for all. For just as by the one man's disobedience the many were made sinners, so by the one man's obedience the many will be made righteous.
>
> (Romans 5:18–19)

Bell argues that the passage has a "mythical perspective" (2002, p. 430). Both Adam and Christ are mythical figures for Paul. They are each representatives of humankind. In the case of Adam, we have the myth of humans participating in an event prior to their birth; and in the case of Christ, we have humans participating in an event prior to their coming to faith in Christ (2002, p. 425, fn. 51). The text does not qualify the scope of the effects of each man's action. Both Adam

---

[6] Apart from Clement of Alexandria, Origen of Alexandria, and Gregory of Nyssa, others with at least universalist tendencies include Didymus the Blind, Diodore of Tarsus, and Macrina the Younger. Gregory of Nazianzus considers the doctrine and remains unsettled about the matter.

[7] For an accessible and brief discussion of the views of Clement, Origen, and Gregory (and also Gregory of Nazianzus) on universal redemption, see J. Sachs, "Apocatastasis in Patristic Theology," *Theological Studies* Vol. 54 (1993): 617–640.

and Christ are "understood universally" (Boring 1986, p. 286). All are condemned in Adam and all are made righteous in Christ (Tuckett 2014, p. 157).

Some wish to qualify the "all." But that by "all" Paul means "some" strains credulity. M. Eugene Boring's response to E.P. Sanders (1977) is helpful here:

> The thrust of the passage as a whole points to universal salvation, for Paul repeatedly makes the point that Christ is not simply parallel to Adam but his deed is *much more* significant than Adam's. Paul's main point would be wiped out if, in fact, the "real" meaning of the passage as a whole is that sin and death ultimately prevail over most of humanity, for in that case the saving deed of Christ would be "much *less*" than the condemning deed of Adam.
>
> (Boring 1986, p. 285)

Actual universal reconciliation lies in the eschatological future. This is not to say that some are not reconciled now owing to their faith. But if confessing that Christ is Lord and believing he was raised from the dead is sufficient for salvation (Rom. 10:9), then Phillipians 2:10–11 implies that all will finally be saved given that "every knee should bend" and "every tongue confess that Jesus Christ is Lord" (NRSV). It is only particularist assumptions that would lead one to read this passage as implying that those not justified antemortem would be insincerely paying obeisance (cf. Boring 1986, p. 282).

But what about the particularist passages? Space constraints and the goals of this chapter will not allow me to offer a proper response to the worry some may have that the overall soteriological thrust of the Christian scriptures, and especially the Pauline corpus, is particularist. There are arguably more texts that imply limited salvation. So should we advocate soteriological particularism over universalism? Boring argues that it is a mistake to read the juridical texts in question as picking out a portion of humanity condemned to hell as retribution. He writes that:

> Those who are pictured as the enemy subjugated by the assertion of God's eschatological kingly power are not one of the two groups into which humanity is ultimately divided, not a group of nonelect or nonbelieving human beings, but superhuman powers, every [*arche* – principality], [*exousia* – authority], and [*dunamis* – power] that has kept God's creation from being what it was intended to be, such as [*thanatos* – death], the last enemy. They are defeated; their power is taken away. All creation becomes subject to the gracious kingly rule of God. Not only is there no room left for hell in this picture; there is no room for destroyed annihilated creatures who have been defeated by sin and death.
>
> (1986, p. 281)

While he finds Boring's argument attractive, Christopher Tuckett adopts a different approach. He asks whether it could be that "other things said elsewhere provide the qualifier which in turn provides a logical, and perhaps chronological, sequel" to assertions about those not in Christ "perishing" (2014, p. 168). So such statements should be taken with a grain of salt. Tuckett concludes that, "it is entirely possible that Paul may have had a basic idea that some 'eschatological' events, e.g., apparently consigning some people to what might otherwise appear to be final and definitive rejection or destruction is not the final word, or the final event, in the eschatological drama to unfold at the End" (2014, pp. 168–169). So while some may be described now as "perishing" or "condemned" that is not God's final word (Tuckett 2014, p. 169). Going further, some may choose separation from God postmortem, and, in virtue of their choice, may be described as "perishing" or "condemned," but that state of affairs is by no means one that is settled. But, if we take the universalistic passages in the Christian scriptures at face value, then it seems that the final state of those who choose separation from God in hell is, in fact a settled affair. They will all finally be redeemed.

The foregoing was all rather quick. And, again, I do not pretend to be a systematic theologian or a New Testament scholar. I am a philosopher with some theological training. So what I am most interested in is the general line of reasoning we get from scriptural sources. I believe the following approximates an accurate summary of the general line of reasoning that we get from my brief excursion into Pauline soteriology and eschatology.

1. All of humankind participate in the disobedience of Adam and they all participate in the righteousness of Christ.
2. Everyone will finally confess Christ as Lord.
3. So (1) and (2).
4. If (3), then all of humankind will finally be saved.
5. So all of humankind will finally be saved.

Again, I am open to the possibility that the foregoing line of reasoning fails to track the overall thrust of Pauline soteriology and eschatology (and the broader New Testament). But I think we have at least *prima facie* reason for accepting that universalism reflects the soteriological message of the Christian scriptures.

So what does any of the foregoing have to do with escapism as a doctrine of hell? In developing our escapist account of hell, Allen Plug and I remained officially agnostic on the question of whether anyone ever leaves hell and if hell would ever be finally emptied of its denizens. That said, we argued that escapism is consistent with the possibility of universal salvation (Buckareff and Plug 2005, 2015). We argued that this possibility is a strength of escapism over other alternatives given that "universal reconciliation without divine coercion is not merely a logical possibility but may be a likely state of affairs in the eschaton" (Buckareff and Plug 2005, p. 50). The philosophical argument we made was from God's moral character and motivational states to the conclusion that hell would be a place of separation provided by God out of love for those who do not wish to be with God. Our argument was from certain claims about the divine nature to a conclusion about what God's policies must be like toward those who reject the offer of reconciliation antemortem (or postmortem, for that matter). But we remained silent on whether there was good reason to accept universalism because we saw any argument for universalism as resting on a different set of premises. In particular, the premises would be ones derived from scripture and tradition. The case from tradition is mixed, and leans heavily in favor of particularism. But there are prominent exceptions, as noted earlier with my examples from patristic sources. The case from scripture is stronger. Coupled with the philosophical arguments for rejecting hell as retributive punishment, we can derive a strong *prima facie* case for a "weak universalism" in which (a) philosophical arguments render it an open possibility that all will be saved and (b) the biblical case suggests that all will, in fact, be saved.

> **Box 11.11**
>
> Note here how the author raises possible objections to his position. Good writers will think of possible objections in advance, and then address them. In this case, however, since the author has addressed them in detail previously, he will cite his previous work and give a brief review of his response.

I can imagine a possible interlocutor declaring that the foregoing is all fine and good, but why should we even bother with escapism (see Box 11.11)? Why not adopt a view of hell that is purgatorial? It may be argued that, if God is as described in the argument for escapism, then universalism follows as a matter of necessity. I will not engage with any such arguments here. I believe that Allen Plug and I have already made an adequate case for denying a strong version of universalism. We have rejected any kind of divine coercion, arguing that it is inconsistent with the divine character. And, while we have allowed that hell may be purgatorial in a very loose sense since at least some who are finally in heaven would have taken the long route through hell before going to heaven, we have argued that hell as characterized by escapism lacks two essential features of the traditional doctrine of purgatory. First, purgatory is a place for those already destined for heaven to become morally fit to reside in heaven. Second, purgatory traditionally involves some purifying pain aimed at rectifying the moral shortcomings of its inhabitants (Brown 1985, p. 16). Escapism has neither feature. Regarding the first features, those in hell are not already destined for heaven in virtue of being denizens of hell. While I have contended that they will all be in heaven eventually, they are not in hell for the purpose of preparing them for heaven. They are in hell because they prefer not to be in communion with God. And, with respect to the second feature, the purpose of hell is neither the moral rehabilitation of its residents nor their punishment (Buckareff and Plug 2005, p. 49). That said, it may be that, if one decides to enter into communion with God in heaven, they may have to undergo a period of moral rehabilitation (assuming they are not transformed immediately upon repenting) to render them fit to be citizens of heaven (see Buckareff and Plug 2010).

> **Box 11.12**
>
> Here the author describes the advantages his approach enjoys relative to the alternative position (a stronger universalism) he is rejecting.

Suppose my interlocutor agrees that the foregoing is all fine and good (see Box 11.12). They concede that escapism is consistent with the weak universalism I articulated earlier and it is not just purgatory with window dressing. Why should we prefer the weak universalism we can get if we accept escapism over the stronger universalism endorsed by those who offer philosophical arguments that start from the evil of hell and the divine character and conclude that universal salvation follows as a matter of either logical or metaphysical necessity? I think the chief strength enjoyed by escapism over alternatives (and the one on which I will focus here) is that escapism helps us better address the tension between the particularist and universalistic passages in the New Testament.

As mentioned earlier, those who initially elect to be separated from God can be described as "perishing" postmortem given that, in the words of the answer to the first question of the *Westminster Shorter Catechism*, they are failing to fulfill their primary purpose as humans, which is to "glorify God and enjoy [God] forever." A view of hell that sees it as being, as a matter of metaphysical necessity, a mere stop-off point on the way to guaranteed salvation fails to capture this aspect of their condition, especially if they agree with the escapist that any separation from God is owing to God's being motivated by love for humankind.

If we suppose, as I have, that the utility of those in hell may be positive, the state of their existence is vastly inferior to that of those in communion with the divine. The latter group are fulfilling their divine purpose, while the former group, insofar as they are separated from God owing to their choice, are not. It is not a given that those in hell will be finally reconciled with God. That they will be is arguably a contingent state of affairs owing to the work of Christ and the uncoerced choice of those agents. The Christian scriptures simply report what will occur and do not argue for it on the basis of premises about the divine nature and the evil of hell as punishment.

> **Box 11.13**
>
> In his final point, the author here rejects divine manipulation as being incompatible with his understanding of God. Note that once again the author provides a very generous interpretation of the position he opposes.

Before I wrap things up, I should say something about divine manipulation (see Box 11.3). For strong versions of universalism, including sophisticated universalism, there is some manipulation of recalcitrant agents by God that results in their choosing heaven. One species of divine manipulation is relatively innocuous and the other is more problematic. I will start with the more problematic form of divine manipulation. In making the case for her version of sophisticated strong universalism, Marilyn McCord Adams goes on the offensive against "the idol of human agency." Adams argues that a realistic picture of human agency will take into account how humans begin their lives as agents in an immature state and, owing to environment and history, their free agency by adulthood is impaired. She reaches two conclusions:

> [F]irst, such impaired adult human agency is no more competent to be entrusted with its (individual or collective) eternal destiny than two-year-old agency is to be allowed choices that could result in its death or serious physical impairment; and, second, that the fact that the choices of such impaired agents come between the divine creator of the environment and their infernal outcome no more reduces divine responsibility for the [*sic*.] damnation than two-year-old agency reduces the responsibility of the adult caretaker.
>
> (1993, p. 313)

Adams is open to God bringing about changes in agents with impaired agency to ensure that they will choose communion with God (1993, pp. 318–319).

There are at least two ways God could bring about changes in impaired agents to ensure that they choose communion with God. The first involves a kind of direct manipulation of agents' minds in such a way as to guarantee an outcome. The second involves removing internal and external impediments to making a choice that involves the exercise of an agent's repaired capacity to appreciate and respond to practical reasons (including prudential, moral, and other normative considerations). I will call the former kind of activity "outcome-oriented divine manipulation" and the latter "structural-impediment divine manipulation."

Adams comes closest to endorsing outcome-oriented divine manipulation for at least some agents. She indicates that she "does not share the worries of free will defenders about how God can make sure to win human cooperation without violating our freedom." Recognizing that the misuse of created agency has resulted in "producing one horrendous mess after another," she contends that God will not only rehabilitate agents, enabling them to make better decisions, but allows that God may "causally determine some things to prevent everlasting ruin." She contends that "this is not more an insult to our dignity than a mother's changing a baby's diaper is to the baby" (1999, p. 157). If any cases of things causally determined by God *qua* agent include the decision-making of agents, then such divine activity amounts to outcome-oriented divine manipulation. This sort of divine manipulation not only vitiates an agent's capacity for *free* agency but it may also undermine their more general capacity for intentional agency. The reason is that, in such a case, the process of exercising agency would not just involve the manifestation of the human agent's relevant powers constitutive of their capacity for intentional agency. Rather, in the extreme cases, divine intentions would be among the powers manifested in the process of an agent making a decision to turn to God. So the process of decision-making would be guided not just by the executive capacities of the human agent but also God's relevant capacities. In principle, the decision-making may take eons, but the outcome is guaranteed by the divine agent who will take steps along the way to guide the process so it conforms to the divine will . This sort of manipulation strikes me as unacceptable and incompatible with the picture we get of God's motivation and policies on escapism.[8]

In contrast to outcome-oriented divine manipulation is structural-impediment divine manipulation. Thomas Talbott has defended a version of sophisticated universalism that is committed to this type of manipulation by God. On this sort of account, God removes the external barriers and repairs the practical capacities of agents postmortem, enabling them to make informed decisions that they would otherwise not make given their antemortem impairments.

Agents can thus make decisions with their eyes wide open, with a proper understanding of the nature of God and what it would mean to be apart from God. Talbott has contended that assuming that agents are thusly repaired postmortem, "given the Christian understanding of God, the very idea of someone making a free and fully informed decision to reject God forever, or of someone freely embracing an eternal destiny apart from God, is deeply incoherent and therefore logically impossible" (2001, p. 421). I maintain that such a claim is much too strong. This is in part because there is nothing logically inconsistent about someone making such a decision and doing so freely, especially if they have strong preferences not to be with God. It certainly is logically possible that such agents are necessarily motivated to choose communion with God (where this motivation was not present antemortem), but that motivation is not sufficient to trump other considerations that they take to have greater normative force. That said, if we understand claims about what is metaphysically possible or impossible as being made true by the causal powers of objects, including human agents, then I am inclined to agree that any such decision may be *metaphysically* impossible, especially if the environmental and psychological factors that impair one's agency are removed and the agent's relevant practical capacities are repaired. In particular, I assume that such an agent would be strongly responsive to reasons. An agent who is strongly responsive to reasons is such that their relevant practical mechanism or capacities active in decision-making would conform to what the agent recognizes as being dictated by their practical reasons.[9] Of course, an agent would have to *recognize* certain considerations as not only reason-giving but also as having greater normative force than other considerations. It may take time, owing to the standing preferences and policies of an agent, for the agent to recognize that certain reasons are better than others. That said, it does not seem like a stretch to hold that repaired agency, exercised with complete information and *full understanding* of the implications of the options presented to an agent, should result in choices that result from practical capacities that are strongly responsive to reasons. I take it that full understanding will require a proper

---

[8] Readers familiar with the free will literature may assume that it is because such manipulation undermines libertarian free agency that I regard it as incompatible with escapism. But that would be a mistake. Allen Plug and I have always remained neutral in our publications on hell about whether libertarian versus compatibilist views of free will are correct. That said, we have maintained that theological determinism would undermine free agency given that such determinism involves manipulation by another agent (namely, God). That said, for those familiar with the literature, I am an actual-sequence compatibilist about free will; but I deny that any species of free will is compatible with determination by another agent for reasons having to do with the type-identity conditions for exercises of individual agency that would preclude interventions by other agents.

[9] My use of "strong reasons-responsiveness" is influenced by J. Fischer and M. Ravizza, *Responsibility and Control: An Essay on Moral Responsibility* (New York: Cambridge University Press, 1998). I part company with them, however, and am closer to Wolf in preferring to characterize responsiveness to reasons in terms of capacities. See the following: S. Wolf, *Freedom within Reason* (New York: Oxford University Press, 1990). J. Aguilar and A. Buckareff, "A Gradualist Metaphysics of Agency," in *Agency, Freedom, and Moral Responsibility*, ed. A. Buckareff, C. Moya, and S. Rosell (New York: Palgrave-Macmillan, 2015), 30–43.

appreciation of the weight of some reasons over others. And this sort of full appreciation of the normative force of some reasons can take time, no matter how repaired the relevant capacities of agents might be. Thus, structural-impediment divine manipulation is indirect and involves empowering agents to make autonomous decisions by removing the structural impediments to their making decisions involving the manifestation of a capacity for executive agency that is strongly responsive to reasons. Importantly, God does not guide the process of the agent's decision-making to ensure an outcome. As a result, depending upon the values and character of an agent, there may not be immediate recognition of the overwhelming normative force of reasons that favor deciding to enter into communion with God. But, given the testimony of Scripture, I assume that such divine manipulation is done with the knowledge that such empowerment will, in the final analysis, result in everyone making the choice to leave hell in favor of heaven.

Conclusion

Whether or not I have convinced readers that the traditional retributive doctrine of hell should be abandoned in favor of a version of issuantism, specifically, escapism, is not my primary concern. Moreover, if I have convinced any readers to endorse escapism and they resist the further move to accepting the sort of weak sophisticated universalism, then I will not count the foregoing as a failure.[10] What matters most to me is that readers appreciate the dialectic and understand that the traditional doctrine of hell is, if not untenable, at least susceptible to some serious objections. And what is just as important is that they understand that there are alternatives.[11]

---

[10] Truth be told, while I am a Christian, I am skeptical about the tenability of traditional theism of any sort and have my doubts about an afterlife. Owing to a commitment to metaphysical naturalism, worries about the problem of evil, and other considerations, I am most inclined to accept a "personal pantheistic" metaphysic of the divine and understand resurrection in this-worldly terms. If there is an afterlife, I'm most attracted to a story I think is more compatible with such commitments. For details, see the following: A. Buckareff, "Omniscience, the Incarnation, and Knowledge de se," *European Journal for Philosophy of Religion* Vol. 4 (2012): 59–71; A. Buckareff, "Pantheism and Saving God," *Sophia* Vol. 55 (2016a): 347–355; Andrei Buckareff, "Theological Realism, Divine Action, and Divine Location," in *Alternative Concepts of God: Essays on the Metaphysics of the Divine*, ed. A. Buckareff and Y. Nagasawa (New York: Oxford, 2016a), 213–233; Andrei Buckareff, "Theistic Consubstantialism and Omniscience," *Religious Studies: An International Journal for the Philosophy of Religion* Vol. 54 (2018): 233–245; Andrei Buckareff, "Unity, Ontology, and the Divine Mind," *International Journal for the Philosophy of Religion* Vol. 85 (2019): 319–333; Andrei Buckareff, "Pantheism and the Possibility of Surviving Death," in *Death, Immortality, and the Afterlife*, ed. T.R. Byerly (New York: Routledge, 2021). That said, *if* some version of traditional theism gets things right, then I am convinced that the foregoing account is closer to the truth than the existing alternatives. I am further convinced that getting things right about such matters cannot be what determines our final state. If any readers of this chapter assume that getting things right is a prerequisite for being on good standing with the divine, and they assume that God is morally perfect, then I think there is a reductio argument that can be run on their position. How such an argument would go is something I will leave to those readers as an exercise. I believe I have provided a blueprint in this chapter.

[11] In working on this chapter I received helpful feedback from John Knight, Ian Markham, and Leigh Vicens. I wish to thank them for their comments.

Works Cited

Adams, M. (1993). The Problem of Hell: A Problem of Evil for Christians. In: *Reasoned Faith: A Festschrift for Norman Kretzmann* (ed. E. Stump), 301–327. Ithaca, NY: Cornell University Press.

Adams, M. (1999). *Horrendous Evils and the Goodness of God*. Ithaca, NY: Cornell University Press.

Aguilar, J. and Buckareff, A. (2015). A Gradualist Metaphysics of Agency. In: *Agency, Freedom, and Moral Responsibility* (ed. A. Buckareff, C. Moya, and S. Rosell), 30–43. New York: Palgrave Macmillan.

Barth, K. (1989). The Humanity of God. In: *Karl Barth: Theologian of Freedom* (ed. C. Green). London: Collins.

Basinger, D. (1996). *The Case for Freewill Theism: A Philosophical Assessment*. Downers Grove, IL: Intervarsity Press.

Bell, R. (2002). Rom 5.18–19 and Universal Salvation. *New Testament Studies* Vol. 48: 417–432.

Boring, M.E. (1986). The Language of Universal Salvation in Christ. *Journal of Biblical Literature* Vol. 105: 269–292.

Brown, D. (1985). No heaven without purgatory. *Religious Studies* Vol. 21: 447–456.

Buckareff, A. (2012). Omniscience, the Incarnation, and Knowledge *de se*. *European Journal for Philosophy of Religion* Vol. 4: 59–71.

Buckareff, A. (2016a). Pantheism and Saving God. *Sophia* Vol. 55: 347–355.

Buckareff, A. (2016b). Theological Realism, Divine Action, and Divine Location. In: *Alternative Concepts of God: Essays on the Metaphysics of the Divine* (ed. A. Buckareff and Y. Nagasawa), 213–233. New York: Oxford University Press.

Buckareff, A. (2018). Theistic Consubstantialism and Omniscience. *Religious Studies: An International Journal for the Philosophy of Religion* Vol. 54: 233–245.

Buckareff, A. (2019). Unity, Ontology, and the Divine Mind. *International Journal for the Philosophy of Religion* Vol. 85: 319–333.

Buckareff, A. (2021). Pantheism and the Possibility of Surviving Death. In: *Death, Immortality, and the Afterlife* (ed. T.R. Byerly). New York: Routledge.

Buckareff, A. and Plug, A. (2005). Escaping Hell: Divine Motivation and the Problem of Hell. *Religious Studies: An International Journal for the Philosophy of Religion* Vol. 41: 39–54.

Buckareff, A. and Plug, A. (2009). Escapism, Religious Luck, and Divine Reasons for Action. *Religious Studies: An International Journal for the Philosophy of Religion* Vol. 45: 63–72.

Buckareff, A. and Plug, A. (2010). Value, Finality, and Frustration: Problems for Escapism? In: *The Problem of Hell: A Philosophical Anthology* (ed. J. Buenting), 77–90. Aldershot, UK: Ashgate.

Buckareff, A. and Plug, A. (2013). Hell and the Problem of Evil. In: *Blackwell Companion to the Problem of Evil* (ed. D. Howard-Snyder and J. McBrayer), 128–143. Malden, MA: Wiley-Blackwell.

Buckareff, A. and Plug, A. (2015). Escaping Hell But Not Heaven. *International Journal for the Philosophy of Religion* Vol. 77: 247–253.

Buckareff, A. and Plug, A. (2017). Divine Love and Hell. In: *Palgrave Handbook of the Afterlife* (ed. B. Matheson and Y. Nagasawa), 197–214. New York: Palgrave-Macmillan.

Fischer, J. and Ravizza, M. (1998). *Responsibility and Control: An Essay on Moral Responsibility*. New York: Cambridge University Press.

Himma, K. (2010). Birth as a Grave Misfortune: The Traditional Doctrine of Hell and Christian Salvific Exclusivism. In: *The Problem of Hell: A Philosophical Anthology* (ed. J. Buenting), 179–198. Burlington, ON: Ashgate.

Jones, R. (2007). Escapism and Luck. *Religious Studies* Vol. 43: 206–216.

Kershnar, S. (2005). The Injustice of Hell. *International Journal for Philosophy of Religion* Vol. 58: 103–123.

Kvanvig, J. (1993). *The Problem of Hell*. New York: Oxford University Press.

Kvanvig, J. (2011). *Destiny and Deliberation: Essays in Philosophical Theology*. New York: Oxford University Press.

Lewis, D. (2007). Divine Evil. In: *Philosophers without Gods: Meditations on Atheism and the Secular Life* (ed. L. Antony), 231–242. New York: Oxford University Press.

Lucas, J.R. (1976). Forgiveness. In: *Freedom and Grace*. Grand Rapids: Eerdmans.

Matheson, B. (2014). Escaping Heaven. *International Journal for the Philosophy of Religion* Vol. 75: 197–206.

Murray, M. (1999). Three Versions of Universalism. *Faith and Philosophy* Vol. 16: 55–68.

Sachs, J. (1993). Apocatastasis in Patristic Theology. *Theological Studies* Vol. 54: 617–640.

Sider, T. (2002). Hell and Vagueness. *Faith and Philosophy* 19: 58–68.

Stump, E. (1986). Dante's Hell, Aquinas's Moral Theory, and the Love of God. *Canadian Journal of Philosophy* Vol. 16: 181–196.

Swan, K. (2009). Hell and Divine Reasons for Action. *Religious Studies* Vol. 45: 51–61.

Swinburne, R. (1983). A Theodicy of Heaven and Hell. In: *The Existence and Nature of God* (ed. A. Freddoso), 37–54. Notre Dame: University of Notre Dame Press.

Swinburne, R. (1989). *Responsibility and Atonement*. New York: Clarendon.

Talbott, T. (2001). Freedom, Damnation, and the Power to Sin with Impunity. *Religious Studies* Vol. 37: 417–434.

Tuckett, C. (2014). Paul and Universalism. In: *Revealed Wisdom: Studies in Apocalyptic in Honour of Christopher Rowland* (ed. J. Ashton), 155–169. Boston: Brill.

Walls, J. (1992). *Hell: The Logic of Damnation*. South Bend Ind: University of Notre Dame Press.

Wolf, S. (1990). *Freedom within Reason*. New York: Oxford University Press.

12

Christ Will Come Again

Keith Ward

RESEARCH LEVEL 2

Editors' Introduction

Beliefs about the second coming of Jesus are often very opaque. Some take the language very literally; others tend to take it as symbolic. There are plenty of theologians who want to affirm the significance of the language yet are very unclear as to precisely what they are imagining at the "end of the age." In this article, Keith Ward provides a careful critique of the Biblical language and argues that the purpose of this discourse is to point to the divinely intended purposes of creation.

Introduction

"He [Jesus Christ] shall come to judge the quick and the dead." These words from the Apostles Creed express the widespread Christian belief that Jesus will return to Earth fairly soon, while there are still living human beings (the "quick") on the planet, to pass judgment on the wicked and redeem all who repent. I take this belief to be mistaken, yet I can still say the Apostles' Creed with a straight face. I aim to explain how this is possible, and to recommend this possibility to you.

New Testament scholars argue about whether Jesus thought of himself as the Messiah, and whether he actually taught that he would return after his death in glory with hosts of angels in the near future. But there is no doubt that parts of the gospels state that Jesus thought of himself as the "Son of Man" who would descend from heaven to end world history in a spectacular fashion (Matt. 26, 64, for instance).

For thinking Christians this poses a problem. Not only did Jesus not shortly after his death return in glory but we now know that the universe is vastly bigger than anyone in Jesus's time thought, and consequently that the end of this planet would not be the end of creation.

Faced with this problem, there are four main responses which seem to be possible. The first is to dismiss all talk of Jesus's "second coming" as pure myth or legend, and give up that part of the Apostles' Creed. The second is to accept the accounts in the New Testament as literally true in all its details. The return has not happened yet, but it might do so at any time. The third is to allegorize the accounts, saying that they are literally false, but they are still wholly true as allegories, that is, in a sense which reflection can spell out. I suspect that most Christian churches do this. The fourth is to say that they are literally false narratives, but they do express basic spiritual truths. However, it would be a mistake to try to make every detail stand for something true, and some parts of the narratives may need to be abandoned.

These responses can be paralleled by responses to the accounts of creation given in the opening chapters of Genesis. This is not surprising, since the doctrine of the return of Christ is really a doctrine about the end or goal of the universe, and the Genesis account is a doctrine about the beginning or ontological status of the universe.

I will not spend time discussing the "pure myth" interpretation. If the universe is created by God, and if it has a goal set by God, then there is something true about the biblical accounts. The universe was intentionally created by God and it has a goal of great value. The New Testament states that Christ was centrally involved both in the creation and in the final goal of the universe. Since it seems that this is a very basic Christian affirmation, I will begin by exploring it, especially in the light of our modern expanded view of the nature of the universe. This will turn out to exclude a literal interpretation of relevant biblical texts. To help in understanding the other interpretations that are available, I shall look at how prophetic statements about "the end" are used in the Old Testament. My conclusion will be that detailed allegorical interpretations (as in Augustine) are implausible. This, amazingly enough, will lead to my own view, that statements about "the coming of Christ in judgment" use imaginative verbal pictures to convey a belief that there is a divinely intended goal of creation, that the Christ who was incarnate in Jesus will then be fully revealed in glory, that what we do now will be judged in the light of that revelation, and that (what unfortunately the Apostles' Creed is not quite clear about) finally all creation will be united in the life of the eternal Christ (see Box 12.1).

Box 12.1

The paper begins with a blunt statement that may sound shocking – it is meant to attract a reader's attention. It then goes on to give what is in effect a short abstract of what the paper will say, so that the reader can see the plan of what is coming.

The Final Unity of All Things in Christ

How is Christ involved in the goal of the universe? The writer of the letter to the Ephesians says, "He [God] has made known to us the mystery of his will … as a plan for the fullness of time, to gather up all things in him [Christ], things in heaven and things on earth" (Eph. 1, 9, 10).[1]

Box 12.2

The author is making it clear where he stands on the interpretation of the "apocalyptic" in the New Testament and that he is aware of the main debate. He shows that at least one main early Christian tradition was concerned with cosmic themes, as the cosmos was then understood. The point is to show that many Christian beliefs were not primarily political or concerned only with the story of a Jewish apocalyptic preacher.

---

[1] Most scholars believe the text was written in the late first century by a second-generation follower of Paul's. A minority contend that it could have been written by Paul at the end of his ministry. See Jennifer K. Berneson, "The Letter of Paul to the Ephesians," in *The New Oxford Annotated Bible: New Revised Standard Version with the Apocrypha*, 4th edn., ed. Michael D. Coogan (New York: Oxford University Press, 2010), 2052–2053.

This passage, and others like it, takes a wide cosmological view (see Box 12.2). It is about "all things ... in heaven and ... earth." What did the writer mean by *all things*? Probably he had a view of the universe like that recorded in Genesis, which is a modification of Babylonian cosmology.[2] The Earth was a flat disc floating on a great sea; the sky was a dome holding back a great sea above it; and the stars were "sanctuary lamps" set in the dome of the sky (the "firmament"), their movements controlled by angels or spirits. The writer may, however, have taken a Ptolemaic view of cosmology,[3] for which the Earth is a sphere at the center of the universe, and the sun, moon, and stars, placed on a number of crystalline spheres, controlled by angels, circle around it. Heaven, wherever it was, probably above the outermost sphere, was filled with spiritual beings, angels, archangels, thrones, dominions, and powers, both fallen and unfallen. So there were lots of extra-terrestrials, and they too were to be gathered up in Christ.

Whatever this Christ is, Christ is not a human being, however glorified. For a human being is still a finite part of the universe, and Christ is that in which the whole universe, material and spiritual, is gathered up. Christians naturally believe that Jesus *is* the Christ, but the human being Jesus is not capable of containing the universe.[4] So presumably what is being said is that Jesus is the human form or expression of a supra-cosmic power, the reality of which extends far beyond all human or created forms.

It is said that this power "contains" the universe. Obviously, as a spiritual reality, it does not physically contain the universe, though there may be a relic here of the Babylonian/Genesis view that heaven is beyond the outer sphere of the cosmos. Perhaps we could say that the physical universe is not totally distinct from the spiritual reality of Christ, but is part of, or one expression of, that spiritual reality, and for the writer of the letter so is the world of angels.

This thought is also found in the letter to the Colossians:[5] "In him [Christ] all things in heaven and on earth were created ... all things have been created through him and for him" (Col. 1, 16). Christ is the reality in, through, and for whom all things were created. The paragraph in which this sentence occurs contains the difficult phrase that Christ is "the first-born of all creation." The phrase is difficult because in traditional Christian thought Christ is not part of creation at all, but is uncreated and, as the Gospel of John puts it, was always "with God and was God" (Jn. 1, 1).[6]

---

[2] For further description see F. Rochberg, "Mesopotamina Cosmology," in *Cosmology: Historical, Literary, Philosophical, Religious, and Scientific Perspectives* (New York: Garland, 1993), 40–45.

[3] For further description see Norriss S. Hetherington, "The Presocratics," in *Cosmology: Historical, Literary, Philosophical, Religious, and Scientific Perspectives* (New York: Garland, 1993), 105–144.

[4] The Council of Chalcedon reconciled the differences between the Alexandrian school which emphasized the unity of the two natures of Christ, and the Antiochian school which emphasized the distinctiveness of the natures of Christ. The work of nineteenth-century theologian Herman Bavinck articulates a Christology that provides a synthesis between these ancient schools and reformed theology that typifies more recent mainstream Christian dogmatic theology. See J. Ryan Davidson, "Nicaea and Chalcedon After Modern Christologies: Herman Bavinck as Exemplar in Engaging Christological Developments," *Bulletin of Ecclesial Theology* Vol. 6, No. 1 (2019): 59–68, accessed February 28, 2020, https://0-search-ebscohost-com.librarycatalog.vts.edu/login.aspx?direct=true&AuthType=ip,cookie,url,uid&db=a6h&AN=ATLAiA14190722000804&site=eds-live.

[5] The Letter to the Colossians (unlike Ephesians – see footnote 1) is commonly believed to have been composed either during Paul's life or shortly after his death by one of his followers. See Jennifer K. Berneson, "The Letter of Paul to the Colossians," in *The New Oxford Annotated Bible: New Revised Standard Version with the Apocrypha*, 4th edn., ed. Michael D. Coogan (New York: Oxford University Press, 2010), 2067–2068.

[6] Also as evidenced in the Nicean Creed, common to many of the various expressions of Christianity.

It makes sense, however, if one thinks of Christ as the pattern of creation existing in God, like a thought in the mind of God (this is one way of translating the Greek word *logos* that John uses[7]). Perhaps, since Christ is a personal reality, one should say that Christ is God existing in the mode of rational intelligence, and as such Christ contains the archetype or model of this created cosmos. This thought is realized or embodied as the "container" or the all-embracing spiritual reality within which the created universe is to exist. The pattern in the mind of Christ becomes the actual ground-plan of creation (see Box 12.3).

Box 12.3

The idea that Christ is God existing in a particular mode or way is an echo of Karl Barth's idea that Christ is one *Seinsweise* (way of being) and Karl Rahner's idea that Christ is one *Subsistenzweise* (way of subsisting) of God. They hold that such expressions may be less misleading to contemporary readers than the traditional term 'person,' which may imply that there are three distinct minds and wills in God, for the second member of the Trinity. This is a controversial point.

This can be seen as a sort of first incarnation of the divine in the universe – a thought which is expressed in Maximus the Confessor, among others – a first outflowing of what is in the divine mind into physical reality. The creation is through Christ, because all things come into being in accordance with the divine pattern, and are formed within the spiritual reality which is the foundation of their being.[8] As the text goes on to say, "in him all things hold together" (Col. 1, 17).

If we think in this way of Christ as a supreme spiritual power enfolding the universe and bringing all things to a form of unity within it, we are in a very different thought-world from that of those who think of Jesus only as a man who will descend very soon on a cloud to found a new political state (the "new Jerusalem") on planet Earth.[9] This throws doubt on any fully literal interpretation of the relevant New Testament passages.

Yet there is a link between these thought-worlds, and it is made explicit in the Gospel of John. The Prologue of that gospel begins not with the birth of a man, but with the eternal Word of God, through whom all beings, life, and light, came into being. This is a vast cosmological picture of the universe, not as the product of chance and necessity alone, but through a rational and intelligible expression of a supreme moral will.

For John, reality is vast in extent, for it includes myriads of spiritual beings. But *physical* reality is centered on the Earth, and what happens on Earth is a central focus of interest for the angelic host. When the Word becomes flesh, it takes physical form at the center of and sole home of created persons in the physical universe. What happens on Earth is in this way of great significance for the whole of the physical universe.

---

[7] J.M. Dillon, J.D.G. Dunn, and T.E. Pollard, "Logos" in *The Cambridge Dictionary of Christian Theology*, 285–286, ed. Ian A. McFarland (Cambridge: Cambridge University Press, 2011), accessed March 2, 2020, https://0-web-a-ebscohost-com.librarycatalog.vts.edu/ehost/ebookviewer/ebook/bmxlYmtfXzM2NjEzMF9fQU41?sid=ec75c508-aba9-40c2-8ccb-c72c65d26936@sessionmgr4008&vid=0&format=EB&rid=1.

[8] Maximus of Constantinople, *Quaestiones ad Thalassium*, 22.

[9] The popular *Left Behind* series provides a modern expression of the contemporary Christian groups that continue to hold a literal view of the rapture. For a detailed analysis of scriptural misapplication of this view, see B. Bingaman, "Learning from Left Behind? A Call for Coherent Accounts of Scripture," *Anglican Theological Review* Vol. 91, No. 2 (Spring 2009): 255–272, accessed February 28, 2020, https://0-search-ebscohost-com.librarycatalog.vts.edu/login.aspx?direct=true&AuthType=ip,cookie,url,uid&db=rlh&AN=39659468&site=eds-live.

Moreover, the history of the universe is short – counting up the biblical genealogies, the whole physical universe only began a few thousand years ago. There is no sense that it will ever evolve, and indeed it is probably going to be destroyed, at least in its present form, when God's purpose for it has been fulfilled. In this context, it was natural to see that fulfillment in Jesus, so that Jesus inaugurated "the last days," the prelude to the final realization of God's plans for the physical universe. And it was natural, for Jews at least, to see the destiny of Israel as the most important concern in the whole physical universe.

In the modern world that link has been decisively broken. In 1924, Edwin Hubble established that beyond the Milky Way there were other galaxies of stars.[10] We now know that there are billions of them – one recent estimate is that there may be 500 billion galaxies beyond the Milky Way, many of them billions of light years beyond, each containing billions of stars and planets. In 1931, Father Georges Lemaître proposed that our universe originated with a "Big Bang" about 15 billion years ago.[11] The universe will indeed cease to exist, but only after many billions of years, when it will at last run out of energy. Our universe has expanded vastly in time and space beyond that envisaged by the biblical writers.

No longer is the Earth the center of the universe, humans being the center of God's attention in creation. How are we to place Jesus, one rather short-lived human being crawling about on the thin crust of a small and short-lived planet in a tiny part of a vast cosmos? How can such a person any longer be of central importance in the scheme of things?

The Prophetic Imagery of the Bible

In addressing this question, it may be helpful to consider the nature of prophetic language in the Hebrew Bible, language which helped to determine the context in which Jesus lived. We may then see better how such language was used in the New Testament to interpret the life of Jesus, and to proclaim his central role in the created cosmos (see Box 12.4).

Box 12.4
The author now turns to a consideration of Old Testament prophecy. This will examine the nature of such prophecy, suggesting that it was not primarily concerned with the 'end of the world," but with particular political situations, and specific moral demands. However, it did also refer, in very picturesque terms, to the fulfillment of God's purpose in creation. Relevant readings are: George Caird, *The Language and Imagery of the Bible*, John Robinson, *In the End, God*, as well as Claus Westermann, *What Does the Old Testament Aay About God?* (SPCK, 1979), and Abraham Heschel, *The Prophets*.

Our interpretation of Jesus will have to change in view of our new knowledge of the created universe, but it may be that such a shift in interpretation is not as great as one might at first think, and that it might even prove to provide a deeper and wider view of the divine purpose in creation.

---

[10] Alexander S. Sharov and Igor D. Novikov, *Edwin Hubble, The Discoverer of the Big Bang Universe* (Cambridge: The Cambridge University Press, 1989), 101.

[11] Georges Lemaître, "Expansion of the Universe, The Expanding Universe," *Monthly Notices of the Royal Astronomical Society*, Vol. 91, No. 03/1931: 490–501.

The images that existed in Judah at the time of Jesus were images drawn by the prophets and dreamers and visionaries whose concerns were with the trials and destiny of the people of Abraham and Isaac among the nations of the world. Their images had a double focus, firstly on the historical situation of the Jews, and secondly on the cosmic purpose of the whole created universe. Somehow these were bound together, but naturally with their limited knowledge of the universe, they were in no position to say how, with any scientific plausibility. They had difficulty even in including American and Chinese people in their vision of God's plan for creation, let alone possible beings in other galaxies.

The prophetic books of the Old Testament embody very different visions and viewpoints, but there are some repeated themes. Though the prophecies recorded in the books were made in differing historical situations, they all have to deal with the fact that Judah and Israel, the only remnants of the twelve tribes, have continually been oppressed, occupied, and carried into exile. How could the people with whom God had made an eternal covenant suffer in this way? One common prophetic response is to foretell terrible and catastrophic judgments on the oppressors of the Jews. Thus, Micah writes, "O daughter Zion ... you shall beat in pieces many people, and shall devote their gain to the Lord" (Micah 4, 13). And Zechariah says, "the clans of Judah ... shall devour to the right and to the left all the surrounding peoples" (Zech. 12, 6). Judah will have revenge on her enemies, and "strangers shall stand and feed your flocks, foreigners shall till you land and dress your vines" (Is. 61, 5). All foreign oppressors will be destroyed, or will serve Israel and come to worship Israel's God.

Sometimes this destruction is taken to the utmost extent: "I will utterly sweep away everything from the face of the earth, says the Lord ... I will cut off humanity from the face of the earth" (Zeph. 1, 3). It sounds as if there will be nothing left. Even the animals, birds, and fish will be swept away. Isaiah goes even further: "All the host of heaven shall rot away, and the skies roll up like a scroll" (Is. 34, 4). And Joel adds, "The sun and moon are darkened and the stars withdraw their shining" (Joel 2, 10). It looks as if the whole universe will be destroyed.

It is obvious that matters have got slightly exaggerated. Zephaniah goes on to say, "Perhaps you may be hidden on the day of the Lord's wrath" (Zeph. 2, 3), and Zechariah says, "Many peoples and strong nations shall come to seek the Lord of hosts in Jerusalem" (Zech. 8, 22). There are some people left after all. Isaiah (or one of the writers of this part of Isaiah) even has God saying, "Blessed be Egypt my people, and Assyria the work of my hands, and Israel my heritage" (Is. 19, 25). There will be a time of peace and blessing: "The Lord will comfort Zion ... and will make her wilderness like Eden, her desert like the garden of the Lord; joy and gladness will be found in her" (Is. 51, 3).

The prophets swing between saying that Israel will destroy all her enemies, and that there is a remnant of Israel who will live in a renewed and fruitful Zion, and that all nations will come to serve Israel joyfully.

It may seem unfair to patch such prophetic passages together, as though they are all parts of one agreed message. My point, however, is precisely to show that there is no agreed message. What different prophets are saying is that evil will be confounded and peace and justice will come. But they have very different ideas about how and when this will happen.

It should also be said that the main prophetic message is to call the people of Judah to a renewed commitment to morality and obedience to God's purpose. "Is not this the fast that I choose: to loose the bonds of injustice, to undo the thongs of the yoke, to let the oppressed go free ... to share your bread with the hungry, and bring the homeless poor into your house?" (Is. 58, 6, 7). Some prophets even criticize the sacrificial Temple rites: "I hate, I despise your festivals ... even though you offer me your burnt offerings and grain-offerings, I will not accept them ... but let justice roll down like waters, and righteousness like an ever-flowing stream" (Amos 5, 21–24).

The point is that this is the background to the New Testament passages which some have taken to be about the end of the world. The first thing to say is that they are not all literally true, and indeed that they do not all say one consistent thing. There is huge exaggeration and use of *poetic imagery*. The second thing is that they are not about the end of the world. They are primarily concerned with events in the history of Israel and Judah, with warnings of disaster and promises of peace if the people repent. The third thing is that the prophetic call is to renewed righteousness; the message is primarily a moral one, not a set of precise oracular predictions about the future. The prophets of Judaism were proclaiming the moral demands of God, the judgment of God upon evil, and the promises of God, together with warnings about the price of disobedience as it is perceived in very specific historical situations.

If Jesus stood in this prophetic tradition – and it would seem likely that he did – we would expect these things to be true of his message also.

Box 12.5

The author's claim is that Jesus's teaching on "the end" should be seen in the light of Hebrew prophetic teaching. It will therefore be primarily moral, symbolic, and historically specific, though it will also reflect a general belief in divine judgment and the promise of salvation. There follows a short exposition of the New Testament apocalyptic passages, aiming to show that these elements are to be found in them.

The teaching would be hyperbolic (highly exaggerated) and metaphorical (not literal); it would be concerned with the specific historical situation of Judah under Roman domination, with warnings of the danger of impending political catastrophe; and it would be primarily a call to moral reform and commitment to a God of justice and mercy, and an assurance of hope that the will of God would be ultimately realized in a new creation (see Box 12.5).

So it is. Apocalyptic themes are not dominant in the gospels, and they almost disappear in John's Gospel. But there is a similar apocalyptic section in the first three gospels, with some variations (Matt. 24, Mk. 13, and Lk. 21). A major part of these sections is concern with damping down overexcitement at the thought of an imminent "end of history." There will be troubles, wars, and earthquakes, but people should not think the end has come, and should patiently go on enduring and practicing compassion and mercy. There are specific warnings not to follow false Messianic claimants, or to think that Christ has returned. If there is an end, it will be immediate, unmistakable, and "like a lightning flash."

Then there is a section on the destruction of the Temple, and warnings of terrible suffering that would come upon the Jewish people. These warnings were validated when the Temple was destroyed in 70 CE, and in 135 CE the nation of Israel ceased to exist.

Finally, there is a brief reference to the fall of the stars from heaven and the Son of Man coming on clouds to gather his elect from heaven and Earth. One puzzling and much debated feature of the gospels is that in the synoptic gospels, Jesus most often refers to himself as the Son of Man. There is dispute among scholars as to whether he did so; and if he did, of what exactly he meant (see Box 12.6).

Box 12.6

The trouble with theology it that talking about one part of faith will sooner or later involve saying something about many other issues. You can't do everything in one paper, and it is important not to try to do everything at once. So stick to the main theme, with perhaps a brief reference to other relevant literature.

It may seem presumptuous of me to take a view on this when I depend almost wholly on biblical scholars for my knowledge of these things. However, there is one view that has some scholarly backing, and that I have found helpful in thinking about the apocalyptic sayings attributed to Jesus.

In its main Old Testament occurrence, the expression "Son of Man" is used in the book of Daniel as a symbol not primarily of an individual, but of a group or community, "the holy ones of the most High" (Daniel 7, 13–14, 18), who would usher in the rule of justice and mercy, which will supplant the militaristic rule of Babylon, Media, Persia, and Greece, symbolized by four beasts from the sea. It seems possible that Jesus could have referred to himself as "Son of Man," meaning that he and the saints who are with him would establish a new age of peace and righteousness, supplanting the militaristic power of the Roman Empire. This would be a new age, ending the age of Temple sacrifices, and also ending the existence of Israel and later of Rome as worldly powers. It would be a terrible "Day of the Lord" for Jews, and Jesus's mission was to turn Jews to the true and inward worship of God instead of relying on external conformity to the Divine Law, and to enter into the new age of the Kingdom of God (see Box 12.7).

Box 12.7

The next section is controversial. It takes elements from the 'realized eschatology' of C. H. Dodd, and from the 'liberal' theology of Adolf von Harnack, without being committed wholly to either of these views. The previous sections about the nature of Biblical prophecy, and our revolutionized scientific knowledge of the cosmos, are meant to lead to seeing this interpretation as plausible. The author's main postulate is that Jesus was not mistaken, but this requires that we see his alleged teachings as symbolic and as having a 'double focus.'

But there was a new twist to this story. The Davidic monarchy was not restored; an age of peace and justice did not begin. The new kingdom, it became clear, would not be a politically revived Jewish kingdom, and maybe it was always a misunderstanding on the part of some of Jesus's followers that it would. The Kingdom would be the rule of God in the hearts of men and women, and God would rule through self-sacrificial love, not through conquest and the sword. As such, it would come "with power" within the lifetimes of some of those who heard him preach–as it did, arguably, with Pentecost. Such an interpretation might help to make sense of many otherwise mysterious uses of the imagery of the "day of the Lord" and the coming of Christ on the clouds of heaven. Such imagery would be an echo of Daniel's dream visions, which referred to events in political and religious history, not literal predictions of the end of the world.

The Vision of the Cosmic Christ

Box 12.8

The author seeks to pull the various strands of his paper together, by relating together the new cosmology, the nature of prophetic language, and an understanding of the Christ as a supreme cosmic power who wills to liberate all beings and unite them to the spiritual life of God.

Biblical Christianity was not just a new moral teaching or a commentary on historical events and probabilities (see Box 12.8). It had a cosmology. It was concerned with events in human history, but it was also interested in Jesus's relation to the whole of physical and spiritual reality. It postulated that Christ was the fundamental spiritual force embracing and gathering all things to union with the divine. But it turns out that the biblical conception of physical reality was much too small. We now know that we live on a small planet in a small solar system in a small galaxy among billions of others. Earth has existed for 4 billion years, and scientists at SETI estimate that there are billions of planets in the universe which could be suitable for the evolution of living organisms.

Whether there is any other intelligent life in the universe is a matter of speculation. But the thought that there could be, and our appreciation of the sheer vastness of the physical universe, must cause us to rethink the implications of modern cosmology for Christian belief. In the earliest days of Christianity, there was already argument between flat Earth cosmology and the Ptolemaic cosmology, but by the ninth century Ptolemy had won. When Copernicus revolutionized both views in 1543, cosmological disputes arose again, and this time the Roman Catholic Church backed the wrong horse, and placed his book, *On the Revolution of the Heavenly Spheres*, on the index of prohibited reading until 1835. Now, however, Krakow cathedral, where he was a Canon, contains a sculptured model of the Copernican hypothesis. The Church moves slowly, but, like the Earth and the Sun, it moves.

What Copernicus did was to remove our planet from the center of the physical universe, and make a literal reading of Genesis impossible. It was already impossible on Ptolemy's cosmology, and Augustine knew this. Augustine held, for instance, that the six "days" of creation were not literal days. God did not take six days to create the universe, and then have to rest and recover on the seventh day. For Augustine, God created the universe from the beginning to the end of time in one non-temporal act. Much of Genesis therefore has to be given an allegorical interpretation, Augustine thought. It is very difficult to say just what he thought the six "days" of creation represent. It must be said that the specific allegories he suggests are extremely implausible, even fantastic. He nevertheless spent much time on trying to reconcile the facts of the science of his day with Scripture. But the science of his day still assumed that the Earth was the center of the universe. Now, however, we know that we are very unlikely to be the center or most important thing in God's creation. We are, to put it bluntly, probably not God's major concern in creation.

It has now become obvious that Genesis does not give a scientific account of the creation of the universe. As such it has been outdated three times, once by Ptolemy, once by Copernicus, and once by Edwin Hubble. Genesis gives a creation story influenced by contemporaneous Middle Eastern creation stories.[12] Its significance is that, unlike the Babylonian story, for instance, it proposes that there is just one God who creates the universe, and who ensures that in this universe creatures emerge who are in the image of God, that is, who have intellectual understanding, creative freedom, and moral responsibility. Those creatures – us – have a responsibility for tending and cultivating their planet, as if it was a garden treasured by God. The Genesis story enshrines these truths in an imaginative and picturesque narrative that does not compete with later scientific accounts of the origin of the universe since it is not a scientific account at all. It is a story which enshrines the truth that humans are responsible for caring for the Earth as the beloved creation of God.

Box 12.9

Moving toward a conclusion, the author explicitly relates the Biblical creation stories to modern scientific thought about the cosmos, develops an interpretation of the doctrine of creation, and argues that the apocalyptic material in the New Testament is primarily about the fulfillment of creation, which will be beyond our present spacetime.

---

[12] Alexander Heidel, *The Babylonian Genesis* (Chicago: University of Chicago Press, 1951).

As Christian theologians thought about creation, they realized that the idea of creation is not really an idea about how things began (see Box 12.9). It is more importantly the idea that every moment in spacetime depends upon some reality beyond spacetime, some reality which is conscious, of supreme value, and purposive. Creation is the dependence of every time on a supra-temporal and spiritual reality. It does not much matter how the universe originated and developed. It could have done so in many ways. In fact, scientists now think that it originated with a dimensionless point of immense heat and energy, and expanded into more and more complex integrated forms over billions of years, ending (so far, and on this planet) in the existence of communities of carbon-based intelligent organisms.

Since the universe is created by a conscious and wise God, it has a purpose, and this leads naturally to speculation on what that purpose may be. The Bible speaks of this by using the same sort of imaginative and picturesque narrative as does the book of Genesis. It does not give a scientific account, which would mean disclosing the second law of thermodynamics, which governs the ultimate future (and death) of the physical universe, and at least hinting that there are billions of galaxies in the universe. The Bible does not do those things. The New Testament draws a picture of the gathering up of all things in Christ. This is a communion of conscious and intelligent beings who are united in creative relationship and love, beyond the domain of present physical laws, but alive within an all-encompassing spiritual reality, fulfilled in mutual relationship and bliss. This is pictured as "a new creation," the *Parousia* or known and felt presence of the eternal Christ, or the "return of Christ in glory with all the saints."

This is not primarily a story about the end of our spacetime, just as Genesis was not primarily about the beginning of our spacetime. It is a story about the relationship of every time to the spiritual reality which supports it, and upon which it totally depends. As creation tells us that we derive at every moment from an eternal Spirit, so stories about the end of time tell us that every moment of our lives is taken up into the eternal realm, where it finds either its fulfillment or, insofar as it is evil, its negation and transformation.

The story of tending a garden in Genesis is like a dream image that demands that we care for the Earth. So the story that we find in the New Testament of rising to meet Christ in the air and be with him forever is a dream image that promises that our labors, and the Earth itself, despite all its apparent failures and setbacks, will be fruitful and fulfilled in the God whose nature and purpose is revealed in Christ.

There is a tension of expectations and hopes among early Christians. On the one hand, they hoped that evil and persecution, and the cruel deaths of martyrs, would be ended soon. On the other hand, they hoped that there might be many more good things the Earth yet had to offer, and that there would be many more souls to be saved before "the end."

In a literal understanding of the Biblical universe, Christ would descend from the heavens beyond the dome of the sky, upon which the stars hang, destroy evil, and take the righteous and repentant to himself. For many, they expected that he would be the Davidic King, reuniting the twelve tribes and bringing them back to Jerusalem, where the Temple would be the center of the true worship of God. That might happen very soon.

But that view began to change even in the first generation of Christians.

Mark's Gospel says, "The good news must first be proclaimed to all nations" (Mk. 13, 10), which is very unlikely to happen within one generation. Jesus was seen as the Savior of the whole world, and all people were to be included in the new relation to God which Jesus offered. That would take much longer.

In our universe, the picture has changed again, by expanding enormously. Now Christ is the archetype and fulfillment of the whole cosmos. All times will be included yet transfigured by being taken into Christ. Christ is the spiritual presence and goal of the cosmos, in which what creatures do is eternalized, and either negated or fulfilled. The cosmos will not end soon – that thought has to go. Even the destruction of our planet would leave the rest of the cosmos largely untouched. But the cosmos is included in the spiritual reality of Christ, where there is both negation and fulfillment. "Christ will come again" becomes "Christ will fulfill your life by taking your life into his."

Following the example of the "double focus" of many prophecies recorded in the Hebrew Bible, the events portrayed in New Testament imagery about the coming of the Son of Man would partly be a warning about the coming destruction of Israel and the age of Temple sacrifices, and would partly present the hope of an ultimate goal of creation, the trans-historical fulfillment of the divine purpose for creation, in which all created persons can share. The Son of Man who comes to establish the rule of the Spirit in the hearts of men and women who followed him in Galilee and Jerusalem is also the Son of Man who at the end of time gathers all things in in the universe in the cosmic Christ.

One implication of modern scientific discoveries is the knowledge that life on this planet may in fact end at any moment, and we may be responsible for its ending. The Christian message is that if it does, there will still be a fulfillment of human, and perhaps of all sentient life on Earth, in Christ. In that sense, even if the worst happens to us, it will not be the end of the human story. Christ will "come again" at the end of human life on this planet. When that will be, we cannot know. Those who think the end of human life and Christ's appearing to us in glory may be soon, are not absurdly wrong. They are, however, wickedly wrong if they think that in the meanwhile they need not do all they can to prevent the destruction of the planet.

Yet there is a more expansive story to be told, of worlds far from us in time and space, and of God's love for them. Every moment of time in the whole cosmos enters into and becomes part of the building up of the completion of God's purpose for the universe. That completion will contain each moment of time, so one can live as if the consummation is "at hand," present both in time and in eternity, held in the mind of God until the fulfillment of all things is complete. Our expanded vision of the universe is also an expansion of our understanding of the purpose and the providence of God, an understanding which was inaugurated in the historical life, the death and resurrection appearances, of Jesus. Those who look for the coming of Christ are those who hope for the apotheosis of each moment of their lives in the completed purpose of the whole of creation, when all things in heaven and earth will finally be united in the cosmos – including Christ.

Works Cited

Augustine. (1982). *The Literal Meaning of Genesis*. Translated and Annotated by J.H. Taylor. New York: Newman Press.
Caird, G.B. (1980). *The Language and Imagery of the Bible*. Philadelphia: Westminster Press.
Dodd, C.H. (1961). *The Parables of the Kingdom*. New York: Charles Scribner's Sons.
Heschel, Abraham. (2001). *The Prophets*. New York: Harper.
Rahner, Karl. (1997). *The Trinity*. Translated by Joseph F. Donceel. New York: Crossroad.
Robinson, John. (1968) *In the End, God*. New York: Harper & Row.
von Harnack, Adolf. (1908). *What is Christianity?* Trans. Thomas Bailey Saunders. New York: G.P. Putnam's Sons.
Ward, Keith. (1996). *Religion and Creation*. Oxford: Clarendon Press.
Westermann, Claus. (1979). *What Does the Old Testament Say about God?* London: SPCK.
Wright, N.T. (2019). *History and Eschatology*. Waco, TX: Baylor University Press.

Part VI

Method in Theology

13

Theological Language and Method in Liberal Theology

Schubert Ogden's Response to the Falsification Controversy

John Allan Knight

RESEARCH LEVEL 4

Editors' Introduction

In this essay, Knight is attempting to show that there is a relationship between a theologian's understanding of theological language and how they think theology should be done (their theological method). Rather than giving us a deductive proof, or a reductio ad absurdam, Knight gives us an argument to the best explanation. He takes a premier example of a liberal theologian (Schubert Ogden) and tries to show that Ogden's response to a raging debate in the middle of the twentieth century (the theology and falsification controversy) is motivated by his understanding of theological language.

Knight first contextualizes his essay by situating it within his attempt to understand and analyze the divide between liberal and postliberal theologies in the latter part of the twentieth century. This provides some reason for viewing Ogden as a liberal theologian. Thus, if his response to falsification theorists reveals his understanding of religious and theological language, this can yield more insight into liberal theological method as it was practiced in the middle to late twentieth century.

Knight then turns to what he calls a descriptivist view of language. This was the dominant view of language during the theology and falsification controversy, and Knight sets out its requirements for the meaningful use of language. Undergirding these requirements were Bertrand Russell's requirements for two types of knowledge – knowledge by acquaintance and descriptive knowledge. Falsification theorists have argued that theologians could not meet these requirements, and therefore that talk about God was meaningless.

Knight then describes Ogden's theological method and argues that it allows him to respond to the falsification theorists, arguing that the way he talks about God meets the requirements set out by descriptivists for meaningful language about God. If Knight's argument is successful, while it doesn't prove that a theologian's method will be related to their understanding of theological language, it will provide evidence for believing there to be such a relationship.

Box 13.1
The author begins with a broad contextualization, to show where this study fits in with the arc of the liberal versus postliberal divide North American theology in the twentieth century.

The Craft of Innovative Theology: Argument and Process, First Edition. Edited by John Allan Knight and Ian S. Markham.
© 2022 John Wiley & Sons Ltd. Published 2022 by John Wiley & Sons Ltd.

For the past one hundred years, at least in North America, theology has been marked by what I have called the great divide – the divide over how to validate Christian theological claims (see Box 13.1). It was instigated by Karl Barth's revolt against his teachers, the great nineteenth-century liberal theologians like Harnack and Hermann and their mentors dating back to Schleiermacher. For theologians such as Barth and his followers, the only validation needed by any theological claim is a showing that it comports with God's self-revelation in Jesus Christ. On this view, to validate theological claims by appeal to any other criteria, including criteria that Christians and non-Christians alike could share, is to forsake the central Christian affirmation that "Jesus is Lord." Liberal theologians, on the other hand, argue that God's self-revelation in Christ cannot be the sole criterion of validation, because this yields only a determination of whether the claim under investigation is distinctively Christian, but cannot determine whether such a claim is true. Liberal theologians are concerned about the truth of theological claims and seek a way of doing theology that can legitimate or validate such claims as being true. They insist on validating theological claims by reference to criteria that are general (i.e. that are not limited to particular fields of discourse) and argue that any theological claims that cannot meet such criteria are arbitrary. Barthian theologians, on the other hand, and especially Barth's postliberal heirs, are skeptical that any such criteria can be articulated. Indeed, they argue that any attempt to meet such criteria distorts the claims of Christianity. Liberals, then, insist on general criteria of meaning and validation, while Barthians insist on the particularity of claims, especially concerning Jesus.[1]

This essay is part of an ongoing attempt to understand this divide and its ramifications.[2] One of the more neglected ramifications of the great divide involves the relationship between the meaning of theological language and theological method (see Box 13.2).

Box 13.2

Here the author gets more specific about one way to analyze the liberal/postliberal divide.

And we can gain much insight into this relationship by re-visiting a very active dispute that arose in the middle of the twentieth century over the nature of religious and theological language, often called the theology and falsification controversy. No consensus emerged, but the dispute highlighted the relationship between the meaning of theological language and theological method.

Box 13.3

Here the author gives a roadmap of his planned argument so that the reader knows what is coming. Not every author likes such a roadmap, but it does help readers to critically assess whether the author has done what he has set out to do.

In this essay, I want to provide an example that illustrates this relationship (see Box 13.3). First, I shall briefly outline the descriptivist understanding of language that motivated the theology and falsification dispute and then discuss the dispute itself. I will then move to Schubert Ogden, in my view a clear and pre-eminent example of liberal theological method. I shall first describe his theological method and then show how it yields an understanding of language that satisfies the requirements imposed by descriptivism for successful reference to God.

---

[1] Note that this understanding of "liberal" in theology might in fact describe a number of theologians that in popular parlance are most often dubbed "conservative".

[2] See my *Liberalism Versus Postliberalism: The Great Divide in Twentieth Century Theology* (New York: Oxford University Press, 2013).

Meaning, Reference, and the Falsification Controversy

> **Box 13.4**
>
> The author begins to describe the falsification challenge. See the glossary for "referent" and "reference."

Falsification theorists such as Antony Flew argued that claims about God could not be assigned any meaning, because there was no way to identify the **referent** of the term "God" (see Box 13.4). And because the referent of "God" remained indeterminate, statements about God remained strictly meaningless. Many thinkers saw the falsification challenge as a straightforward application of the falsifiability principle to theological or religious statements. But the challenge posed by the falsification theorists ultimately relied less on the falsifiability thesis of logical positivism than on the descriptivist requirements specified by Bertrand Russell for successful reference. Russell's view of language (which included his descriptivist theory of reference) remained dominant long after the demise of logical positivism as a viable philosophical project.

To understand the falsification challenge, we need to understand the descriptivist understanding of language that was dominant until the advent of Kripke's critique in 1970. In any assertion, the subject of the sentence will contain a name or singular term or definite description, which are *referring* terms or expressions that are intended to pick out, or *refer* to, the object about which a speaker or writer is going to say something. For those holding descriptivist views, a name or other singular term succeeds in referring to an object if and only if it stands for one or more definite descriptions that (either singly or together) *uniquely* describe the referent object.[3] That is, of the descriptions that a speaker takes to describe an object, the speaker takes one or some to belong uniquely to that object. The *meaning* of the referring expression is not identical with its referent. Rather, the meaning of a referring expression is a descriptive sense that provides necessary and sufficient conditions for determining its reference. If, however, no object uniquely satisfies one or some of the descriptions for which the name stands, then the purportedly referring expression does not refer. If the referring expression in the subject does not refer, neither the term nor the sentence that contains it has any meaning. As for predicate terms (such as *green* in "The car is green") their meaning consists of a descriptive condition satisfaction of which by an object is necessary and sufficient for the predicate to be true of the object.[4] And this means that on the descriptivist view, the meaning of a sentence is constituted by its truth conditions.

This descriptivist view of language was well established by the time the falsification controversy broke out in the middle of the century.[5] Compounding the problem was the closely related

---

[3] On some such views, the constitutive descriptions are just the meaning of the name.

[4] For a more extensive description, see Scott Soames, *Reference and Description: The Case Against Two-Dimensionalism* (Princeton: Princeton University Press, 2005), 1–2.

[5] By 1950, Strawson and other ordinary language philosophers, under the influence of Wittgenstein's intermediate and later thought, had begun to challenge Russell's views. Other philosophers, such as Kripke, Ruth Barcan Marcus, Peter Geach, Michael Dummett, Hilary Putnam, Paul Grice, Keith Donnellan, David Kaplan, and others, were raising challenges from other quarters. Nonetheless, descriptivism remained the dominant view prior to 1970.

role played by descriptions in Russell's account of knowledge. The combination of his accounts of language and knowledge formed a unified program that was used by falsification theorists in their challenge to theology.

> **Box 13.5**
>
> Epistemology is the study of, or discourse about, knowledge.

Russell deploys two epistemological concepts, the most basic of which is the relation of "acquaintance": a momentary qualitative experience of sense data (see Box 13.5). An acquaintance relation is a *non-propositional, immediate relation* to an object.[6] "Object" here does not include physical objects, but it is not strictly limited to sense data.[7] Acquaintance is immediate knowledge – not mediated by a description or any other conceptual apparatus. It is not by acquaintance that we know any other physical object in the world. Acquaintance thus stands in contrast to the second basic epistemological relation, that of description. "We have descriptive knowledge of an object when we know that it is the object having some property or properties with which we are acquainted; that is to say, when we know that the property or properties in question *belong to one object and no more*, we are said to have knowledge of that one object by description, whether or not we are acquainted with the object."[8] For most of the important things we know, our knowledge is by description,[9] and Russell therefore held that "common words, even proper names, are usually really descriptions."[10]

> **Box 13.6**
>
> The author has now set out the assumptions that will cause problems for theology – descriptivist understandings of language and Russell's epistemological concepts. In the next section he will describe how the falsification theorists use those assumptions to issue their challenge to theology.

We can immediately see what Russell's view implies for the knowledge of God. If it is only some universals, sense data, and possibly ourselves that we can know by acquaintance, then insofar as we can know anything of other beings, it can only be by description. And this applies *a fortiori* to God, who (at least mostly), incites no sense data at all. More importantly, even to have descriptive knowledge of God, we must be able to specify one or more properties, with which we are acquainted, that belong *only* to God. Russell imposes a twofold requirement

---

[6] "I say that I am *acquainted* with an object when I have a direct cognitive relation to that object, that is, when I am directly aware of the object itself. When I speak of a cognitive relation here, I do not mean the sort of relation which constitutes judgement, but the sort which constitutes presentation." Bertrand Russell, "Knowledge by Acquaintance and Knowledge by Description," *Proceedings of the Aristotelian Society* Vol. 11 (1910–1911): 108–28.

[7] Ibid., 112, 126. "We have acquaintance with sense-data, with many universals, and possibly with ourselves, but not with physical objects or other minds".

[8] Ibid., 127 (emphasis added).

[9] "Common words, even proper names, are usually really descriptions. That is to say, the thought in the mind of a person using a proper name correctly can generally only be expressed explicitly if we replace the proper name by a description." Russell, "Knowledge by Acquaintance," 114.

[10] Ibid.

therefore on anyone who purports to have knowledge of God: first, there must be some property or properties that are unique to God, and second, the knower must have knowledge of that property or those properties by acquaintance. At least at first glance, this would seem to rule out properties such as omnipotence, of which knowledge by acquaintance is hard to come by.

Further, in order to *refer* successfully to some object or being, we have to have some knowledge of the object to which we are attempting to refer. And, since we can know other beings only by description, in order to refer successfully to God, we will have to satisfy Russell's two requirements for descriptive knowledge. This will mean that we must have knowledge (by acquaintance) of some descriptive condition that is both necessary and sufficient to pick out God as the unique referent of the term "God."

Wisdom's Parable and the Descriptivist Argument that Statements about God are Meaningless

For falsification theorists such as Antony Flew, these descriptivist requirements meant that reference to God could not succeed. To make his point, he adapts John Wisdom's story of two friends, a Believer and a Skeptic, who happen upon a garden in the middle of a woods. The Believer thinks some gardener must tend the garden; the Skeptic does not. In Flew's adaptation of Wisdom's story, the two friends undertake further empirical investigation using bloodhounds, electric fences, etc., but there is no direct sign of the gardener.

> Yet still the believer is not convinced. "But there is a gardener, invisible, intangible, insensible to electric shocks, a gardener who has no scent and makes no sound, a gardener who comes secretly to look after the garden which he loves." At last the Skeptic despairs, "But what remains of your original assertion? Just how does what you call an invisible, intangible, eternally elusive gardener differ from an imaginary gardener or even from no gardener at all?"[11]

This parable illuminates, Flew argues, typical theological utterance: a Believer, he says, will not allow any fact that the friends are able to observe to count against his belief that a gardener exists. But just this feature, Flew concludes, means that the Believer's putative assertion that an invisible gardener exists and tends the garden is really no assertion at all.[12]

Flew conflates two distinct issues here – verification (or falsification) and reference. It's one thing to argue that whatever one says about God can't be verified (or falsified) and thus shouldn't be believed; it's another to argue that a putative reference to God can't succeed.[13] But for Flew, if an assertion cannot be falsified, then it does not really assert anything and is strictly meaningless. Flew argues that statements about God are very much like the Believer's statement about

---

[11] Antony Flew, "The University Discussion," in *New Essays in Philosophical Theology*, ed. Antony Flew and Alasdair MacIntyre (London: SCM Press, 1955, reprint 1958), 96 (page references are to reprint edition).

[12] As Flew puts it, "if there is nothing which a putative assertion denies then there is nothing which it asserts either: and so it is not really an assertion." Ibid., 98.

[13] Notice that Flew makes a subtle assumption that the Believer is unlikely to share – namely, that if there is no *observable state of affairs* that p denies, then there is no *state of affairs at all* that p denies. But whatever the Believer may assert about the gardener being invisible, etc., surely there is at least one state of affairs that the Believer denies – namely, *that there is no gardener*.

the invisible gardener. Theological utterances, he says, may seem like assertions, but since the theist won't allow any empirical observation to count decisively against them, such putative assertions are not really assertions at all, but are meaningless.

What allows Flew to conflate these two issues is descriptivism – which includes theories of both meaning and reference. When Flew argues that theistic statements don't count as assertions because the people who make them don't allow anything to count against them, what he's saying is that they fail to fulfill the descriptivist requirements for meaningful language use. When he argues that theists can't distinguish God from an imaginary god or no god at all, he's saying that theistic claims do not set out any set of descriptive conditions that will allow us to determine that "God" refers to God and not to anything else, such as an imaginary god.

Further, even if reference to God could be established, Flew argues that theistic claims do not set out necessary and sufficient conditions that will allow us to test whether the claim is true of God. This, I think, is the point Flew is trying to make in the following example: "Someone tells us that God loves us as a father loves his children. … But then we see a child dying of inoperable cancer of the throat. His earthly father is driven frantic … but his Heavenly Father reveals no obvious sign of concern." Given no miraculous intervention, Flew asks, "Just what would have to happen not merely (morally and wrongly) to tempt but also (logically and rightly) to entitle us to say 'God does not love us' or even 'God does not exist'?"[14] Flew can be interpreted in at least two ways. Flew might have used the example to argue against the reasonableness of the belief that God loves us. On this interpretation, the lack of empirical evidence of God's concern deprives the belief in God's love of (at least some of) its epistemic justification. Instead, Flew's example suggests that the qualifications made to the statement that God loves us have eroded the statement to the point "that it was no longer an assertion at all."[15] And if it no longer counts as an assertion, that is because it can't be assigned a meaning. And the reason it can't is that it does not describe a set of conditions that must be satisfied for the statement to be true.[16]

Schubert Ogden on the Task and Method of Theology

Box 13.7
What the author really wants to describe is Ogden's response to the falsification challenge. But by setting out Ogden's method before his response, the author is hoping that the reader will see how his response grows out of his method.

Turning now to Ogden, in this section I'll describe his views on the task and method of theology (see Box 13.7). In section 13.4, I'll show how his method allows him to meet the descriptivist requirements for meaningful statements about God. Ogden argues that the theologian's task is to "translate" the meaning of the church's proclamation into the language and thought forms of her own day.[17] Such an exercise in translation presupposes "the correlation of the Christian

---

[14] Flew, "University Discussion," 98.

[15] Ibid.

[16] Flew challenges his interlocutors to set out such conditions: "I therefore put to the succeeding symposiasts the simple central questions, 'What would have to occur or to have occurred to constitute for you a disproof of the love of, or of the existence of, God?'" Flew, 99.

[17] Schubert M. Ogden, "The Lordship of Jesus Christ: The Meaning of Our Affirmation," *Encounter* Vol. 21 (Autumn 1960): 408–422, 410.

witness of faith and human existence ... ."[18] Precisely because of the correlational structure of theology, the theologian will have to answer two central questions: What does it mean to say that Jesus is the Christ? And is this statement about Jesus true? These two questions Ogden seeks to answer by applying his dual criteria of theological adequacy.[19] Theological claims must be *appropriate* to Jesus Christ, and *credible* to common human experience and reason.[20]

Ogden's criteria of adequacy derive from his understanding of the nature of religious claims, about which he makes two important points. First, Ogden defines religion as "the primary form of culture in terms of which we human beings explicitly ask and answer the existential question of the meaning of ultimate reality for us."[21] And this "existential question," asks "how we are to understand ourselves and others in relation to the whole if ours is to be an authentic existence?"[22] Ogden maintains that we ask and answer the existential question, at least implicitly, in everything we say or do. A religious claim, though, is one that *explicitly* asserts an answer to the existential question.[23]

Second, religious assertions, like all other assertions, claim to be true, "and true not in some utterly different sense from that in which anything else is true, but in essentially the same sense, in that it, too, can be verified in some way or other by common human experience and reason (see Box 13.8)."[24]

Box 13.8

Ogden's point that religious assertions claim to be true in the same sense as any other assertion does, by appeal in some way or other to common human experience and reason, is what Knight has in mind when he characterizes Ogden as emblematic of liberal theological method.

---

[18] Schubert M. Ogden, "What Is Theology?" *Journal of Religion* Vol. 52 (1972): 22–40, reprinted in *On Theology* (San Francisco: Harper & Row, 1986; reprint, Dallas: Southern Methodist University Press, 1992), 1–21: 3 (page citations are to reprint edition).

[19] Ibid., 4.

[20] See Schubert M. Ogden, "Toward Bearing Witness," *Religious Studies Review* Vol. 23 (1997): 337–340, 338. Ogden has always maintained that these two criteria of systematic theology are "logically independent and mutually irreducible." Ogden, *Doing Theology Today*, 9.

[21] Schubert M. Ogden, *Is There Only One True Religion or Are There Many?* (Dallas, TX: Southern Methodist University Press, 1992), 5. In an earlier work, Ogden argued that religion is "neither simply a metaphysics nor simply an ethics, [but] it is in a peculiar way both." This means that "religion is at once an understanding of the ultimate reality of self, others, and the whole and an understanding of our own possibilities of existing and acting in relation to this ultimate reality." Schubert M. Ogden, *Faith and Freedom: Toward a Theology of Liberation* (Nashville, TN: Abingdon Press, 1979; rev. edn. 1989), 32 (page citations are to revised edition).

[22] Ogden, *Is There Only One True Religion?*, 6.

[23] Some theological claims might be better characterized as, for example, historical (if they made assertions about the dating of Jesus's death) or philosophical (if they made methodological assertions about validation of religious claims). But other theological claims explicitly assert answers to the existential question, and one might contend that these theological claims would be religious claims. For Ogden, however, while a religion is a *primary* form of culture, theology is a *secondary* form of culture in that it is "critical reflection on the validity claims of some specific religion ... ." Ogden, *Is There Only One True Religion?*, 8. Nonetheless, I can see no reason why a theological claim that interprets or reflects upon a religious claim cannot itself serve as a religious claim. In what follows, I shall consider all claims that assert answers to the existential question to be religious claims.

[24] Ogden, "The Enlightenment is Not Over," 326. That is, a religion "affirms both the right and the responsibility of reason to validate critically all claims to validity, including its own claims to truth and unique authority." Ogden, "Enlightenment," 326–327.

This means that all phases of theological reflection must be carried out in a secular manner – secular in the Enlightenment sense that the autonomy of rational discourse is preserved.[25]

Let's now turn to Ogden's two criteria of adequacy. In his latest work, Ogden works these criteria into a broader description of the theologian's task as occurring in three stages.[26] The first phase is a historical phase, whose task is to identify the "formally normative witness" that can validate theological claims as appropriate to Jesus Christ.[27] It is not Scriptures as a whole, nor the New Testament, but the earliest strand of apostolic witness, or the "Jesus-kerygma," that Ogden takes to be the formally normative or authorizing witness to Jesus Christ.[28]

The second phase is a hermeneutical phase, in which the theologian is to interpret the formally normative witness. Because theology is a secondary form of culture, on Ogden's construal, all theological claims serve as part of the enterprise of reflection upon the claims of a particular religion. It is these religious claims that are primary, and, consequently, the norm of appropriateness must be construed as an answer to the same question as that to which religious claims assert an answer. The formally normative Christian witness must therefore be articulated as an answer to "the existential question about the meaning of ultimate reality for us."[29] This existentially interpreted formal norm is the criterion Ogden uses to determine whether a claim is appropriate to Jesus Christ.

The third phase of theological reflection is its most explicitly philosophical phase, in which the principal objective is to establish the second criterion necessary to validate theological claims.[30] In Ogden's view, "Any witness at all makes or implies the claim to be adequate, and hence makes or implies the further claims to be credible as well as appropriate."[31] Thus, this second criterion will be used to assess whether theological statements are successful in their claim to be credible to what Ogden takes "to count as the truth about human existence."[32] But because of the nature of the primary religious claims upon which theology reflects, what counts here is not any and all truths about human existence but the *existential* truth about the *meaning or significance* of ultimate reality for us (see Box 13.9).

Box 13.9

If Ogden's language about "the existential truth about the meaning or significance of ultimate reality for us" makes you wonder if he's influenced by Bultmann, the answer is an unqualified yes. His first book, based on his doctoral dissertation, was *Christ Without Myth: A Study Based on the Theology of Rudolf Bultman* (Dallas: Southern Methodist University Press, 1961).

---

[25] See Schubert M. Ogden, "The Reality of God," in *The Reality of God and Other Essays* (New York: Harper & Row, 1966; 2nd edn. Dallas: Southern Methodist University Press, 1992), 1–70: 7.

[26] Ogden, *Doing Theology Today*, 13–17.

[27] Ogden distinguishes between a witness that is "formally normative" from one that is "substantially normative." A substantially normative witness may validate some, but not all, theological claims as being appropriate to Jesus Christ. Still, a substantially normative witness will agree with all other appropriate witnesses. A formally normative witness, on the other hand, can validate the appropriateness of all theological claims, in that all theological claims must agree with it if they are to be appropriate to Jesus Christ. See Ogden, *Is There Only One True Religion?*, 12–13.

[28] Again, determining the identity of this formally normative witness is a secular activity, in that the norms of historical criticism and investigation must guide the theologian's determination of the formal norm. Ogden, *Doing Theology Today*, 11–12.

[29] Ogden, *Doing Theology Today*, 14; see *supra* note 8.

[30] Schubert M. Ogden, "The Nature and State of Theological Scholarship and Research," *Theological Education* Vol. 24 (Autumn 1987): 120–131, 125.

[31] Ogden, *Doing Theology Today*, 18.

[32] Ibid., 15.

How does Ogden arrive at and articulate this existential truth about human existence? Recall that Ogden insists that the theological reflection involved in all three phases must be thoroughly secular,[33] which means that no religious or theological claim can be judged credible (or incredible) through any appeal to either scripture or tradition or any kind of authority other than human reason and experience alone. For Ogden, the great achievement of the Enlightenment is "the consistent affirmation of the unique authority of human reason over all other putative authorities."[34] If human reason is to have this unique authority, it must be because there is a common aspect to the experience of all human beings to which reason can refer or appeal in validating claims.[35] That is, Ogden intends "common human experience" to refer to whatever is common to *any and all* experiences or acts of thought (i.e. whatever is common to human subjectivity).[36] Therefore, when he says that theological claims can be judged to be credible (or not) by reference to the "existential truth" that is "given only through common human experience," he means that the criterion of credibility is a (non-empirical) transcendental criterion.[37]

If Ogden is to derive his norm of credibility from an examination of whatever is common to any and all human experiences or acts of thought, he will need an account of the *a priori* elements of human experience. Ogden has such an account, which he derives from Whitehead.[38] A transcendental analysis of human experience reveals an unavoidable faith in the worth or value of our lives and the necessary existence of God, who is constituted by boundless love for all humanity, as the ground of this basic faith. To be credible, religious claims must be consistent

---

[33] "In its philosophical aspect, in which it validates this further claim of Christian witness to be credible, systematic theology necessarily presupposes philosophical theology as an independent secular, or nontheological, discipline. In fact, unless philosophical theology were thus independent of Christian theology, it could not be the critical reflection that systematic theology requires in order to validate the claim of Christian witness to be credible as well as appropriate." Ogden, "The Nature and State of Theological Scholarship and Research," 125.

[34] Ogden, "The Enlightenment is Not Over," 322.

[35] "No matter what the claim is or who the claimant may be, whether or not it is valid can be determined only by … discourse or argument somehow grounded in our common experience simply as human beings." Ibid., 322–323. See also Schubert M. Ogden, "The Reformation that We Want," *Anglican Theological Review* Vol. 54 (October 1972): 260–273, 262.

[36] Although one can discern a consistent trajectory of Ogden's use of the norm of credibility, his phrasing of it has varied. In the early 1970s, he argued that the credibility of a claim is established by "the meaning and truth universally established with human existence." Ogden, "What Is Theology?," 22–40, 25. A few years later, the norm sounded slightly more empirical. See, e.g., Schubert M. Ogden, "Sources of Religious Authority in Liberal Protestantism," *Journal of the American Academy of Religion* Vol. 44 (1976): 403–416, 412, 415–416. But by the mid-1980s, he would clarify that theology's claims are "not subject to any strictly empirical mode of verification." Schubert M. Ogden, "The Experience of God: Critical Reflections on Hartshorne's Theory of Analogy," in *Existence and Actuality: Conversations with Charles Hartshorne*, ed. John B. Cobb, Jr. and Franklin I. Gamwell (Chicago: University of Chicago Press, 1984), 16–37: 18. Ogden's varied statements of the norm caused at least one commentator to conclude that Ogden's use of experience is misleading, implying some kind of empirical claim while Ogden intended "a very specific philosophical interpretation of experience … ." Owen C. Thomas, "Theology and Experience," *Harvard Theological Review* Vol. 78, No. 1–2 (1985): 179–201, 186.

[37] Ogden, *Doing Theology Today*, 16.

[38] For an explication of Ogden's account, see my *Liberalism Versus Postliberalism* (New York: Oxford University Press, 2013), 88–89.

with this understanding of ourselves and all others as equally the object of God's boundless love.[39] More can be said about Ogden's criterion of credibility, but sufficient for my purposes is that Ogden has derived his criterion only through an analysis of common human experience and reason. As such, claims proposed as candidates for the "existential truth about human existence" are transcendental and require a transcendental argument for their validation.[40]

Schubert Ogden's Response to the Falsification Challenge

Box 13.10

Having set out Ogden's theological method, the author now turns to Ogden's response to the falsification challenge.

On my reading, Ogden accepts the basic descriptivist approach to language presupposed by Flew, and he is confident that theology can meet Flew's challenge (see Box 13.10).[41] In so doing Ogden takes religious language to acquire meaning in the descriptivist manner we have been discussing.

---

[39] Ogden argues that the norm of credibility must have two prongs. Christian theological claims must be theoretically credible; and they must be practically credible in the face of the contemporary quest for justice. Theoretical credibility requires (negatively) demythologizing, or (positively) existentialist interpretation. Practical credibility has a structure analogous to theoretical credibility. It requires (negatively) "de-ideologizing," or (positively) political interpretation. Ogden, *The Point of Christology*, 93–95. See also Ogden, *Faith and Freedom*, 55.

[40] Ogden acknowledges that there is no consensus regarding just what is the existential truth about human existence, nor regarding what criteria should be used to adjudicate between rival claimants to the title of existential truth. Nor has there ever been, and today obtaining such a consensus is, Ogden realizes, "an all but impossible job … ." Ogden, *Doing Theology Today*, 17. But this by no means implies that the job should not be attempted. Indeed, in such a pluralistic situation, it is all the more important at least to attempt to validate the credibility of theological claims, for "no claims to truth are likely to be regarded as exempt from the requirement of critical validation." Ibid., 19. See also Ogden, "What is Theology?," in Ogden, *On Theology*, 1–21: 11.

[41] Though his concerns do not run in precisely the same directions as mine, I am indebted to Mark McLeod for the collection of sources and synthesis of Ogden's various comments and thoughts on religious language. See Mark S. McLeod, "Schubert Ogden on Truth, Meaningfulness, and Religious Language," *American Journal of Theology and Philosophy* Vol. 9 (Summer 1988): 195–207. On McLeod's reading, Ogden uses "empirical" in three senses: (1) a positivistic sense, (2) a sense that includes both sensuous and nonsensuous experience, and (3) a Whiteheadian sense in which every experience includes an experience of both ourselves and another, of value, and of the whole (or of Deity). Ibid., 197–198. These three senses of experience correspond to three kinds of claims: (1) factual claims, (2) contingent existential claims, and (3) necessary existential claims. Each kind of claim, McLeod argues, has its own test of meaningfulness. Factual claims acquire meaning positivistically

As we have seen, Ogden conceived the theologian's task as that of a translator, translating the Church's confessions into the language and conceptualities of her own day. Ogden's understanding of theology's task implies that there were certain ideas or notions formulated in the past, which now need to be reformulated using different language. But this reformulation need not change the meaning of the idea. And if different language can express the same idea, then it is the idea itself that gives meaning to the language, insofar as the language points to it. To use the vocabulary of descriptivism, we can restate Ogden's position as follows: the theological confession formulated by theologians in the past described a set of conditions, the satisfaction of which were necessary and sufficient for the confessions to be true. The theologian's task, as Ogden conceives it, is to use contemporary language to describe those same set of conditions. And the meaning of the confessions consists in the descriptive senses, satisfaction of which are necessary and sufficient conditions for the confessions to be true.

This understanding of language is shared by Antony Flew, and Ogden's response to Flew at least implicitly accepts it.[42] Ogden construes Flew's challenge as involving three assertions regarding theism. First, a theist cannot identify to what the concept of God applies; second, she cannot speak of God in terms of a valid analogy; third, God cannot be conceived as infinitely powerful, wise, and good and as also having a will that can be disobeyed, and even if God could be so conceived, the claim that God exists is refuted by the existence of evil in the world.[43] Here I want simply to make two points regarding Ogden's use of language and experience.[44]

Box 13.11

When Ogden uses the term "experiential," this is a clue that he is attempting a transcendental argument or analysis. See the glossary for a definition of transcendental, including transcendental arguments and transcendental analysis.

First, Ogden distinguishes between "empirical" and "experiential," which is a broader term (see Box 13.11). On Ogden's usage, "'empirical' means applying through some but *not all* possible experience, while 'experiential' means applying through *at least some* possible experience, and perhaps all (see Box 13.12)."[45] For Ogden, the claims of metaphysics apply not only through

---

(presumably through truth conditions). Contingent existential claims, he says, are falsifiable by conceivable, nonsensuous experience. McLeod does not say, however, just how this goes, or how it is distinguishable from acquiring meaning through truth conditions. So far as I can see, such statements also acquire meaning through truth conditions; but those truth conditions are of a different sort. Necessary existential claims are falsifiable only by showing that they are confused or self-contradictory. "Accordingly, whenever one shows a particular assertion to be meaningful, one also shows it to be true." Ibid., 200. This just means that such statements acquire meaning through their truth conditions as well. Consequently, though the three types of claims may have different ways of testing their truth and meaning, they all acquire meaning the same way – through their truth conditions.

[42] See Schubert M. Ogden, "God and Philosophy: A Discussion with Antony Flew," *Journal of Religion* Vol. 48 (April 1968): 161–168, 161.

[43] Ibid., 163.

[44] I do not wish to give an analysis of Ogden's arguments against Flew, though they seem to me successful. Perhaps the most telling argument advanced by Ogden is that Flew's "falsification test," which for Flew spells the defeat of the concept of God, also defeats the claim that the universe exists. Ibid., 169.

[45] Ibid., 172 (emphasis in original).

some but through all possible experience. That is to say, such claims concern states of affairs that are either necessary or impossible. And the question of the existence of God, Ogden says, is a metaphysical question.[46] This means, in Ogden's judgment, that if the concept of God is meaningful, no empirical argument could ever disprove the existence of God.[47] Recall Russell's view that we have knowledge by acquaintance with some universals (abstract concepts) and the relations between them. When Ogden says that the question of the existence of God is a metaphysical question, he is also saying that answering the question asserts knowledge by acquaintance with abstract concepts and the relations between them. So, to use Russell's terms, Ogden takes Flew to be making a category mistake in failing to take account of knowledge by acquaintance.

> **Box 13.12**
>
> Ogden's distinction between "empirical" and "experiential" is important because experiential (but not empirical) criteria allow Ogden to set out his transcendental argument for the existence of God, and thus for the meaningfulness of theological language.

Second, after taking issue with the method of Flew's falsification test, Ogden argues that the constitutive assertions of Flew's atheistic position "are without clear experiential significance."[48] More specifically, Flew's position fails "sufficiently to relate its terms and assertions to the experience which *alone* gives them any sense."[49] The implication of a statement such as this is that language gets its meaning or sense by its ability to point to or describe an experience, though that experience need not be empirical experience. The non-empirical experience Ogden has in mind here encompasses the transcendental conditions of the possibility of any and all experience. So long as the assertion provides a descriptive sense, satisfaction of which provides necessary and sufficient conditions for the assertion to be true, the assertion will be meaningful. And its meaning will be constituted by that descriptive sense. This requirement holds both for empirical claims and for claims involving abstract concepts as well. In speaking of Flew's notion of "order in the universe," Ogden argues that there must be some experience that gives the phrase meaning.[50] That experience is what gives meaning to an assertion, insofar as the assertion is capable of pointing to it by means of a description. Ogden's descriptivist position on language is not merely incidental or unintended or simply assumed. Instead, one of Ogden's principal criticisms of Flew depends on it. Flew had argued that the "order in the universe" need not be explained by reference to a divine Orderer. On Ogden's view, if Flew's understanding of order has meaning, this can only be derived by reference to some experience. This experience, in turn, is less than adequately understood if it is not understood as an experience of God. Thus:

> [T]he only experience of which I have any inside experience, and *by reference to which, therefore, my idea of order finally has whatever meaning it has*, is the order exhibited by my own

---

[46] "[T]heistic argument, properly understood, is not at all a matter of generalization from instances, for the decisive reason that it is not an empirical or scientific kind of argument but is strictly conceptual or metaphysical." Ibid. 175, n.16.

[47] Ibid., 172–173.

[48] Ibid., 174.

[49] Ibid., 175 (emphasis added).

[50] "What, as Hume might ask, is the impression from which his idea of order is derived and by reference to which it must ultimately be shown to have such meaning as it has?" Ibid., 175. This is the kind of question that fundamental or philosophical theology should ask. "Hence the *reductio ad absurdam* character of all the theistic arguments, which, if they succeed, leave theism as the only reasonable position, because the non-theistic alternatives are shown to be absurd, experience furnishing no coherent meaning for them." Ibid., 175, n.16.

occasions of experience as a self or person. Consequently, when I try to conceive what might be meant by speaking of "cosmic order," I find that I have no success at all unless I conceive of a *cosmic experience* and that in having this conception I already have everything of the theistic idea but the name. Flew's position, by contrast, seems to me to have the defect of non-theistic positions generally in that it makes use of ultimate conceptions such as order without sufficiently attending to the meaning actually given them by experience.[51]

Ogden's critique is that Flew's language lacks meaning because of its inability to give an adequate description of an experience that could imbue it with meaning (see Box 13.13). More precisely, the experience to which it points is more accurately described as in some sense an experience of God.[52] So Ogden takes language about God to get its meaning by describing aspects of our experience. The function of religious or theological language, in Ogden's view, "is to re-present symbolically, or at least at the level of full self-consciousness, this underlying sense of ourselves and others as of transcendent worth."[53] Ogden's requirement of experiential verification means that these symbolic re-presentations provide the descriptive senses satisfaction of which provide the necessary and sufficient conditions for the truth of the assertions. And the meanings of the assertions are constituted by their descriptive senses.[54]

Box 13.13

In the argument that follows, the author will reinterpret Ogden's response to Flew in the descriptivist terms of the requirements for successful reference and meaningful assertion.

---

[51] Ibid., 176 (emphasis added).

[52] Ibid., 176. This understanding of language is apparent in a contemporaneous essay in which Ogden argues that theology concerns the proper use of religious or theological language. Schubert M. Ogden, "Present Prospects for Empirical Theology," in *The Future of Empirical Theology*, ed. Bernard Meland (Chicago: University of Chicago Press, 1969), 65–88. In using such religious or theological language, Ogden assumes that a valid objection to any theological argument is that it relinquishes "the certainty that experience alone is able to provide as to the meaning and truth of any of our assertions." Ibid., 71. For Ogden, experience gives meaning to the language in which assertions are formulated, by serving as the referents to which such assertions point. In turn, it is by means of their descriptive senses that assertions point to, or refer to, their referents. Elsewhere he is explicit about this: "I hold that it is this complex experience of existence – of myself, others and the whole – which is the experience out of which all religious language arises and to which it properly refers." Schubert M. Ogden, "How Does God Function in Human Life?" in *Theology in Crisis: A Colloquium on the Credibility of "God,"* ed. Charles Hartshorne and Schubert M. Ogden (New Concord, OH: Muskingham College, 1967), 34–35, (quoted in David R. Mason, "Selfhood, Transcendence and the Experience of God," *Modern Theology* Vol. 3 (July 1987): 293 314, 305).

[53] Ogden, "Present Prospects for Empirical Theology," 86.

[54] After his debate with Antony Flew was largely over, Ogden again addressed the issue of religious language in response to a proposal by Alastair McKinnon that sought to address the charges surrounding the alleged unfalsifiability of religious claims. Schubert M. Ogden, "Falsification and Belief," *Religious Studies* Vol. 10 (1974): 21–43. McKinnon's proposal is elucidated in Alastair McKinnon, *Falsification and Belief* (The Hague: Mouton, 1970). Several years later, Ogden returned to the problem of religious language in a discussion of the Wittgensteinian philosopher of religion D.Z. Phillips. Schubert M. Ogden, "Linguistic Analysis and Theology," *Theologische Zeitschrift* Vol. 33 (September–October 1977): 318–325. I don't have space to treat these efforts here; for discussion, see my *Liberalism versus Postliberalism: The Great Divide in Twentieth Century Theology* (New York: Oxford University Press, 2013), 68–77.

Thus, Ogden's view is that the ultimate criterion for judging the truth or falsity of any claim at all is human experience. Clearly, he differs with Flew and other falsification theorists about what comprises human experience. Still, human experience remains the criterion for judging the truth or adequacy of theological claims (and all other claims as well). To say this is also to say that human experience provides the truth conditions of an assertion. These truth conditions consist of the necessary and sufficient conditions for determining the referent of the subject term of the assertion, as well as necessary and sufficient conditions that must be satisfied for the predicate of the assertion to be true of the subject. These conditions are specified by the descriptive senses provided by the language of the assertion. We can therefore say that, for Ogden, these truth conditions imbue the assertion with its meaning.[55] And they do this by means of a description.

Recall that Flew's position on reference is that theists are unable to identify a descriptive sense to the term "God" that would pick out one being or object (God) and no others, not even imaginary others. Ogden accepts this view of reference and, in his argument for the reality of God, he attempts to identify a descriptive condition that is necessary and sufficient to pick out God and no other object. In his argument for the reality of God, he argues that human beings cannot avoid asserting that their actions, and indeed their very lives, are valuable. The experience of value, then, is a constitutive and undeniable part of human experience. Humans cannot avoid having confidence in the final worth of our existence, and this confidence Ogden calls faith. In Ogden's view this unavoidable faith must have an "objective ground in reality." And since our faith is unavoidable, if it needs an objective ground, that objective ground exists necessarily. The function of the term "God," Ogden writes, is to refer to the objective ground in reality itself of this unavoidable faith.[56] God, then, is the being that meets the description *the objective ground in reality of human persons' unavoidable faith in the worth of their lives*. And since God is the only being that exists necessarily, Ogden holds that God is the only being that meets this identifying description. No imaginary God or mere idea of God could satisfy this descriptive sense. Consequently, he believes he has met Flew's challenge and has identified a descriptive sense of the term "God" that provides necessary and sufficient conditions for the term "God" to refer to God.

---

[55] It must be admitted that inferring Ogden's position on linguistic meaning, when he has not articulated one explicitly, is hazardous. It might be possible, for example, to argue that Ogden would defend the position that truth conditions are necessary but not sufficient to imbue assertive sentences with meaning (and he might take non-assertives to be another matter altogether). In a private conversation in fact he has indicated that he takes non-assertives to be a different, or at least a more complicated, matter. He might also, for example, want a communication community to play some role in the establishment of linguistic meaning. He has given some indication of a move in this direction by his approving references to Habermas and Apel. See *Doing Theology Today*, ix. My own interests, however, are less exegetical than constructive and analytical. What I hope to show is what I take to be the relationship between descriptivist theories of meaning and reference and the kind of transcendental method Ogden pursues.

[56] Ogden, "The Reality of God," 1–70: 37.

Concluding Remarks

During the formative years of Ogden's theological career, and in particular when he was developing his argument for the reality of God, a descriptivist understanding of both meaning and reference was dominant. So it would be reasonable to expect that this understanding of reference could be detected in his writings. And indeed it can be. One can see it particularly clearly in his reference to God, his most important reference (see Box 13.14). Schubert Ogden therefore provides a good example of how a theologian's understanding of the meaning and reference of language will often be consistent with their theological method and can provide insight into it. Of course, to the extent that her understanding of language is flawed, her method may need to be revised as well.[57] But that's a topic for another day.

Box 13.14
Here the author states his conclusion, noting that it is about the relationship between method and theological language. But at the end, he gives a hint that, though he believes Ogden to have responded successfully to Flew, he nonetheless believes the view of language that they both share to be flawed.

---

[57] For an argument that all truth-conditional theories of meaning are fatally flawed, see my "Why Not Davidson? Neopragmatism in Religious Studies and the Coherence of Alternative Conceptual Schemes," *Journal of Religion* Vol. 88 (Apr. 2008): 159–189.

14

Does Culture Determine Belief?

The Relationship between the Social Sciences and Theology

Martyn Percy

RESEARCH LEVEL 3

Editors' Introduction

The temptation for a person of faith is to imagine that their account of God and the world is simply the truth, while all other accounts are misguided. Martyn Percy challenges this picture of faith. Instead he argues that all accounts of faith are shaped by culture. He starts by drawing an analogy between the construction of maps and the constructions of religious beliefs. Drawing on the work of Kathryn Tanner, he suggests that the concept of "ecclesial terroir" (church beliefs are grounded in a certain soil and texture of life). He then illustrates how such a concept can make sense of certain denominational differences and how, more broadly, this links to the rich insights of H. Richard Niebuhr.

Box 14.1

This is the lens through which the author invites us to see the issues. The author provides a powerful illustration of the connection between accounts of God and accounts of the world. Everyone imagines that a map is neutral and accurate; he illustrates that maps say as much about the culture from which they come as the world that they seek to describe.

Looking at old maps of the world is, as I have discovered, a more illuminating exercise than may be at first apparent (see Box 14.1). I recall a day, not so long ago, when one of our alumni brought in his own exceptional and valuable collection of cartographical books and charts. I was mesmerized by each one. There was the first known map of Virginia. In another ancient leather-bound volume, there was a medieval map of the world that had the bottom half of Africa missing, and seemed to have no knowledge of India, and yet a vague knowledge of China and Japan. Indonesia and the Philippines were also inferred. There were maps that showed no knowledge of Australasia or New Zealand. Another old map that gave us a hesitant, feint sketch of the Eastern Seaboard of what is now the US, which looked like educated guesswork based on some travel, yet long before Columbus set sail. In other maps there was no South America or Canada. Or California. In another old map, California was thought to be an island. Many of these maps were a blend of the reasonably accurate and the purely speculative. Others sketched what was outside the lands that were currently known – mythical peoples and beasts dwelt there, surrounded by oceans of chaos. Little was to scale. Oh, and the world was flat.

The Craft of Innovative Theology: Argument and Process, First Edition. Edited by John Allan Knight and Ian S. Markham.
© 2022 John Wiley & Sons Ltd. Published 2022 by John Wiley & Sons Ltd.

What these maps showed is what we ought to remind ourselves of in the study of religious belief. Namely, that there is a relationship between the world around us and the God whom we think is behind this world; or above, beneath, or wholly beyond it. Maps illustrate – to a scale, and using signs and symbols – what people think they know; but they also reveal what people don't know. Some maps – a bit like some beliefs and theologies – are decent educated guesses. But they are of their time.

So what are maps? The answer is not as simple as one might at first suppose. They are not simply about navigation. Rather, they are also about orientation, imagination, and innovation. They are aids to reflection and potential ways of seeing:

> A world view gives rise to a world map; but the world map in turn defines its culture's view of the world. It is an act of exceptional symbiotic alchemy.[1]

Maps reveal not so much a world that might be encountered, but rather, how the cartographer chose to view and guide us through the world. Scale, symbol, demographics, topography, geography – indeed, any number of factors – play their part. The mapmaker, in many ways, is a narrator and a guide, and trying to attempt something similar to the sociologist of religion, every time they venture into the field:

> At the risk of shocking sociologists, I should be inclined to say that it is their job to render sociological or historical content more intelligible than it was in the experience of those who lived it. All sociology is a reconstruction that aspires to confer intelligibility on human existence, which, like all human existences, are confused and obscure.[2]

Mapmakers do not just reproduce the world they see. Indeed, they cannot do that. They *create* a view of that world – constructing through sifting information, drawing lines, selecting colors and tones, devising symbols, choosing scales and relations – and invite viewers to share in that construction of reality. A map always *manages* the reality it is trying to convey.[3] No map ever perfectly captures the territory it surveys. There is too much to see; too much to weigh and discern; too much to be interpreted and then refracted back. All maps are partial interpretations of reality. Theology cannot claim much more than this, in my humble opinion.[4]

So, does culture "shape" theology? The short answer to this complex question is "yes" (see Box 14.2).

Box 14.2

The question is asked and then answered. The author is taking a position. This position will be demonstrated as true through a whole host of illustrations in the paper. The author creates a cumulative case argument (one where each sub argument may not be persuasive, but taken together a strong case is made).

---

[1] Denis Cosgrove, "Mapping the World," in *Maps: Finding Our Place in the World*, ed. James R. Akerman and Robert W. Karrow (Cambridge: Cambridge University Press, 2007), 65–115.

[2] Raymond Aron, *Main Currents in Sociological Thinking* (London: Penguin, 1970), 207.

[3] Jerry Brotton, *A History of the World in Twelve Maps* (London: Penguin, 2012), 8–9.

[4] On this point, I have benefited enormously from the excellent study by Ernesto Spinelli, *The Interpreted World: An Introduction to Phenomenological Psychology* (London: Sage, 1989 1st edn., 2005 2nd edn.).

Indeed, one could go further, and say that no theology or religious belief lacks a cultural or social reference point and shape. The extent to which a theology or belief is culturally related or culturally relative (note, these are not quite the same things) is a fair question. But it should be obvious (and frankly logical) that there is no "pure" religion, belief, revelation, or doctrine. Everything we say, think, do, believe, and practice about God is mediated through social or cultural agents. These can be artifact, language, music, art, social patterns of polity, celebration or lament, humor or seriousness – all are mediated through material or social agents that are encountered, experienced, and processed.

Equally – and I say this in case you are sensing discomfort at the notion that your religion, revelation, belief, or theology cannot ever be "pure" – God does not communicate with us without using some kind of social, cultural, or natural agent.

> **Box 14.3**
>
> As the author continues to frame the territory of the paper, he, with refreshing clarity, asserts that pure revelation is impossible because God just does not do that. In a lovely use of the Moses call, the author explained that even the burning bush required fire and shrubbery. Some kind of "social, cultural, or natural agent" is always needed.

A burning bush requires fire, and some shrubbery (see Box 14.3). Not every burning bush speaks about God. Actually, very few do. So religion and belief, and our theology, are, like maps: fundamentally, *interpretive* exercises.[5] Theologians and believers may well want to argue about the division between what is description and ascription in relation to God. They may want to debate what is revelation from God, and what is mere (human) projection. The Bible will offer all of these, incidentally – as the Psalms amply testify.

> **Box 14.4**
>
> This is the heart of the author's argument. He wants to hold together an awareness that "revelation is socially or materially mediated" (and therefore the social sciences are important) with an awareness of the importance of the theology. He takes the view that the social sciences and theology are complementary.

All revelation is socially or materially mediated (see Box 14.4). Correspondingly, and to pick two social sciences here, sociology (which concerns itself with people and society) and anthropology (which is concerned with custom, artifact, ritual, etc.) rightly focus on the social and material things, without which there could be no religion, belief, or theology. In saying this, I do not claim – and never would – that social sciences are superior to theologies. Like maps, we are dealing with different ways of interpreting the world around us. Every account in and of faith is an interpretative one. So theological constructions of reality can live alongside social, cosmological, psychological, or anthropological constructions of reality. Social sciences need not compete; they can complement. Our doctrines and beliefs flow from our experiences, or those of our

---

[5] The London Underground Map created in 1931 by Harry Beck is a particularly good example. Beck realized that that as long as the stations were presented in their right sequence with their interchanges marked, scale could be distorted. His underground map adopts the orderly precision of an electrical wiring system that bears little disorderly geography of the London that exists above ground.

ancestors or previous generations. These beliefs – including our common, lived, distilled experience over age and time – are transformative, and stable. But they are also living, and they change too. Time erodes some things, and adds to others. Beliefs come and go. So what is "theological material" and what is peripheral is not always obvious.

> **Box 14.5**
>
> Every author builds on a literature. At this point, Percy introduces one of his important conversation partners – Kathryn Tanner. Later in the article, he considers at length the classic *Christ and Culture* by H. Richard Niebuhr. Good research writing always shows a familiarity with the key texts in the field.

Kathryn Tanner (see Box 14.5) notes that religious beliefs are "a form of culture, inextricably implicated in the material practices of daily social living on the part of those who hold them … [I]n the concrete circumstances in which beliefs are lived … actions, attitudes, and interests are likely to be as much infiltrated and informed by the beliefs one holds as beliefs are to be influenced by actions, attitudes and interests."[6] In other words, doctrines practice us; practices are not just things that Christians do in the light of doctrine: "practices are what we become as we are set in motion in the space of doctrine."[7] Theology is performative, and it "gains power and meaning insofar as it is embodied in the total gestalt of community life and action."[8] But there is an irony here for the theologian, and for the Church. For in gaining an understanding of how the worlds of belief and practice begin to cohere, one immediately sees that they in fact do not necessarily do so easily. For every example of clarity and directness, there is one of obliquity and indirectness.

> **Box 14.6**
>
> The author uses quotes sparingly. This is a case where the author has already summarized Tanner's general argument and then uses the Tanner quote as a summary of her position, which he seeks to endorse for his own argument. The quote is carefully selected, precise, and clear.

As Tanner says (see Box 14.6):

> Christian practices do not in fact require (1) much explicit understanding of beliefs that inform and explain their performance, (2) agreement upon such matters among the participants, (3) strict delimitation of codes for action, (4) systematic consistency among beliefs or actions, or (5) attention to their significance that isolates them from a whole host of non-Christian commitments. More often than not, Christian practices are instead quite open-ended in the sense of being undefined in their exact ideational dimensions and in the sense of being always in the process of re-formation in response to new circumstances.[9]

---

[6] Kathryn Tanner, *Theories of Culture* (Minneapolis, MN: Fortress Press, 1992), 9.

[7] Miroslav Volf and Dorothy C. Bass eds. *Practicing Theology* (Grand Rapids, MI: Eerdmans, 2002), 75.

[8] George Lindbeck, *The Nature of Doctrine* (Philadelphia: Westminster Press, 1984), 36.

[9] Kathryn Tanner, "Theological Reflection and Christian Practices," in *Practicing Theology*, ed. Miroslav Volf and Dorothy Bass (Grand Rapids MI: Eerdmans, 2002), 229.

So the theologian stands within a complex nexus of issues, contexts, concerns, narrative streams and socio-cultural situations. As Rowan Williams remarks, "the theologian is always beginning in the middle of things ... there is a practice of common life and language already there."[10] Theologians do not and cannot start with a blank page, or one pure moment of revelation. All theologians have to work with, and work on, is mediated. Indeed, this is one central tenet of Christianity: God is among us, taking our flesh. Jesus is Jewish, Galilean, and Palestinian. He was born and raised at a specific time and ministers in specific locations. Jesus is a dweller in occupied territories. He is an educated Rabbi.

True, Jesus is indeed the "field and terms of interpretive enterprise"[11] and engages in prescient deconstructions of the religious and social practices around him at the time. But that was then and this is now. Moreover, Jesus was (and is) a person too, who in his incarnation ate, spoke (more than one language), engaged with others, took action, walked, wandered, and wondered – so he can *also* be subject to *some* interpretative deconstruction. This is no bad thing. After all, God likes to be understood. That's why the burning bush has to be *interpreted* to Moses.[12]

Grounding Doctrine and Belief

Box 14.7

The subheading "Grounding Doctrine and Belief" is introduced. The author invites the reader to make the transition. This is the heart of the author's argument. With illustration after illustration, the case will be made that doctrine and belief are grounded in historical and sociological realities.

(See Box 14.7). Because all doctrine and belief are rooted and grounded in confessional communities, congregations, and denominations, it is likely that the places and peoples from which beliefs and practices emerge might have some influence in shaping theology for their time and for future generations. Those who might also be slightly niggled by this opening sentence in this section, might be harboring high "Catholic" ideas of truth (i.e. it's the same wherever you are, and does not change), or could be ultra-orthodox or even fundamentalistic (i.e. the Bible or Church never changes, and has always meant the same – the reader must obey and adapt, and not presume to reinterpret for their time). While this is an interesting position for people of faith to

---

[10] Rowan Williams, *On Christian Theology* (Oxford: Blackwell, 1999), xii.

[11] Rowan Williams, *Dwelling of the Light* (Grand Rapids MI: Eerdmans, 2003), 6–7.

[12] See Exodus chapter 3. The encounter takes place on Mount Horeb. See also Ernesto Spinelli, *The Interpreted World: An Introduction to Phenomenological Psychology* (London: Sage, 1989/2005). Spinelli highlights the differences between straightforward and reflective experience, and objective or external reality and subjective consciousness. Clearly, any experience processed or described as "religious" or "spiritual" is interpreted as such, and belongs more to subjective consciousness than to objective, external reality. This is not to say that God is only known in personal-centered ways, or that all religion is relative, and spirituality subjective. It is, rather, to affirm that all we say about God is contextual. All language has to be adequate for the times we inhabit, and it is subject to some degree of relative change. The Word may well be eternal; but all other words are temporal.

adopt, it is almost deliberately naïve and crude. Take language as an example. English can be understood in many parts of the world. Yet there are enormous variations on accents, phrases, and vocabulary – even in England. Moreover, English words don't mean the same, necessarily, from one country to the next. Culture takes everything and adapts it. But don't be too concerned by this, because religion does the same. And religion and culture are quite a mix, with some seriously effervescent synergies.

Box 14.8

With the invention of the concept of "ecclesial terroir," the author is advancing the discussion. Drawing on a notion used primarily in wine production, he suggests that you can make sense of denominational differences by looking at the way in which the denominations take root in cultural life.

One way to understand this better is to take a non-English word, and here I choose the term "terroir (see Box 14.8)." The Gallic terroir is an evocative word that refers to the mélange of environmental, situational, and human factors, from soil, to vine, to barrel, that define each wine; and accounts for how two glasses of Burgundy, for example, originating from the same village could taste so different to a discerning and well-trained palate. Terroir applies to coffee too. Discovering and accounting for the terroir is analogous to localizing an ecclesial identity; and requires the same skill both in being able to recognize and draw out these seemingly incidental factors, and ascertaining their consequences, through patient reflection. Some might object here, and while acknowledging that churches can individuate and proliferate, doctrine and belief do not. This is partly true, but still naïve. What are churches, after all, other than a social articulation of what the theology and beliefs of groups and peoples imagine God to be, and who and how that God is to be worshiped and followed.

So, when considering what I call the "ecclesial terroir" of church life, one must at once hold in the same frame the cultural elements that have interacted with beliefs and theology. Some of the factors include history, ethos, practice, both physical and organizational architecture, in addition to the local subtleties and regional accents that make each center of worship unique and distinctive. The ability to read these elements requires attention and commitment, in order to cultivate depth and sensitivity.[13]

This is where the social scientific study of religion can make a modest contribution. On the ground, as it were, it attempts categorization "establishing normative epoches" for meaning.[14] The social sciences concern themselves with describing phenomena in common-sensical ways, creating categories of meaning and knowledge in order to give a "social" account of what it sees. Thus, "religion" tends to be treated like a "thing" – an "object" of scientific analysis – and deconstructed accordingly.

Correspondingly, religion can find itself feeling like a patient at a hospital being subjected to a multidisciplinary medical analysis. The patient might have thought they were just an average person

---

[13] See Martyn Percy, *Shaping the Church: The Promise of Implicit Theology* (London: Routledge, 2010), 13, 102–238.

[14] Gavin D'Costa, "The End of 'Theology' and 'Religious Studies'?," *Theology* Vol. 99, No. 791 (September 1996): 338–351.

with not much wrong with them. But diagnosis and prognosis from our imaginary multidisciplinary medical panel will talk about skin, bones, nerves, heart, lungs, and other organs. The panel may go on to discuss mental health, or weight, diet, exercise, and obesity. The panel might be able to tell you how long you are likely to live for, and even what risks you carry now. Inside and outside, the patient is still the same person. But they are before a group that has, almost literally, carved up the patient, dividing organs from social life, and nerves from psychological fears. Similarly, social scientific surveys of religion break religion into useful constituent parts (e.g. sacred-profane, etc.), or refer to faith in rather functional terms (e.g. "social legitimization," "projection," etc.). Social sciences, however, often fail to see *themselves* as a construction of reality, social or otherwise.

As Catherine Bell points out: "That we construct 'religion' and 'science' is not the main problem: that we forget we have constructed them in our own image – that is a problem."[15] In saying this, Bell is suggesting that, like a good map, a "pure" or "comprehensive" description of phenomena is not possible. Both the social sciences and theology are engaged in an interpretative task, and describe what they see according to the prescribed rules of their grammar of assent. In the case of the sociology of religion, for example, this has often tended to assume a humanist-orientated perspective, which has sometimes imagined itself to be a "neutral" perspective. Thus, sociologists and anthropologists describe what they see, while theologians and religious people are said to "ascribe" meaning to the same phenomena. On the other hand, those who have had religious experiences feel that what they experience is "real," and the sociological or anthropological account is therefore deemed to be at best complementary, and at worst reductive to the point of being unrepresentative. Invariably, both approaches forget that "religion" is something of a complex word with no agreed or specific definition.

What though, can theology gain from sociology? Obviously and principally, it is gaining a partner in dialogue that can enrich its self-understanding, and help avoid the narcissism of "interior enquiries" that are often uncritical and self-serving. Certainly, it cannot afford to assume that sociology is concerned with "relationality," while theology is only to do with God. Ninian Smart's claim that "traditional theology has focused, naturally enough, on God as its subject-matter"[16] misses the point that all theology is to do with that which *relates* to God – there are no "pure" studies of God.

Ecclesial Culture

> **Box 14.9**
>
> The section on ecclesiology presses us to "read" churches as social reifications of theological texts. The author suggests that all theology is practiced, and so social science can help us understand these belief-based-behaviors.

As someone who essentially specializes in ecclesiology – the study of the shape, practices, and form of churches in the world, and how their beliefs are reified in "thought, word and deed" (intentionally), and yet also through "ignorance, weakness, and their own deliberate fault" – I am

---

[15] Catherine Bell, "Modernism and Postmodernism in the Study of Religion," *Religious Studies Review* Vol. 22, No. 3 (1996): 179–190.

[16] Ninian Smart, *The Science of Religion and the Sociology of Knowledge* (Princeton: Princeton University Press, 1973), 10.

acutely conscious of the mysterious symbiotic alchemy that takes place between Christianity and culture (see Box 14.9). Even a simple concept such as sin (!) has a checkered ecclesial-cultural history. We cannot understand the doctrine apart from its cultural performance down the ages. Moreover, many of the actions we now regard as sinful were not previously thought to be so, and some behaviors we once thought of as sinful are now quite normal, and may indeed go unremarked in churches. Example of this include divorce, remarriage, human sexuality, borrowing or lending money, owning a slave, or how we spend our time on the Sabbath – assuming you, the reader, know what a Sabbath day is.[17]

In 2005, Graham Ward explored the role of habitus in the work of the theologian Karl Barth – a rapport that has been critically underexplored.[18] Put simply, a theology appearing from the socio-cultural and political conditions that birthed the work of Barth (Switzerland) might not be as easy to cultivate or replicate in other contexts. For example, South American liberation theologians such as Leonardo Boff or Jon Sobrino developed their distinctive theological approach from the "terroir" (or conditions) of political oppression that they experienced. Terroir may bring some more subtle flavoring to denominational proclivity. For example, aspects of Scottish Free Presbyterianism invite some examination of how environment, discourse and practice blend together. The ascetic and somber character of the ecclesial polity seems indivisible from the austere and discipline-demanding climate of northern Europe. Equally, Caribbean theologian Kortright Davis notes:

> Western theologians are attempting to educate themselves about the new theological surges emanating from the Third World. They have finally realized that there is no universal theology; that theological norms arise out of the context in which one is called to live out one's faith; that theology is therefore not culture free; and that the foundations on which theological structures are built are actually not transferable from one context to another. Thus although the Gospel remains the same from place to place, the means by which that Gospel is understood and articulated will differ considerably through circumstances no less valid and no less authentic.[19]

So while some may be tempted to distance theology from the influence of cultural conditions, keeping the "purity" of its source, we can see that by investing in the idea of context and locality, we can gain crucial insights into our understanding of ecclesial identities and the role of culture in theological production. A significant historical example of this is the movement of the Anglican position on families in the early twentieth century. The Church began to phase out their support of the large family in favor of smaller households, and by extension supporting the use of contraception in response to the changing needs of their communities and congregants.[20] Recognizing the potential economic benefits and greater social control to be gained by individuals, particularly for women, with the aid of family planning, the Church embraced and endorsed it for the greater good of the communities they served.

---

[17] See Martyn Percy, "Falling Far Short: Taking Sin Seriously" in *Reinhold Niebuhr and Contemporary Politics*, ed. Richard Harries and Stephen Platten (Oxford; Oxford University Press, 2010), 116–128.

[18] Graham Ward, *Christ and Culture: Challenges in Contemporary Theology* (Malden, MA: Blackwell Publishing, 2005).

[19] K. Davis, *Emancipation Still Comin': Explorations in Caribbean Emancipatory Theology* (MaryknollNew York: Orbis Books, 1990), 70.

[20] Simon Szreter, *Fertility, Class and Gender in Britain, 1860–1940: Cambridge Studies in Population, Economy, and Society in Past Time no. 27* (Cambridge, UK: Cambridge University Press, 1996).

In addition to historicizing their approach, sociologists of religion look to lay the foundations of their research on evidence, whether experimental or experiential.[21] This approach underpins inference from large-scale narrative with solid, evidence-based conclusions. In this spirit, sociologists examining congregants in the US have made the connection between class and denominational identity. An anecdote related by Max Weber supplies an illustration of the invisible link between class and denomination.[22] A German dentist who had moved to the US was taken aback when a patient, before disclosing any other perhaps more pertinent information such as medical history, informed him of their denomination, to convey what they thought he needed to understand of their own situation: a concept perhaps alien to a European. The patient wanted to prove their own social standing, perhaps their wealth, to their health care provider – and in their eyes, this was the quickest route to this understanding.

It seems despite the diversity of offerings for churchgoers, and the increased ability of individuals to cast their net as widely as possible in terms of transportation, class-denominational symbolism, unaffected by locale, persists. Across North American, Episcopalians, Presbyterians, and Methodists are thought of as the "upper" denominations of class, and Baptists and Evangelicals are considered "lower." This helps to explain the rather snide and classist remark in the opening of Norman Maclean's 1976 novella, *A River Runs Through It*: "my father (a Presbyterian minister) always told me that a Methodist was a Baptist that had been taught to read."[23]

Denominational identity is therefore entwined with ideas of wealth, and by extension, social standing. Additionally, the "spectrum" of denomination is informed by ethnicity: many Pentecostal and "Gospel" churches are composed primarily of African American worshippers; while denominations on the Protestant end of the scale see majority White congregations. H. Richard Niebuhr's research examines how these factors shape congregations, as a "practical contribution to the ethical problem of denominationalism."[24] He perceived the formation of congregations as fundamentally dialectical: faith and culture, disinherited and established, nationalist and sectionalist, immigrant and of "the color line." In interrogating these oppositions, Niebuhr was looking to uncover deeper unities between congregations that draw from such distinct political and social identities. Niebuhr wishes to prove that American Christianity crystallized around not only ecclesial and doctrinal proclivities, but the wider social-economic-political forces working within communities. Methodists and Baptists, for example, by merging their identity with a "frontier ethos" in the south and west of the US, gained greater popularity among potential worshippers than more reserved and established denominations (e.g. Episcopalians and Presbyterians).

To account for the persistence of factors of class and race in shaping North American religious affinity, we can cast an eye over the demographics of the colonies. The East Anglian Puritans settling in what became Massachusetts, Quakers of the north Midlands in Pennsylvania and as Fischer describes, the Royalists of the Southern Counties, who fled to Virginia during the Civil War,[25] all brought to their fledgling communities their own ideas of how to live, how to be

---

[21] Meredith B. McGuire, *Religion, the Social Context* (London: Wadsworth, 2002).

[22] Max Weber, *The Protestant Ethic and the Spirit of Capitalism* (Routledge: London/New York, 1930).

[23] Norman Maclean, *A River Runs Through It, and Other Stories* (Chicago: University of Chicago Press, 1976).

[24] H. Richard Niebuhr, *The Social Sources of Denominationalism* (New York: Henry Holt and Co.,1929).

[25] David Hackett Fischer, *Albion's Seed: Four British Folkways in America* (New York/Oxford: Oxford University Press, 1992).

a citizen, and how to worship. The strong markers of identity that drove those people to seek out unknown territory in which to freely forge their own unchallenged ways of worship and governance have left their trace in subsequent generations, in both implicit and explicit forms of leadership in both congregations and wider communities.

We can furthermore find more specific illustrations of this in the history of festivity in the "New World." The development of new communities afforded the freedom to keep or dispatch with traditions. Cromwell's staunchly Puritan England looked to end the celebration of Christmas with the threat of fines; which was replicated in the New World by loyal followers. Puritan celebrations, in keeping with their outlook, were frugal and prudent. Pennsylvanian Quakers went further to distance themselves from frivolity and hedonism, by sweeping clean the calendar of any markers of festivity. Months became numbered instead of named; the Sabbath or Sunday became the "first day," as "all days are alike holy in the sight of God."[26] The Quakers also carried the spirit of their deeply held commitment to social justice in their food preferences; refusing sugar because of its dependence on the slave trade; and salt for the belief that the salt tax paid for military activity.

In contrast, the decadent, transposed Cavaliers of Virginia were keenly and extravagantly observant of the full Christian calendar: Christmas, Whitsun, Shrovetide, Hocktide, and Twelfth Night were richly celebrated with feasts and festivity. Fischer's account paints the picture of a jubilant society that embraced "parties, dances, visits, gifts and celebrations,"[27] and delicacies such as fried chicken and fricassee.

If such large-scale organizers of duration and action such as food and the scheduling of seasons were subject to such cultural distinctions, it is not hard to imagine granular units of social order such as economy, rank and power, and leading worship being subject to cultural and class distinctions as well. Signifiers of class distinction, such as the position of a seat and the company kept in church, clothing, and conventions in behavior and manners upheld were as rife in the "New World" in the sixteenth century as in Medieval England; and what's more, were encountered in each denomination – certainly in the aforementioned settlements. Underlying this visible stratification of status through social cues, symbolism, and mannerisms were the invisible, implicit theological assumptions that this mirrored a Divine Order – thereby regulating society according to both a worldly and otherworldly logic.

Theology and Culture

Box 14.10
The flow of the chapter is now reaching its climax. From maps, to denominations, and now to the deeper connections between faith and culture. H. Richard Niebuhr's text is a classic. The author wants to explore the ways in which faith and culture can and do intersect. He notes the irony that Niebuhr's own discussion reflects the culture of the 1950s and liberal Protestantism.

Niebuhr's classic 1951 study, *Christ and Culture*, offers a crucial late-modern analysis of how faith and culture were and are two complex realities (see Box 14.10). The work is a call to recognize that "an infinite dialogue must develop in the Christian conscience and the Christian

---

[26] Ibid., 561.
[27] Ibid., 370.

community."[28] Niebuhr's thesis shared with Ernst Troeltsch a foundational acceptance that Christianity and Western culture are indivisible from each other; reflecting his further position that "culture" is too great to be neatly contained in one definition. Niebuhr assessed the theological responses to culture, and perceived three mainstream ideologies: that culture is entirely neutral to Christ; that culture is hostile to Christ; or that culture was solidly based on a natural, rational knowledge of God or God's law (i.e. enculturated).

In creating a definition of culture, to then find other ways for Christians to engage with it, Niebuhr turned to the work of Bronislaw Malinowski to prove it as a human-made, "artificial, secondary environment." Culture is therefore secondary to what is then called the "natural": "language, habits, ideas, beliefs, customs, social organization, inherited artifacts, technical processes and values."[29] The defining characteristics of culture which Niebuhr offered, drawing on Malinowski, were that it is social; it is a human achievement; it is value-based (and furthermore, driven by their realization and conservation); and it exists in plurality.

Niebuhr's study went on to find theological responses to how a Christian might engage with culture. Firstly, he saw one dominant response in cultivating distance between Christ and culture, after Tertullian, typified by "missionaries who require their converts to abandon wholly the customs and institutions of so-called 'heathen' societies." The second was the opposite view: that "there is a fundamental agreement between Christ and culture." This view was supported by liberal Protestantism, including figures such as Schleiermacher. These are opposing views for the dialectical argument on religious resilience and sustainability. The former sees resilience in terms of resistance to culture. The latter is for the embracing of culture.

Niebuhr identified a third response, in the lineage figures such as Hooker and Aquinas who operate by laws and principle, but with the understanding that neither can supplant revelation. In this view, culture can lead worshippers to Christ, but Christ remains apart from or above culture.[30] A fourth response identified by Niebuhr, with Luther as "the greatest representative of this type,"[31] was a variant on the first type. Here, secular society is subordinate to Christ's claims, but staying obedient to the requirements of civil authorities in this society is nonetheless willed by the Divine. A fifth and final response Niebuhr held was exemplified by the likes of Calvin and Augustine, and is conversionist. Here, the worshipper is simultaneously within and without culture, and yet Christ is at the center of culture. These latter three types, Niebuhr pointed out, were close in spirit – as they perceived some *mediation* between Christ and culture that rendered each distinct in some way, but in his analysis, he supported the idea of fluidity between the five types of response, as "strange family resemblances may be found along the whole scale."[32] Niebuhr's own world view resonated most strongly with the second type, with sympathy for the third and fourth. Niebuhr's study proved pioneering in trying to seriously engage and grapple with culture. His finale signals a hope for the reception of his analysis:

> This faith has been introduced into our history, into our culture, our church, our human community, through this person [i.e. Christ] … In that faith we look to make decisions in our existential present, knowing that the measure of faith is so meagre that we are always

---

[28] H. Richard Niebuhr, *Christ and Culture* (New York: Harper, 1951).

[29] Cf. Bronisław Malinowski, "Culture" in *The Encyclopedia of Social Sciences IV* (London: Macmillan, 1931), 541–549; and Jacques Maritain, *Religion and Culture: Essays in Order, No. 1* (London: Sheed & Ward, 1931).

[30] Niebuhr, *Christ and Culture*, 42 and chapter 4.

[31] Ibid., 43 and chapter 5.

[32] Ibid., 40, 43, and chapter 6.

combining denials with our affirmations of it. Yet in faith in the faithfulness of God we count on being corrected, forgiven, complemented, by the company of the faithful and by many others to whom He is faithful though they reject Him ... To make our decisions in faith is to make them in view of the fact that no single man or group or historical time is the church; but that there is a church of faith in which we do our partial, relative work and on which we count. It is to make them in view of the fact that Christ is risen from the dead and is not only the head of the church but the redeemer of the world. It is to make them in view of the fact that the world of culture - man's achievement – exists in the world of grace – God's kingdom[33]

Niebuhr's sifting and defining of "types" of responses to culture from a theological point of view is incredibly useful and provides us with vital frames of reference in this field. But as previously mentioned, there is far more fluidity between these approaches in practice.

Niebuhr's work suffers from the same fate as that of all theologians, including me: our relevance to the field is subject to fashion and fluctuation. The lineage Niebuhr draws from, namely the liberal Protestantism of Ernst Troeltsch, to Paul Tillich's *Theology of Culture*,[34] positions his theology as pliable and progressive. Or put another way, adaptive. Yet we see the embers of that approach in a variety of approaches to theology and culture in the twenty-first century. Rowan Williams accounts for the "cultural bereavement" of a changing environment and society for loosing grip on realities such as charity, childhood, and remorse.[35] Zigmunt Bauman too assesses the loss of what were previously untouchable realities of culture, perceiving a "widespread aversion to grand social designs, the loss of interest in absolute truths, privatisation of redemptive urges, reconciliation with the relative ... value of all life techniques, acceptance of [the] irredeemable plurality of the world."[36] Put another way, I would say that all study of religion is a study of culture. And all studies of culture will encounter significant difficulties if excluding religion. Correspondingly, social sciences and religion need to work together, in a manner that is illuminating and complementary. That has been the goal of my theological enterprise.

Conclusion

Box 14.11
The author concludes, ironically, by appealing to religious tradition to validate his interpretive theological-social-science "hybrid" model of analysis. The reader should pause at this point and ask: Was this a sufficiently convincing lens through which to explore the relationship between theology, culture, religion, and the social sciences?

As we began with maps, so we conclude (see Box 14.11). Cartography has many uses, and maps serve as a useful guide to what to expect on arrival, should you choose to journey there. There

---

[33] Ibid., 255–256.
[34] Paul Tillich, *Theology of Culture* (Oxford: Oxford University Press, 1959).
[35] Rowan Williams, *Lost Icons: Reflections on Cultural Bereavement* (Harrisburg, PA: Morehouse Publishing, 2003).
[36] Zygmunt Bauman, "Modernity and Ambivalence," in *Global Culture: Nationalism, Globalization and Modernity: Theory, Culture & Society*, ed. Mike Featherstone (London: Sage, 1990), 97. Cf. Jean-Francoise Lyotard, *The Postmodern Condition: A Report on Knowledge* (Manchester: Manchester University Press, 1984), xxiii. "I define postmodern as incredulity toward metanarrative ...".

are maps that mark landscapes and terrain; empires and territories; borders and boundaries. But there are other kinds of maps too, and these may be just as significant for what we might term "religious geography" and local cultural productions of theology. Some maps chart oppression, inequality, racial division and more besides. Might these kinds of maps also help us, as Niebuhr suggested,[37] to chart the social sources of denominationalism, and therefore of distinctive theological proclivity? I think so.

In the UK, obesity is now one of our biggest threats to health, and one of our biggest killers. Yet it is not a disease of the rich but of the poor. Maps of the UK spell out the demographics of obesity plainly. The concentrations of obesity lie in our poorest and most disadvantaged communities. A map of Scotland, taken from September 2014,[38] showed that the concentrations of population voting "yes" to Scottish independence correlated almost precisely with maps that charted concentrations of obesity, unemployment, and underlying social concerns connected to indices of poverty.[39] These maps then charted the health-related consequences – cancers, heart conditions, and diabetes – following in their wake.

The areas in Scotland that voted "no" to independence were, unsurprisingly, the wealthiest and healthiest. The map has too many similarities to the patterns of voting "yes" for "Brexit."[40] That map, in turn, looked very similar to the ones where we observe the "concentrations" of COVID-19. The poorer and more densely populated parts of London feature heavily, which have less communal space and shoddier housing. These areas have higher concentrations of ethnic minorities, and therefore of minority faiths and denominations formed from recent diaspora and waves of immigration. There is little escape for deprived urban priority areas.[41]

"Terroir," then, is a fertile motif for contemplating the cultural production of theology – or at least the partial role of prevalent socio-economic and political conditions played in giving theologies and denominations their distinctive local, regional, or national "flavoring." In closing, I briefly draw on a classic social-anthropological text. In *The Interpretation of Culture* by Clifford Geertz, he observed that:

> The concept of culture I espouse ... is essentially a semiotic one. Believing, with Max Weber, that man is an annual suspended in webs of significance he has himself spun, I take culture to be those webs.[42]

One significant legacy of Geertz's work was his concerted movement toward symbolism and interpretation in the field of cultural studies – itself rooted in the culture of that time.[43] The extended "web" metaphor he draws on here is notable, pointing to how religion and society weave together in thick reticulate patterns and points of intersection, and that the production of both contemporary religion and culture remain unavoidably and absolutely intermingled and interdependent.

---

[37] H. Richard Niebuhr, *The Social Sources of Denominationalism* (New York: Henry Holt and Co., 1929).

[38] Christine Jeavens, "In Maps: How Close Was the Scottish Referendum Vote?" BBC News, September 19, 2014, http://www.bbc.co.uk/news/uk-scotland-scotland-politics-29255449.

[39] "Map Highlights 'Obesity Hotspots,'" BBC News, August 27, 2008, http://news.bbc.co.uk/1/hi/health/7584191.stm.

[40] https://www.bbc.co.uk/news/uk-politics-36616028.

[41] https://www.covidlive.co.uk.

[42] Clifford Geertz, *The Interpretation of Culture* (New York, NY: Basic Books, 1973).

[43] See, for example, George Steiner, *Grammars of Creation* (London: Faber and Faber, 2001).

A personal anecdote illuminates this point. Some years ago, distant relatives of mine took a couple of children from an even more distant part of the family for a day trip to Bath Abbey. The adults were worshippers there, and the children they took on the tour of the Abbey belonged to an unusual ultra-conservative Roman Catholic sect. At the end of the tour, the adults asked the children if they had enjoyed the tour. They had. But, remarked the older child, it was odd that so many different people had been involved in the construction of Bath Abbey over the ages. Because, as he opined, the church he and his parents attended was "built by Jesus."

Religious faith is, of course, "built" by the cultures in which it emerges and practiced, as much as it might be by founders and other people. In turn, religion shapes cultures. Roman Catholicism retains some "ecclesial DNA" that comes from ancient Roman imperialism. Anglicanism, in its English form, draws on the broad polity of the Elizabethan Settlement that is tolerant and careful not to ask too many questions about private practices. Anabaptists were dissenters. But over time non-conformists became quite conformist. Pentecostals can be mellow. Culture and belief change.

If we examine the "fabric" of any culture or civilization, religion appears in the strands, woven in. Another aspect of this "weave" of culture is that it is unending and requires constant renewal and reproduction to ensure new strands, and new intersections, and therefore fresh meanings and interpretative possibilities. We can see through this metaphor that the sacred and secular cultures are impossible to divide. Christians see themselves to be in the world but not of it. This paradox was expressed by the unknown author of the late second century *Epistle to Diognetus* in this way:

> Christians are not distinguished from the rest of mankind by either country, speech or customs; the fact is that they nowhere settle in cities of their own; they use no peculiar language; they cultivate no eccentric mode of life ... Yet while they dwell in both Greek and non-Greek cities, as each one's lot was cast, and conform to the customs of the country in dress, food, and mode of life in general, the whole tenor of their way of living stamps it as worthy of admiration and extraordinary. They reside in their respective countries, but only as aliens. They take part in everything as citizens and put up with everything as foreigners. Every foreign land is their home, and every home a foreign land ... In a word: what the soul is in the body, that Christians are in the world. The soul is spread through all the members of the body, and the Christians throughout all the cities of the world. The soul dwells in the body, but is not part and parcel of the body; so Christians dwell in the world, but are not part and parcel of the world[44]

Christianity, in fact, gives shape to "secular" culture: even in its freedom to marginalize and reject religion. This position is shaped from normative incarnational doctrines. Namely, the Word made flesh; yet as part of God's economy of grace, followers are offered the total freedom to respond to or reject this revelation. To paraphrase a familiar cliché, "creation is dictated by God, but not signed." As William Hart notes, culture is "a negotiated enterprise – a product of consent, accommodation, resistance and transformation."[45] Indeed, this is a description that could also serve for religion itself. Religion is not something archaic or residual that was somehow left in culture – but the very life that culture has grown from.[46]

---

[44] Anonymous, "The Epistle to Diognetus," in *The Ancient Christian Writers No. 6*, ed. James A. Kleist (New York, Newman Press, 1948), 138–140. Op Cit. Michael Warren, *Communications and Cultural Analysis: A Religious View* (Westport, CT: Bergin & Garvey, 1992).

[45] William Hart, *Edward Said and the Religious Effects of Culture: Cambridge Studies in Religion and Critical Thought* 8 (Cambridge: Cambridge University Press, 2000).

[46] See, for example, Marcel Danesi and Paul Perron, *Analysing Cultures: An Introduction and Handbook* (Bloomington, IN: Indiana University Press, 1999) where religion is treated as a "separate" area of culture from other fields such as politics or nationalism.

15

Theological Reference and Theological Creativity in Judaism
Cass Fisher

RESEARCH LEVEL 4

Editors' Introduction

In this chapter, Cass Fisher draws on recent developments in philosophy of language in order to create a space for Jewish theology in the discourse over the nature of Jewish studies. To do creative Jewish theology, he argues, requires successful reference to God (theological reference). But this has been stymied by the dominant view of rabbinic literature as based on practices (in the case of halakhah) or edifying, sermonic literature (aggadah) that is not aimed at truth. To support this view, a number of scholars draw on Wittgenstein's approach to religious language as language that religious people use to provide guidance to their lives, rather than to make assertions about God or God's relation to the world. To counter this dominant view, Fisher will need to argue that at least some religious language does make statements about God, and in order to do this, he will need to show that theological reference is possible. Fisher points to recent developments in the theory of reference that provide substantial resources for showing that theological reference is indeed possible, and with it, the possibility of discourse about God. The effort is crucial for Jewish theology, he argues, because the alternative is to accept the impossibility of speaking about God. But "[i]f we cannot speak truthfully about God," he asks, "why bother at all?"

Introduction: Theological Creativity and the Peculiar Contours of Jewish Theology

Creative thinking imagines new possibilities that stretch current patterns of thought in terms of both form and content. As much as creative thinking is an imaginative extension of thought, it is, by necessity, also an informed mode of thinking. This fact is particularly evident with respect to theology. Creative theological reflection requires familiarity with the resources available to contemporary theology and understanding the current parameters and restrictions on theological discourse. How else can one set forth innovative theological ideas without having the requisite tools at one's disposal and the knowledge of what constitutes a forward advance in theological reflection? While these requirements hold for creative theological thinking across traditions, the impediments to theological innovation are particularly severe in Judaism such that Jewish theology becomes a test case for the very possibility of creative theology.

The Craft of Innovative Theology: Argument and Process, First Edition. Edited by John Allan Knight and Ian S. Markham.
© 2022 John Wiley & Sons Ltd. Published 2022 by John Wiley & Sons Ltd.

Discussions of Jewish theology must begin by acknowledging that theology assumes distinct forms in Judaism, a religion that eschews dogmatic and systematic formulation of belief. Accordingly, Judaism requires a broad definition of theology such as *reasoned discourse about God and the divine–human relationship*. For theology to be about God, it must be possible to refer to God. Challenging this fundamental requirement of theology, historians, philosophers, and theologians have argued that Jewish tradition does not refer to God in a manner that produces truth claims about the divine. To be sure, all theistic traditions have faced challenges from modern and postmodern philosophy and their critiques of metaphysics and onto-theology. Jewish studies, however, has drawn its principal philosophical resources from German idealism and later forms of continental philosophy, which are particularly inimical toward metaphysics and theology. Consequently, critiques of theology have exerted a pronounced influence on the study of Judaism. In addition, the desire among nineteenth-century scholars of Judaism to procure citizenship for the Jewish people and intellectual respectability for Judaism led them to present Judaism as a religion ideally suited for the modern world that requires no irrational beliefs. So, while all theistic traditions have faced challenges since the Enlightenment, Judaism absorbed and deployed anti-theological arguments in a uniquely intensive manner.

Theology is too diverse within and across traditions to allow for many generalizations. While it may not be universally true, a feature common to most theologies is that they give serious consideration not only to our capacity to speak about God but also to the limits of our knowledge and language about God. What is peculiar about Judaism is the insistence by scholars studying diverse historical strata of the tradition that Judaism either does not or cannot make truth claims about God. It takes little reflection to appreciate how astounding this position is. Consider the Hebrew Bible. Even though the Hebrew Bible is a document written over a period of 800 years representing diverse religious and political interests, it is indisputably a defining feature of the text that God enters into relationship with the Israelites. It is quite peculiar that a tradition founded on the possibility of the divine–human relationship would adopt views that sharply limit or even negate the role of theology. How is it possible to understand, maintain, and develop the divine–human relationship if little or nothing can be said about God? Surely the nature of God and how we are to orient ourselves toward the divine are matters in need of significant explication but many approaches to Jewish theology block such inquiry from the start by denying our ability to refer to God.

It is not just the challenges to theological language in Judaism that make it an interesting test case for creative theology; theology has a diverse array of functions within Judaism that encourage wide participation in theological reflection. Jewish theology, as I have noted, largely eschews systematic and dogmatic expression. It is also the case that theology in Judaism does not fall within the domain of a magisterium. On the contrary, any Jew engaged in the study of written and oral Torah will find themselves inexorably drawn into theological reflection. Jewish liturgical readings of the Torah and Haftarah, the reading of the Passover Haggadah, the communal reading of the scrolls on holidays like Purim and Tisha B'Av, the all-night study on Shavuot, and the penitential process of the High Holidays strongly encourage active theological engagement. The contours of theology within Judaism become visible when one considers its functions. Jewish theology has theoretical and formative functions and the study and production of Jewish theology is a form of spiritual exercise.[1] At the theoretical level, Jewish theology articulates and defends the Jewish worldview as it relates to God and the divine–human relationship. Here Jewish theology not only informs practitioners about God but it also justifies Jewish practice by

---

[1] For more on the functions of Jewish theology see Cass Fisher, *Contemplative Nation: A Philosophical Account of Jewish Theology* (Stanford: Stanford University Press, 2012), 65–100.

detailing how our conceptions of God map onto the life of religious observance. Closely related to the theoretical and justificatory aspects of Jewish theology is the function of Jewish theology as a formative discourse. Religious language is inherently rhetorical as it seeks to persuade practitioners to adopt the beliefs, practices, and values that structure and sustain the religious world set forth in the text. A third function of Jewish theology is that the production, transmission, and study of classic Jewish texts was and is a spiritual exercise. Taking these points together, theological reflection in Judaism has a strongly communal and ritualized nature such that the question of theological creativity bears on matters of practice relevant to all observant Jews.

Judaism, it would then seem, is subject to two opposing forces. From one perspective, post-Biblical Judaism seeks to preserve and develop the divine–human relationship that is central to the Hebrew Bible. This effort requires active theological engagement from Jewish practitioners. An alternative force, arguably the one that is currently dominant, insists that theology plays a negligible role in Judaism; that in fact it is Judaism's distaste for theology that makes it the modern religion par excellence. It is neither necessary nor possible here to trace in full the vicissitudes of Jewish theology. A brief sketch of the principal factors that have led to the marginalization of Jewish theology will suffice. Such a survey will indicate that the problem of theological reference has played a central role in the de-theologizing of Judaism and that efforts toward a creative revitalization of Jewish theology require new resources to preserve and defend theological reference (see Box 15.1).

Box 15.1

The author provides a helpful signpost. He explains the structure of the paper. At this point, the reader notes that this is a major challenge to current approaches in Jewish studies. The author stresses the irony that a biblical tradition that endlessly talks about God has become a Jewish tradition that is very nervous about talking about God. In the next section, he will explain why this is the case.

Theological Reference and Rabbinic Theology

Box 15.2

The author stresses a key distinction found in the rabbinic literature – halakhah and aggadah. He notes how the rabbinic focus on the practice of Judaism – the commandments and their observance – has made theology (talk about God) much less important. This is an important section. The author sets out in some detail the precise reasons for theological nervousness. This emphasis gets combined with a Jewish studies interest in accounts of religious language that avoid theological reference to God. Wittgenstein, a philosopher who spent much of his time at the University of Cambridge (UK) is a major influence. For Wittgenstein, religious language is a way of looking at life, not a way of describing the world.

Efforts to diminish the role of theology in rabbinic Judaism often begin by identifying two basic forms of discourse in rabbinic literature, halakhah, which deals with the commandments and their observance, and aggadah, a grab-bag term for everything else including theology, ethics, legends, and folk material (see Box 15.2). While contemporary scholarship has done much to undermine this dichotomy, the distinction between halakhah and aggadah has served to privilege rabbinic discussions of law over theology. The motivations for identifying rabbinic theology as a secondary discourse are complex but, undoubtedly, a significant factor is scholars' embarrassment over the rabbis' anthropomorphic and anthropopathic depictions of God. Could the rabbis really have believed that God wept at the destruction of the temple or that God laughed when the rabbis usurped God's interpretive authority over the Torah? Elevating halakhah over aggadah paved the way for the further diminishment of aggadah as a homiletic discourse. Aggadah appears throughout classical rabbinic literature but it is a central component in rabbinic scriptural commentaries called *midrash* (pl. midrashim). Contemporary scholarship divides the rabbis' midrashic literature into several categories including halakhic midrash, exegetical midrash, and homiletic midrash. The halakhic midrash are the earliest midrashim but despite being designated as "halakhic" they in fact contain significant amounts of aggadah. The exegetical and homiletic midrashim are associated with the second generation of rabbis, the amoraim. The difference between the exegetical and homiletic midrashim is that while the exegetical midrashim appear to be straightforward commentaries on Scripture, the homiletic midrashim are organized around the liturgical readings of the Torah and the calendar of holidays. The identification of aggadic midrash with sermons has had the deleterious effect of casting all aggadah as an edifying discourse that is not aimed at truth. The basic outlines of this view are expressed by one of the greatest contemporary scholars of rabbinic literature, David Weiss Halivni, who says: "Rabbinic theology is not categorical nor easily categorized, and is more prone to homiletical discourse than to carefully groomed, neatly disciplined speculation. Rabbinic theology is often packaged and shrouded in aggada, within a folkloric context, functioning more as hortatory and pedagogic than as speculative literature."[2]

The claim that if rabbinic theology is neither systematic nor dogmatic, which it clearly is not, then it must be homiletic has profound implications for rabbinic theology. Understanding rabbinic theology on such terms entails that the rabbis are not interested in getting at the truth about God and the divine–human relationship; instead, they seek to shape the religious lives of the laity. While this view distances the rabbis from the anthropomorphic and anthropopathic views of God, which they appear to espouse, the homiletic approach to rabbinic theology does not align with contemporary historical research on the rabbinic movement nor textual analyses of rabbinic literature. Historians now believe that the rabbinic movement was small, insular, and exerted little social control, even over the synagogue, for many centuries after the destruction of the second temple.[3] Furthermore, regarding the rabbinic texts that appear to be collections of

---

[2] David Weiss, Halivni, *Peshat and Derash: Plain and Applied Meaning in Rabbinic Exegesis* (New York: Oxford University Press, 1991), 89. For more on the homiletic approach to rabbinic theology see Cass Fisher, "Beyond the Homiletical: Rabbinic Theology as Discursive and Reflective Practice," *The Journal of Religion* Vol. 90, No. 2 (2010): 199–236.

[3] On the social formation of the early rabbinic movement, see Catherine Hezser, *The Social Structure of the Rabbinic Movement in Roman Palestine* (Tübingen: Mohr Siebeck, 1997); Shaye Cohen "Epigraphical Rabbis," *The Jewish Quarterly Review* Vol. 72, No. 1 (1981): 1–17; Shaye Cohen, "The Rabbis in Second-Century Jewish Society," in *The Cambridge History of Judaism* Vol. 3, ed. William Horbury, W.D. Davies, and John Sturdy (Cambridge: Cambridge University Press, 1999), 922–990; Hayim Lapin, "The Origins and Development of the Rabbinic Movement in the Land of Israel," in *The Cambridge History of Judaism* Vol. 4, ed. Steven T. Katz (Cambridge: Cambridge University Press, 2006), 206–229; Hayim Lapin, "The Rabbinic Movement," in *The Cambridge Guide to Jewish History, Religion, and Culture*, ed. Judith R. Baskin and Kenneth Seeskin (Cambridge: Cambridge University Press, 2010), 58–84; Stuart Miller, *Sages and Commoners in Late Antique 'Erez Israel: A Philological Inquiry into Local Traditions in Talmud Yerushalmi* (Tübingen: Mohr Siebeck, 2006); Seth Schwartz, *Imperialism and Jewish Society, 200 B.C.E. to 640 C.E.* (Princeton: Princeton University Press, 2001).

sermons, scholars of rabbinics now identify these works as scholastic collections.[4] Stated succinctly, current research on the rabbinic movement and its literature does not support the view that rabbinic theology is an edifying discourse intended for the laity but the misidentification of rabbinic theology as a sermonic literature persists nonetheless.

Box 15.3

The author now gives an extended account of the views of Max Kadushin. Kadushin is a key conversation partner for the author. He is one of the best defenders of the position that the author thinks is mistaken. In making his case, the author will seek to be fair and accurate in his description of Kadushin's views; and he explains what motivates Kadushin to take his position.

That the homiletic account of rabbinic theology revolves around the issue of reference is apparent upon reflection (see Box 15.3). According to such a view, the rabbis are not asserting truth claims about God with their theology, rather, they are shaping the religious lives of their purported followers. Among scholarly engagements with rabbinic theology, the influential work of Max Kadushin in the middle part of the twentieth century is most explicit about the impossibility of theological reference. Kadushin bases his approach to rabbinic theology on what he calls "value concepts," the central examples of which are "God's justice, God's love (or mercy) Torah, and Israel."[5] Kadushin argues that, with only a few exceptions, all other rabbinic concepts are sub-concepts of these four. What makes the rabbinic conceptual system "organismic" is that the nature of the conceptual terms prevents them from being used propositionally and so the whole conceptual system lacks logical order. Kadushin argues that "organismic rabbinic concepts ... are not objects, qualities, or relations in sensory experience." Neither are they philosophical or scientific concepts. As he explains, "philosophic and scientific concepts depend upon definitions, whereas rabbinic concepts are connotative only, and hence are not amenable to formal definition."[6] Because rabbinic concepts are not definitional, their meanings cannot be given once and for all. Instead, the concepts emerge and develop in relation to other concepts. It is on this basis that Kadushin argues that rabbinic thought is "organismic." The organismic nature of the rabbinic conceptual system, according to Kadushin, is a strength not a weakness. He says that the rabbinic value concepts:

> exhibit an order infinitely more complex than can be devised by an individual, an order infinitely more flexible and thus more suitable to everyday needs. The organismic order

---

[4] See Richard S. Sarason, "The Petiḥtot in Leviticus Rabba: Oral Homilies or Redactional Constructions?" *Journal of Jewish Studies* Vol. 33, No. 1–2 (1982): 557–567; Burton L. Visotzky, "The Misnomers *Petihah* and 'Homiletic Midrash' as Descriptions for Leviticus Rabbah and Pesikta De-Rav Kahana," *Jewish Studies Quarterly* Vol. 18, No. 1 (2011): 19–31. For a helpful survey of the research on rabbinic preaching, see Günter Stemberger, "The Derashah in Rabbinic Times," in *Preaching in Judaism and Christianity: Encounters and Developments from Biblical Times to Modernity*, ed. Alexander Deeg et al. (Berlin: de Gruyter, 2008), 7–21.

[5] Max Kadushin, *Rabbinic Mind* (New York: Block Publishing, 1952), 15.

[6] Max Kadushin, *A Conceptual Approach to the Mekhilta* (New York: Jewish Theological Seminary of America, 1969), 28.

which they exhibit is something which is native to man, completely in keeping with the rest of his organismic nature, part and parcel of that nature. Contrasted with the religious values typified by the rabbinic concepts, philosophic systems are seen to be stiff, brittle and artificial.[7]

Part of what motivates Kadushin's organismic approach to rabbinic value concepts is his understanding of rabbinic theology as fundamentally homiletic. Along these lines he argues: "Because of the intimate relation of the Rabbis to the folk, rare among creators of written literature, the sermons of the Rabbis as preserved in the Haggadah constitute a unique literature. Informed by the value concepts common to the whole people, these sermons reflect the manner in which the value concepts functioned in everyday speech and action."[8] According to Kadushin, rabbinic theology is a sermonic discourse that expresses value concepts that were shared by the rabbis and the laity. Kadushin likens these rabbinic sermons to poetry with the difference that the rabbis' sermons focus on "valuational significance" rather than "aesthetic significance."[9] With their sermons, Kadushin claims that the "rabbis trained the folk by means of stories."[10] A crucial caveat is that these stories do not contain "crystallized beliefs."[11] On the contrary, rabbinic theology is marked by what Kadushin calls "indeterminate belief." Regarding indeterminate belief, Kadushin says:

> What kind of belief is this that can be surrendered so casually, that can accept ideas and stories and then dismiss them so lightly? A belief of this kind can only be an indeterminate belief … Indeterminacy of belief is doubtless a difficult thing for the modern mind to comprehend. It does not seem to be within our ken or within the range of our experience. Indeterminacy of belief is the only climate, as we have said, in which haggadic concretization of value-concepts can freely grow.[12]

Rabbinic value concepts, which are the core of rabbinic theology, do not denote God, are not used propositionally, and come to expression in a manner that does not culminate in religious beliefs. The rabbis' theological reflections are the stuff of stories and images that flash across our mind but require no cognitive commitments as they tell us nothing about God.

If, pace Kadushin, some theological language does assume propositional form and successfully refers to God, claims about divine perfection are a good candidate as they uniquely pick out God. Looking at how Kadushin addresses divine perfection provides a helpful example of what is at stake in his approach to rabbinic theology. In a work titled *A Conceptual Approach to the Mekilta*, Kadushin applies his organismic account of rabbinic theology in a reading of the early rabbinic commentary on the book of Exodus, *Mekhilta of Rabbi Ishmael*. God's command to the Israelites in Exodus 12:7 to place the blood of their paschal lambs on their doorposts and the rabbis' response to this directive provide insight into Kadushin's treatment of divine perfection. The questions arise for the rabbis whether the blood was to be put on the outside or the inside of the doorpost and for whom the blood was meant to be a sign? In Exodus 12:13 God

---

[7] Kadushin, *Rabbinic Mind*, 32.
[8] Ibid., 95.
[9] Ibid., 112.
[10] Ibid., 141.
[11] Ibid., 142.
[12] Ibid., 138.

says, "when I see the blood I will pass over you," and Rabbi Ishmael interprets this to mean that the blood is on the inside of the doorpost as only God can see it. Putting his interpretation in God's own words, Rabbi Ishmael has God say, "the blood that is seen by Me and not by others." It appears that Rabbi Ishmael is disturbed by the idea that God's knowledge is so inadequate that God would need a sign to mark the Israelites' dwellings and so he offers a creative interpretation that underscores God's omniscience. However, for Kadushin, Rabbi Ishmael's creative exegesis is not a claim about God's knowledge but, rather, an assertion of God's "otherness." Kadushin simply says:

> R. Ishmael gives expression here to the rabbinic emphasis on the otherness of God. God is not like man: what would be hidden from man is not hidden from God. This idea has nothing in common with the philosopher's aversion to anthropomorphism, for the latter involves metaphysical conceptions which belong to a non-rabbinic universe of discourse.[13]

In a second discussion of this same topic in the *Mekhilta of Rabbi Ishmael*, Kadushin is even more explicit in his rejection of the idea of God's perfection. When Rabbi Ishmael comes to interpret Exodus 12:13 directly, he offers a more forceful claim about God's omniscience. The *Mekhilta* has the following commentary on the phrase "when I see the blood":

> Rabbi Ishmael used to say: "Is not everything revealed before him, as it is said: 'He knows what is in the darkness and the light dwells with him' (Dan. 2:22)? And it says 'even darkness is not dark for you' (Ps. 139:12). Why does scripture say 'when I see the blood'? This can only mean that in the reward of the commandment you are doing [i.e. placing the blood on the doorpost] I will reveal myself and protect you as it says 'and I will pass over you' Ex. 12:13)"

In this second effort to understand God's command to place the paschal blood on the doorposts, Rabbi Ishmael offers a radical reinterpretation of the incident that preserves God's perfection and highlights the rabbinic system of reward and punishment based on the observance of the commandments. According to Rabbi Ishmael, scripture clearly asserts that God is all-knowing and so the blood on the doorposts cannot be a sign for God. Instead, the purpose of the command is to provide the Israelites with the opportunity to acquire the merit necessary for their redemption. Comparing Rabbi Ishmael's two interpretations of this incident, Kadushin says:

> In the [passage] given earlier, the blood is still a sign for God, whereas now it has no such function. Moreover, although the earlier interpretation expresses the idea of the otherness of God, it does so by means of a specific instance. Now, however, in the question, "Is not everything revealed before Him?" this idea is expressed in a less specific manner. The question is, in fact, tantamount to the idea of God's omniscience, but neither that idea nor the more inclusive one of God's otherness is crystallized in a conceptual term in rabbinic thought.[14]

Kadushin's organismic account of rabbinic theology gives pride of place to the four value concepts that are demarked by their own conceptual terms. Where there is no evident term for Kadushin, there is no concept. Regardless of Rabbi Ishmael's claims about God's possessing all

---

[13] Kadushin, *A Conceptual Approach to the Mekilta*, 83–84.

[14] Ibid., 97–98.

knowledge, such ideas cannot play a central role in rabbinic theology because they do not have an associated conceptual term. At best, Kadushin suggests that God's omnipresence, omnipotence, and omniscience are what he calls "auxiliary ideas."[15] While it is certainly true that the rabbis' approach to divine perfection lacks the systematic and dogmatic concerns that drive much Christian theology, relegating God's perfection to a set of auxiliary ideas significantly distorts rabbinic theology by diminishing the rabbis' efforts to praise God and reflect on God's greatness.

In arguing that rabbinic theology is not propositional, that it only elicits indeterminate beliefs, and that divine perfection is, at most, an auxiliary idea for the rabbis, one might falsely assume that Kadushin sought to undermine rabbinic theology. Our historical and intellectual distance from the middle of the twentieth century, when Kadushin wrote his works, makes it easy to mistake a defender of theology for an opponent. With the critiques of metaphysics and theology that accompanied the rise of logical positivism in the middle part of the last century, religious thinkers were compelled to find creative ways to preserve the core theological insights of their traditions. In Judaism, these strategies of theological preservation often came at the expense of theological reference. That Kadushin's cognitively constrained approach to rabbinic theology is in fact a coy defense is most apparent in his discussions of what he calls "normal mysticism." Normal mysticism, according to Kadushin, is an experience of God that is not mediated by the senses. Instead, normal mysticism finds expression in value concepts that occur in daily life that promote a "mystical consciousness of relationship to God," often through activities such as prayer and blessing.[16] In Kadushin's view, "from almost every page of the rabbinic texts it is evident that the Rabbis *experienced* God." He goes on to say:

> The actual experience of God is personal; the ways or modes of experiencing God, however, are common to the group as a whole. Being common to the entire group, the modes of God-experience are expressed in value-concepts, among them such concepts as prayer, repentance, the study of Torah. The personal experience of God through the modes crystallized by these and other value-concepts can be characterized ... as normal mysticism.[17]

In keeping with Kadushin's limitations on theological language, value concepts provide the possibility of speaking about our encounter with God without making assertions about God.[18] He cites a number of rabbinic texts in which the Israelites speak of God using various epithets, from which he concludes:

> Passages like these, depict a warm personal relationship to God, but reflect the normal mysticism which the Rabbis, and the people as a whole, experienced in everyday life. And in the expression of that normal mysticism, the appellatives and epithets themselves are an important factor. They are used as names for God, names applied to him out of feelings of unbounded reverence and love; they are, in fact, just so many tributes of reverence and love, and hence their multiplicity. Being thus names alone for God, not generalizing concepts, the appellatives represent a personal relationship to God, the sheer consciousness of Him, more poignantly perhaps than do the names for God that are also conceptual terms.[19]

---

[15] Ibid., 51.
[16] Kadushin, *Rabbinic Mind*, 272.
[17] Ibid., 194.
[18] Ibid., 215.
[19] Ibid., 205.

According to Kadushin, the divine epithets in rabbinic Judaism, e.g. the Holy One Blessed be He, Makom (Place), Heaven, Gevurah (Power), function as names bearing no semantic content. In his view, these divine epithets are a human response to the experience of a personal God but do not characterize God. Kadushin adopts this position because he thinks rabbinic religious experience is ultimately an experience of God's otherness. Along these lines, he says:

> Every experience of God, therefore, brought with it the recognition that God is like none other. It is this recognition of the otherness of God that the generic terms for God point to; they are like no other terms, being neither defined, nor cognitive, nor valuational terms; they are thus, in a sense, the rabbinic terms for the otherness of God. Furthermore, the entire character of normal mysticism leads toward the recognition of the otherness of God. It is mysticism that does not involve sense phenomena, and this in itself would tend to demarcate the experience of God from other experience.[20]

Kadushin seeks to preserve the divine–human relationship that he finds in rabbinic literature but his strategy for doing so is to denude that experience of its cognitive content. The rabbis he says "were certainly never surpassed and probably never equaled" in their ability to foster an experiential awareness of God's otherness.[21]

Kadushin knew well that his reconstruction of rabbinic theology and religious experience was shaped by his own intellectual commitments. He insightfully cautions at the beginning of *The Rabbinic Mind* that "every modern presentation of rabbinic thought is also an interpretation."[22] While his organismic account of rabbinic theology has few adherents among contemporary scholars, the idea that rabbinic theology is a homiletic discourse akin to poetry remains prevalent. The continued appeal for such readings of rabbinic Judaism does not derive its support from its historical validity; rather, it is the widespread effort among modern and contemporary Jewish thinkers to restrict Jewish theological language that lends credence to non-cognitive interpretations of rabbinic thought. As I will briefly sketch, many of these efforts to restrict Jewish theological language do so by either limiting or renouncing our capacity to refer to God. For Jewish thinkers interested in advancing creative theological positions, it is imperative that they acknowledge this fundamental impediment to Jewish theology so that they can properly assess the resources for revitalizing Jewish theological reflection.

The Restriction of Theological Reference in Modern and Contemporary Jewish Thought

Box 15.4
This section is crucial. It is here that the author wants to explain the extent of the "united front" of opposition to any serious Jewish theology. There are a variety of factors – religious language, modern science, and Wittgenstein. In this section, he coins a label "theo-realism." He is inventing a term that will help us place two giants in the Jewish tradition – Martin Buber and Abraham Joshua Heschel. Theo-realists, he says, "are realists about God, but not about theological language." So theo-realists are halfway there, but Fisher will need more help to get to realism about theological language.

---

[20] Ibid., 304.

[21] Ibid., 259.

[22] Ibid., 8.

A broad swath of modern and contemporary Jewish philosophers and theologians have one significant position in common, the belief that Jewish theology is not a theoretical discipline that discloses the truth about God and the divine-human relationship (see Box 15.4).[23] It is a perplexing fact that Jewish thinkers, with otherwise divergent philosophical and theological commitments, agree that Jewish theology does not inform us about God. Why is the rejection of theology as a theoretical discourse a unifying force for Jewish thinkers? In some cases, the arguments limiting theological predication are clear and decisive. Hermann Cohen, for instance, declares that God's uniqueness is the "essential content of monotheism"[24] and that "the uniqueness of God consists in incomparability."[25] We cannot know God, we can only acknowledge God.[26] Knowledge of God relates only to morality; God's essence is concealed from us and God's "attributes of action" are "moral archetypes" that refer to humans rather than God.[27] According to Cohen, these attributes "do not give any knowledge of God's being. Because they are only ethical, and not at the same time logical attributes, they cannot be adequate to God's being."[28] Emmanuel Levinas adopts a similar position arguing that "our relation with the Metaphysical is an ethical behavior and not theology, not a thematization, be it a knowledge by analogy, of the attributes of God."[29] We cannot participate in God conceptually or experientially; to claim otherwise is a "denial of the divine."[30] Contemporary adherents of negative or apophatic theology also renounce our capacity to refer to God. Kenneth Seeskin offers a stringent reading of Maimonides in which "the most negative predicates provide is an approximation, a set of very general directions for how to think about God. In Maimonides' opinion, they take us to the limit of what the human mind is capable of understanding but stop short of literal truth."[31] On this view, theological language "is not referential but heuristic," disclosing to us the inadequacy of our language for God and leading us to silent contemplation.[32] Elliot Wolfson adopts an equally intensive form of negative theology and seeks an "apophasis of apophasis."[33] According to Wolfson, a "theolatrous impulse ... lies coiled in the crux of theism" that insists on cognizing the transcendent.[34] In his view, divine transcendence "cannot be enclosed within the

---

[23] For an extended discussion of this topic see Cass Fisher, "Religion without God? Approaches to Theological Reference in Modern and Contemporary Jewish Thought," *Religions* Vol. 10, No.1 (2019): 1–25.

[24] Hermann Cohen, *Religion der Vernunft aus den Quellen des Judentums: Eine Jüdische Religionsphilosophie* (Wiesbaden: Fourier Verlag, 1995), 41; Hermann Cohen, *Religion of Reason out of the Sources of Judaism*, trans. Simon Kaplan (Atlanta: Scholars Press), 35.

[25] Cohen, *Religion der Vernunft*, 51/Cohen, *Religion of Reason*, 44.

[26] Cohen, *Religion der Vernunft*, 58/Cohen, *Religion of Reason*, 50.

[27] Cohen, *Religion der Vernunft*, 411/Cohen, *Religion of Reason*, 353.

[28] Cohen, *Religion der Vernunft*, 480/Cohen, *Religion of Reason*, 414.

[29] Emmanuel Levinas, *Totality and Infinity: An Essay on Exteriority*, trans. Alphonso Lingis (Pittsburgh: Duquesne University Press, 1969), 78.

[30] Ibid., 78.

[31] Kenneth Seeskin, "Sanctity and Silence: The Religious Significance of Maimonides' Negative Theology," *American Catholic Philosophical Quarterly* Vol. 76, No. 1 (2002): 7–24, 14.

[32] Ibid, 9.

[33] Elliot Wolfson, *A Dream Interpreted within a Dream: Oneiropoiesis and the Prism of Imagination* (New York: Zone Books, 2011), 32.

[34] Elliot Wolfson, *Giving Beyond the Gift: Apophasis and Overcoming Theomania* (New York: Fordham University Press), 260.

boundaries of what may be experienced or comprehended."[35] Borrowing a term from Buber, Wolfson says it is "theomania" that compels thinkers to turn the transcendent into an object of thought and that this "theolatrous" tendency extends to apophatic theology. Along such lines, he argues that "What is necessary, although by no means easy, is the termination of all modes of representation, even the representation of the nonrepresentable, a heeding of silence that outstrips the atheological as much as the theological, the saying of an unsaying that thinks transcendence as the other beyond theism and atheism."[36] For Wolfson, "the exigency of the moment … demands a sweeping and uncompromising purification of the idea of the infinite from all predication."[37]

While some Jewish philosophers and theologians, like those just mentioned, limit our capacity to refer to God out of fear that our conceptual categories compromise God's transcendence, other thinkers question the cognitive status of theology and its relevance to Jewish religious life. A common position among modern philosophers and theologians is that science has displaced theology as a source of theoretical knowledge. Mordecai Kaplan, for instance, argues that:

> Modern science has again reconstructed our picture of the universe and destroyed the dichotomy of body and soul, matter and spirit, physical and metaphysical, which characterized the Middle Ages. We cannot conceive of God any more as a sort of invisible superman, displaying the same psychological traits as man, but on a greater scale. We cannot think of him as loving, pitying, rewarding, punishing, etc.[38]

For Kaplan, science is destructive of theology. According to him, nearly all "healthy-minded persons" have abandoned the idea of "God as a personal agent."[39] The shift in our paradigms of knowledge undermines theology but not Judaism as Judaism is not a theologically oriented religious tradition. Kaplan says:

> The Jewish religion, in which the prophetic impulse still throbs, is fundamentally not a system of metaphysical beliefs about God, His existence, His infinitude, omniscience, and the whole string of algebraic adjectives which fill the theological works of the Middle Ages. The Jewish religion is an attempt to set forth the God idea by selecting those purposes and possibilities in the life of the Jewish people in which there is most promise of good, and making God, as it were, sponsor for them.[40]

Theology, on this view, is the language Jews use to maximize human flourishing rather than a theoretical discourse about the nature of God. For Kaplan, science challenges theology as a source of knowledge, but Judaism avoids the presumptive crisis because its theological language is not actually about God. Kaplan was long associated with Conservative Judaism before founding the Reconstructionist movement. It is noteworthy that the privileging of scientific over religious

---

[35] Ibid., 30.

[36] Wolfson, *A Dream Interpreted within a Dream*, 31. Cf. Wolfson, *Giving Beyond the Gift*, 152, 235.

[37] Wolfson, *A Dream Interpreted within a Dream*, 30.

[38] Mordecai Kaplan, *The Meaning of God in Modern Jewish Religion* (Detroit: Wayne State University Press, 1937), 88.

[39] Mordecai Kaplan, *Judaism without Supernaturalism: The Only Alternative to Orthodoxy and Secularism* (New York: The Reconstructionist Press, 1958), 25.

[40] Kaplan, *Meaning of God*, 305.

knowledge would find expression not only in the work of a liberal-minded thinker like Kaplan but also in the work of an orthodox one such as Yeshayahu Leibowitz. For Leibowitz, who was a biochemist and a neurophysiologist, the ascendance of scientific knowledge comes naturally. He argues:

> Our source of information is science. To the extent that we possess any real knowledge it is by way of scientific cognition. Psychologically, the information it supplies is forced upon the consciousness of all who understand it, for a human being is unable not to know what he knows. But the constitutive element of religious feeling and consciousness is not information which is derivable from religion. The essence of religion is not the information it provides but the demand made of man to worship God. Undoubtedly this aspect of religious faith has always been the essence of Judaism, but today it is likely to be more conspicuous than in the Middle Ages, when informative significance was attached to religion.[41]

As with Kaplan, science is determinative of human knowledge, but, once again, this fact has no adverse consequences for Judaism, a religion Leibowitz associates with commandment. According to Leibowitz, "faith, in Judaism, is the religion of mitzvot [commandments], and apart from this religion Jewish faith does not exist."[42] Insofar as Judaism is oriented to the observance of the commandments and not to theology, Leibowitz says that the Jewish religious practitioner "tries to refer minimally to God, who has no image at all, and makes an effort to direct his religious consciousness to himself as recognizing his duty to God."[43] When theology makes no theoretical contribution to our understanding of God, the question of whether we can refer to God is no longer a pressing issue.

Ludwig Wittgenstein advanced an antitheoretical approach to religious language that has found numerous proponents among contemporary Jewish thinkers.[44] Wittgenstein sought to defend religious language by arguing that there can be no conflict between science and religion because religious language makes no theoretical claims about the nature of reality. Instead, religious language consists of images or pictures that guide our lives. Although Wittgenstein considers these pictures "unshakable" for the religious practitioner, they are not upheld by reason. They are supported by the entire "form of life" or "language game." Along these lines, Alan Mittleman argues that "The word God does not make a claim about the furniture of the universe. Rather, to speak of God is to underwrite a form of life that allows us to respond with love and courage and hope to the mystery out of which we come and toward which we progress."[45] Theological language does not refer to God; rather, it is a means of articulating the fundamental actions and values that shape our lives. Avi Sagi brings to clear expression the consequences for Jewish theology in endorsing Wittgenstein's antitheoretical account of religion. Sagi, in his book *Jewish Religion after Theology*, asserts that "Truth claims about the world, about God, and about

---

[41] Yeshayahu Leibowitz, *Judaism, Human Values, and the Jewish State*, ed. Eliezer Goldman (Cambridge: Harvard University Press, 1992), 136.

[42] Ibid., 38.

[43] Ibid., 76.

[44] For more on the reception of Wittgenstein in Jewish philosophy and theology see Cass Fisher, "The Posthumous Conversion of Ludwig Wittgenstein and the Future of Jewish (anti-) theology," *AJS Review* Vol. 39, No. 2 (2015): 333–365.

[45] Alan Mittleman, "Asking the Wrong Question," *First Things* Vol. 189 (2009): 15–17, 17.

crucial events such as the Sinai theophany, are religiously irrelevant. In other words, religion is a value system that neither relies upon nor reflects metaphysical assumptions or factual data that could be translated into truth claims."⁴⁶ While some philosophers of religion find resources in Wittgenstein's thought for more affirmative positions on theological language, for Sagi and many other Jewish thinkers the appeal of Wittgenstein's thought lies in his rejection of religious language as a theoretical discourse. On this reading, religion has nothing to say about the nature of reality, including God. Sagi says regarding God and theology that: "The Key question concerning God, then, is not his objective character, his existence or identity, but the way in which human beings, in their language and in their lives, use the concept of God."⁴⁷ For Sagi, it is evident that Jews do not use theological language to understand God and the divine–human relationship.

Despite appearances, the efforts of Jewish philosophers and theologians to restrict or renounce theological reference are not necessarily motivated by the desire to sunder the divine–human relationship. Kadushin, for instance, rejects the idea that we can speak propositionally about God, yet a key component of his account of rabbinic theology is the preservation of a form of religious experience he identifies as "normal mysticism." Two of the most prominent Jewish thinkers of the twentieth century, Martin Buber and Abraham Joshua Heschel, embraced a similar position, which I refer to as "theo-realism." Theo-realists like Buber and Heschel are realists about God but not about theological language. Buber's realism about God is evident in his claim that "If one dares to turn toward the unknown God, to go to meet Him, to call to Him, Reality is present."⁴⁸ Along the same lines, Heschel asserts: "The existence of God is not real because it is conceivable; it is conceivable because it is real."⁴⁹ While God is the ultimate reality for Buber and Heschel, God's reality impedes rather than facilitates human cognition of the divine. Buber succinctly states that God "eludes direct contemplation."⁵⁰ Heschel says "we have neither an image nor a definition of God. We have only His name. And the name is ineffable."⁵¹ Along with their theo-realism, Buber and Heschel also share an intermediate position on theological reference. They contend that while our language does not refer to God, we are able to point to the divine via ostensive reference. Heschel says, "while we are unable either to define or to describe the ineffable, it is given to us to point to it. By means of indicative rather than descriptive terms, we are able to convey to others those features of our perception which are known to all men."⁵² Again, arguing along similar lines, Buber says, "The religious communication of a content of being takes place in paradox. It is not a demonstrable assertion (theology which pretends to be this is rather a questionable type of philosophy), but a pointing toward the hidden realm of existence of the hearing man himself and that which is to be experienced there and there alone."⁵³

Two points of reflection on Buber's and Heschel's theo-realism can guide subsequent discussions of Jewish theology. First, Buber and Heschel are surely correct that defending the reality of God

---

[46] Avi Sagi, *Jewish Religion after Theology*, trans. Batya Stein (Boston: Academic Studies Press, 2009), 27.

[47] Ibid., 132.

[48] Martin Buber, *Eclipse of God: Studies in the Relation between Religion and Philosophy* (Amherst, New York: Humanity Books, 1952), 28.

[49] Abraham Joshua Heschel, *Man is not Alone: A Philosophy of Religion* (New York: Farrar, Straus and Giroux, 1951), 91.

[50] Buber, *Eclipse of God*, 14.

[51] Heschel, *Man is not Alone*, 97.

[52] Ibid., 21.

[53] Buber, *Eclipse of God*, 43.

requires that we possess the capacity to refer to God in one way or another. What difference does it make if God is real or not if we cannot speak about or somehow indicate whom we are referring to? A second point relates directly to the matter of theological creativity. Like many of the thinkers I have discussed, Buber and Heschel offer a solution to the critiques of religious language that preserves what they take to be of paramount importance, the divine–human relationship. Solutions such as these may be intellectually creative, but they are theological conversation-stoppers. Heschel claims that the proper cognitive response to God is wonder and Buber argues that the I–Thou relationship is not productive of knowledge. The outcome of their positions is that everything that can be said about God has been said. As far as God and the divine–human relationship go, Buber's and Heschel's positions can only be advanced by way of critique. Only by arguing that more can and must be said about God is it possible to invoke Buber and Heschel in further theological creativity.

Theories of Reference as a Source for Jewish Theological Creativity

Box 15.5
The author will now develop his alternative approach. He wants to defend the legitimacy of theological reference – in other words, he wants to defend the idea that you can refer to God. His sources here are interesting. He does not draw only on more familiar literature on the theory of reference, but also on more recent conversation partners. He wants to show that a belief in divine transcendence does not make it impossible to talk about God. Interestingly, a key image is from Francois Recanati and his library files.

The Jewish philosophers and theologians I have surveyed restrict, declare irrelevant, or renounce theological reference (see Box 15.5). Curiously, scholars developed these positions independently of discussions in the philosophy of language on the theory of reference. For the first part of the twentieth century, views on reference were closely associated with Bertrand Russell's distinction between knowledge by acquaintance and knowledge by description. For Russell, knowledge by acquaintance is limited to that which we know directly, such as our sense data, memories, introspection, and universals. Knowledge of everything else is dependent on definite descriptions. In the 1960s and early 1970s, an important advance in the theory of reference emerged with the idea of direct or causal reference. Ruth Barcan Marcus, Saul Kripke, and others argued that reference occurs through an original designation of a name, often referred to as a "baptism," and that the name then becomes a "rigid designator," naming the object in every possible world.[54] While the attribution of a name in an "initial baptism" can occur through ostension or description, what is important for theological purposes is that names can be shared and learned through social communication. Philosophers of religion have been quick to point out that this account of how names are fixed and transmitted reflects the way religions often cultivate beliefs about God. Religious practitioners typically do not acquire their initial beliefs by learning a definite description that uniquely picks out God. Instead, they learn to use the word God and other divine names through religious education and practice.

---

[54] Ruth Barcan Marcus, "Modalities and Intensional Languages," *Synthese* Vol. 13, No. 4 (1961): 303–322; Saul Kripke, *Naming and Necessity* (Cambridge, MA: Harvard University Press, 1972). Quentin Smith, "Marcus, Kripke, and the Origin of the New Theory of Reference," *Synthese* Vol. 104, No. 2 (1995): 179–189.

While many Jewish philosophers and theologians have endeavored to minimize theological reference, analytic philosophers of religion, both Christian and Jewish, have pushed back against the criticisms of theological language. In contrast to the non-cognitive approach common to many Jewish thinkers, Christian thinkers such as William Alston and Nicholas Wolterstorff have argued that God is precisely the kind of being one can identify by means of description. Alston says, "purely qualitative uniquely identifying descriptions (if they are exemplified at all) are much more plentiful for God than for other objects of attempted reference."[55] Wolterstorff also holds that nothing prevents us from using definite descriptions with respect to God. He wryly argues: "Well, here's a way of fixing the reference of the term 'God': use a definite description. Find some property with which one is acquainted and that is uniquely exemplified by God, compose a definite description expressing that property, and then declare that 'God' refers to what fits that definite description."[56] Among Jewish philosophers of religion, no scholar has made a greater contribution to the issue of theological reference than Jerome Gellman. As just one example, Gellman's article, "Naming, and Naming God," is a tour de force in which he defends our capacity to refer to God through both definite descriptions and causal reference.[57] Not only does Gellman buck the trend of restricting reference in modern and contemporary Jewish thought, he also offers an array of arguments that God could be the proper object of causal reference, a possibility that is excluded by secular approaches to causal reference. Gellman's engagement with the theory of reference in order to secure philosophical resources for theological reflection has propelled his extraordinary theological creativity. The most recent evidence of this theological creativity is a trio of monographs: *God's Kindness has Overwhelmed Us: A Contemporary Doctrine of the Jews as the Chosen People*; *This Was from God: A Contemporary Theology of Torah and History*; and *Perfect Goodness and the God of the Jews: A Contemporary Jewish Theology*.[58]

Continuing in the path set by Gellman, recent developments in the theory of reference offer a host of new resources for Jewish theology. Much of the resistance to theological reference among Jewish thinkers is couched in terms of the problem of God's transcendence: How can finite human language contain something divine? The matter of God's transcendence reflects a basic concern within the theory of reference regarding the means by which language hooks on to reality. Recent work in theory of reference has moved away from thinking about how lan-

---

[55] William Alston, "Religious Language," in *The Oxford Handbook of Philosophy of Religion*, William J. Wainwright (Oxford: Oxford University Press, 2005), 220–244, 229.

[56] Nicholas Wolterstorff, *Practices of Belief: Selected Essays Vol. 2*, ed. Terence Cuneo (Cambridge: Cambridge University Press, 2010), 370.

[57] Jerome Gellman, "Naming, and Naming God," *Religious Studies* Vol. 29, No. 2 (1993): 193–216. Other important contributions by Gellman on theological reference include: "The Name of God," *Noûs* Vol. 29 (1995): 536–543;"Religion as Language," *Religious Studies* Vol. 21 (1985): 159–168; "Identifying God in Experience: On Strawson, Sounds and God's Space," in *Referring to God: Jewish and Christian Philosophical and Theological Perspectives*, ed. Paul Helm (New York: Routledge, 2000), 71–89.

[58] Jerome Gellman, *God's Kindness has Overwhelmed Us: A Contemporary Doctrine of the Jews as the Chosen People* (Boston: Academic Studies Press, 2013); Jerome Gellman, *This was from God: A Contemporary Theology of Torah and History* (Boston: Academic Studies Press, 2016); Jerome Gellman, *Perfect Goodness and the God of the Jews: A Contemporary Jewish Theology* (Boston: Academic Studies Press, 2019).

guage captures reality and instead sees reference as an essential tool in communication.[59] A good starting point in exploring this work is a new theory of reference developed by John Perry and Kepa Korta. Perry first set forth the theory in his 2001 monograph, *Reference and Reflexivity*, and further developed it with Korta in the 2011 monograph, *Critical Pragmatics: An Inquiry into Reference and Communication*.[60] Perry and Korta synthesize elements of descriptivist and causal theories of reference but seek to push past both by focusing their theory on the roles of cognition and communicative intention. In his earlier work, Perry argues that reference is part of a collective and public exercise that occurs through what he calls "notion networks." He describes the accumulation of notions around a single referent as the process of assembling a file. For Perry and Korta, the goal of reference is not to pick out objects; rather, we use referential language to convey beliefs and attitudes. According to Perry and Korta, "the use of a definite description does not imply that the speaker refers to the object in question, but that he designates the object in question with the intention of imparting a belief with a referential cognitive fix. It is not a matter of the speaker referring, but a matter of the speaker designating with a target intention of imparting a referential belief."[61] Using a suggestive metaphor, Perry and Korta say of a medical file that "the importance of the accuracy of the information in the file is not to secure reference to the object, but to enable appropriate treatment of the patient it is a file of."[62] Because the problem of how human language can capture the divine has proven so vexing for Jewish thinkers, an account of reference that emphasizes communication offers significant resources for revitalizing Jewish theology. Embracing Perry's and Korta's theory of reference means we no longer have to construe theological reference as the struggle of a lone individual to haltingly capture the transcendent in words and thought. On the contrary, theological reference is a collective endeavor to produce, evaluate, and transmit beliefs about God. To appreciate the importance of this shift in understanding reference for Jewish theology, consider how different our picture of rabbinic theology is if the rabbis were engaged in producing, testing, and communicating their beliefs about God in contrast to the idea that the rabbis used beliefs they did not hold to shape the religious lives of people over whom they had little authority or interest. Clearly, updating our account of reference not only provides resources for contemporary theology; it can also significantly improve our historical understanding of Judaism and the place of theology within it.

Perry and Korta's theory contains additional features beneficial to the study of Jewish theology. Importantly, their account of reference does not require individuals to hold particular theoretical views in order to successfully refer. All that is necessary is that the person has access to the "notion network." As Perry and Korta point out, "we can use names to ask the most basic of questions about what they stand for, and to make statements about them that reflect ignorance of the most basic facts about what they are or who they are."[63] The idea that reference can succeed in non-ideal circumstances allows for an approach to theological language that does not

---

[59] In addition to the work of John Perry, Kepa Korta, and Francois Recanati that I discuss here, Imogen Dickie also offers an account of reference that emphasizes communication that holds potential resources for Jewish theology. Imogen Dickie, *Fixing Reference* (Oxford: Oxford University Press, 2015).

[60] John Perry, *Reference and Reflexivity* (Palo Alto: Center for the Study of Language and Information, 2001); Kepa Korta and John Perry, *Critical Pragmatics: An Inquiry into Reference and Communication* (Cambridge: Cambridge University Press, 2011).

[61] Korta and Perry, *Critical Pragmatics*, 96.

[62] Ibid., 38.

[63] Ibid., 82.

privilege the elite over the laity. In my view, there is much to be gained by adopting philosophical positions that do not undercut the laity's ability to think and speak about God. This is particularly true within Judaism where theology is deeply integrated into religious practice. Another benefit of Perry and Korta's theory is that conceiving of reference as the building of a file lays the groundwork for a response to criticisms that Jewish theology is neither systematic nor dogmatic. According to Perry and Korta, files undergo a buffer stage in which beliefs are accumulated, sorted, contested, and merged. Much Jewish theology from the Hebrew Bible forward closely resembles this process of constructing a file about God through the amassing of alternative conceptions of the divine. Perry and Korta's theory of reference also provides resources for addressing another pivotal issue in Jewish theology: the rabbis' penchant for figurative language. As we have seen, the rabbis' use of parables has led scholars to view their theology as a homiletical discourse directed at the laity rather than a theoretical discourse aiming to disclose truths about God and the divine–human relationship. Perry and Korta's theory offers a solution to the problematic identification of the rabbis' figurative language with preaching. Their account of reference allows for successful communication even when speakers "use a description that neither the speaker nor hearer thinks accurately picks out the speaker's intended referent."[64] In words that I think reflect the rabbis' communicative intentions in their use of figurative language, Perry and Korta speak of such linguistic acts as "an invitation for the hearer to come up with an alternative description, or identifying condition, in the course of figuring out the speaker's intention."[65] They see no inherent problem with the fact that sometimes we say something false in order to convey something true. Accordingly, we do not have to assume that the figurative nature of rabbinic theology negates its theoretical aspirations.

Francois Recanati also conceives of reference as a system of files and his 2013 monograph, *Mental Files*, offers further resources for understanding Jewish theology.[66] In Recanati's view, one advantage of thinking of reference as a file system is that it allows different forms of reference to function together. Each file is linked to its referent through acquaintance relations that are "epistemically rewarding" in their own way.[67] Thus, reference based on perception, communicative chains, or indexicals can work together. According to Recanati, "mental files are 'about objects': like singular terms in the language, they refer, or are supposed to refer. They are, indeed, the mental counterparts of singular terms. What they refer to is not determined by properties which the subject takes the referent to have (i.e. by information – or misinformation –in the file), but through the relations on which the files are based."[68] What makes the file account of reference so flexible is that reference does not depend on descriptions that the object must satisfy. Instead, reference succeeds when the file is in the right epistemic relation to its object. Recanati's theory permits a range of epistemic relations, what he refers to as "multiple anchors."[69] This position is consonant with the view that Jewish theology consists of multiple forms of theological language each arising out of distinct belief-forming practices.[70] Like Perry's and Korta's theory, Recanati advances an epistemically egalitarian account of reference that would serve religious

---

[64] Ibid., 99.

[65] Ibid., 99.

[66] Francois Recanati, *Mental Files* (Oxford: Oxford University Press, 2012).

[67] Ibid., 20.

[68] Recanati, *Mental Files*, 35.

[69] Ibid., 253.

[70] For such an account of the forms of Jewish theological language see Fisher, *Contemplative Nation*, 21–101.

purposes well. The individual using a file does not have to possess reflective knowledge on the relevant epistemic relation for reference to succeed; all that is required is that the file has the right relation to its object.[71]

One aspect of Recanati's theory can help us imagine what a "God" file might look like. Recanati's notion of a file is based on indexicals in that every file has a unique cognitive path similar to the way indexicals such as I, you, she, and now are distinguished from each other. There are, however, files that operate at a more general level, which he calls "encyclopedic files."[72] Unlike generic files that have a single epistemic relation, encyclopedic files collect information gathered from the diverse epistemic relations of multiple files. Interestingly, Recanati says that encyclopedic files function more like names than indexicals. Our theological language about God is best understood as an encyclopedic file in that we form beliefs about God through a range of distinct belief-forming practices. A second way in which Recanati's theory could be usefully adapted to Jewish theology relates to his allowing for "imagined" or "anticipated" reference. Not only does Jewish theological language have multiple forms and functions but we should also be quick to acknowledge that individuals use theological language differently. Whereas for some, reference to God is secured by firm epistemic relations, other practitioners can only hope for an acquaintance relation with God and thus their reference is anticipated but not actual. In Exodus 24:7, the Israelites reply to God, "we will do and we will hear," which established a spiritual principle in Judaism that action brings understanding. In allowing for the possibility of anticipated reference, Recanati's theory has the advantage of being applicable across the long continuum of "doing in order to hear" that Jewish practitioners commonly traverse.

Conclusion

Box 15.6

The author reaches his conclusion. For those in Judaism who want to think and write in creative ways in theology, he identifies three options. The first is to just ignore the traditional Jewish resistance to theology. The second is to follow an option that religious language is not intended to refer to God. Or the third, which he commends, is to appropriate recent philosophical resources that are useful for arguing that theological reference is possible.

As I have attempted to sketch, a pronounced resistance to theological reference is prevalent in the study of rabbinic Judaism and in modern and contemporary Jewish thought (see Box 15.6). What is a constructive Jewish theologian to do? I see three possibilities. First, one can simply ignore the resistance to theological reference and get on with one's work. Second, one can adopt positions that circumvent the criticism of theological reference such as Kadushin's value concepts, theo-realism, or a Wittgensteinian emphasis on forms of life rather than truth claims about God. Third, one can utilize the philosophical resources developed in the theory of reference to overcome the prejudice against theological language in Judaism. The problem with ignoring the challenges to theological reference is that by doing so one greatly reduces one's conversation partners. Jewish theology may eschew systematic and dogmatic expression, but it has always been based in communal conversation. The Hebrew Bible is marked by inner-biblical

---
[71] Recanati, *Mental Files*, 37.
[72] Ibid., 73.

exegesis and rabbinic literature depicts the rabbis conversing with each other across geographic and temporal distances. Furthermore, from the rabbis forward every stage of the Jewish tradition is an engagement with earlier layers of the tradition extending back to the Torah. A defining feature of much modern Jewish thought is its dialogical nature. To turn aside from the criticism of theological reference is to conduct one's theological reflection in isolation and subvert the collective mode of Jewish theology. Skirting the issue of theological reference by embracing non-theoretical approaches to theology comes at the extraordinarily high price of accepting that we are incapable of speaking truthfully about God. Does not such a position ensure theology's ultimate irrelevance? If we cannot speak truthfully about God, why bother at all? Surely, the best alternative is to address the matter of theological reference directly. Engaging with work on the theory of reference, past and present, can secure the legitimacy of Jewish theology by restoring its place in earlier layers of the tradition, resolving long-standing questions about the particular nature of Jewish theology, and providing resources for advancing creative Jewish theological reflection.

16

Marshall's Slingshot
Truth Theory, Realism, and Liberal Theological Method

John Allan Knight

RESEARCH LEVEL 4

Editors' Introduction

In this essay, Knight defends correspondence theories of truth from a particular critique (the slingshot argument) developed by Bruce Marshall. Though the author himself prefers an alternative view of truth to a correspondence view, he thinks it important to show that the slingshot argument is fatally flawed. It's important, in his view, because if the slingshot works, it will also defeat any realist view of truth that is compatible with a liberal approach to theology. After describing Marshall's slingshot argument and his critique of it, Knight closes by offering some features of an account of truth he would prefer.

Introduction

> **Box 16.1**
>
> The author begins by contextualizing the essay, describing why he's writing it and how it fits with his larger project.

This essay is a small part of an attempt to defend a distinctly liberal theological method (see Box 16.1). Part of any theological method is to assess theological claims for their truth or falsity. And one of the things that marks a theological method as liberal, on my construal, is this: when assessing a theological claim, "truth" is understood in the same way as it is when assessing any other claim. Such an assessment, that is, must be done in a way that preserves the autonomy of rational judgment.[1] A liberal theology cannot assume that once we determine that a theological assertion is characteristically or traditionally Christian, it is *eo ipso* true. Yet in the late twentieth century, a number of theologians reexamined what it means to say that a theological statement is true, and some wanted a

---

[1] Note that this understanding of "liberal" in theology might in fact describe a number of theologians that in popular parlance are most often dubbed "conservative".

distinctly theological definition of "truth." Bruce Marshall is exemplary here. Christians, he says, "should have their own ways of thinking about truth."[2] Now Marshall seeks to uphold realism in theology, but he is suspicious of any non-theological correspondence theory of truth. Yet he thinks that some version of a correspondence view is required for any realist construal of theology. Marshall's criticism of the correspondence theory has been well received, and it is incumbent on those of us hoping to defend both a liberal approach to theology and realist theories of truth compatible with liberal theology to defend them against his critique. I will argue that correspondence theories of truth withstand his criticism. But to defend correspondence theories against Marshall's criticism is not to defend them *tout court*. Indeed, in my own view, realism in theology is better served by truthmaker theory than by correspondence.

Box 16.2
Here the author sets out the specific motivating reason for his critique of Marshall.

Still, it's important to address Marshall's criticism, because if his criticism is correct, it defeats not only correspondence theories, but any and all realist views of truth that are compatible with liberal theological method (see Box 16.2). So this essay will remain devoted to addressing Marshall's criticism rather than offering my own view of truth. But in the conclusion, I will gesture in the direction of an alternative to the truth theories considered here that I believe introduces less confusion into the discourse about truth.

Marshall, Postliberal Theology, and Correspondence

Box 16.3
The author places Marshall in the postliberal stream of twentieth century theology, explaining briefly what motivates Marshall to object to correspondence theories of truth.

Marshall's most sustained critique of correspondence theories is set out in *Trinity and Truth*, and I'll limit my comments to that nuanced and erudite text (see Box 16.3).[3] Marshall wants to preserve the central aspects of the theological method Frei and Lindbeck appropriated from Barth. Frei in particular maintained that to argue for the truth of any theological claim by reference to some independent notion of truth is to submit to an "all fields-encompassing scheme" that inevitably distorts the Christian message. Yet Frei wanted to remain a theological realist, and Marshall follows him in this (Marshall 2000, p. 117). Much of Marshall's book on truth is concerned with the epistemic justification of theological beliefs. He doesn't focus on the concept of truth until chapter 8 (the penultimate chapter). And there, the first section in the chapter is "Realism in search of a truth-bearer." By the end of the chapter he will say that a theological account of truth will need some version of correspondence, for he wants to defend postliberal theology as realist when it comes to truth. And the most common way to preserve realism in truth theory is via a

---

[2] Bruce D. Marshall, *Trinity and Truth* (Cambridge: Cambridge University Press, 2000), xi.
[3] Ibid. For a broader treatment of Marshall's understanding of truth, and how it compares with Kevin Hector and Stephen Long, see my "The Return of Truth: Defending the Correspondence Theory After the Liberal/Postliberal Divide," *Religious Studies* vol. 56 (2020) : 578–595.

correspondence theory. So Marshall does not want correspondence theories (and a fortiori the notion of truth) to be "annihilated." But he does want them to be "radically disciplined and changed," because, he argues, no (non-theological) correspondence theory of truth can work unless it is subjected to Trinitarian discipline (Marshall 2000, p. 242; quoting MacKinnon[4]).

For assistance in making this argument, Marshall turns to Donald Davidson.[5] Marshall uses Davidson's famous "slingshot" argument to describe what Marshall takes to be fatal deficiencies in any non-theological correspondence theory of truth.[6] This type of argument was developed long before Davidson and often has been seen as establishing limits on metaphysical theories regarding facts. In consequence, it has been appropriated in criticisms of a variety of theories that have facts as a constituent, such as theories of truth, correspondence, and the like.[7] Davidson, and Marshall following him, uses it to argue that correspondence theories of truth are "not so much false as empty," as Marshall summarizes it, "and so useless for saying what truth is." (Marshall 2000, p. 226).[8]

---

[4] Donald MacKinnon, "The Problem of the 'System of Projection' Appropriate to Christian Theological Statements," in *Explorations in Theology 5: Donald MacKinnon* (London: SCM Press, 1979), 81.

[5] Marshall is also indebted to Thomas Aquinas, and he notes that Aquinas thought of truth as a sort of correspondence. For Aquinas, truth primarily concerns the intellect and its judgments. Yet, on many occasions, Aquinas speaks of truth in relation to sentences or utterances. And it is sentences that Marshall treats as the primary truth-bearers of correspondence theories (at least prior to Trinitarian discipline). He doesn't treat propositions or beliefs in order to avoid unnecessary controversy. See Marshall, *Trinity*, 222. Though everyone agrees that sentences are truth-bearers, the existence and nature of propositions or other "various types of non-linguistic mental entities" is contested. Marshall then argues thus: "But if mental entities can no longer fruitfully be regarded as truth vehicles, does it still make sense to think of truth as the correspondence of mind to reality? And if it turns out that the truth borne by interpreted sentences cannot be that of correspondence, how should we think about truth?" (Marshall, *Trinity*, 223). The notion that only sentences can be plausibly regarded as truth bearers is not only highly contested, but most likely a minority view. See the following: Alexis G. Burgess and John P. Burgess, *Truth* (Princeton, NJ: Princeton University Press, 2011), 10–15; Scott Soames, *Understanding Truth* (New York, NY: Oxford University Press), 32–39; William P. Alston, *A Realist Conception of Truth* (Ithaca, NY: Cornell University Press, 1995), 5–30.

[6] Marshall describes epistemic accounts of truth and their criticisms of correspondence theories. On epistemic accounts, "In order to be accessible, truth itself has to be epistemic: for a sentence to be true just is for people to be justified in believing it." (Marshall, *Trinity*, 225). Marshall is not persuaded by such criticisms and takes epistemic accounts to be plagued by similar problems as well as others all their own (Marshall, *Trinity*, 225).

[7] There is actually a fairly broad family of slingshot-style arguments used for different purposes. For a concise overview of the ways slingshot arguments have been used, see J. Brandl, "Some Remarks on the 'Slingshot Argument,'" in *Advances of Scientific Philosophy*, ed. G. Dorn and G. Schurz (Amsterdam: Rodopi, 1991), 421–437. For an in-depth study of slingshot arguments and their history, as well as a sympathetic assessment, see Stephen Neale, *Facing Facts* (Oxford: Clarendon Press, 2001).

[8] Marshall's statement of the slingshot is derived from Davidson. See Donald Davidson, "True to the Facts," in *Inquiries into Truth and Interpretation*, ed. Donald Davidson (Oxford: Clarendon Press, 2001), 37–54; Davidson, "The Structure and Content of Truth," *Journal of Philosophy* Vol. 87 (1990): 279–328. Marshall states that his reading of Davidson's slingshot argument is indebted primarily to Simon Evnine, *Donald Davidson* (Palo Alto, CA: Stanford University Press, 1991), 136, 180–182. See Marshall, *Trinity*, 228, n. 25.

The Slingshot Argument

> **Box 16.4**
>
> The author gives a very brief background to the slingshot argument, and describes two crucial assumptions that allow it to work.

The slingshot argument seems to have originated with Alonzo Church,[9] who developed it using certain ideas of Frege (see Box 16.4).[10] The argument turns on two crucial assumptions. First, logically equivalent sentences have the same reference.[11] This is an extrapolation from the formal Principle of Substitutivity for Logical Equivalents (PSLE). Second, the reference of a sentence does not change if a component singular term is replaced by another with the same reference. Again, this is an extrapolation from the formal Principal of Substitutivity for Singular Terms (PSST). Using these two assumptions, proponents of the slingshot will identify two sentences with different meanings and attempt to show that they refer to the same fact.[12] This is exactly the way Marshall uses it. According to PSST, coreferential singular terms can be substituted *salva veritate* (without any change in truth value) in sentences that create an "extensional context" (Marshall 2000, p. 228). As for PSLE, as Marshall explains it, "in an extensional context, logically equivalent sentences, like co-extensive terms, may be substituted without changing the truth value of the expression in which the substitution occurs." (Marshall 2000, p. 228). Two questions naturally arise: "What is an extensional context?" and "Do factual contexts count as extensional?" As Marshall suggests, extensional contexts can be simply defined as those in which substitution of coreferential terms necessarily preserves truth value. Unfortunately, Marshall is imprecise when explaining PSLE. He says that "sentences are logically equivalent which must always have the same truth value." (Marshall 2000, p. 228). According to the standard definition of logical equivalence, however, "two sentences are logically equivalent if and only if they are true in precisely the same models or possible worlds." (Young 2002, p. 124). In defining extensional contexts, Marshall uses the term "must," but leaves out the modal term "necessarily."

> **Box 16.5**
>
> The author here provides a foreshadowing of a major problem with Marshall's use of the slingshot argument, and raises a question central to his argument: Do factual contexts count as extensional contexts?

---

[9] Alonzo Church, review of Carnap's *Introduction to Semantics*, *Philosophical Review* Vol. 52 (1943): 298–304; idem. *Introduction to Mathematical Logic* vol. 1 (Princeton, NJ: Princeton University Press, 1956).

[10] Gottlob Frege, "On Sense and Reference," trans. Max Black, *The Philosophical Review* Vol. 57 (1948): 207–230, reprinted in *Readings in the Philosophy of Language*, ed. Peter Ludlow (Cambridge, MA: MIT Press, 1997), 563–583.

[11] Jon Barwise and John Perry, *Situations and Attitudes* (Cambridge, MA: MIT Press, 1983; reprint Stanford, CA: CSLI Publications, 1999), 24. Note that for Frege, sentences that make assertions refer either to "the False" or "the True".

[12] James O. Young, "The Slingshot Argument and the Correspondence Theory of Truth," *Acta Analytica* Vol. 17 (2002): 124.

This is potentially important, because, as we will see, the facts Marshall uses as evidence that factual contexts are extensional are not necessarily true (see Box 16.5). Thus, since Pam and Ted are married, are the two sentences "Pam threw the ball to Ted" and "Pam threw the ball to her husband" logically equivalent? They have the same truth value in the actual world. But there is a possible world W in which Ted is Pam's cousin and not her husband, and in which Pam did indeed throw the ball to Ted. In W, then, the two sentences have different truth values, and this shows that they are not logically equivalent.

But what about factual contexts? Do they count as extensional contexts? Marshall thinks so based on the following example. Since St. Olaf College is located in Northfield, the definite description "the town where St. Olaf is located" can be substituted (at least in the actual world) for Northfield and retain the same truth value. So, Marshall concludes that the sentential operator "corresponds to the fact that" creates an extensional context. An extensional context, he quite rightly says, is typically contrasted with an "intensional" (or "hyperintensional," as some philosophers call it) context, in which substitution of coreferential terms does not necessarily preserve truth value. For example, "Mary believed Pam hit her husband with the ball" may or may not be substituted for "Mary believed Pam hit Ted with the ball." If Mary believed that Ted were Pam's cousin, then substituting one sentence for the other would not preserve truth value. In drawing this contrast, and as his discussion proceeds, Marshall drops even his allusions to the mode of necessity in discussing extensional contexts. Thus: 'The goal of the slingshot argument is to establish the truth of the general point, suggested by our example, that in expressions of the form "the sentence s corresponds to the fact that p, the values of s and p can be any true sentences." (Marshall 2000, pp. 228–229). I'll return to this line of criticism later. For now, let's see how Marshall sets up his argument.

Marshall's Use of the Slingshot Argument

Box 16.6
Here the author gets specific in his description of Marshall's slingshot argument.

Marshall structures his argument as a *reductio ad absurdam* (see Box 16.6). It goes like this:

(1) "Northfield is east of Lonsdale" corresponds to the fact that Northfield is east of Lonsdale
(Premise)
(2) "Northfield is east of Lonsdale" corresponds to the fact that the town where St. Olaf is located is east of Lonsdale[13]
(PSST)

---

[13] Marshall needs another premise here: Northfield is the town where St. Olaf is located. Though it is easily remedied, the necessity of the premise is a clue to what's wrong with the argument, as I will argue later.

(3) $x(x = x$ and Northfield is east of Lonsdale$) = x(x = x)$ [14]
(PSST)
(4) Northfield is east of Lonsdale = (3)
(PSLE)
(5) "Northfield is east of Lonsdale" corresponds to the fact that $x(x = x$ and Northfield is east of Lonsdale$) = x(x = x)$
(PSLE)
(6) "Northfield is east of Lonsdale" corresponds to the fact that $x(x = x$ and Red Square is in Moscow$) = x(x = x)$
(PSST)
(7) $x(x = x$ and Red Square is in Moscow$) = x(x = x)$
(PSST)
(8) Red Square is in Moscow = (7)
(PSLE) … and finally,
(9) "Northfield is east of Lonsdale" corresponds to the fact that Red Square is in Moscow.
(PSLE) (Marshall 2000, pp. 229–230).

What conclusion does Marshall draw from this? Marshall says that the correspondence theory "is supposed to explain truth; … [to tell] us something about truth which we would not otherwise know." (Marshall 2000, p. 230).[15] But, he says, as an explanation of truth for sentences, the correspondence theory is hopeless. It "tells us nothing useful we do not already know, and know better, from whatever grasp of 'true' we already have." (Marshall 2000, p. 231). On Davidson's (and my own) view, though, the correspondence theory is not designed to explain something about truth we don't already know. Rather, it articulates a pre-theoretical understanding of truth that realists about truth do indeed already have. But in addition, it creates a relationship between semantics and ontology.

Problems with Marshall's Slingshot

Box 16.7

Having described Marshall's argument, the author begins his critique.

Be that as it may (see Box 16.7), Marshall's gloomy prognosis for the correspondence theory presupposes the success of the slingshot argument. Yet, in its Davidsonian instantiation, it is not successful, which is why few analytic philosophers have followed Davidson in using it to attack

---

[14] To state this in plain English, $x(x = x)$ can be read as "the set of objects x that are identical with themselves." This obviously includes all objects. $x(x = x$ and Northfield is east of Lonsdale$)$ can be read as "the set of objects x such that they are identical with themselves and that Northfield is east of Lonsdale".

[15] Despite his reliance on Davidson's slingshot, Davidson does not regard truth theories as explanatory. Rather, their job is to theorize T-sentences, which are supposed to be our pre-theoretical understanding of truth.

the correspondence theory.[16] There are a couple of obvious responses that on their own should make us suspicious about Davidson's and Marshall's use of the slingshot. First, if the slingshot works in this context, it would work not only on the sentential operator "corresponds to the fact that" but also equally well on "is true if and only if... ." That is, Marshall argues that the slingshot shows that "in the expressions of the form 'the sentence s corresponds to the fact that p,' the values of s and p can be any true sentences." (Marshall 2000, pp. 228–229). If Marshall is right, then the slingshot would also show that in expressions of the form "the sentence s is true if and only if p" [i.e. T-sentences], the values of s and p can be any true sentences as well.

Box 16.8

This is the real threat if Marshall's argument is successful.

And if that's the case, then the slingshot could be thought to undermine not only the correspondence theory, but any theory at all about truth (see Box 16.8). Now this would not bother Davidson (though it might trouble Marshall), since Davidson is famously a primitivist about truth – he takes the concept of truth to be properly primitive, or basic, and not subject to definition, explanation, or explication at all.[17] Thus, Davidson's use of the slingshot is closely related to his program of truth-conditional semantics. Davidson famously maintains that the meaning of a sentence is constituted by its truth conditions. And if that's the case, then to know the meaning of a sentence is to know the sentence's truth conditions. But one can't know what any sentence's truth conditions are without possessing the concept of truth. Thus, Davidson says, the concept of truth is a primitive, or basic, concept.[18]

---

[16] He's not devoid of followers, though. See, e.g. Gonzalo Rodrigues-Pereyra, "Searle's Correspondence Theory of Truth and the Slingshot," *Philosophical Quarterly* Vol. 48 (1998): 513–522. As Andrew McFarland has pointed out, Davidson uses at least three separate slingshots. In "Truth and Meaning," Davidson argues that expressions cannot refer to their meanings since the slingshot would show that all expressions with the same semantic extension end up having the same meaning, an obviously unacceptable result. Donald Davidson, "Truth and Meaning," *Synthèse* Vol. 17 (1967): 304–323. In "The Logical Form of Action Sentences," Davidson argues that we should reject Hans Reichenbach's analysis of the logical form of action sentences, since the slingshot shows that on Reichenbach's proposal there is only one event. See Davidson, "The Logical Form of Action Sentences," in *The Logic of Decision and Action*, ed. Nicholas Rescher (Pittsburgh, PA: University of Pittsburgh Press, 1966), 81–95. The third and most famous, from Davidson, "True to the Facts," is the one I discuss in the text. See Andrew McFarland, "Misfired Slingshots: A Case Study in the Confusion of Metaphysical and Semantic Considerations," *Logos & Episteme* Vol. IV (2013): 419.

[17] Alexis G. Burgess and John P. Burgess, *Truth* (Princeton, NJ: Princeton University Press, 2011), 84–90.

[18] Donald Davidson, "The Folly of Trying to Define Truth," *Journal of Philosophy* Vol. 93 (1996): 263–278, reprinted in Donald Davidson, *Truth, Language and History* (Oxford: Clarendon Press, 2005), 19–37.

Though I don't have time to argue the point here, the trouble with the Davidsonian program in semantics is that no truth-conditional theory of meaning has any hope of succeeding.[19] That in itself should make us suspicious of Davidson's (and Marshall's) claim that the slingshot tells us anything about truth (at least as it applies to natural languages).[20] But we should also be suspicious of the slingshot's prospects of success in accomplishing what Davidson and Marshall want it to accomplish. Marshall argues that if the slingshot works, then "Northfield is east of Lonsdale" corresponds to the fact that Red Square is in Moscow. He takes it to work, and that therefore "Northfield is east of Lonsdale" corresponds to the fact that Red Square is in Moscow. And what this accomplishes, Marshall argues, is to demonstrate that correspondence theories tell us nothing about truth. But, to borrow Alvin Plantinga's quip, one person's *modus ponens* is another's *modus tollens*. Thus (see Box 16.9), I could agree that if the slingshot works, then

---

Box 16.9

Knight here deploys what is sometimes called "**the G.E. Moore shift.**"

"Northfield is east of Lonsdale" corresponds to the fact that Red Square is in Moscow. But it should be obvious that "Northfield is east of Lonsdale" does not correspond to the fact that Red Square is in Moscow. Therefore, the slingshot does not work. We could refine the argument somewhat by substituting "factual contexts are/are not extensional" for "the slingshot works/does not work." If factual contexts are not extensional, and neither Marshall nor Davidson provide any adequate reason to believe that they are, then the slingshot cannot undermine the correspondence theory.

Box 16.10

The author moves to his next critique.

A slightly more technical reason to believe that the factual contexts are not extensional has to do with PSLE used by Marshall and Davidson (see Box 16.10). As I have mentioned, "two sentences are logically equivalent if and only if they are true in precisely the same models or possible worlds." (Young 2002, p. 124). Yet several statements in Marshall's argument are not logically equivalent in this way. And the reason is quite straightforward. Marshall says that "corresponds to the fact that" creates an extensional context so that PSST and PSLE will

---

[19] John Allan Knight, "Why Not Davidson? Neopragmatism in Religious Studies and the Coherence of Alternative Conceptual Schemes," *Journal of Religion* Vol. 88 (April 2008): 159–189; idem. *Liberalism vs. Postliberalism: The Great Divide in Twentieth Century Theology* (New York: Oxford University Press, 2013), 229–234. See also Scott Soames, "Truth, Meaning, and Understanding," *Philosophical Studies* Vol. 65 (1992): 26–29.

[20] If it were to succeed, the most it could do is provide a semantic constraint on the referents of sentences. It still could not tell us anything about what facts (however construed) have to do with the truth of sentences or propositions.

apply. And to demonstrate this, he notes that "we may safely infer" (2) from (1), since Northfield is the town in which St. Olaf College is located. But it's obviously a contingent fact that St. Olaf is located in Northfield. There are any number of possible worlds in which Northfield is east of Lonsdale, but St. Olaf is not located in Northfield. At the very least, then, we'd need more than inferring (2) from (1) in the actual world to establish that factual contexts are extensional.

Indeed, not many philosophers have endorsed Davidson's slingshot argument, and many are unwilling to allow Davidson's and Marshall's assumption that factual contexts are extensional.[21] Particularly dubious is the phrase "the x such that" or "the set x such that." Philosophers such as Nathan Salmon argue that these operators are nonextensional and that expressions within the scope of such operators are not amenable to substitutivity.[22] Others object to Davidson's assumption that facts are extensions or can be treated as such.[23] Still others contest the assumption that the correspondence relation is essentially a reference relation.[24] Indeed, Davidson himself seemed to reject this assumption in his earlier use of the slingshot.[25] Finally, if one adopts a Russellian quantificational account of definite descriptions, rather than a referential account, PSST won't apply to such

---

[21] The seminal essay is Jon Barwise and John Perry, "Semantic Innocence and Uncompromising Situations," *Midwest Studies in the Philosophy of Language VI* (1981): 387–403. Even after the Barwise and Perry essay, though, Davidson stuck by it and found some advocates. See, e.g. Rodrigues-Pereyra, "Searle's Correspondence," 513–522.

[22] Nathan Salmon, *Frege's Puzzle* (Cambridge, MA: MIT Press, 1986, 6; idem, "The Very Possibility of Language,: in *Metaphysics, Mathematics and Meaning: Philosophical Papers* Vol. 1 (Oxford: Oxford University Press, 2001), 349. Idem, Reference and Essence, 2nd edn. (Amherst, MA: Prometheus Books, 2005).

[23] Lorenz Kruger, "Has the Correspondence Theory of Truth Been Refuted? From Gottlob Frege to Donald Davidson," in *Why Does History Matter to Philosophy and the Sciences? Selected Essays*, ed. Thomas Sturm, Wolfgang Carl, and Lorraine Daston (Berlin: Walter de Gruyter, 2005).

[24] Given that the slingshot is usually said to have originated with Frege (who did not use the term "slingshot"), this assumption is odd. For Frege is famous for distinguishing the referent of an expression from its content. See Frege, "Sense and Reference," 207–230. One fairly obvious alternative, which abstracts from any metaphysical commitments on facts, characterizes the correspondence relation as "simply the relation of being true if and only if certain conditions obtain." See Young, "Slingshot," 123. It could also be a truthmaking relation. See Andrew McFarland, "Misfired Slingshots: A Case Study in the Confusion of Metaphysical and Semantic Considerations," *Logos & Episteme* Vol. IV (2013): 430, n. 59.

[25] Recall that in 1967 Davidson used the slingshot to argue that expressions do not refer to their meanings. Davidson, "Truth and Meaning," 19. Yet Davidson notoriously argues in the same article that the meaning of a sentence just is its truth conditions. But the truth conditions of a sentence are just whatever facts would have to obtain to make the sentence true. See Young, "Slingshot," 122. So, part of Davidson's argument in "Truth and Meaning" is that sentences don't refer to facts, whereas in "True to the Facts," he assumes that they do.

descriptions, and the slingshot won't work (see Brandl 1991; Read 1993).[26] One might argue that Davidson (and Marshall) could avoid this critique by simply adopting a referential account of descriptions. Perhaps so, but a correspondence theorist could also avoid the slingshot by adopting a Russellian account.[27]

> **Box 16.11**
>
> Here the author moves to his final critique, which he signposts by the use of "finally." It's an important critique, because someone might wonder why the slingshot argument worked for Frege, Church, and Gödel, but not for Davidson. The key is that Davidson shifts the referents of sentences to facts, and this defeats the slingshot, in Knight's view, because factual contexts are not extensional.

Finally, contrary to his earlier use of the slingshot, in his argument against the correspondence theory, Davidson makes the substantive assumption that sentences refer to facts. In this, he departs from the classic slingshot arguments used by Frege, Church, and Gödel. Their arguments advanced only a semantic thesis – namely, that sentences with the same truth values have the same referents. All true sentences refer to *the true*, while all false sentences refer to *the false*.[28] But these are both unique semantic entities and abstract completely from any metaphysical commitments. By switching the referents of sentences to facts, and then assuming that the context will remain extensional, Davidson smuggles a metaphysical conclusion into what is essentially a semantic argument. Thus, he is only able to draw metaphysical conclusions from the argument (viz, that there is only one Eleatic fact) by building into the argument precisely those

---

[26] A definite description is a phrase of the form "the *A*." Examples include "the cat in the kitchen," "the woman in the corner drinking champagne," or "the present King of France." On Russell's theory, a sentence of the form [The *A* is *B*] has the logical form [there exists some *x* such that *x* is *A* & *x* is *B*]. Therefore, definite descriptions are devices of quantification, and Russell's account is usually called a quantificational account.Russell developed this theory in order to reject the view that every object of thought must have some kind of being. On this view, things such as Santa Claus, the Great Pumpkin, or the current king of the US must have some kind of being even though they don't exist. If they did not have some kind of being, there would be no propositions about them, and therefore we could not make any statements expressing such propositions. Such statements are called "negative existentials," examples of which include these: "The Great Pumpkin doesn't exist." "White crows don't exist." "There is no king of the US." Russell's theory allows him to argue that in the case of a sentence such as "White crows do not exist" the logical form of the proposition it expresses is something like this: "For every object *x*, either *x* is not a crow or *x* is not white." See S. Read, "The Slingshot Argument," *Logique & Analyse* Vol. 36 (1993): 195–218.

[27] At least one commentator has argued that a Russellian semantics for definite descriptions could be developed that would not doom Gödel's version of the slingshot. See Stephen Neale, "The Philosophical Significance of Gödel's Slingshot," *Mind* Vol. 104 (1995): 794. But Gödel's version is different than Davidson's.

[28] Gottlob Frege, "The Thought: A Logical Inquiry," trans. A.M. and Marcelle Quinton, *Mind* Vol. 65 (1956): 289–311, reprinted in *Readings in the Philosophy of Language*, ed. Peter Ludlow (Cambridge, MA: MIT Press, 1997), 563–583.

assumptions he needs for the argument to work. Consequently, as Andrew McFarland argues, however interesting the semantic results of properly deployed slingshots, "they tell us very little (if anything) about metaphysics." (McFarland 2013, p. 432).

> **Box 16.12**
>
> In the next six paragraphs, Knight will describe John Searle's objections to the slingshot argument, along with Marshall's responses. Knight then describes what he thinks is wrong with Marshall's responses.

Marshall responds to only one objection to the slingshot, that of John Searle (see Box 16.12).[29] Searle argues that any set of logical constraints must take into account features of the meaning of "fact" set out by the particular correspondence theory to which it is applied. And on Searle's account, a fact is that which makes a statement true or in virtue of which a statement is true. In other words, a fact is a truthmaker. In addition, any set of logical constraints must respect the intuitive features of "true" and "correspond." But the slingshot fails to do this, Searle argues, in applying principles such as PSLE. Another way to put the objection, Searle says, is that PSLE does not preserve the identity of facts. And it should be obvious that the self-identity of all objects has nothing to do with the fact that Northfield is east of Lonsdale.

Marshall's response is twofold. First, he says that an objection that blocks the inference from (1) to (5) would also block the inference from (1) to (2). In consequence, he says, Searle effectively treats the operator "corresponds to the fact that" as extensional in (2) but intensional in (5) (Marshall 2000, pp. 231–232). But so far as I can see, Marshall is wrong about this. For the inference from (1) to (2) to be valid, we must assume a suppressed premise: namely, that Northfield is the town where St. Olaf is located. And the reason we need this suppressed premise is that it's a contingent fact about Northfield that St. Olaf is located there. But given this premise plus (1), we can infer (2) whether or not the context is extensional. But without the suppressed premise, we can't infer (2) from (1), and that in itself should make us suspicious of the notion that the correspondence operator creates an extensional context.

Marshall's second response challenges Searle's method of differentiating one fact from another. "The difficulty remains," he says, "of individuating facts or states of affairs and of specifying when they are identical." (Marshall 2000, p. 232). The most obvious initial reply, he says, is to say that facts are differentiated by true statements. And he notes that Searle himself advocates this reply.[30] Marshall argues that when facts are individuated in this way, the correspondence theory fails as a strategy for explaining truth, because we must already understand the concept of truth in order to identify the fact that makes a statement true. For his part, Searle seems to recognize this but is untroubled by it: "Facts in short are not extralinguistic things, but facts already have the notions of statement and truth built into them, because in order to specify a fact

---

[29] Searle actually raises several objections. John Searle, *The Construction of Social Reality* (New York, NY: The Free Press, 1995), 221–226.

[30] "Once we have identified the statement and the fact, we have nothing further to do by way of comparing them, because *the only way to identify a fact is to make a true statement*." Searle, *Social Reality*, 205. Marshall quotes the italicized portion of this passage, Marshall, *Trinity and Truth*, 232, n. 30; see also Searle, *Social Reality*, 201–212 (also cited by Marshall).

we have to have a true statement." (Searle 1995, p. 205).[31] This construal of facts is contested, of course, but it indicates that Searle's correspondence theory is an articulation of our already (somewhat) understood, pre-theoretical notion of truth.

Marshall also objects to Searle's perceived violation of Occam's razor. Individuating facts this way leads to an infinitely multiplying Platonic menagerie of facts. He illustrates this with the following examples:

(10) Northfield is 10 miles east of Lonsdale.
(11) Northfield is 16 kilometers east of Lonsdale.
(12) Lonsdale is 10 miles west of Northfield.

Now (10) to (12) all describe an aspect of the geographic relationship between Northfield and Lonsdale. Yet, at least on Marshall's reading of Searle, they all describe different facts – too many facts for Marshall's taste. For every true statement, we have a separate corresponding fact, and in this situation, he says, "substitution which preserves identity of fact becomes impossible" (Marshall 2000, p. 232). Marshall takes this to imply that Searle's method for individuating facts is untenable as a way to distinguish which substitutions are acceptable and which are not, and thus we have "no clear idea what is wrong with the slingshot argument." (Marshall 2000, p. 233). So far as I can see, though, Marshall's conclusion is too extreme. We have a very good idea about what is wrong with Marshall's Davidsonian slingshot argument, and I've mentioned several things wrong with it. The basic problem, though, which Searle and others have pointed out in different ways, is that we have no reason to assume that factual contexts are extensional, especially in the absence of any argument that they are. But beyond that, I think Marshall's dispute with Searle highlights a broader point. When the coreferential principle is applied to sentences (or propositions) rather than singular terms, it creates problems whose analysis is clarifying. And what it clarifies is that disputes between realists and antirealists over truth are often derivative from differences over other philosophical notions (see Soames 1998, pp. 32–39). And indeed, here Marshall's dispute with Searle seems to be as much about the metaphysical status of facts as it is about truth.[32]

> **Box 16.13**
>
> The author moves to his final critique, and along the way he will offer a criterion of fact identity.

There is one final flaw in Marshall's use of the slingshot that I'd like to highlight (see Box 16.13). And this, so far as I can see, is a fatal flaw in Marshall's and Davidson's use of the slingshot, as well as any use that deploys the sentential operator "corresponds to the fact that." That is not so much the move from (4) to (5) (which I do think problematic as well), but the move from (5) to (6). So to recall:

(5) "Northfield is east of Lonsdale" corresponds to the fact that $x(x = x$ and Northfield is east of Lonsdale) $= x(x = x)$
   (PSLE)

---

[31] I should note that Searle considers facts to be representational. They are what true statements or beliefs represent.
[32] This is highlighted by the fact that immediately following this discussion of Searle, Marshall begins a discussion of "Truth without realism or anti-realism." Marshall, *Trinity*, 233.

(6) "Northfield is east of Lonsdale" corresponds to the fact that $x(x = x$ and Red Square is in Moscow$) = x(x = x)$
(PSST)

Let's let N = "Northfield is east of Lonsdale" and R = "Red Square is in Moscow." Then we can restate the steps as follows:

(5) N corresponds to the fact that $x(x = x\ \&N) = x(x = x)$
(6) N corresponds to the fact that $x(x = x\ \&R) = x(x = x)$

Marshall takes (6) to follow from (5) as a result of PSST. That can only be the case if $x(x = x\ \&N) = x(x = x)$ and $x(x = x\ \&R) = x(x = x)$ are coreferential – in nontechnical terms, if they are names for the same fact. Consequently, to defeat the slingshot, all a correspondence theorist needs to do is to find some criterion of fact identity according to which the two facts are not identical. And we don't need to search too far to find one. One quite plausible criterion is the existential criterion of fact identity set out by Kenneth Olson, according to which two facts are identical if and only if they are instantiated in exactly the same possible worlds.[33] Now Olson's biconditional raises some potentially thorny problems, so let's modify the criterion such that existing in the same possible worlds is a necessary but not sufficient condition of fact identity.[34] But since N and R are both contingent facts, there will be possible worlds in which N is instantiated but R is not, and vice versa. And this means in turn that there are possible worlds in which $x(x = x\ \&N) = x(x = x)$ is false but $x(x = x\ \&R) = x(x = x)$ is not. And therefore it is possible that in (5) N corresponds to some fact, while in (6) N corresponds to nothing. Consequently, substitution is not warranted, and the slingshot fails. As a result, I see no reason to accept Marshall's conclusion "that a view like Davidson's, which accepts realism's fall but not anti-realism's rise, is the most plausible outcome currently available of the long philosophical debate about what truth is." (Marshall 2000, p. 241).

---

[33] Kenneth R. Olson, *An Essay on Facts* (Stanford, CA: CSLI Publications, 1987).

[34] The problems I have in mind have to do with entailments. So, for example, in every world in which right triangles exist, there also exist triangles in which the square of the length of the hypotenuse equals the sum of the square of the length of the sides. Yet these are separate facts – that is, every right triangle has a right angle, and every right triangle conforms to the Pythagorean theorem. Yet conforming to the Pythagorean theorem and having a right triangle are distinct facts notwithstanding that they are instantiated in every right triangle. James Young has also proposed this as a possible modification, calling it the "weak existentialist criterion." For those who wish to retain the existentialist criterion of fact identity, Young has pointed out several additional strategies that work to defeat the slingshot. Young, "Slingshot," 128–131. Andrew Newman has criticized Olson's criterion on different grounds. In Newman's view, it yields possible worlds that differ from each other absolutely rather than compositionally. Andrew Newman, *The Correspondence Theory of Truth: An Essay on the Metaphysics of Predication* (Cambridge: Cambridge University Press, 2002), 166–167. Newman prefers the much more complex compositional view of facts set out by D.M. Armstrong, *A World of States of Affairs* (Cambridge: Cambridge University Press, 1997), 133. It's not clear that Newman is right about this result following purely from Olson's criterion of fact identity. But be that as it may, Newman's concerns are substantially mitigated by my modification, for even on Armstrong's more compositional account, two facts are not identical if they do not exist in the same possible worlds.

Concluding Remarks

> **Box 16.14**
>
> In his concluding remarks, the author will not only repeat his conclusion that Marshall's slingshot argument fails but will also point out some consequences for theology. He will also point to some features of a theory of truth he hopes to develop in future work.

On my reading (see Box 16.4), Marshall's dislike of non-theological correspondence theories arises from concerns distinct from the correspondence relation itself. Marshall wants realism in truth theory to be dependent on Christology, taking as his clue one statement about truth in John's Gospel: "If Jesus Christ is the truth, then truth is borne, not only or chiefly by sentences and beliefs, but by a person. More than that: if the New Testament is right, then in the end truth *is* a person." (Marshall 2000, p. 242). I don't have space in this essay to scrutinize Marshall's theological disciplinary proposal – that will have to await another paper. But let me simply suggest the anticipated direction of that paper. Marshall argues that his disciplinary proposal is necessitated by two things: first, that some version of correspondence is needed for a theological understanding of truth; and second, that philosophical versions of the correspondence theory have been crippled by Davidson's slingshot argument. I've tried to show in this paper why I think the correspondence theory has withstood the slingshot attacks. If I'm right, this opens the door to a different kind of Trinitarian gloss on the notion of truth than that put forward by Marshall.

Rather than the kind of intellectual gymnastics required to defend the notion that the primary *truth-bearer* is Jesus, why not say that the primary or ultimate *truthmaker* is the Trinitarian God?[35] Certainly at first glance, this would seem as consistent with the enigmatic Johannine statements about truth as the notion that the primary truth-bearer is a person. As an added bonus, it would take us into a conversation about ontology, which is what we are doing when we are discussing a concept or doctrine of God. And out of that conversation about truthmakers, we can address disputes over differing accounts of facts or states of affairs.[36] I can't address those issues here. Instead, I've simply tried to show why I remain unpersuaded by both Marshall's and Davidson's objections to correspondence theories of truth.

Yet to say that I'm not persuaded by such objections is not to defend any particular correspondence theory, and especially not any and all of them. So I shall close simply by pointing in the direction of the kind of account I would hope to articulate and defend in future work. I would begin with the basic truthmaker thesis:

---

[35] A *truth-bearer* is something that *bears* a truth value (there are only two truth values – true and false), typically propositions, assertive sentences, beliefs, etc. Note that some sentences have no truth value – e.g. questions, commands, etc. A *truthmaker* is whatever *makes* a true statement (proposition/belief, etc.) true. So if the assertion "Ian is in his office" is true, then Ian's being in his office is the assertion's truthmaker.

[36] D.M. Armstrong, *Truth and Truthmakers* (Cambridge: Cambridge University Press, 2004), 48–49; Hubert Hochberg, "Facts and Relations: The Matter of Ontology and of Truth-Making," in *Truth and Truth-Making*, ed. E.J. Lowe and A. Rami (Montreal, Kingston and Ithaca: McGill-Queens University Press), 158–184; Andrew Newman, *The Correspondence Theory of Truth: An Essay on the Metaphysics of Predication* (Cambridge: Cambridge University Press, 2002), 140–171.

[TM]: Every true proposition is made true by something.[37]

This thesis can be understood as a basic, minimum articulation of realism in truth theory, sometimes called truthmaker minimalism. It will be compatible with some correspondence theories and not with others. But generally correspondence theories will involve three components: truth-bearing representations (including propositions, statements, beliefs), facts, and a correspondence relation. Following truthmaker theories, my preference would be to substitute the truthmaking relation for the correspondence relation.[38] To defend any account of each of these components will involve answering a number of objections, which I don't have space to attempt here. But it seems most promising to me to adopt a rather minimalist version of each component. Thus, a proposition is simply the content of an assertion or propositional attitude. This is our basic intuition about propositions, though it is not an explanation. I would not take them as having any mode of being independent of illocutionary acts or propositional attitudes, or, as William Alston would say, "independent of their content-bearing involvements."[39]

Regarding facts, Andrew Newman says that generally speaking there are two approaches to facts: compositional views (such as those of Russell, the early Wittgenstein and Armstrong) and linguistic views (more like Austin's) (Newman 2002, p. 140). A linguistic view, Newman says, "starts with certain linguistic expressions and singles out some as describing states of affairs, states of affairs being introduced merely as what those expressions describe, and then facts are explained as states of affairs that obtain" (Newman 2002, p. 154). My own view is closer to the linguistic approach. To put it more colloquially, a fact is simply a slice of the actual world identified under a description. It seems to me that a fact bears a mereological relation to the actual world similar to the relation that my left leg bears to me. Yet this linguistic view of facts doesn't imply that they are not real, but only that the identification of a fact does not on its own increase the inhabitants of the world.

And finally, the correspondence relation can be articulated in a variety of ways, but, to use George Pitcher's distinction,[40] very often it is done in either of two ways. The first is "correspondence-as-correlation," in which facts and propositions are correlated according to some rule or function. The second is "correspondence-as-congruity," in which facts and propositions correspond just in case they have the same components and these components are related to each other in the same or sufficiently similar way – i.e. they have the same or similar structure (David 2009, pp. 139–143). My own preference would be to abstract from these for purposes of an account of truth, as William Alston has done. For Alston, all that is needed for a minimal but sufficient account of correspondence is:

(p) The proposition that p is true *iff* it is a fact that p (Alston 1996, p. 38).

Such an understanding of correspondence may seem trivially obvious and uninformative, and it certainly doesn't tell us all we might want to know about correspondence. But it does play an important role. First, requiring that the same substitution be made for "p" on both sides of the

---

[37] Alternative formulations include, "For every true proposition, there is something that makes it true" and "Every true proposition has a truth-maker." According to Marian David, these formulations are treated as interchangeable and functionally equivalent. Marian David, "Truth-making and Correspondence," in *Truth and Truth Making*, ed. E.J. Lowe and A. Rami (Montreal, Kingston and Ithaca: McGill-Queens University Press, 2009), 138.

[38] On most accounts the truthmaking relation would be an *internal relation*.

[39] William P. Alston, *A Realist Conception of Truth* (Ithaca, NY: Cornell University Press, 1996), 19.

[40] George Pitcher, "Introduction," in *Truth*, ed. George Pitcher (Englewood Cliffs, NJ: Prentice Hall, 1964), 1–15.

biconditional guarantees that however one construes the correspondence relation, it will be truth-preserving. Thus, "it is enough to assure us that truth and correspondence are tightly connected" (Alston 1996, p. 39). Second, although it is neutral regarding competing metaphysical accounts of facts, it is compatible with those views that regard them as real parts of "the extralinguistic, extraintentional world" (Alston 1996, p. 39).

All this requires further articulation, of course. But I would envision a rather minimal correspondence theory of truth that is metaphysically neutral on a variety of issues, though perhaps not all issues. Even better would be to substitute for the correspondence relation a truth-maker relation that is similarly metaphysically neutral. That neutrality leaves theologians free to articulate a theistic ontology unconstrained (or less constrained) by the requirements of a more metaphysically involved truth theory. A correspondence theory, even a minimal one, identifies a truthmaker for true propositions. Conflicts can arise out of the thought that there is only one truthmaker (a particular fact) for true propositions. But truthmaker theorists generally argue that there may be a number of truthmakers for true propositions. Thus, they are complementary, so that truthmaker theory connects a realistic ontology with truth theory. Indeed, truthmaker theory is explicitly concerned to preserve metaphysical realism. And for any doctrine of God that views a Trinitarian God as the creator of all that is, since true propositions may have more than one truthmaker, a truthmaker theory leaves open the possibility that such a God can be construed as the Maker of all truth.

Works Cited

Alston, William P. (1996). *A Realist Conception of Truth*. Ithaca, NY: Cornell University Press.
Brandl, J. (1991). "Some Remarks on the 'Slingshot Argument,'" in *Advances of Scientific Philosophy*, 421–437, ed. G. Dorn and G. Schurz. Amsterdam: Rodopi.
David, Marian. (2009). "Truth-making and Correspondence," in *Truth and Truth Making*, ed. E.J. Lowe and A. Rami. Montreal, Kingston, and Ithaca: McGill-Queens University Press.
Marshall, Bruce D. (2000). *Trinity and Truth*. Cambridge: Cambridge University Press.
McFarland, Andrew. (2013). "Misfired Slingshots: A Case Study in the Confusion of Metaphysical and Semantic Considerations," *Logos & Episteme* Vol. IV, No. 4: 407–432.
Newman, Andrew. (2002). *The Correspondence Theory of Truth: An Essay on the Metaphysics of Predication*. Cambridge: Cambridge University Press.
Read, S. (1993). "The Slingshot Argument," *Logique & Analyse* Vol. 36: 195–218.
Searle, John. (1995). *The Construction of Social Reality*. New York, NY: The Free Press.
Soames, Scott. (1998). *Understanding Truth*. New York, NY: Oxford University Press.
Young, James O. (2002). "The Slingshot Argument and the Correspondence Theory of Truth," *Acta Analytica* Vol. 17: 121–132.

Glossary

allegorical Exegetical method that ascribes symbolic, sometimes hidden, meaning of embedded in Scripture.

antecedent Something that precedes another.

anthropocentric Belief that humanity is the most important element of creation.

anthropomorphism Attributing human qualities to a nonhuman being.

anti-miscegenation laws Laws preventing marriage or intimate relationships between members of different races.

apophasis/apophatic Rhetorical method that raises a point by denying or opposing it. In theology, the apophatic tradition holds that God's otherness to us as humans means that we cannot make positive affirmations about God.

apotheosis Metaphorically, the culmination or high point of something. Traditionally used to refer to persons who have been elevated to divine or god-like status. Sophocles, the Greek tragic poet, for example, underwent an apotheosis after his death and was worshipped on the Acropolis.

autopoesis A self-organizing or self-producing system.

bezoar (Bezoar Ibex) A species of wild goat found in Asia and the Middle East.

biconditional Joins two statements (an antecedent X and a consequent Y) in the form of a sentence "X if and only if Y." Note that each variable follows from the other; i.e. X follows from Y AND Y follows from X.

centripetal/centrifugal Centripetal is the force that moves and object in arced circular motion; centrifugal is the force experienced by the object in an arced circular motion that pushing it outwardly away from the center point of rotation.

Christology Theological study of the person and nature of Jesus Christ.

coreferential Two or more terms are coreferential if they refer to the same thing.

correspondence theory of truth Truth of a statement is determined by whether it corresponds to a fact about the world.

deconstruction A method of reading and analyzing literary and philosophical texts that doubts the possibility of finding a fixed meaning in them. Instead, deconstructive analysis looks for a multiplication of possible meanings, an "excess of meaning," that appear to undo themselves as soon as we try to fix them. It was developed in the middle of the twentieth century by the French philosopher Jacques Derrida.

definite descriptions   A phrase that describes a person or object. According to Bertrand Russell, to be meaningful, a definite description must describe one and only one person or object.

descriptivism   An approach to philosophy of language in which the meaning of a referring expression (e.g. a name or singular term) is a descriptive sense that provides necessary and sufficient conditions for determining its reference. Such referring expressions successfully refer to an object if and only if the expression stands for one or more descriptions that uniquely describe the referent object.

dialectical   Concerned with the logical analysis of ideas or opinions, especially oppositional concepts.

docetic-Monophysite   Heretical movement that asserted Christ had only a divine nature, not human, which was in opposition to the Council of Chalcedon.

dualism   Dividing something into opposed and distinctly contrasting categories.

Durkheimian   Pertaining to the work of David Émile Durkheim (1858–1917), a French positivist, foundational to modern social science.

ecclesial/ecclesiastical   Related to the Church, usually the institutional church.

Elizabethan Settlement   1559 document issued during the reign of Elizabeth I to settle and establish a religious compromise between warring Roman Catholic and Protestant factions. Essentially this document was foundational to the forming of the Church of England.

emic   Field research done from the perspective within a social context.

eo ipso   Latin, "by the thing itself."

epistemology/epistemic   Discourse about knowledge and what it means to have knowledge.

escapism   In the context of soteriology, this is the idea that eventual reconciliation to God remains possible even after a soul has been consigned to hell. This is a variant of issuantism.

eschaton   The end of the world; the final judgment.

etic   Field research done from the perspective from external observation of a social context.

exclusivism   In a religious context, the belief that there is only one true religion.

exegesis/exegetical   Critical interpretive analysis of text; in this context usually sacred scripture.

existential(ism)   Related to the nature of human existance. Existentialism is a branch of philosophy that analyzes the nature of human existence through the range of human experience.

extensional context   This is a concept in philosophy of language that has two features. First, A context is extentional if a sub-sentential expression can be replaced by another expression with the same extension while necessarily preserving the truth-value (true statement remains true or false statement remains false). Second, existential generalization necessarily preserves truth value. Thus, if "Pam threw the ball to Ted" is true, then, necessarily, it is true that "There exists some actual person that threw the ball to Ted."

fallibilism   The idea that no belief can ever be proven conclusively and beyond all doubt.

falsifiability principle   A principle developed by logical positivists that a statement has to be disprovable in order to be meaningful.

Golden Rule   Conceptually universal to most of the world's major religions, in Christianity it is articulated as "In everything do to others as you would have them do to you; for this is the law and prophets" (NRSV: Matthew 7:12).

hermeneutics/hermeneutical   The branch of knowledge related to interpretive understanding.

heuristic   Enabling self teaching or discovery.

Hocktide Medieval festival falling on the second Tuesday after Easter Sunday. One of the few vacation days granted to peasants working the land for the lord of the manor.

horatory An exhortation.

humanist A philosophy that shifts focus away from the supernatural and divine, to the primary importance and goodness of human beings.

illocutionary acts A speech act that is intended to communicate some content. Thus, suppose a German friend asks me about the weather in Frankfurt, and I reply, "Es regnet." My reply is an illocutionary act. In contrast, If I utter the same sentence while practicing my German pronunciation, that would not be an illocutionary act.

imago Dei Latin literally "image of God," from Genesis the idea that humans were made in God's image.

Incarnation/Incarnate/Incarnate Word Pertaining to the belief that Christ, the second person of the Trinity, became fully human in the person of Jesus of Nazareth. "Word" refers to the John 1:14 in which this is described as "the Word became flesh."

inchoate Not fully formed or developed.

inclusivism From a Christian perspective, this is the belief that the Trinitarian God is present in other religions and therefore they are within the purview of salvation.

indexical A word or phrase whose meaning is dependent upon context. "I," "he," "they" are examples of indexicals.

instantiation A demonstration of an instance of some property. Thus, my green car is an instantiation of greenness in the actual world.

interlocutor A dialogue partner.

issuantism The idea that holds that hell is a preferable option for those who do not wish to be reconciled and in union with God. In other words, eschatalogical outcome is a matter of human agency.

kenotically/kenotic Petaining to kenosis, which in Christian theology is Christ's subjugation and emptying of self to the will of the Father.

logically equivalent sentences Sentences are logically equivalent if they have the same truth value in exactly the same possible worlds.

Magisterium In the Roman Catholic Church, the central authoritative body made up of the Pope and the bishops.

mereological Related to the study of parts and whole, ie. how parts relate to the whole, how the whole relates to parts, how parts relate to each other, etc.

metaphysics/metaphysical The branch of philosophy related to foundational concepts: being, space, time, cause, identity, etc.

midrash(ic) Collection of ancient commentary on Hebrew scripture (plural is midrashim).

modus ponens Logic rule that states if the statement "if p, then q" is accepted as true and p is known to be true, then q must also be true.

modus tollens Logic rule that states if the statement "if p, then q" and q is known to be false, then p must also be false.

mouflon A sub species of wild sheep.

mutatis mutandis Literally "when things changed that should be changed." Used to refer to an argument that allowing for necessary alterations to be made, the main point remains unchanged.

mysterification Ascribing understanding to mystery rather than an explanation utilizing careful analysis

neo-Platonic Group of philosophers originating in the third century AD building upon the ideas of Plato.

ontological Philosophical understanding of existence and how elements in existence are related.

onto-theology Theologicial ontology of God and being.

parapsychology The study of mental phenomena that occur outside of rational or scientific psychological explanation.

pedagogy/pedagogic Related to teaching method or theory.

pericope The over arching content or context in which a particular text passage, especially Scripture, is found.

Platonic menagerie A metaphorical phrase deriving from Plato's theory of the Forms. It refers (usually in a derogatory way) to metaphysical views that take there to be really existing things that have no instantiation in the actual world. For example, Plato understood the Form "Chair" to exist before any actual chair. Views that take Ideas, propositions, universals like "redness," etc., to be really existing entities might be said by critics to posit a Platonic menagerie.

pluralism In a religious context, existence of many different religious traditions in any given context.

polity Form or process of governance.

polysemy Language having multiple meanings.

positivism Requires that for any assertion to be justifiable, it must be verifiable or provable. Rejects the metaphysical and theistic.

possible worlds Used in modal logic. A possible world is simply a way of describing one way the world might have been, usually focusing on one or more possibilities. Since Trump's election in 2016 is a contingent fact about the world, if certain things had been otherwise, Clinton would have been elected. Thus, there is a possible world (which in this case is not the actual world) in which Clinton is president.

Prelapsarian/postlapsarian Occuring in time relative to the Fall of humanity.

prima facie Literally "first face." The initial or superficial impression or appearance of something.

Principal of Substitutivity for Singular Terms (PSST) If two terms A and B have the same extension (they refer to the same things), they can be interchangeably used in a sentence without altering the truth or falsity of the sentence.

Principle of Substitutivity for Logical Equivalents (PSLE) If two terms A and B can be used interchangeably in all models or possible worlds, they are said to be logical equivalents.

propositional attitude The attitude of an agent towards a proposition. So, toward the proposition "ghosts inhabit my house," I may one or more of the following attitudes: belief, disbelief, suspicion, contempt, acceptance, etc. Such attitudes are often expressed through indirect discourse reports: "Jim believed that Agnes loved him."

Pyrrhonian skepticism School of thought that believes because nothing can be known for certain, those who are wise avoid controversy contingent upon certain knowledge.

qua Acting in the capacity as.

reductio ad absurdam Literally "reduction to absurdity." A means of proving an idea is false because the eventual logical conclusion is absurd or incoherent.

reductionism Analyzing complex issues or entities through representations at a simpler or more fundamental level.

reference The connection between a proper name and the object to which it refers. Normally understood in the context of names or expressions that refer to some object in the world. But Frege famously held that assertive sentences referred to their truth value (either "the True" or "the False").

referent A referent is that which is designated by a referring expression. Thus, in the sentence, *The cat on the mat is hungry*, "The cat on the mat" is a referring expression, and its referent is the cat that is on the mat.

scylla and charybdis From Greek mythology, two dangerous perils, a deadly whirlpool and a monster, between which ships would have to pass. Used figuratively to refer choosing between two equally perilous options.

sentential operator Any expression used to form new compound sentences from other sentences (that may be simple or compound).

sentient Capable of sensation or feeling.

singular term A linguistic expression that names a particular object.

sophialogy Field of biblical research which explores the female imagery of wisdom and God in scripture.

soteriological/soteriology Pertaining to salvation.

speculative Expressing conjecture or opinion.

stigmatization Regarding a person, group, or entitiy as disgraced or unworthy of respect.

substitutivity The concept that words that refer to the same thing can be substituted for each other in a sentence without affecting the truth value of the sentence.

theistic Relating to a belief in a divine being(s).

theodicy/theodical An attempt to answer the question of why God allows evil.

theolatrous Pertaining to the worship of a diety or dieties.

transcendence Beyond the realm of normal experience or existence.

transcendental argument A method of a priori metaphysical argumentation that works backward, if you will, from an experience that all human beings share (e.g. that we all perceive things or make judgments) to determine the conditions of the possibility of having such experiences.

truth-bearer Something (usually a proposition, sentence, or utterance) that is said to have a truth value.

truth-conditional semantics A programme in philosophy of language that views meanings (of sentences or propositions) as being reducible to their truth conditions.

truthmaker theory A branch of metaphysics that takes truth to depend on the way the world is, rather than vice versa. So, for example, if the proposition that "there are houses on the campus of Virginia Seminary" is true, it is made true by the houses that exist on the campus of Virginia Seminary.

Index

a
Abel 121
Adams, Marilyn McCord 111–112, 168–169, 178, 181
Adams, Robert 105, 111, 112
Adams, Tony 143
Aguilar, J. 179, 181
Afterlife 60, 151–157, 159–163, 166–167, 180–181
Allen, Peter 134
Alston, William P. 240, 247, 259–260
Amadeo, Kimberly 129
Anderson, Elisha 130
Annihilation or Annihilationism 160
Anselm 21–23, 27
Anti-Miscegenation Laws 34
Anthropomorphism 117–119, 232
Anthropocentric 69–72
Anthropology 65–69, 72–76, 78, 80, 87, 139, 214
Anyoha, Rockwell 57
Apophatic 6, 235–236
Acquaintance 200, 208, 239, 242–243
Aquinas, Thomas 6, 22–23, 27, 61, 65–69, 77–79, 138, 166, 182, 222, 247
Aron, Raymond 213
Artificial Intelligence (AI) 50–51, 55, 57–58, 61–62, 87
Attfield, Robin 94
Attraction 5, 9, 10
Attributionism or Attributionist 104
Armstrong, D.M. 257–259
Atwater, P.M.H. 153
Augustine 6–7, 65–69, 78, 91, 102, 184, 191, 193, 222
Augustine of Hippo 6, 66
Autopoesis 13, 15

b
Baggett, Marybeth Davis 135
Bailey, Sarah Pulliam 133
Banks, Adelle M. 46, 133
Barnes, Albert 35–36
Barnes, Corey L. 23
Barrett, Justin 85
Barth, Karl 27, 70, 93, 172, 181, 186, 198, 219, 246
Barton, Stephen C. 6, 24, 25, 28
Barwise, Jon 248, 253
Basic Desert 103–107
Basinger, David 170
Bauckham, Richard 70
Bauman, Zygmunt 223
Bavinick, Herman 185
Beachman, Lateshia 134
Beardsley, Monroe 10
Bechtel, Trevor 114–126
Beck, Glenn 132

The Craft of Innovative Theology: Argument and Process, First Edition. Edited by John Allan Knight and Ian S. Markham.
© 2022 John Wiley & Sons Ltd. Published 2022 by John Wiley & Sons Ltd.

Beck, Harry   214
Bell, Catherine   218
Bell, Richard   174
Bell, Rob   162
Benezet, Anthony   35–36
Bennett, Christopher   108, 112
Bentham, Martin   134
Bentley, Paul   90
Berneson, Jennifer K.   184–185
Berger, Lee   73
Berinato, Scott   132
Berkeley, George   54
Berry, R.J.   71
Bhaktin, Mikhail   10
Biblical Christianity   190
Bingaman, B.   186
Bishop Clement of Alexandria   138
Blanchard, Kathryn D.   127–144
Blanchard, Isabella   30
Blow, Charles M.   144
Bochner, Arthur   144
Boff, Leonardo   219
Bonhoeffer, Dietrich   105
Boring, M. Eugene   175
Brandl, J.   247, 260
Brightman, Edgar   54
Brotton, Jerry   213
Brown, W.P.   84
Buber, Martin   234, 236, 238–239
Buckareff, Andrei A.   164–182
Bulgakov, Sergei   93
Burdett, Michael   87
Burgess, Alexis G.   247, 251
Burgess, John P.   247, 251

C

Cain   121, 126
Caird, George   187
Callahan, Allen   37
Calvin, John   138
Camosy, Charlie   76–77
Canal, Emily   131
Caruso, Gregg   105, 112
Centrifugal   9–11
Centripetal   9–11
Chamie, Joseph   147
Chappell, David L.   42

Christian *or* Christianity   5–7, 10, 11, 13–20, 26–30, 33–43, 45–48, 61–62, 66, 70–72, 79, 81–96, 99–104, 106–110, 112–116, 127–141, 143, 145–148, 151–157, 159, 169, 171–172, 174–177, 179–181, 183–186, 190–193, 198, 202, 204–206, 215–216, 219–222, 225, 230, 233, 240, 245–247
Christian Theism, 171
  Christian Theist   172
Christology   20–21, 23–27, 29–30, 65–66, 77, 79–80, 185, 206, 258
Christological   79, 88, 185
Chomsky, Noam   131
Chua, Linus   132
Church, Alonzo   248
Churchland, Patricia   57
Churchland, Paul   57
Clarke, Randolph   106
Clement of Alexandria   3, 138, 174
Clooney S. J., Francis X.   11
Clough, David   76–77, 88
Coates, J.   113
Cohen, Hermann   235
Cohen, Shaye   229
Colarossie, Natalie   141
Conger, Kate   132
Consciousness   50–52, 58, 60–62, 78, 117, 123, 140, 142, 153, 216, 233, 237
Contingency   5, 9
Contingent Materialism   50, 60–61
Conway Morris, Simon   86
Cooper, David   36
Copernicus   191
Correspondence Theory   8, 246–248, 250–258, 260
Corporate Social Responsibility   131
Cosgrove, Denis   213
Cosmology   191
Couenhoven, Jesse   104, 112
Creation   9, 12–13, 25–26, 79–82, 84–86, 88–89, 91–96, 116, 120–122, 126, 138, 140, 155, 157, 163, 168, 175, 183–193, 225
Creationism   81
Crick, Francis   85
Crisp, Oliver   19, 102–103, 112

Crouse–Dick, Christine E. 143
Culp, Kristine A. 89
Cunningham, David 78
Cyr, Taylor 110

d

D'Costa, Gavin 217
Danesi, Marcel 225
Darwin, Charles 71, 81–83, 85, 87, 92, 95, 140
   Darwinian 90, 94–95
Davidson, Donald 54, 247, 250–254, 256–258
Davidson, J. Ryan 185
Davies, Brian 22
Davis, Ellen 70
Davis, Kortright 219
Davison, Andrew 79, 86
Dawkins, Richard 85–86
Deane–Drummond, Celia 24–25, 65–80, 93
Dembski, William 91
Deme, Daniel 21
Dennett, Daniel 85
Denomination *or* Denominations 33–35, 39, 41, 43–45, 47, 49, 133, 216–217, 220–221, 224
   Denominatonal Identity 220
   Denominationalism 220, 224
DeRose, Keith 111–112
Descartes, Rene 52, 117
Description 200
Dialectical 11
Dickie, Imogen 241
Didymus the Blind 174
Dietary Law 123
Diodore of Tarsus 174
Divine 6–7, 16, 21–26, 30, 35–37, 66, 68, 77–79, 84–89, 92–95, 186
   Manipulation 178–179
   Widsom 24
Docetic–Monophysite 21
Doctrine 215–216
Dodd, C.H. 190
Dodda, Michael D. 142
Domestication *or* Domesticated 123, 125
Douglas, Mary 16, 122
Doughnut Economics 141
Dred Scott 33, 38, 46
Dunn, James D.G. 25
Durkheimian 142

e

Ecclesial Terroir 212, 217
Ecclesiology 51, 218
Ecology 140
Ecotheology 70
Ehrman, Bart 29
Elliott, Charles 35–36
Ellis, Carolyn 143
Emic 4, 10
Empirical 208
Epistemic 5, 7
Epistemology 16
Escapism 164–167, 170–173, 176–177, 179–181
Eternal Word 19
Etic reference 4
Evnine, Simon 247
Experiential 208
Evolution 81–82, 92
   Covergent Evolution 86
Exclusivism 5
Exegesis 77
Existential 70

f

Factory Farming 117–119, 125
Fagan, Brian 116, 124
Fallibilism 5–7, 13
Falsification 197–203, 206–210
Falwell, Jr., Jerry 135
Faria–e–Castro, Miguel 144
Farwell, James 24, 30
Federer, Roger 83
Fedor, Lauren 129
Feminist Theologian 19, 26
Fisher, Cass 226–244
Fisher, David Hackett 220
Fischer, John Martin 106, 153, 179
Flew, Antony 199, 201, 207, 209
Flourishing 116
Fontrodona, Joan 143
Fossey, Diane 118
Franck, Thomas 130
Frankfurt, Harry 101, 112
Frege, Gottlob 248, 253–254
Frei 246
Freud 10
Frost, Gary L.45
Fuentes, Agustin 69, 73

g

Functionalism 54
Furman, Richard 37

Gadamer 10
Galdikas, Birute Mary 118
G.E. Moore Shift 252
Geertz, Clifford 224
Gellman, Jerome 240
Ghemawat, Pankaj 147
Giles, Keith 159
Giuseffi, Benjamin Sievert 142
Glickman, Lawrence 134
God 3–8, 10–14, 16–19–30, 35–36, 39–41, 43, 46–48, 51, 56, 60–61, 65–72, 76–96, 99–101, 108–111, 120–122, 126, 131–132, 134, 136–138, 140–141, 145–147, 157–182, 184–193, 197–202, 204–211, 212–215, 216–218, 221–223, 226–244, 258, 260
Gödel 254
Goffman, Erving 47
Golden Rule 33–38, 43–44, 47, 145
Gonzalez, Frank J. 142
Goodall, Jane 118
Goostman, Chatbot Eugene 58
Gorman, Michael 22
Gould, Stephen Jay 86
Graziano, Michael S. A. 59
Green, Emma 49
Gregersen, Niels 77
Gregory of Nazianzus 174
Gregory of Nyssa 174
Griffin, David Ray 153
Grumett, David 90
Gunton, Colin 28

h

Hachikō 117–120
Haag, Matthew 131
Haidt, Jonathan 142
Halivni, David Weiss 229
Hankins, Barry 45
Hanson, John Wesley 158
Harlan, John Marshall 39
Harnack 198
Harrison, Peter 70
Harvey, Paul 48
Hart, David Bentley 159
Hart, William 225
Hawks, John 73
Hawkins, Barney 30
Hawkins, Ellen 30
Hawley, Erin M. 138
Hazell, Peter 141
Hearne, Vicki 117
Hector, Kevin 246
Hedley Brooke, John 83
Heidel, Alexander 191
Hermann 198
Hermeneutic 10
Hermeneutical 96, 204
Herron, George 139
Herzfeld, Noreen 87
Herzog, Hal 118
Heschel, Abraham Joshua 187, 234, 238–239
Hetherington, Norriss S. 185
Hezser, Catherine 229
Hibbing, John R. 142
Hick, John 155
Hieronymi, Pamela 104, 112
Hill, Jonathan 30
Hill, Thomas 105, 111–112
Himma, Kenneth 169
Hlavinka, Elizabeth 144
Hochschild, Arlie 142
Hopkins, Jasper 21
Horsely, Scott 147
Hubble, Edwin 187, 191
Humility 5–7
Hurtado, Larry W. 29
Hutson, Matthew 58–59

i

Imago Dei 20, 51, 65–66, 68, 76–78, 80, 87–90, 166
Imbert, Fred 130
Incarnate *or* Incarnated 13, 19–21, 23, 25, 28–29, 77, 88, 146, 184
Incarnation 17, 19–20, 22–23, 26–30, 77, 88, 180–181, 186, 216
Inchoate 12, 17
Inclusivism 5
Indeterminism 7–9
   Indeterminacy 5, 9
Industrial Farming 117
Ingold, Tim 74
Issuantist 171
   Issuantism 171–172, 180

Instantiation 9
Interreligious 4
Irony 4, 5, 13, 14, 21

j
Jablonka, Eva 82
James, William 8, 13
Jaspers, Karl 114
Jeavens, Christine 224
Jenkins, Jack 133–134
Jenkins, Willis 70
Jersak, Bradley 159
Jim Crow 33–34, 38–43, 47
Johnson, Elizabeth 26
Jones, Pamela D. 33–49
Jones, R. 165
Jones, Stacy Holman 143
Jordan, Miriam 132

k
Kadushin, Max 230–234, 243
Kahneman, Daniel 142
Kaplan, Mordecai 236
Kasparov, Gary 57
Kass, Leon 120
Kelsey, David 76
Kenotically 9
Kerns, Christopher 130
Kershnar, Stephen 168, 171
Kierkegaard 8, 13, 14
Kilner, John F. 87
Kim, Jaegwon 51
King, Matt 106, 112
King, Jr., Martin Luther 42
Kingsley, Charles 82
Kissel, Marc 73
Kittle, Simon 101
Klender, Joey 131
Knight, John Allan 180, 197–211, 245–260
Knowledge
    Divine 21–22
    Experimental 22–23
    Human 22
    Propositional 24
Kohn, Eduardo 74
Kolbert, Elizabeth 144
Korta, Kepa 241–242
Kramer, Mark R. 131
Kripke, Saul 199, 239

Krishna 19
Kruger, Lorenz 253
Kvanvig, Jonathan 166, 171

l
Lamarck 83
Lamb, Marion J. 82
Lambert, Lance 129
Lamoureux, Denis 92
Lapin, Hayim 229
Largen, Kristin Johnston 19
Leibowitz, Yeshayahu 237
Lemaître, Georges 187
Leneman, Leah 124
Levinas, Emmanuel 235
Levine, Amy–Jill 137
Levy, Neil 106
Levy, Paul 131
Lewens, Tim 73
Lewis, David 168, 170–171
Limit Situations 114–115
Lindbeck, George 7, 215, 246
Lindsley, Art 136
Linker, Damon 147
Lipka, Michael 49
Lloyd, Michael 91, 93
Long, Stephen 246
Loury, Glenn 47
Louth, Andrew 6
Love 156–157
Lucas, J.R. 172
Luter, Jr., Fred 46
Luther, Martin 138

m
MacKinnon, Donald 247
Maclean, Norman 220
Mahoney, John 71
Mair, Simon 144, 146–147
Mak, Aaron 132
Malinowski, Bronislaw 222
Mandik, Pete 52
Manis, Zachary 110, 112
Marcina the Younger 174
Marcus, Ruth Barcan 239
Markham, Ian S. 19–30, 50–62, 77, 180
Marshall, Bruce 245–247, 249, 251–258, 260
Marshall, Christopher 105, 109, 111–112
Marshall, David 71

Materialism   24, 50, 53, 55, 57, 60–61
  Contingent Materialism   50, 60–61
Mawson, T.J.   60
Maximus the Confessor   186
Mccool, Martin   58
McDaniel, Jay   94
McDonald, William   13
McFarland, Andrew   251, 255, 260
McFarland, Ian   84
McGuire, Brian   58
McGuire, Meredith B.   220
McKenna, M.   112
McLeod, Mark S.   206
Meijer, Ava   118
Mélé, Domènec   143
Mendel, Gregor   83
Mercer, Joyce   24, 30
Merritt, Jonathan   45
Messer, Neil   93, 95–96
Metaphor *or* Metaphorical   7, 10–12
Metzger, Bruce   137
Middleton, J. Richard   87
Miller, Kenneth   92
Miller, Stuart   229
Mills, Mark   142
Mittleman, Alan   237
Mohler, Albert   45
Monogenism   90
Moo, Douglas   99, 101, 113
Moore, Gorden   57
Moore, Russell   49, 145
Morisette, Alannis   14
Morris, Conway   87
Morris, Stephen   105, 112
Morris, Thomas   23
Mortensen, Vigo   17
Moritz, Joshua   93
Moss, Candida   133
Murray, Michael   173
Mysterification   96

n
Naughtie, Andrew   132
Neo–Platonic   66
Neale, Stephen   254
Newell, Allen   57
Newman, Andrew   257, 260
Newman, Mark   41
Newmarker, Chris   131

Niche Construction Theory (NCT)   75–76, 80
Niebuhr, Gustav   45
Niebuhr, H. Richard   212, 215, 220–224
Niebuhr, Reinhold   151
Noah   121
Noll, Mark   38
Nomadism   121
Noponen, Martin   147
Normal Mysticism   233, 238
Northcott, Michael   71
Novikov, Igor D.   187
Nussbaum, Martha   38

o
O'Collins, Gerald   23
Ogden, Schubert M.   197, 202–211
Omniscient *or* Omniscience   20
Ontological   68
Oord, Thomas J.   151–163
Origen of Alexandria   174

p
Page, Ruth   76, 86
Pancevski, Bojan   130
Pandemic   131, 135
Pannenberg, Wolfhart   21
Parapsychology   153
Paris, Peter, J.   39
Pascal   101
Patterson, Paige   45
Percy, Martyn   212–225
Pereboom, Derk   103–105, 107, 113
Perlow, Becky   46
Perper, Rosie   134
Perron, Paul   225
Perry, John   241–242, 248, 253
Personhood   36, 50, 60–61
Philosophy of Mind   50–53, 57
Pilkington, Ed   144
Pitcher, George   259
Plantinga, Alvin   252
Plato   12–13, 154
Plug, Allen   165–167, 169–172, 176–177, 179, 181
Pluralism *or* Religious Pluralism   3, 4, 5, 15
Poetic *or* Poesis *or* Poiesis   5, 9, 11
  Autopesis   13, 15
Polychroniou, C.J.   131

Polysemy 7
Pope, Alexander 66
Porter, Eduardo 140
Positivism 16
Prelapsarian 91
Princes Elisabeth of Bohemia 52
Principle of Substitutivity for Logical Equivalents (PSLE) 248, 250, 252, 255–256
Priori 14, 16
Prophetic 188–189
Ptolemy Cosmology 191
Purgatory 177
Purity 16–18
   Codes 122
Putnam, Hilary 54

q
Quinn, Philip 102, 113

r
Racial Stigma 33–34, 38, 41, 47
Radical flexibility 7
Radical risk 13
Rahner, Karl 186
Ravenscroft, Ian 51–54
Ravizza, M. 179
Raworth, Kate 141
Rea, Michael 102, 113
Recanati, Francois 239, 242–243
Reddy, Raj 58
Reductive Physicalism 53–54
   Non–reductive Physicalism 54
Reductionism 85
Referent 199
Reincarnation 151–152
Reichenbach, Hans 251
Relentless Love 161–162
Religious Language 237
Reno, R.R. 134
Restoration (*apokatastasis*) 174
Retributivism 164, 167, 170–171
   Retributivist 173
Richardson, Herbert 21
Ricoeur, Paul 10
Robinson, John 187
Rochberg, F. 185
Rock, Marcus Baynes 75
Rodrigues-Pereyra, Gonzalo 251
Rollin, Bernard 117
Rolston, Holmes 93
Rorty 8, 12
Rosenberg, Stanley 87, 91
Rozsa, Matthew 132
Ruparell, Tinu 3–18
Russell, Bertrand 197, 199–200, 202, 208, 239
Russell, Robert J. 95
Ryle, Gilbert 52–53

s
Sachs, J. 174
Safran Foer, Jonathan 118
Sagi, Avi 237–238
Salmon, Nathan 253
Sanchez, Aaron 139
Sanders, E.P. 175
Sarason, Richard S. 230
Schleiermacher 198
Schleidt, Wolfgang M. 124
Schneider, John R. 136
Schrotenboer, Brent 132
SchÜssler Fiorenza, Elisabeth 26
Schwartz, Seth 229
Schweitzer, Don 27
Scientific Reductionism 52
Scylla 8
Searle, John 251, 253, 255–256, 260
Second Coming 183
Seeskin, Kenneth 235
Semitic 5, 16, 18
Sengupta, Somini 147
Settled Agriculture 121
Shalter, Michael D. 124
Sharov, Alexander S. 187
Shaw, Cliff 57
Shaw, Rosalind 17
Shuttlesworth, Jonathan 134
Sider, Ted 168
Silliman, Daniel 133
Simon, Herbert 57
Sin 99, 102
   Original Sin 103
Singer, Peter 72
Slattery, John 71
Slave *or* Slavery 33–39, 43–49, 72, 126
Slingshot Argument 245, 247–258, 260
Smart, J.J.C. 53–54

Smart, Ninian 218
Smith, Adam 146
Smith, Angela 104–106, 108, 113
Smith, J.Z. 4
Smith, James K.A. 71, 91, 96
Smith, Kerri 142
Smith, Kevin B. 142
Smith, Quentin 239
Snyder-Belousek, Darrin 115
Soames, Scott 199, 247, 252, 256, 260
Sobrino, Jon 219
Socrates 12, 14, 154
Solle, Dorothee 47
Sollereder, Bethany 91
Soskice, Janet Martine 7, 10
Soteriological 5
Southgate, Christopher 81–96
Southern Baptist Convention (SBC) 33–35, 37–44–49
Spinelli, Ernesto 213, 216
St. Francis of Assisi 138
Stackhouse, Max L. 143
Steiner, George 224
Stenmark, Mikael 78
Stemberger, Günter 230
Stigmatization 35, 46–48
Strawson, Peter 107, 113
Stuart, Charles 17
Stump, Elenore 22
Subjectivity 8, 9, 14
Substance Dualism *or* Interactive Substance Dualism 52
Swinburne, Richard 101, 113, 166
Syncretism *or* Syncretic 16–17
Szreter, Simon 219

t

Talbert, M. 113
Talbott, Thomas 101, 113, 179, 182
Tankersley, Jim 130, 140
Tanner, Kathryn 212, 215
Tanner, Kristi 130
Tarki, Atta 131
Teilhard de Chardin, Pierre 90
Theistic 85, 227
Theodical 6
Theodicy 87, 94
Theodrama 78–79
Theoharis, Liz 145
Theological
 Anthropology 66–68, 76, 78, 139
 Language 40, 197–198, 209, 211, 227, 231, 233–238, 240–243
 Method *or* Methodology 77, 87, 95, 197–198, 204, 209, 211, 245–246
Theology 4–19, 23, 26–27, 30, 69–73, 76–81, 83–88, 92–96, 99, 101, 103–104, 112–115, 120, 128, 136, 167, 174, 182, 185–186, 189–190, 197–198, 200–210, 212–219, 221, 223–224, 226–228, 235–238, 240–247, 252, 258
 Jewish 26, 146, 226–228, 234–235, 237–238, 240–244
 Liberation 26, 139
 Pluralistic 5–6, 8–18
 Rabbinic 228–234, 238, 241–242
Theo-realism 234
Theory of Truth 8
Thomas, Elisabeth Marshall 75
Thornwell, James Henley 37
Thracians 3
Tillich, Paul 223
Tognazzini, N. 113
Tomašev, Nenad 58
Transcendence 6, 7, 16
Troeletsch, Ernst 223
Trump, Donald J. 133
Truth 4, 5, 8, 9, 13, 16, 22, 28
Tuckett, Christopher 175
Turing, Alan M. 55–58

u

Universal Reconciliation 164, 175–176
Universalism 110–112, 159–160, 164, 173–180, 183
Urs van Balthasar, Hans 77, 79

v

van den Toren, Benno 87
van Huyssteen, J. Wentzel 87
van Wouderberg, René 82
Vargas, Manuel 107, 113
Vegan *or* Veganism 124–126
Vegetarian *or* Vegetarianism 121
Vicens, Leigh 90, 99–113, 180
Villegas, Isaac 139
Virtue of the absurd 13–14
Visala, Aku 73

Visotzky, Burton L.   230
Voloshinov   10
von Harnack, Adolf   190
Vroom, Hendrik   16

W
Walker, David   35–36
Wallace, Alfred Russel   71
Wallis, Jim   130–131, 145, 166
Ward, Graham   219
Ward, Keith   30, 60–61, 183–194
Watson, Gary   99, 113
Weber, Max   220
Weed, Laura   51
Weeks, Stuart   24
Weise, Karen   132
Weiss, David   229
Weiss, Jeff   131
Wenham, Gordon J.   77
Wesleyan Quadrilateral   128
West, Cornel   128
Westermann, Claus   187
White, Lynn   70
White Supremacy   33–34, 38, 41, 47–48
Williams, Rowan   216, 223
Willis, Dave   130
Wilson, Edward O.   84–85

Winter, Reddy, R.   58
Wisdom, John   201
Wittgenstein, Ludwig   199, 209, 226, 228, 234, 237–238, 243, 259
Wolf, S.   179
Wolfson, Elliot   235–236
Wolterstorff, Nicholas   240
Woo, Stu   130
Woolman, John   35–36
Wright, Christopher   137

X
Xenophanes   3

Y
Young, Frances   89
Young, James O.   248, 260

Z
Zalta, Edward N.   13
Zeder, Melinda   124
Zhang, Christine   129
Zillman, Claire   130
Zizioulas, John   79
Zylstra, Sarah Eekhoff   48

www.ingramcontent.com/pod-product-compliance
Lightning Source LLC
LaVergne TN
LVHW081523060526
838200LV00044B/1987